LINPACK

INPACK

NPACK

PACK

ACK

CK

K

USERS' GUIDE

J.J. Dongarra C.B. Moler
J.R. Bunch G.W. Stewart

	CO	FA	SL	DI
SGE	*	*	*	*
SGB	*	*	*	*
SPO	*	*	*	*
SPP	*	*	*	*
SPB	*	*	*	*
SSI	*	*	*	*
SSP	*	*	*	*
CHI	*	*	*	*
CHP	*	*	*	*
STR	*		*	*
SGT			*	
SPT			*	

	DC	SL	UD	DD	EX
SCH	*		*	*	*
SQR	*	*			
SSV	*				

First letter

S	Real	C	Complex
D	Double precision	Z	Complex*16

Second and third letters

GE	General	SI	Symmetric indefinite
GB	General band	SP	Symmetric indefinite packed
PO	Positive definite	HI	Hermitian indefinite
PP	Positive definite packed	HP	Hermitian indefinite packed
PB	Positive definite band	CH	Cholesky decomposition
TR	Triangular	QR	Orthogonal triangular decomp.
GT	General tridiagonal	SV	Singular value decomposition
PT	Positive definite tridiagonal		

Fourth and Fifth letters

FA	Factor	DC	Decompose
CO	Estimate condition	UD	Update
SL	Solve	DD	Downdate
DI	Determinant, inverse, inertia	EX	Exchange

LINPACK

Users' Guide

J. J. Dongarra
Argonne National Laboratory

C. B. Moler
University of New Mexico

J. R. Bunch
University of California, San Diego

G. W. Stewart
University of Maryland

siam
Philadelphia/1979

ISBN: 0-89871-172-X
Library of Congress Catalog Card Number: 78-78206.

Second printing 1980.

No warranties, express or implied, are made by the publisher that the programs contained in this volume are free of error. They should not be relied on as the sole basis to solve a problem whose incorrect solution could result in injury to person or property. If the programs are employed in such a manner, it is at the user's own risk and the publisher disclaims all liability for such misuse.

Table of Contents

"R.T.F.M." -- Anonymous

Preface

In June of 1974 Jim Pool, then director of the research section of the Applied Mathematics Division of Argonne National Laboratory, initiated a series of informal meetings to consider the possibility of producing a package of quality programs for the solution of linear systems and related problems. The participants included members of the Laboratory staff, visiting scientists, and various consultants and speakers at the AMD colloquium series. It was decided that there was a need for a LINPACK and that there was a secure technological basis for its production. Accordingly, a proposal was submitted to the National Science Foundation, which agreed to fund the project for three years beginning January 1976; the Department of Energy also provided support at Argonne.

The LINPACK project had a number of objectives. In the first place, it represented research into the mechanics of software production; to our knowledge no package has been produced in quite the way we have done it, and some of the many things we have learned from the effort will appear in subsequent publications. Secondly, we hope that we have provided a yardstick against which future mathematical software projects can be measured. Third, we hoped to produce a package that would be used, both as library subroutines and by people who wish to modify or extend the code to handle special problems (however, to protect the innocent, we request that anyone who modifies a LINPACK code also change the name of the subroutine and comment the modifications). Finally, we hope that LINPACK and this guide will be of value in the classroom.

These goals have imposed constraints on the code and its documentation. We have tried to make the code both machine independent and efficient. Although these two objectives are often at odds, we feel that in LINPACK we have gone far toward achieving both. The code itself has to be in Fortran, which is the language of scientific programming in the United States. We have tried to mitigate the unclarity of Fortran codes by carefully structuring our programs and adopting indentation conventions that reflect the structure. In addition the programs share a common nomenclature and uniform typing and commenting conventions. In documenting LINPACK we have tried to serve both the casual user and the person who must know the technical details of our programs. We have done this by segregating user oriented material for any particular set of programs into the first three sections of each chapter of the documentation, leaving the technical material for later.

The mechanics of designing and producing the package were somewhat unusual. Three of us (Bunch, Moler, Stewart) worked separately at our various institutions. Once a year in June we met for a month at Argonne National Laboratory, which provided the central computer and software support under the supervision of our fourth colleague (Dongarra). Later some of the work was done at Los Alamos Scientific Laboratory. The arrangement worked smoothly, but we suspect that LINPACK is about as large a project as can be handled in this anarchistic way.

A magnetic tape containing the Fortran source code for LINPACK is available from either of two sources:

National Energy Software Center
Argonne National Laboratory
9700 South Cass Avenue
Argonne, IL 60439
(Phone: 312-972-7250)

International Mathematical and Statistical Libraries, Inc.
Sixth Floor, GNB Building
7500 Bellaire Boulevard
Houston, TX 77036
(Phone: 713-772-1927)

Information regarding distribution charges and tape formats can be obtained directly from either source.

The LINPACK project supports these routines in the sense that detailed information on the testing procedures is available, and reports of poor or incorrect performance in conventional Fortran operating environments will gain immediate attention from the developers. Reports of suspected errors, descriptions of interesting applications and other comments should be sent to:

LINPACK Project
c/o J. J. Dongarra
Applied Mathematics Division
Argonne National Laboratory
9700 South Cass Avenue
Argonne, IL 60439

The developers intend that support of LINPACK shall continue indefinitely. Such support is, of course, contingent upon the continued interest and assistance by those agencies which have made the program possible.

Our efforts have been aided by many people, but no group has contributed as much as the personnel of the Applied Mathematics Division of Argonne National Laboratory. Jim Pool and Wayne Cowell have provided administrative support and sheltered us from many routine tasks. Jim Boyle and Ken Dritz adapted their TAMPR system to the needs of LINPACK, providing us with automatic type conversion and formatting. Judy Beumer typed the manuscript for this document, and Doris Pahis and Pat Berglund were always on hand to help us when we needed it. We are particularly grateful to our friends in the AMD for making our yearly visits to ANL enjoyable and fruitful.

LINPACK would have been impossible without the help of the people at our test sites who twice nursed our test drivers through their systems and reported the results. A list of the sites follows this preface. In several cases, LINPACK testing has helped uncover bugs in Fortran compilers, operating systems, and even hardware. We suggest that LINPACK test drivers can be used to check out new versions of Fortran systems.

Many individuals have contributed to LINPACK in various ways. Lapses of memory no doubt have made the following list incomplete, and we apologize in advance to anyone who has been left out. We wish to particularly thank Valerie Barr, Mary Ann Berg, Garrett Birkhoff, Jim Boyle, Ed Block, Alan Cline, George Davis, Don Doerner, Bo Einarsson, Joseph Fahle, Mike Frantz, Burt Garbow, David Gay, Joseph Glover, Gene Golub, Tom Goodman, Eric Grosse, Len Hardin, Richard Hanson, Karen Haskell, Alan Hinds, Molly Hindman, David Husnian, Linda Kaufman, Tom Jordan, Barbara Kerns, Charles Lawson, Yih Ling, Alan Moy, Michael Saunders, Brian Smith, Ned Tanhauser, Bob Veroff, Mike Wester, and Steve White.

Finally, special thanks go to Jim Wilkinson, whose generous assistance has benefited the project at every stage.

LINPACK Test Sites

Facility	Computer
Argonne National Laboratory	IBM 370/195
Bell Telephone Laboratories	Honeywell 6080
College of William and Mary	IBM 370/158
International Mathematical and Statistical Libraries (IMSL)	Eclipse C330
Iowa State University	Itel AS/5
Lawrence Livermore Laboratory	CDC 7600
Los Alamos Scientific Laboratory	CDC 7600 CRAY-1
Monash University, Australia	Burroughs 6700
NASA Langley Research Center	CDC Cyber 175
National Center Atmospheric Research	CDC 7600 CRAY-1

Naval Weapons Center, China Lake	Univac 1110
Northwestern University	CDC 6600
Oak Ridge National Laboratory	IBM 360/91
Purdue University	CDC 6500
Stanford University, SLAC	IBM 370/168
University of California, San Diego	Burroughs 6700
University of Kentucky	IBM 370/158
University of Illinois, Chicago Circle	IBM 370/158
University of Illinois, Urbana	CDC Cyber 175
University of Michigan	Amdahl 470/V6
University of Texas, Austin	CDC 6600/6400
University of Toronto, Toronto, Canada	IBM 370/165
University of Wisconsin, Madison	Univac 1110
Yale University	DEC KL-20 DEC KA-10

A Note on the Second Printing

This reprinting incorporates corrections of a number of typographical and grammatical errors present in the first printing. No substitute changes have been made.

Magnetic tapes continue to be available from the sources given on page vi.

Introduction

1. Overview

LINPACK is a collection of Fortran subroutines which analyze and solve various systems of simultaneous linear algebraic equations. The subroutines are designed to be completely machine independent, fully portable, and to run at near optimum efficiency in most operating environments.

Many of the subroutines deal with square coefficient matrices, where there are as many equations as unknowns. Some of the subroutines process rectangular coefficient matrices, where the system may be over- or underdetermined. Such systems are frequently encountered in least squares problems and other statistical calculations. Different subroutines are intended to take advantage of different special properties of the matrices and thereby save computer time and storage.

The entire coefficient matrix will usually be stored in the computer memory, although there are provisions for band matrices and for processing large rectangular matrices row by row. This means that on most contemporary computers, LINPACK will handle full matrices of order less than a few hundred and band matrices of order less than several thousand. There are no subroutines for general sparse matrices or for iterative methods for very large problems.

Most linear equation problems will require the use of two LINPACK subroutines, one to process the coefficient matrix and one to process a particular right hand side. This division of labor results in significant savings of computer time when there is a sequence of problems involving the same matrix, but different right hand sides. This situation is so common and the savings so important that no provision has been made for solving a single system with just one subroutine.

We make a somewhat vague distinction between a matrix "factorization" and a matrix "decomposition". For either, a given matrix is expressed as the product of two or three matrices of various special forms which subsequently allow rapid solution of linear systems and easy calculation of quantities useful in analyzing such systems. With a factorization, the user is rarely concerned about the details of the factors; they are simply passed from one subroutine to another. With a decomposition, the user will often be interested in accessing and manipulating the individual factors themselves. For the most part, factorizations are associated with standard problems involving square matrices and decompositions with more esoteric problems involving both square and non-square matrices.

A subroutine naming convention is employed in which each subroutine name is a coded specification of the computation done by that subroutine. All names consist of five letters in the form TXXYY . The first letter, T , indicates the matrix data type. Standard Fortran allows the use of three such types:

S	REAL
D	DOUBLE PRECISION
C	COMPLEX

In addition, some Fortran systems allow a double precision complex type:

Z	COMPLEX*16

The next two letters, XX , indicate the form of the matrix or its decomposition:

GE	General
GB	General band
PO	Positive definite
PP	Positive definite packed
PB	Positive definite band
SI	Symmetric indefinite
SP	Symmetric indefinite packed
HI	Hermitian indefinite
HP	Hermitian indefinite packed
TR	Triangular
GT	General tridiagonal
PT	Positive definite tridiagonal
CH	Cholesky decomposition
QR	Orthogonal-triangular decomposition
SV	Singular value decomposition

The final two letters, YY , indicate the computation done by a particular subroutine:

FA	Factor
CO	Factor and estimate condition
SL	Solve
DI	Determinant and/or inverse and/or inertia
DC	Decompose
UD	Update
DD	Downdate
EX	Exchange

The following chart shows all the LINPACK subroutines. The initial S in the names may be replaced by D , C or Z and the initial C in the complex-only names may be replaced by a Z .

	CO	FA	SL	DI
SGE	√	√	√	√
SGB	√	√	√	√
SPO	√	√	√	√
SPP	√	√	√	√
SPB	√	√	√	√
SSI	√	√	√	√
SSP	√	√	√	√
CHI	√	√	√	√
CHP	√	√	√	√
STR	√		√	√
SGT			√	
SPT			√	

	DC	SL	UD	DD	EX
SCH	√		√	√	√
SQR	√	√			
SSV	√				

The remaining sections of this Introduction cover some software design and numerical analysis topics which apply to the entire package. Each of the chapters 1 through 11 describes a particular group of subroutines, ordered roughly as indicated by the preceding chart. Each chapter includes Overview, Usage and Examples sections which are intended for all users. In addition many chapters include additional sections on Algorithms, Programming Details and Performance which are intended for users requiring more specific information. In order to make each chapter fairly self-contained, some material is repeated in several related chapters.

2. Software Design

The overall design of LINPACK has been strongly influenced by TAMPR and by the BLAS. TAMPR is a software development system created by Boyle and Dritz (1974). It manipulates and formats Fortran programs to clarify their structure. It also generates variants of programs. The "master versions" of all the LINPACK subroutines are those which use complex arithmetic; versions which use single precision, double precision, and double precision complex arithmetic have been produced automatically by TAMPR. A user may thus convert from one type of arithmetic to another by simply changing the declarations in his program and changing the first letter of the LINPACK subroutines being used.

Anyone reading the Fortran source code for LINPACK subroutines should find the loops and logical structures clearly delineated by the indentation generated by TAMPR.

The BLAS are the Basic Linear Algebra Subprograms designed by Lawson, Hanson, Kincaid and Krogh (1978). They contribute to the speed as well as to the modularity and clarity of the LINPACK subroutines. LINPACK is distributed with versions of the BLAS written in standard Fortran which are intended to provide reasonably efficient execution in most operating environments. However, a particular computing installation may substitute machine language versions of the BLAS and thereby perhaps improve efficiency.

LINPACK is designed to be completely machine independent. There are no machine dependent constants, no input/output statements, no character manipulation, no COMMON or EQUIVALENCE statements, and no mixed-mode arithmetic. All the subroutines (except those whose names begin with Z) use the portable subset of Fortran defined by the PFORT verifier of Ryder (1974).

There is no need for machine dependent constants because there is very little need to check for "small" numbers. For example, candidates for pivots in Gaussian elimination are checked against an exact zero rather than against some small quantity. The test for singularity is made instead by estimating the condition of the matrix; this is not only machine independent, but also far more reliable. The convergence of the iteration in the singular value decomposition is tested in a machine independent manner by statements of the form

```
TEST1 = something not small
TEST2 = TEST1 + something possibly small
IF (TEST1 .EQ. TEST2) ...
```

The absence of mixed-mode arithmetic implies that the single precision subroutines do not use any double precision arithmetic and hence that the double precision subroutines do not require any kind of extended precision. It also implies that LINPACK does not include a subroutine for iterative improvement; however, an example in Chapter 1 indicates how such a subroutine could be added by anyone with easy access to mixed-mode arithmetic. (Some of the BLAS involve mixed-mode arithmetic, but they are not used by LINPACK.)

Floating point underflows and overflows may occur in some of the LINPACK subroutines. Any underflows which occur are harmless. We hope that the operating system sets underflowed quantities to zero and continues operation without producing any error messages. With some operating systems, it may be necessary to insert control cards or call special system subroutines to achieve this type of underflow handling.

Overflows, if they occur, are much more serious. They must be regarded as error situations resulting from improper use of the subroutines or from unusual scaling. Many precautions against overflow have been taken in LINPACK, but it is impossible to absolutely prevent overflow without seriously degrading performance on reasonably scaled problems. It is expected that overflows will cause the operating system to terminate the computation and that the user will have to correct the program or rescale the problem before continuing.

Fortran stores matrices by columns and so programs in which the inner loop goes up or down a column, such as

```
      DO 20 J = 1, N
         DO 10 I = 1, N
            A(I,J) = ...
   10    CONTINUE
   20 CONTINUE
```

generate sequential access to memory. Programs in which the inner loop goes across a row cause non-sequential access. Sequential access is preferable on operating systems which employ virtual memory or other forms of paging. LINPACK is consequentially "column oriented". Almost all the inner loops occur within the BLAS and, although the BLAS allow a matrix to be accessed by rows, this provision is never used by LINPACK. The column orientation requires revision of some conventional algorithms, but results in significant improvement in performance on operating systems with paging and cache memory.

All square matrices which are parameters of LINPACK subroutines are specified in the calling sequences by three arguments, for example

```
      CALL SGEFA(A,LDA,N,...)
```

Here A is the name of a two-dimensional Fortran array, LDA is the leading dimension of that array, and N is the order of the matrix stored in the array or in a portion of the array. The two parameters LDA and N have different meanings and need not have the same value. The amount of storage reserved for the array A is determined by a declaration in the user's program and LDA refers to the leading, or first, dimension as specified in this declaration. For example, the declaration

```
REAL A(50,50)
```
or
```
DIMENSION A(50,50)
```

should be accompanied by the initialization

```
DATA LDA/50/
```

or the statement

```
LDA = 50
```

The value of LDA should not be changed unless the declaration is changed. The order N of a particular coefficient matrix may be any value not exceeding the leading dimension of the array, that is $N \leq LDA$. The value of N may be changed by the user's program as systems of different orders are processed.

Rectangular matrices require a fourth argument, for example

```
CALL SQRDC(X,LDX,N,P,...)
```

Here the matrix is called X to adhere to the notation common in statistics, LDX is the leading dimension of the two-dimensional array, N is the number of rows in the matrix, and P is the number of columns. Note that the default Fortran typing conventions must be overridden by declaring P to be an integer. This conforms to usual statistical notation and is the only argument of a LINPACK subroutine which does not have the default type.

Many of the LINPACK subroutines have one or two arguments with the names JOB and INFO . JOB is always an input parameter. It is set by the user, often by simply including an integer constant in the call, to specify which of several possible computations are to be carried out. For example, SGESL solves a system of equations involving either the factored matrix or its transpose, and JOB should be zero or nonzero accordingly.

INFO is always an output parameter. It is used to return various kinds of diagnostic information from LINPACK routines. In some situations, INFO may be regarded as an error parameter. For example, in SPOFA , it is used to indicate that the matrix is not positive definite. In other situations, INFO may be one of the primary output quantities. For example, in SCHDC , it is an indication of the rank of a semi-definite matrix.

A few LINPACK subroutines require more space for storage of intermediate results than is provided by the primary parameters. These subroutines have a parameter WORK which is a one-dimensional array whose length is usually the number of rows or columns of the matrix being processed. The user will rarely be interested in the contents of WORK and so must merely provide the appropriate declaration.

Most of the LINPACK subroutines do not call any other LINPACK subroutine. The only set of exceptions involves the condition estimator subroutines, with names ending in CO , each of which calls the corresponding FA routine to factor the matrix. However, almost all the LINPACK subroutines call one or more of the BLAS. To facilitate construction of libraries, the source code for each LINPACK subroutine includes comments which list all of the BLAS and Fortran-supplied functions required by that subroutine.

3. General Numerical Properties

The purpose of this section is to give an informal discussion of a group of closely-related topics -- errors, detection of singularity, accuracy of computed results, and especially scaling. By scaling we mean the multiplication of the rows and columns of a matrix A by nonzero scaling factors. This amounts to replacing A by $D_r A D_c$, where D_r and D_c are diagonal matrices consisting respectively of the row and column scaling factors. Many matrix problems have mathematically equivalent scaled versions. For example, the linear system

$$Ax = b \tag{3.1}$$

is equivalent to the system

$$(D_r A D_c)(D_c^{-1} x) = (D_r b) \tag{3.2}$$

and this latter system can be solved by applying, say, SGEFA to $D_r A D_c$ and then SGESL to $D_r b$ to give $D_c^{-1} x$.

Scaling is important for two reasons. First, even if two formulations of a problem are mathematically equivalent, it does not follow that their numerical solution in the presence of rounding error will give identical results. For example, it is easy to concoct cases where the use of LINPACK routines to solve (3.1) and (3.2) will give accurate answers for one and inaccurate answers for the other. The second reason is that some of the LINPACK routines provide the user with numbers from which the accuracy of his solutions can be estimated. However, the numbers and their interpretation depend very much on how the problem has been scaled. It is thus important for the LINPACK user to have some idea of what is a good scaling.

For simplicity we shall confine ourselves to the case of a square matrix A of order n , although much of what we have to say applies to the general rectangular matrices treated by the QR and SV routines. The discussion is informal, and the reader is referred to other parts of this guide and to the literature for details.

Scaling problems arise as a consequence of errors in the matrix A . These errors may have a number of sources. If the elements of A have been measured they will be inaccurate owing to the limitations of the measuring instruments. If they have been computed, truncation error or rounding error will contaminate them. Even a matrix that is known exactly may not be representable within the finite word length of a digital computer. For example, the binary expansion of 1/10 is nonterminating and must be rounded.

Subsequent computations performed on A itself may sometimes be regarded as another source of initial error. In particular, most of the LINPACK routines have the property that the computed solutions are the exact solutions of a problem involving a slightly perturbed matrix $A+E'$. We can then lump E' with the other errors in A to get a total error matrix E that accounts for initial errors and all the rounding errors made by the LINPACK routine in question. It will often happen that E' will be insignificant compared with the other errors, in which case we may assert that for practical purposes rounding error has played no role in the computation.

The presence of errors in A raises two problems. In the first place the error matrix E may be so large that $A+E$ can be singular, in which case many of the computations for which LINPACK was designed become meaningless. In the second place, even if E is small enough so that A is nonsingular, the solution of a problem involving $A+E$ may differ greatly from the one involving A . Thus we are led to ask two questions: How near is **A** to a singular matrix, and how greatly does an error E cause the solution to change? The answer to the second question depends on the problem being solved. For definiteness we shall suppose that we are trying to solve the linear system (3.1).

An answer to the above questions can be phrased in terms of a <u>condition number</u> associated with the matrix A ; however, we must first make precise what we mean by such vague phrases as "near", "differ greatly", etc. What is needed is a notion of size for a matrix, so that we can compare matrices unambiguously. The measure of size that we shall adopt in this introductory section is the number $\nu(A)$, which is defined to be the largest of the absolute values of the elements of A ; i.e.

$$\nu(A) = \max\{|a_{ij}| : \ i,j = 1,2,\ldots,n\} .$$

We can now say that E is smaller than A if $\nu(E) < \nu(A)$. In particular, the ratio

$\nu(E)/\nu(A)$ can be regarded as a relative indication of how much smaller E is than A. For example, if all the elements of A are roughly the same size and $\nu(E)/\nu(A) = 10^{-6}$, then the elements of A and A+E agree to about six significant figures.

The LINPACK routines allow the user to estimate a condition number $\kappa(A) \geq 1$ with the following properties. The smallest matrix E for which A+E is singular satisfies

(3.3) $$\frac{1}{f_n \kappa(A)} \leq \frac{\nu(E)}{\nu(A)} \leq \frac{f_n}{\kappa(A)} .$$

Moreover, if x+h denotes the solution of the linear system

$$(A+E)(x+h) = b ,$$

then for all sufficiently small E

(3.4) $$\frac{\nu(h)}{\nu(x)} \leq g_n \kappa(A) \frac{\nu(E)}{\nu(A)} .$$

The coefficients f_n and g_n depend on how κ was estimated, and they tend to make the bounds conservative.

It is instructive to examine the bounds (3.3) and (3.4) informally. If we assume that f_n is about one, then (3.3) says that a relative perturbation of order κ^{-1} can make A singular, but no smaller perturbation can. For example, if the elements of A are roughly the same size and $\kappa(A) = 10^6$, then perturbations in the sixth place of the elements of A can make A singular while perturbations in the seventh will not. If A is known only to six figures, it must then be considered effectively singular.

The second bound (3.4) says that the relative error in x due to the perturbation E is $\kappa(A)$ times the relative error that E induces in A. In the above example, if $\nu(E)$ is 10^{-10}, then $\nu(h)/\nu(x)$ is 10^{-4}, and we should not expect the components of x to be accurate to more than four figures.

Both (3.3) and (3.4) suggest that one may encounter serious problems in dealing with matrices for which κ is large. Such matrices are said to be <u>ill-conditioned with respect to inversion</u>. For properly scaled problems, κ provides a quantitative measure of difficulty we can expect. For example, the bound (3.4) gives the following rule of thumb: if $\kappa(A)$ is 10^k then the solution of a linear system computed in t-digit (decimal) arithmetic will have no more than t-k accurate figures. We stress again that A must be properly scaled for the rule of thumb to apply, a point which we shall return to in a moment.

Estimates for a condition number κ may be obtained from all LINPACK routines with the suffixes CO and DC (for the CHDC and QRDC routines, the pivoting option must be taken with JPVT initialized to zero). The details are as follows.

In CO routines take

$$\kappa \cong 1/\text{RCOND}, \quad (f_n = n,\ g_n = n^2).$$

In SVDC routines take

$$\kappa \cong S(1)/S(N), \quad (f_n = \sqrt{n},\ g_n = n).$$

In CHDC routines take

$$\kappa \cong (A(1,1)/A(N,N))**2 \quad (f_n = \sqrt{n},\ g_n = n),$$

where A is the output array.

In QRDC routines take

$$\kappa \cong A(1,1)/A(N,N), \quad (f_n = \sqrt{n},\ g_n = n),$$

where A is the output array.

For further details and sharper bounds in terms of norms, see the documentation for the individual routines.

A weak point in the above discussion is that the measure $\nu(E)$ attempts to compact information about the size of the elements of E into a single number and therefore cannot take into account special structure in E. If some of the elements of E are constrained to be much smaller than $\nu(E)$, the bounds (3.3) and (3.4) can be misleading. As an example, consider

$$A = \begin{bmatrix} 1 & 0 \\ 0 & 10^{-6} \end{bmatrix} .$$

It is easily seen that $\kappa(A) = 10^6$, and in fact that bound (3.3) is realistic in the sense that if

$$E = \begin{bmatrix} 0 & 0 \\ 0 & -10^{-6} \end{bmatrix}$$

then $\nu(E) = 1/\kappa$ and $A+E$ is singular. On the other hand, if we attempt to solve the system (3.1) in 8-digit arithmetic, we shall obtain full 8-digit accuracy in the solution -- contrary to our rule of thumb.

What has gone wrong? The answer is that in solving (3.1), we have in effect solved a perturbed system $A+\tilde{E}$, where the elements of $\tilde{E}$ have the following orders of magnitude:

$$\begin{bmatrix} 10^{-8} & 0 \\ 0 & 10^{-14} \end{bmatrix} .$$

Now the estimate $\nu(\tilde{E}) = 10^{-8}$ is unrealistic in (3.4) since it cannot account for the critical fact that $|e_{22}|$ is not greater than 10^{-14} .

The above example suggests that the condition number will not be meaningful unless the elements of the error matrix E are all about the same size. Any scaling D_rAD_c of A automatically induces the same scaling D_rED_c of E . Consequently, we recommend the following scaling strategy.

> Estimate the absolute size of the errors in the matrix A and then scale so that as nearly as possible all the estimates are equal.

The rest of this section is devoted to elaborating the practical implications of this strategy.

In the first place, it is important to realize that the errors to be estimated include all initial errors -- measurement, computational, and rounding -- and in many applications rounding error will be the least of these. An exception is when the elements of A are known or computed to high accuracy and are rounded to accommodate the floating-point word of the computer in question. In this case the error in an element is proportional to the size of the element, and the strategy reduces to scaling the original matrix so that all its elements are roughly equal. This is a frequently recommended strategy, but it is applicable only when the matrix E represents a uniform relative error in the elements of A . It should be noted, however, that "equilibration" routines intended to scale a matrix A so that its elements are roughly equal in size can be applied instead to the matrix of error estimates to obtain the proper scaling factors.

It may be impossible to equilibrate the matrix of error estimates by row and column scaling, in which case the condition number may not be a reliable indicator of near singularity. This possibility is even more likely in special applications, where the class of permissible scaling operations may be restricted. For example, in dealing with symmetric matrices one must restrict oneself to scaling of the form DAD in order to preserve symmetry. As another example, row scaling a least squares problem amounts to solving a weighted problem, which may be impermissible in statistical applications.

Finally, although we have justified our scaling strategy by saying that it makes the condition number meaningful, the same scaling can have a beneficial effect on the numerical behavior of a number of LINPACK routines, in particular all routines based on Gaussian elimination with pivoting (i.e. GE and SI routines). However, the numerical properties of other routines are essentially unaffected by some types of scaling. For example, scaling of the form DAD will not change to any great extent the accuracy of solutions computed from PO routines. Likewise, QRDC is unaffected by column scaling, as also are the GE and GB routines.

Chapter 1: General Matrices

Subroutines: SGECO, SGEFA, SGESL, SGEDI

1. Overview

Purpose. The LINPACK subroutines in this chapter operate on general square nonsymmetric matrices. The operations performed include the triangular factorization of matrices, the estimation of the matrix condition number, the solution of simultaneous linear equations and the calculation of determinants and inverses. Operations on symmetric matrices, band matrices, triangular matrices and rectangular matrices are covered in other chapters.

Background. Let A be a real or complex square matrix of order n. There is an upper triangular matrix U and a matrix L which is the product of elementary lower triangular and permutation matrices such that $A = LU$. This factorization can be used to solve linear equations $Ax = b$ by solving successively $L(Ux) = b$; to compute the determinant of A as $\det(L)\cdot\det(U)$; and to compute the inverse of A as $A^{-1} = U^{-1}L^{-1}$.

The condition number $\kappa(A)$ is a quantity which measures the sensitivity of the solution x to errors in the matrix A and the right hand side b. If the relative error in A is of size ε, then the resulting relative error in x can be as large as $\kappa(A)\varepsilon$. Errors in A can arise in many ways. In particular, the effect of the roundoff error introduced by the subroutines in this chapter can usually be assessed by taking ε to be a small multiple of the rounding unit.

It is possible to efficiently compute a quantity RCOND which is an estimate of the reciprocal condition, $1/\kappa(A)$. If RCOND is approximately 10^{-d} then the elements of x can usually be expected to have d fewer significant figures of accuracy than the elements of A. Consequently, if RCOND is so small that in floating point arithmetic it is negligible compared to 1.0, then x may have no significant figures. On most computers, this condition may be tested by the logical expression

```
1.0 + RCOND .EQ. 1.0 .
```

When this expression is true, the matrix can be considered to be "singular to working precision." As a special case, if exact singularity is detected, RCOND may be set to 0.0.

If A is badly scaled, then the interpretation of RCOND is more delicate. For a detailed discussion of RCOND, including the consequences of unusual scaling in A and errors in b, see sections 4 and 6.

2. Usage

Single precision, general matrices. The four subroutines for single precision, general matrices are SGECO, SGEFA, SGESL, and SGEDI. Ordinarily, SGECO or SGEFA will be called once to factor a particular matrix and then SGESL and SGEDI will be called to apply the factorization as many times as needed.

SGECO uses Gaussian elimination with partial pivoting to compute the LU factorization of a matrix and then estimates its condition. The calling sequence is

```
CALL SGECO(A,LDA,N,IPVT,RCOND,Z) .
```

On entry,

A — is a doubly subscripted array with dimension (LDA,N) which contains the matrix whose factorization is to be computed.

LDA — is the leading dimension of the array A .

N — is the order of the matrix A and the number of elements in the vectors IPVT and Z .

On return,

A — contains in its upper triangle an upper triangular matrix U and in its strict lower triangle the multipliers necessary to construct a matrix L so that A = LU .

IPVT — is a singly subscripted integer array of dimension N which contains the pivot information necessary to construct the permutations in L . Specifically, IPVT(K) is the index of the K-th pivot row.

RCOND — is an estimate of the reciprocal condition, $1/\kappa(A)$. If RCOND is so small that the logical expression 1.0 + RCOND .EQ. 1.0 is true, then A can usually be regarded as singular to working precision. If RCOND is exactly zero, then SGESL and SGEDI may divide by zero.

Z — is a singly subscripted array of dimension N used for work space. If A is close to a singular matrix, then Z will contain an approximate null vector in the sense that $\|Az\| = \text{RCOND}\cdot\|A\|\cdot\|z\|$ (see Section 4).

SGEFA should be used in place of SGECO if the condition estimate is not needed. The calling sequence is

CALL SGEFA(A,LDA,N,IPVT,INFO) ,

On entry,

A is a doubly subscripted array with dimension (LDA,N) which contains the matrix whose factorization is to be computed.

LDA is the leading dimension of the array A .

N is the order of the matrix A and the number of elements in the vector IPVT .

On return,

A contains in its upper triangle an upper triangular matrix U and in its strict lower triangle the multipliers necessary to construct a matrix L so that A = LU .

IPVT is a singly subscripted integer array of dimension N which contains the pivot information necessary to construct the permutations in L . Specifically, IPVT(K) is the index of the K-th pivot row.

INFO is an integer returned by SGEFA which, if it is 0 , indicates that SGESL and SGEDI can be safely used. If INFO = K $\neq$ 0 , then SGESL and SGEDI may divide by U(K,K) = 0.0 . If U has several zero diagonal elements, K will be the index of the last one. Although a nonzero INFO technically indicates singularity, RCOND is a more reliable indicator.

SGECO is usually called first to factor the matrix and estimate its condition. The actual factorization is done by SGEFA which can be called in place of SGECO if the condition estimate is not needed. The time required by SGECO is roughly (1 + 9/N) times the time required by SGEFA . Thus when N = 9 , SGECO costs twice as much as SGEFA , but when N = 90 , SGECO costs 10 percent more.

Since any matrix has an LU factorization, there is no error return from SGECO or SGEFA . However, the factors can be singular and consequently unusable by SGESL and SGEDI . Either RCOND or INFO should be tested before calling SGESL .

SGESL uses the LU factorization of a matrix A to solve linear systems of the form

$$Ax = b$$

or

$$A^T x = b$$

where A^T is the transpose of A . The calling sequence is

CALL SGESL(A,LDA,N,IPVT,B,JOB) .

On entry,

A is a doubly subscripted array with dimension (LDA,N) which contains the factorization computed by SGECO or SGEFA . It is not changed by SGESL .

LDA is the leading dimension of the array A .

N is the order of the matrix A and the number of elements in the vectors B and IPVT .

IPVT is a singly subscripted integer array of dimension N which contains the pivot information from SGECO or SGEFA .

B is a singly subscripted array of dimension N which contains the right hand side b of a system of simultaneous linear equations $Ax = b$ or $A^Tx = b$.

JOB indicates what is to be computed. If JOB is 0 , the system $Ax = b$ is solved and if JOB is nonzero, the system $A^Tx = b$ is solved.

On return,

B contains the solution, x .

If the upper triangular factor of A has a zero element on the diagonal (a situation that will cause INFO ≠ 0 in SGEFA or RCOND = 0.0 in SGECO), a division by zero will occur in SGESL . Technically this means that the matrix A is singular, but it is often caused by incorrect setting of LDA or other improper use of the subroutines.

SGEDI uses the LU factorization of a matrix to compute its determinant and inverse. However, many calculations formulated in terms of matrix inverses can be reformulated in terms of the solution of sets of linear equations. The reformulated versions often require less time and produce more accurate results. Several examples are included in Section 3. The calling sequence of SGEDI is

CALL SGEDI(A,LDA,N,IPVT,DET,WORK,JOB) .

On entry,

A is a doubly subscripted array with dimension (LDA,N) which contains the factorization computed by SGECO or SGEFA .

LDA is the leading dimension of the array A .

N is the order of the matrix A and the number of elements in the vectors WORK and IPVT .

IPVT is a singly subscripted integer array of dimension N which contains the pivot information from SGECO or SGEFA .

WORK is a singly subscripted array of dimension N used for work space.

JOB indicates what is to be computed. If JOB is 11 then both the determinant and inverse are computed. If JOB is 1 only the inverse is computed. If JOB is 10 only the determinant is computed.

On return,

A contains the inverse of the original matrix if requested. If the units digit of JOB is zero, then A is unchanged.

DET is a singly subscripted array with 2 elements which contains the determinant of A in the form det(A) = DET(1)*10.0**DET(2) , although this expression may underflow or overflow if evaluated. DET(1) is normalized so that $1.0 \leq |DET(1)| < 10.0$ or DET(1) = 0.0 . DET(2) contains an integer stored as a real number. If the tens digit of JOB is zero, then DET is not referenced.

Double precision, general matrices. The calling sequences of the double precision, general subroutines DGECO , DGEFA , DGESL and DGEDI are the same as those of the corresponding single precision "S" subroutines except that A , B , RCOND , DET , Z and WORK are DOUBLE PRECISION variables.

Complex, general matrices. The calling sequences of the complex, general subroutines CGECO , CGEFA , CGESL and CGEDI are the same as those of the corresponding single precision "S" subroutines except that A , B , DET , Z and WORK are COMPLEX variables, RCOND is a REAL variable and the system solved by CGESL when JOB is nonzero involves the complex conjugate transpose of A .

Double precision complex, general matrices. In those computing systems where they are available, the calling sequences of the double precision complex, general subroutines ZGECO , ZGEFA , ZGESL and ZGEDI are the same as those of the corresponding single precision "S" subroutines except that A , B , DET , Z and WORK are COMPLEX*16 variables, RCOND is a DOUBLE PRECISION variable and the system solved by ZGESL when JOB is nonzero involves the complex conjugate transpose of A .

3. Examples

The following program segments illustrate the use of the single precision subroutines for general matrices. Examples showing the use of the "D" , "C" and "Z" subroutines could be obtained by changing the subroutine names and type declarations.

The first program factors a matrix, tests for near singularity and then solves a single system Ax = b .

```
      REAL A(50,50),B(50),Z(50),T,RCOND
      INTEGER IPVT(50)
      DATA LDA /50/
      N = ...
      DO 20 J = 1, N
         DO 10 I = 1, N
            A(I,J) = ...
   10    CONTINUE
   20 CONTINUE
      CALL SGECO(A,LDA,N,IPVT,RCOND,Z)
      WRITE(..., ...) RCOND
      T = 1.0 + RCOND
      IF (T .EQ. 1.0) GO TO 90
      DO 30 I = 1, N
         B(I) = ...
   30 CONTINUE
      CALL SGESL(A,LDA,N,IPVT,B,0)
      DO 40 I = 1, N
         WRITE(..., ...) B(I)
   40 CONTINUE
      STOP
   90 WRITE(..., 99)
   99 FORMAT(40H MATRIX IS SINGULAR TO WORKING PRECISION)
      STOP
      END
```

The next program segment replaces C , a matrix with K columns by $A^{-1}C$ without explicitly forming A^{-1} .

```
      CALL SGEFA(A,LDA,N,IPVT,INFO)
      IF (INFO .NE. 0) GO TO ...
      DO 10 J = 1, K
         CALL SGESL(A,LDA,N,IPVT,C(1,J),0)
   10 CONTINUE
```

The next program segment replaces C , a matrix with K rows by CA^{-1} without explicitly forming A^{-1} . Since this involves the rows rather than the columns of C , the device used in the previous example is not applicable.

```
      CALL SGEFA(A,LDA,N,IPVT,INFO)
      IF (INFO .NE. 0) GO TO ...
      DO 30 I = 1, K
         DO 10 J = 1, N
            Z(J) = C(I,J)
   10    CONTINUE
         CALL SGESL(A,LDA,N,IPVT,Z,1)
         DO 20 J = 1, N
            C(I,J) = Z(J)
   20    CONTINUE
   30 CONTINUE
```

The next segment prints out the condition number and the determinant of a matrix. The determinant is printed with a simulated E format that allows a four-digit exponent and avoids underflow/overflow difficulties.

```
      CALL SGECO(A,LDA,N,IPVT,RCOND,Z)
      IF (RCOND .EQ. 0.0) GO TO ...
      COND = 1.0/RCOND
      CALL SGEDI(A,LDA,N,IPVT,DET,Z,10)
      K = INT(DET(2))
      WRITE(..., 10) COND,DET(1),K
   10 FORMAT(13H CONDITION = , E15.5/15H DETERMINANT = , F20.15, 1HE, I5)
```

The next example illustrates how the actual condition number, COND , of a matrix might be computed by forming the matrix inverse. Such a computation would be of interest primarily to numerical analysts who wish to investigate the claim that RCOND returned by SGECO is a good estimate of 1/COND .

```
      ANORM = 0.0
      DO 10 J = 1, N
         ANORM = AMAX1(ANORM, SASUM(N,A(1,J),1) )
   10 CONTINUE
      CALL SGECO(A,LDA,N,IPVT,RCOND,Z)
      IF (RCOND .EQ. 0.0) GO TO ...
```

```
      CALL SGEDI(A,LDA,N,IPVT,DUMMY,WORK,1)
      AINORM = 0.0
      DO 20 J = 1, N
         AINORM = AMAX1(AINORM, SASUM(N,A(1,J),1) )
   20 CONTINUE
      COND = ANORM*AINORM
      RATIO = RCOND*COND
```

The Basic Linear Algebra Subprogram expression

```
      SASUM(N,A(1,J),1)
```

computes

$$\sum_{I=1}^{N} |A(I,J)| \ .$$

The final example is a complete subroutine SGEIM for obtaining a highly accurate solution to a system of linear equations. It uses single precision for most of the calculations and employs the technique of iterative improvement which requires extended precision arithmetic. This implementation uses two of the Basic Linear Algebra Subprograms, SASUM and SDSDOT . The extended precision, in this case double precision, is obtained in SDSDOT .

SGEIM usually returns a solution X which is equal to the exact solution to the input problem to within single precision on the particular computer being used. It also returns an estimate, RELERR , of the relative error in the solution that is obtained by SGESL alone, that is, without iterative refinement. A zero value for INFO indicates success. A negative value of INFO indicates the process did not converge because the matrix is too close to singular. A positive value of INFO indicates that SGEFA detected exact singularity.

SGEIM requires a working array AA of the same dimensions as A and a working vector R of the same length as B and X . The input A and B are not altered.

This subroutine is not included in LINPACK itself for several reasons. The corresponding double precision and complex subroutines would require quadruple precision and complex double precision dot products, respectively. Such extended precision cannot be obtained readily on many computers and cannot be efficiently simulated in standard Fortran. The extra storage requirements make the technique fairly costly for large matrices. The availability of RCOND partially obviates the need for the estimate provided by RELERR . Finally, most problems involve inexact input data and obtaining a highly accurate solution to an imprecise problem may not be justified.

```
      SUBROUTINE SGEIM(A,LDA,N,B,X,RELERR,AA,R,IPVT,INFO)
      INTEGER LDA,N,INFO
      REAL A(LDA,1),B(N),X(N),RELERR,AA(LDA,1),R(N)
      INTEGER IPVT(N)
C
C     EXAMPLE ILLUSTRATING ITERATIVE IMPROVEMENT
C       USES SDSDOT,SASUM,SGEFA,SGESL
C
      REAL XNORM,RNORM,SASUM,SDSDOT
      DO 20 J = 1, N
         DO 10 I = 1, N
            AA(I,J) = A(I,J)
   10    CONTINUE
         X(J) = B(J)
   20 CONTINUE
      CALL SGEFA(AA,LDA,N,IPVT,INFO)
      IF (INFO .NE. 0) GO TO 60
      CALL SGESL(AA,LDA,N,IPVT,X,0)
      XNORM = SASUM(N,X,1)
      RELERR = 0.0
      IF (XNORM .EQ. 0.0) GO TO 60
      DO 50 ITER = 1, 20
         DO 30 I = 1, N
            R(I) = SDSDOT(N,A(I,1),LDA,X(1),1,-B(I))
   30    CONTINUE
         CALL SGESL(AA,LDA,N,IPVT,R,0)
         DO 40 I = 1, N
            X(I) = X(I) - R(I)
   40    CONTINUE
         RNORM = SASUM(N,R,1)
         IF (ITER .EQ. 1) RELERR = RNORM/XNORM
         T = XNORM + RNORM
         IF (T .EQ. XNORM) GO TO 60
   50 CONTINUE
      INFO = -1
   60 CONTINUE
      RETURN
      END

      REAL FUNCTION SDSDOT(N,X,INCX,Y,INCY,C)
      REAL X(INCX,1),Y(INCY,1),C
      DOUBLE PRECISION SUM
      SUM = 0.0D0
```

```
      IF (N .LE. 0) GO TO 20
      DO 10 I = 1, N
         SUM = SUM + DBLE(X(1,I))*DBLE(Y(1,I))
   10 CONTINUE
   20 SUM = SUM + DBLE(C)
      SDSDOT = SNGL(SUM)
      RETURN
      END
```

4. Algorithms

The factorization. The algorithm used to factor a general full matrix or a general band matrix is a version of Gaussian elimination with partial pivoting. The factorization subroutines generate a matrix L^{-1} of the form

$$L^{-1} = L_{n-1}P_{n-1} \cdots L_2P_2L_1P_1$$

such that

$$L^{-1}A = U$$

where U is upper triangular. Each matrix P_k is a permutation matrix obtained by interchanging at most two rows of the identity. Each matrix L_k is an "elementary eliminator" which differs from the identity at most by elements below the diagonal in a single column. More precisely,

$$L_k = I + m_k e_k^T$$

where the first k components of the vector m_k are zero and where e_k is the k-th column of the identity. The elements m_{ik} of m_k are called the negative multipliers and are chosen to introduce zeros into the last $n-k$ components of the k-th column of the matrix. The permutation P_k is chosen to provide numerical stability by insuring $|m_{ik}| \le 1$.

The calculation of $L^{-1}A$ is accomplished by carrying out permutations and elimination operations on A , rather than by actual matrix multiplication. Neither L nor L^{-1} is explicitly formed, but rather the multipliers are stored below the diagonal in the array originally containing A and the indices which specify the permutations are stored in the pivot vector, ipvt.

In outline, the factorization algorithm is:

```
for  k = 1,...,n-1 do
    find ℓ such that |a_{ℓ,k}| = max_{k≤i≤n} |a_{i,k}| ;
    save ℓ in ipvt(k) ;
    if a_{ℓ,k} = 0 then skip to end of k loop;
    interchange a_{k,k} and a_{ℓ,k} ;
    for i = k+1,...,n do
        m_{i,k} = -a_{i,k}/a_{k,k}  (save in a_{i,k} );
    for j = k+1,...,n do
        interchange a_{k,j} and a_{ℓ,j} ;
        for i = k+1,...,n do
            a_{i,j} ← a_{i,j} + m_{i,k}*a_{k,j} ;
    end j
end k .
```

In terms of this outline, P_k is the identity with the k-th and ℓ-th rows interchanged and L_k is the identity with $m_{i,k}$, $i = k+1,\ldots,n$ inserted below the diagonal. The upper triangular matrix U is stored in the upper triangle of A, including the diagonal, when the algorithm has been completed. The quantity $a_{\ell,k}$ which is moved into $a_{k,k}$, is called the pivot. If it is zero, then at the k-th step of the elimination, the entire k-th column must be zero below the diagonal and $P_k = L_k = I$. A zero pivot does not indicate failure of the factorization, but simply that the factor U is singular and cannot be used for solving linear systems.

The only modification necessary for complex arithmetic is to define $|z| = |\mathrm{real}(z)| + |\mathrm{imag}(z)|$. This can be computed more rapidly than the conventional modulus and has all the necessary numerical properties.

The condition estimate. The condition number of A is

$$\kappa(A) = \|A\| \, \|A^{-1}\|$$

using the ℓ_1 norm, that is

$$\|x\| = \sum_{i=1}^{n} |x_i|$$

$$\|A\| = \max_x \|Ax\|/\|x\|$$

$$\|A^{-1}\| = \max_z \|z\|/\|Az\|$$

The ℓ_1 vector norm is chosen because it can be computed rapidly and because the subordinate matrix norm can be computed directly from the columns a_j by

$$\|A\| = \max_j \|a_j\| .$$

The basic task of the condition estimator is to obtain a good approximation for $\|A^{-1}\|$ without computing all the columns of A^{-1} . This is accomplished by choosing a certain vector y , solving a single system $Az = y$, and then estimating

$$\|A^{-1}\| \approx \|z\|/\|y\| .$$

In order to avoid overflow, an estimate of $1/\kappa(A)$ is computed, namely

$$\mathrm{RCOND} = \frac{\|y\|}{\|A\|\,\|z\|} .$$

Since $\|A^{-1}\| \geq \|z\|/\|y\|$, the estimate actually satisfies

$$1/\mathrm{RCOND} \leq \kappa(A) .$$

If this estimate is to be reasonably accurate, it is necessary that y be chosen in such a way that $\|z\|/\|y\|$ is nearly as large as possible. The technique used is described in a paper by Cline, Moler, Stewart and Wilkinson.

In the condition estimation subroutines, y is obtained by solving $A^Ty = e$ where e is a scalar multiple of a vector with components ± 1 . Using the factorization $A = LU$ this involves solving $U^Tw = e$ and then solving $L^Ty = w$. The components of e are determined during the calculation of w so that $\|w\|$ is large. Suppose that $e_1,\ldots,e_{k-1}$ and $w_1,\ldots,w_{k-1}$ have already been obtained. In the process, the quantities

$$t_j = \sum_{i=1}^{k-1} u_{ij}w_i , \quad j = k,\ldots,n$$

are also computed. The equation determining w_k is

$$u_{kk}w_k = e_k - t_k .$$

The two possible choices for e_k are

$$e_k^+ = \mathrm{sign}(-t_k) \quad \text{and} \quad e_k^- = -e_k^+$$

which give

$$w_k^+ = (e_k^+ - t_k)/u_{kk} \quad \text{and} \quad w_k^- = (e_k^- - t_k)/u_{kk} .$$

The t_j's are temporarily updated, $t_k^+ = e_k^+ - t_k$, $t_k^- = e_k^- - t_k$,

$$t_j^+ = t_j + u_{kj}w_k^+ \quad \text{and} \quad t_j^- = t_j + u_{kj}w_k^- , \quad j = k+1,\ldots,n .$$

The probable growth in $\|w\|$ is then predicted by comparing $\sum_{j=k}^{n} |t_j^+|$ with $\sum_{j=k}^{n} |t_j^-|$ and choosing the larger. The resulting + or - is used to specify the choice of e_k and hence w_k . These steps are repeated for $k = 1,\ldots,n$.

The algorithm may produce overflow during division by u_{kk} if it is small and breaks down completely if any u_{kk} is zero. This indicates that $\kappa(A)$ is large or possibly that A is singular. The overflows and divisions by zero are avoided by rescaling e so that $|w_k^+| \leq 1$ and $|z_k| \leq 1$. The resulting value of RCOND may underflow and be set to zero. With this scaling it is not necessary to handle exact singularity as a special case. A singular A will merely produce a small, possibly zero, value of RCOND .

The vector z satisfies

$$\|Az\| = \text{RCOND}\cdot\|A\|\cdot\|z\| .$$

Consequently, if RCOND is small, then z is an approximate null vector of the nearly singular matrix A .

The general outline of the entire process is

compute $\|A\|$

factor $A = LU$

solve $U^T w = e$, choosing e_k as described

solve $L^T y = w$

solve $Lv = y$

solve $Uz = v$

$\text{RCOND} = \|y\|/(\|A\|\,\|z\|)$.

Solving linear systems. With the factorization $A = LU$ the linear system $Ax = b$ is equivalent to the two triangular systems, $Ly = b$ and $Ux = y$. The algorithm thus involves two stages. The first stage, the forward elimination, produces $y = L^{-1}b$ by applying the same permutation and elimination operations to b that were applied to the columns of A during the factorization. The second stage, the back substitution, consists of solving the upper triangular system $Ux = y$. To obtain an algorithm which involves operations on the columns of U , this system can be written

$$x_1\begin{bmatrix} u_{11} \\ 0 \\ 0 \\ \vdots \\ 0 \end{bmatrix} + x_2\begin{bmatrix} u_{12} \\ u_{22} \\ 0 \\ \vdots \\ 0 \end{bmatrix} + \cdots + x_n\begin{bmatrix} u_{1n} \\ u_{2n} \\ \vdots \\ \vdots \\ u_{nn} \end{bmatrix} = y .$$

The components of x are computed in the order $x_n,\ldots,x_2,x_1$.

The implementation overwrites the input b with the solution x . In outline, the solution algorithm for $Ax = b$ is

<u>for</u> $k = 1,\ldots,n-1$ <u>do</u>

  interchange b_k and $b_{ipvt(k)}$;

  <u>for</u> $i = k+1,\ldots,n$ <u>do</u>

    $b_i \leftarrow b_i + m_{i,k}b_k$;

<u>end</u> k;

  (b now contains y)

<u>for</u> $k = n,\ldots,1$ <u>do</u>

  $b_k \leftarrow b_k/u_{k,k}$;

  <u>for</u> $i = 1,\ldots,k-1$ <u>do</u>

    $b_i \leftarrow b_i - u_{i,k}b_k$;

<u>end</u> k;

  (b now contains x) .

The linear system $A^Tx = b$ is equivalent to the two systems $U^Ty = b$ and $L^Tx = y$. For these systems, a column oriented algorithm involves inner products.

<u>for</u> $k = 1,\ldots,n$ <u>do</u>

  $b_k \leftarrow (b_k - \sum_{i=1}^{k-1} u_{i,k}b_i)/u_{k,k}$;

<u>end</u> k ;

<u>for</u> $k = n-1,\ldots,1$ <u>do</u>

  $b_k \leftarrow b_k + \sum_{i=k+1}^{n} m_{i,k}b_i$;

  interchange b_k and $b_{ipvt(k)}$;

<u>end</u> k ;

If the steps involved in computing the inner products were written out, the algorithms for $Ax = b$ and $A^Tx = b$ would be seen to involve identical counts of arithmetic operations.

<u>Determinant</u>. The factorization $A = LU$ allows the determinant $\det(A)$ to be computed from $\det(A) = (-1)^p \prod_{k=1}^{n} u_{k,k}$ where p is the number of times $ipvt(k) \neq k$.

<u>Inverse</u>. The factorization $A = LU$ allows the inverse A^{-1} to be computed from $A^{-1} = U^{-1}L^{-1}$. The first stage involves the replacement of U by U^{-1} using a column oriented algorithm. Let $V = U^{-1}$, let U_{k-1} be the leading $k-1$ by $k-1$ minor of U , let u_k

be the vector consisting of the first $k-1$ components of the k-th column of U and let V_{k-1} and v_k be the corresponding parts of V. Then

$$\begin{bmatrix} U_{k-1} & u_k \\ 0 & u_{k,k} \end{bmatrix} \begin{bmatrix} V_{k-1} & v_k \\ 0 & v_{k,k} \end{bmatrix} = \begin{bmatrix} I_{k-1} & 0 \\ 0 & 1 \end{bmatrix} .$$

Consequently,

$$V_{k-1} = U_{k-1}^{-1} ,$$

$$v_{k,k} = 1/u_{k,k} ,$$

and

$$v_k = -v_{k,k} V_{k-1} u_k$$

The product $V_{k-1}u_k$ is computed as a linear combination of the columns of V_{k-1}, taking advantage of the triangularity. Once U^{-1} has been obtained, then

$$A^{-1} = U^{-1} L_{n-1} P_{n-1} \cdots L_1 P_1 .$$

The complete algorithm for generating A^{-1} from L and U follows. When implemented, the elements v_{ij} of $V = U^{-1}$ overwrite the elements u_{ij} of U in the upper triangle of A and then the elements a_{ij} of A^{-1} overwrite both the v_{ij} and the multipliers m_{ij} which have been saved in the strict lower triangle of A. A single vector of temporary storage is required to save one column of multipliers.

```
for  k = 1,...,n do
    v_{k,k} = 1/u_{k,k} ;
    for  i = 1,...,k-1 do
        v_{i,k} = -v_{k,k}·u_{i,k} ;
    for  j = k+1,...,n do
        v_{k,j} = 0 ;
        for  i = 1,...,k do
            v_{i,j} ← v_{i,j} + u_{k,j}·v_{i,k} ;
    end  j ;
end  k ;
for  k = n-1,...,1 do
    for  i = k+1,...,n do
        retrieve  m_{i,k}  from  a_{i,k} ;
        a_{i,k} ← 0 ;
    end  i ;
```

```
        for j = k+1,...,n do
            for i = 1,...,n do
                a_{i,k} ← a_{i,k} + m_{i,k} v_{i,j};
        end j;
        swap columns  k  and  ipvt(k)  of  A ;
    end  k ;
```

5. Programming Details

SGEFA

The principal loop involves K , the index of the pivot row and column. The subroutine ISAMAX is used to find L , the row index of the largest element below the diagonal in the K-th column. The quantity K-1 must be added to the value returned by ISAMAX since it starts counting at the K-th row. If the largest element is nonzero, it is moved into the K,K position to become the pivot. If the largest element is zero, this indicates that the entire K-th column below the diagonal is already zero and hence the remainder of the loop can be skipped. The emergence of a zero pivot does not mean failure of the triangularization algorithm itself, but that the resulting triangular factors cannot be used by SGESL or the inversion part of SGEDI .

The negative multipliers are obtained by taking the reciprocal of the pivot and then calling SSCAL . This is done because it is expected that one division followed by N-K multiplications is faster than N-K divisions. The division may cause overflow if the pivot is very near the underflow limit and its reciprocal cannot be represented. With the complex versions CGEFA and ZGEFA , some compilers may even produce code which leads to division by zero. Let A(K,K) = x + iy be the complex pivot. This number will pass the test for nonzero if $|x| + |y|$ is nonzero, but if the reciprocal is computed by $(x - iy)/(x^2 + y^2)$, an unnecessary division by zero will occur when x^2 and y^2 underflow. No attempt has been made to compensate for this unfortunately common defect in compilers. The negatives of the multipliers are computed so that the elimination will involve additions, rather than subtractions. The negative multipliers are stored in place of the zeros that would theoretically be created by the elimination. They are not rearranged by any subsequent pivoting.

The elimination portion of the K-th step involves a loop with a column index J running from K+1 to N . The interchanges between the K-th and L-th rows are made and the revised matrix elements obtained by a call to SAXPY . Almost all the time required by SGEFA is taken "inside" SAXPY .

Underflows are possible in SAXPY , but they are harmless if they are quietly set to zero. Overflows are also possible in SAXPY and indicate that some rescaling of the problem is necessary before the matrix can be factored by this subroutine.

SGECO

The ℓ_1 norm of the matrix is obtained by N calls to the subroutine SASUM . The LU-factorization of the matrix is obtained by a call to SGEFA .

The estimate for the norm of the inverse is obtained by the solution of four triangular systems. The first of these, $U^T w = e$, is the most complicated because it also involves the determination of e . The variable EK , which effectively determines the components e_k , is initially set to 1.0 . Its sign will subsequently be changed to cause growth in w and its magnitude will be changed as e is rescaled to avoid overflow. The auxiliary vector Z is initialized to zero. This vector has a dual role; at the K-th step in the solution of $U^T w = e$, the first K components contain the elements of w that have already been determined (although they may be rescaled later), and the remaining elements contain the quantities t_j which are used in determining the sign of e_k and which are described in the previous section. The K-th component of w , stored temporarily in the variable WK , is obtained by a division,

$$WK = (EK - Z(K))/A(K,K) .$$

Before this division is done, the numerator is rescaled if necessary so that the result satisfies $|WK| \le 1.0$. The entire vector Z is scaled, thereby scaling both the emerging w and the remaining t_j's . An alternate candidate, WKM , is also considered. It satisfies $|WKM| \le |WK|$, but it may occasionally lead to larger values of the t_j's and hence probably to larger $\|w\|$. The variables S and SM are used to compute $\sum t_j^+$ and $\sum t_j^-$, respectively. Since only one auxiliary vector is available, the t_j^- are not saved. It is expected that S will usually be larger than SM and so that the t_j^- will not be needed. If SM happens to be larger than S , then the t_j^- have to be recomputed and stored in Z . Finally, w , which is stored in Z , is scaled so that $\|w\| = 1.0$.

The three remaining triangular systems are $L^T y = w$, $Lv = y$, and $Uz = v$. The program segments are the same as those in SGESL (see below), except that rescaling is applied whenever necessary to insure that each component about to be determined will not exceed 1.0 . The column orientation leads to the use of SDOT for the solution of $L^T y = w$ and of SAXPY for the other two systems.

Underflows in SGECO are quite likely but, as usual, are harmless if set to zero. The rescaling should prevent overflows and divisions by zero, even with poorly implemented complex division.

SGESL

The solution of $Ax = b$ using an LU-factorization of A involves the solution of $Ly = b$ and then $Ux = y$. Since L is not explicitly stored, the solution of the first system is best seen as applying the same pivoting and elimination operations to b as were applied to the columns of A by SGEFA using SAXPY . The solution of the second system is a straightforward implementation using SAXPY of the column oriented algorithm presented in the previous section.

The solution of $A^T x = b$ involves the solution of $U^T y = b$ and then $L^T x = y$. Here the column orientation leads to the use of SDOT instead of SAXPY . Again, the pivoting is part of the solution of the system involving L .

Overflows are possible when SGESL calls either SAXPY or SDOT . In almost all cases, they indicate the components of the solution are too large to be represented on the computer being used. Rescaling of the problem is necessary. Divisions by zero resulting from poorly implemented complex division should not occur if the matrix has made it through SGEFA successfully.

SGEDI

The determinant of L is found by checking the number of times IPVT(I) is not equal to I . The determinant of U is found by forming the product of the diagonal elements. Overflows and underflows would be quite likely if this product were formed in the conventional way. Instead, a two-component format is used for DET . The first component is kept between 1.0 and 10.0 in magnitude and the second component is the exponent d of a scale factor 10^d . Although the value of d is an integer, d is stored as a real or complex variable.

The inverse of A is formed in place of its LU-factorization using the column oriented algorithm described in the previous section. Subroutine SAXPY is used to add multiples of columns to other columns. Since L^{-1} occurs on the right in the equation $A^{-1} = U^{-1}L^{-1}$, the pivoting included in L involves the columns of U^{-1} and it is possible to use SSWAP to carry out the interchanges. Other subroutines in this chapter do not use SSWAP since row interchanges are involved. As implemented here, a column oriented algorithm requires a work vector for the temporary storage of each column of multipliers.

6. Performance

Accuracy. Roundoff errors in floating point arithmetic operations usually cause the quantities computed by the subroutines in this chapter to be somewhat inaccurate. The following fairly vague statements give a general idea of the extent of these inaccuracies.

SGEFA produces matrices L and U for which the product LU is almost always within roundoff error of A , no matter how close A is to being singular.

SGESL produces a vector x for which Ax is almost always within roundoff error of b , no matter how close A is to being singular. However, the difference between the computed x and the exact solution $x_* = A^{-1}b$ will usually be large if A is close to singular, that is if RCOND is small. The difference between x and x_* will usually be comparable to the difference caused by roundoff error in the elements of the original A.

SGEDI produces an approximate inverse X for which the product AX will be close to the identity I if the elements of X are "small", but AX might not be close to I if the elements of X are "large".

SGECO has experimentally been shown to produce an estimate RCOND for which 1/RCOND is usually the same order of magnitude as the actual condition number.

To make these statements more precise, we need to introduce the following notation. Let a_j be the columns of A . Let

$$\|x\| = \sum_i |x_i| ,$$

$$\|A\| = \max_x \frac{\|Ax\|}{\|x\|} = \max_j \|a_j\| ,$$

$$\kappa(A) = \|A\| \|A^{-1}\| .$$

Let ε_M be the rounding unit of the particular computer being used, i.e. ε_M is the distance from 1.0 to the next largest floating point number. For a computer with base β and t digits in its floating point fraction, $\varepsilon_M = \beta^{-t}$.

Let A be the matrix of floating point numbers actually input to SGEFA or SGECO . Let U be the upper triangular matrix and let L be the hypothetical matrix which could be constructed from the multipliers and pivot information produced by the SGEFA .

If certain technical assumptions are made which imply that the floating point arithmetic behaves in a "reasonable" way, it is possible to prove there is a coefficient ρ_n, depending upon n, but not upon A, so that

$$\|A-LU\| \leq \rho_n \|A\| \varepsilon_M .$$

The coefficient ρ_n involves the size of the elements possibly encountered during factorization. If ρ_n is not too large, this inequality says the error in the product LU is on the order of roundoff errors in A itself, even if $\kappa(A)$ is large.

Let b be the vector of floating numbers actually input to SGESL and let x be the resulting computed solution, also a vector of floating point numbers. It is possible to prove that

$$\|Ax-b\| \leq \sigma_n \|A\| \|x\| \varepsilon_M$$

where σ_n is another growth coefficient comparable to ρ_n. If σ_n is not too large, this inequality says that the size of the <u>residual</u>, $b - Ax$, is on the order of roundoff errors in A and x, even if $\kappa(A)$ is large. If, in addition, A is nonsingular, let $x_* = A^{-1}b$ be the exact answer. Then it is possible to prove that

$$\|x-x_*\| \leq \sigma_n \kappa(A) \|x\| \varepsilon_M .$$

This says that if $\kappa(A)$ is large, then the <u>relative error</u> in x may also be quite large.

Let X be the approximate inverse computed by SGEDI. It is possible to prove that

$$\|AX-I\| \leq \sigma_n \|A\| \|X\| \varepsilon_M .$$

Since it is usually true that $\|A\|\|X\|$ is comparable with $\kappa(A)$ this says that AX will be close to I if $\kappa(A)$ is small, but may be far from I if $\kappa(A)$ is large.

Let RCOND be the estimate of reciprocal condition computed by SGECO. If the effects of roundoff error are ignored, it is possible to prove that

$$1/\text{RCOND} \leq \kappa(A) .$$

Roundoff errors complicate this result a bit, but if the computed RCOND is not zero, its reciprocal is almost always a lower bound for the true condition number. No rigorous results are known which indicate how close 1/RCOND is to $\kappa(A)$.

These inequalities involve the norms of vectors and matrices and so they may give little information about the individual elements when the problem is badly scaled or when it has a solution whose components vary over several orders of magnitude. Changing the scaling of a problem obviously changes the scaling of the errors as well. Some general comments about scaling are made in the Introduction. We can repeat the recommendation given there that, in the absence of any other information, a satisfactory scaling is one in which the absolute errors in the elements of the input matrix are all about the same size.

The inequalities quoted above are the results of a rigorous roundoff error analysis. They apply to any problem run on any machine which satisfies the assumptions made about the floating point arithmetic. Unfortunately, the coefficients ρ_n and σ_n that must be used to make the results completely rigorous are impractically large -- they grow roughly like 2^n . But a great deal of experience has convinced us that the matrices which lead to the exponentially large coefficients are very rarely encountered in practice.

We have carried out several numerical experiments measuring the element growth and roundoff error in SGEFA and SGESL , as well as the effectiveness of the condition estimator in SGECO . In the most extensive such experiment, 10,000 matrices of orders 10 through 50 were generated randomly, drawing from four different distributions. SGEFA was used to factor the matrices and the element growth encountered during the elimination was monitored. Let a_{ij}^k be the elements stored in A at the k-th step of the factorization. The element growth for a particular matrix is the ratio

$$r = \frac{\max_{i,j,k} |a_{ij}^k|}{\max_{i,j} |a_{ij}|} .$$

This is an important quantity in the error analysis. There do exist matrices for which $r = 2^{n-1}$, but the largest value we observed was $r = 23$ which occurred for a 40 by 40 matrix of 1's, 0's and -1's.

The total roundoff error generated in SGEFA was also measured by computing the ratio

$$\rho = \frac{\|A-LU\|}{\varepsilon_M \|A\|} .$$

It was found that ρ could be well approximated by the linear function $\rho \sim \alpha n + \beta$, rather than the exponential function required by the rigorous analysis. Each of the four distributions lead to different values of α and β , but all four α's were between 0.05 and 0.15.

In a second experiment, 1250 of the random matrices were used to test RCOND . The inequalities

$$\tau\kappa(A) \le 1/\text{RCOND} \le \kappa(A)$$

were found to be valid for $\tau = 0.1$ in all but 3 cases. Lowering τ to 0.062 included all the cases.

The details of these experiments are given in Goodman and Moler (1977).

Timing. To obtain a rough estimate for the execution time required by a particular subroutine on a particular computer, let μ be the time required by that computer to execute the following Fortran statement once

```
Y(I) = Y(I) + T*X(I) .
```

This involves one floating point multiplication, one floating point addition, a few one-dimensional indexing operations, and a few storage references. Let n be the order of matrix involved. Then estimates for the execution times can be obtained from the following table. The estimates may be quite inaccurate for small n , say $n \leq 10$.

Subroutine	Time
SGECO	$(1/3\ n^3 + 3\ n^2)\mu$
SGEFA	$1/3\ n^3\mu$
SGESL	$n^2\mu$
SGEDI (for A^{-1})	$2/3\ n^3\mu$

Estimates for the execution times of the double precision and complex subroutines can be obtained by changing μ appropriately.

An extensive timing experiment has been carried out on the subroutines in this chapter at a number of LINPACK test sites. Results from the following 21 computing environments are presented in this section. Each is identified by its single letter ID in the graphs that follow.

ID	Facility	Computer	Compiler
A	Argonne National Lab.	IBM 370/195	H, OPT=2
B	Bell Laboratories	Honeywell 6080	Fortran-Y Optimizing
C	Nat'l Center Atmos. Res.	Cray-1	CFT, CAL BLAS
D	Univ. Calif., San Diego	Burroughs 6700	H
E	Iowa State Univ.	Itel AS/5 Mod 3	H, OPT=2
F	Nat'l Center Atmos. Res.	Cray-1	CFT, Fortran BLAS
I	U. Illinois, Urbana	CDC Cyber 175	Ext. Ver. 4.6, OPT=1
K	Naval Weapons Center	Univac 1110	Fortran V
L	Lawrence Livermore Lab.	CDC 7600	CHAT, No optimization
M	Univ. Michigan	Amdahl 470/V6	H, OPT=2
N	Nat'l Center Atmos. Res.	CDC 7600	Local

ID	Facility	Computer	Compiler
O	U. Illinois, Chicago	IBM 370/158	G1
P	Purdue University	CDC 6500	FUN
R	NASA Langley Res. Ctr	CDC Cyber 175	FTN, OPT=2
S	Stanford Univ. (SLAC)	IBM 370/168	H, OPT=2
T	University Toronto	IBM 370/165	H Extended, Fast multiply
V	Northwestern Univ.	CDC 6600	FTN 4.6, OPT=2
W	U. Wisconsin, Madison	Univac 1110	Fortran V
X	Univ. Texas, Austin	CDC 6600/6400	RUN
Y	Yale University	DEC KL-20	F20, OPT
Z	Yale University	DEC KA-10	F40

Two additional test sites, Oak Ridge National Laboratory and College of William and Mary, participated in the studies, but our programs did not produce sufficiently reliable data with the particular timing facilities available on their computers.

All the graphs, or scatter diagrams, in this section are intended to compare two related programs and hence present the ratios of their execution times on the various machines. This eliminates the wide variations in the data caused by the wide variations in the basic execution times of the machines and the changing order of the matrices, but it does obscure the actual running times. The "raw data" used to produce the graphs are contained in an appendix, but the user is warned that changes in machines, compilers, operating systems, number of time sharing users, and even the particular matrix elements can have significant effects on timings and so anyone seriously interested in the timing for a particular problem will probably have to measure it independently.

Test matrices of six different orders were used, namely n = 5, 10, 25, 50, 75 and 100. Timing of single precision, double precision and complex versions of the subroutines were done. Some test sites did not run the $n = 100$ cases, and some did not run the double precision or complex subroutines, so their ID's are omitted wherever data are not available.

The asterisks (*) in the graphs and the numerical values given underneath the graphs represent the averages over the machines of the ratios for each order. They indicate the general trend of these ratios as the order is changed.

The first three graphs show the effect of using the BLAS (Basic Linear Algebra Subprograms) in the factorization and solution routines. In Figure 1a, SGEFA is the version of the single precision, general matrix, triangular factorization routine that is ordinarily part of LINPACK. It uses three of the BLAS -- ISAMAX , SSCAL and SAXPY . SGEFA* is a modified version produced automatically by TAMPR in which the calls to the BLAS have been replaced by equivalent in-line DO-loops. For matrices of small order, the version without the BLAS is faster because the overhead of the subroutine calls is eliminated. For matrices of large order the version with the BLAS is usually faster because most compilers are able to produce more efficient code for the loop in SAXPY and most of the time is spent in this loop. The fundamental question is: Where does the crossover from "small order" to "large order" occur? This is signified in the graphs by ratios greater than 1.00 .

The version of SAXPY used in all the tests except for the ID "N" is written in Fortran. It uses one-dimensional subscripting and its loop is "unrolled" so that four components of each vector are processed each time through the loop. This reduces the overhead of the loop test and allows for increased efficiency on machines with hardware features such as cache memories, fast instruction stacks, and overlapped arithmetic units. When the call to SAXPY is replaced by in-line code, two-dimensional subscripting in a conventional DO-loop is used.

In three of the tests, those with ID's "O" , "Z" and "L" , the version using the BLAS becomes more efficient at an order less than 10 and becomes more than twice as efficient by order 50 . Apparently, these three compilers produce much more efficient code for one-dimensional subscripting. In one very special situation, ID "F" , the version using the BLAS actually becomes less efficient as the order increases. This occurs on the CRAY-1 where the unrolled loops in the Fortran SAXPY prevent the generation of vector instructions.

In the other tests, the crossover point where the BLAS become more efficient occurs somewhere between order 25 and order 100 or greater, but the difference in execution times of the two versions is usually less than 20 percent. We expect that use of machine language versions of the BLAS , which are already available for a fairly wide range of machines, will result in crossovers at lower orders.

Figure 2 shows similar results for double precision arithmetic. Only one test site, "O" , with inefficient two-dimensional subscripting, ran the double precision versions. But this is an important case because it involves the frequently occurring situation of an IBM computer with the G compiler and the use of the BLAS increases the efficiency significantly. Except for "I" , all the other tests show the two versions to be about the same speed. We do not know why the ratio for "I" is so low.

Figure 3 shows the results for complex arithmetic. Here the ratios are much closer to 1.0 because both versions require subroutine calls for the complex arithmetic operations.

When evaluating these results, it is important to realize that the computer time required to factor only one matrix of order 100 is about the same as that required to factor 1000 matrices of order 10 or 8000 matrices of order 5 . Consequently, efficiency for low order matrices is important only in situations requiring solution of a large number of small problems.

Figures 1b, 2b and 3b show similar results for the three solve routines, S- , D- and CGESL , with and without the BLAS . The results are somewhat more erratic than those for the factorization routines because the actual times are much less and the discrete nature of the clock has much more effect.

Figure 4 indicates how the cost of the condition estimator varies with the order of the matrix. The ratio of the time for SGECO and CGECO to that of SGEFA and CGEFA is shown. Since CO calls FA , the ratio is always greater than 1.0 . But since the time for FA is proportional to n^3 and the additional time required in CO is proportional to n^2 , the ratio decreases toward 1.0 as n increases. (All the ratios for $n = 5$ and some of the ratios for $n = 10$ are greater than 2.0 , the upper limit chosen for the graph, but the numerical value of the average is given.) It can be seen that the ratios are fairly consistent over the range of machines and for the two types of arithmetic. Moreover, they are quite close to the quantity $1 + \frac{9}{n}$ predicted by the operation counts. Results for the D subroutines are similar and have been omitted.

Figure 5 shows the cost of complex arithmetic. They involve some of the same data as the previous figures, but here the ratio of the time for the complex factorization and solve routines to that of the corresponding real routines is given. If only multiplication time were considered, this ratio would be 4.0 because one complex multiplication requires four real multiplications. In fact, the average ratio for large order is fairly close to 4.0 , but the variation among machines is quite pronounced. Ratios around 2.0 occur for a group of machines where the time for the storage references and possibly the complex additions are apparently the dominating factors. Ratios much larger than 4.0 occur for machines where the time for the linkages to the complex arithmetic subroutines is very significant. Whenever the ratio exceeds 8.0 , it would be faster to replace the complex problem by a corresponding real problem of order $2n$, but this also doubles the storage required.

Figure 6 shows the ratios of the factorization times to a simpler n^3 process, a certain matrix multiplication. The names SXTX and DXTX refer to single and double precision subroutines for forming the product X^TX where, in this case, X is an n by n matrix. Such a product is also used to normalize the timings of the LINPACK subroutines for least squares and other problems described in chapters 8 through 11.

For large n , SGEFA requires about $\frac{1}{3}n^3$ multiplications and, because of the symmetry of the result, SXTX requires about $\frac{1}{2}n^3$ multiplications. The ratio of the multiplication times alone thus approaches $\frac{2}{3}$ as n increases. However, SGEFA uses an outer product algorithm involving SAXPY while SXTX uses an inner product algorithm involving SDOT and so the $\frac{2}{3}$ should be multiplied by the ratio of SAXPY to SDOT time. This ratio is frequently larger than 1.0 because SDOT requires fewer storage references. For two machines, "A" and "N" , the SAXPY/SDOT ratio is exceptionally large. In single precision, only one machine, "B" , gets very near the $\frac{2}{3}$ ratio for large n . In double precision, where the fewer storage references in SDOT are less important, several machines appear to have ratios approaching $\frac{2}{3}$.

Figure 7 shows similar ratios of the solve times to a simpler n^2 process, a matrix-vector multiplication. The multiplication subroutines are called SXTY and DXTY because the application to least squares involves the formation of X^Ty . But in this situation, it can be thought of as the formation of $A^{-1}b$ if A^{-1} has already been computed. In many cases the ratios are significantly greater than 1.0 , even though the number of multiplications and additions in the two processes is the same. This comes from the SAXPY/SDOT ratio and the fact that SGESL has two main loops while SXTY has only one. It shows that for problems involving very many right hand sides, it may be faster to use SGEDI once to get A^{-1} and then apply A^{-1} to the various right hand sides than to use SGESL many times. However, the number of right hand sides has to be quite large before the cost of computing A^{-1} can be justified. Moreover, the solution obtained by computing $A^{-1}b$ may have worse roundoff error.

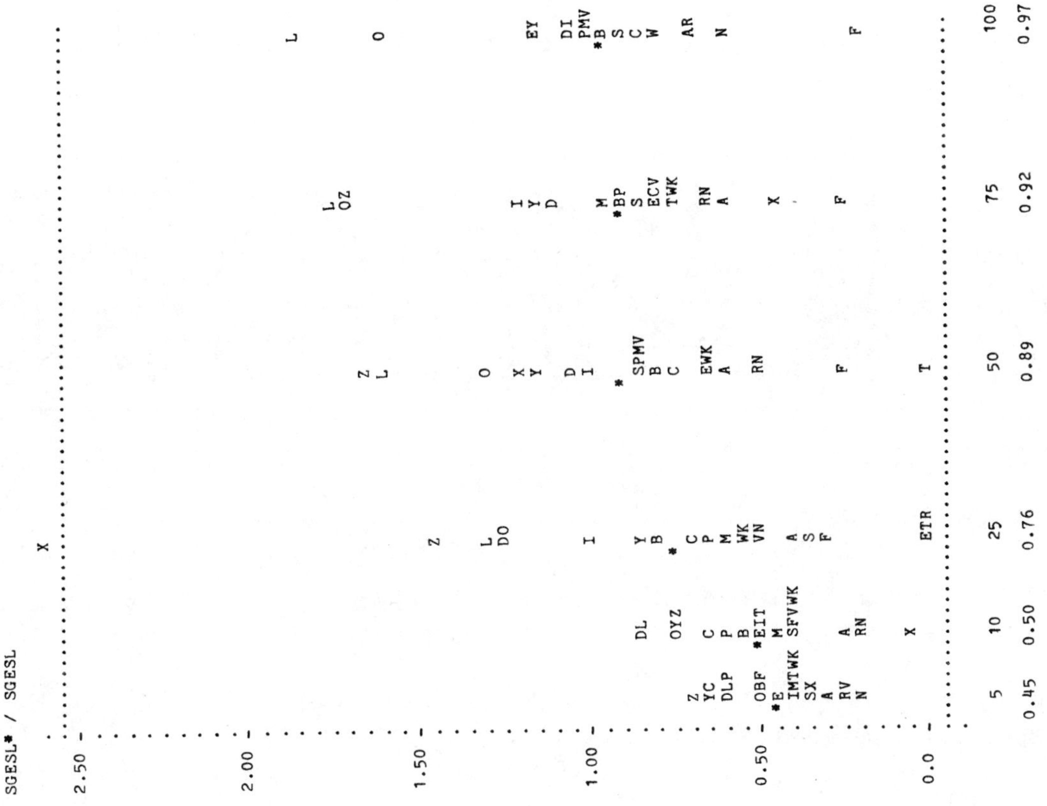

Fig. 1b

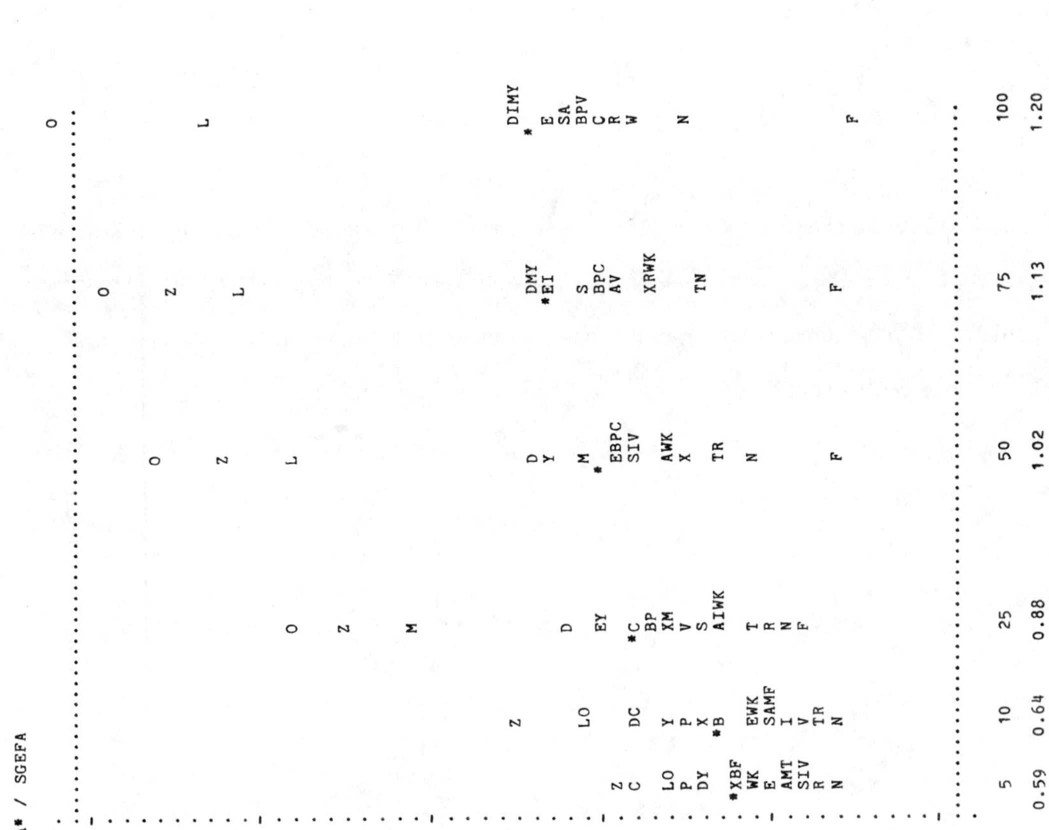

Fig. 1a

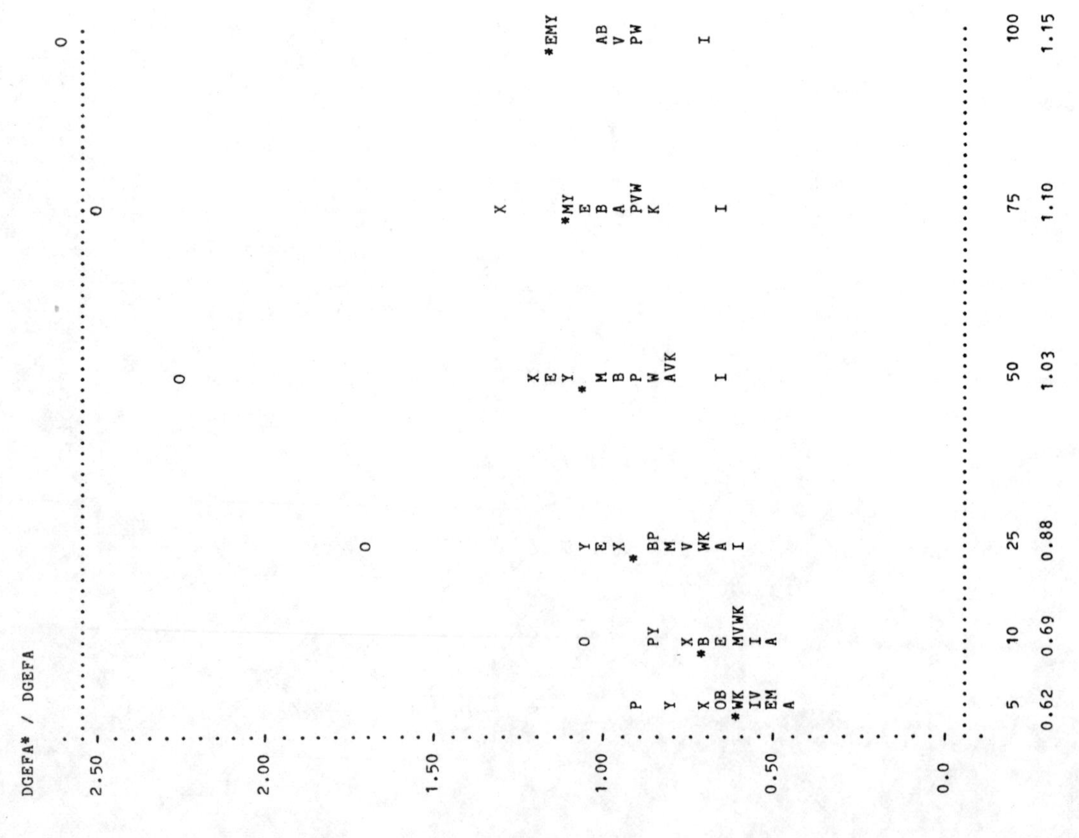
DGEFA* / DGEFA
2.50
2.00
1.50
1.00
0.50
0.0
5
10
25
50
75
100
0.62
0.69
0.88
1.03
1.10
1.15

Fig. 2a

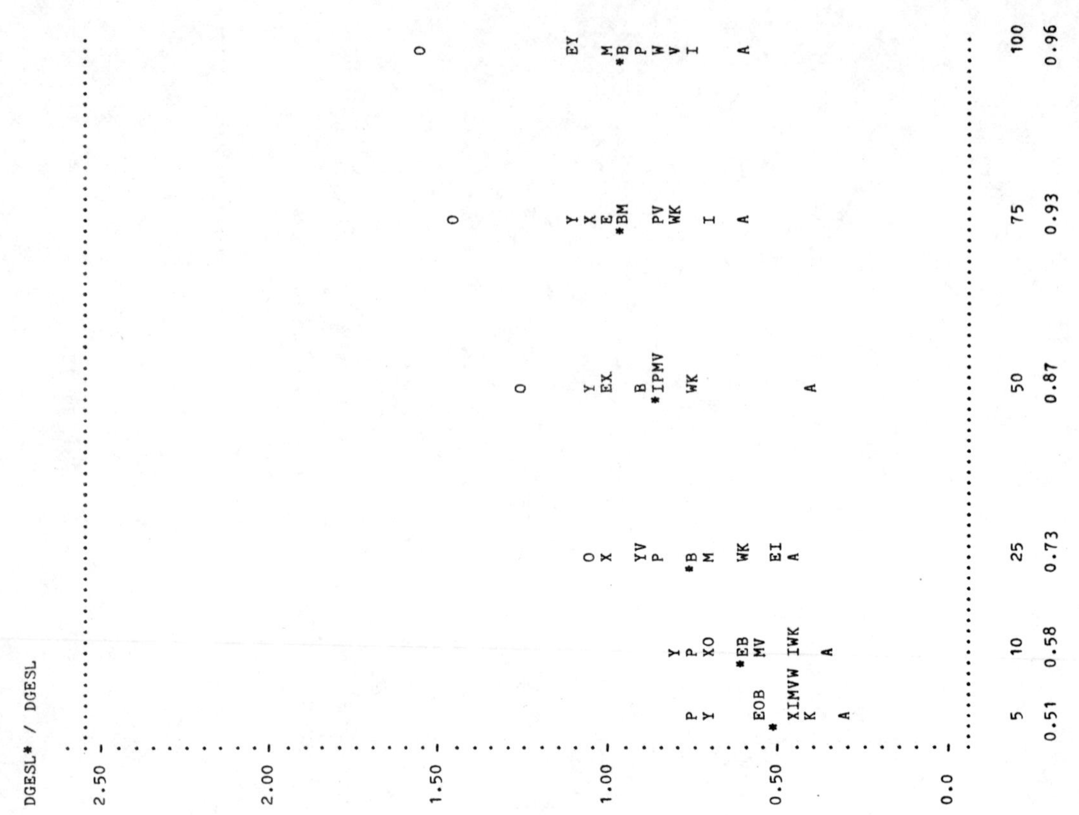
DGESL* / DGESL
2.50
2.00
1.50
1.00
0.50
0.0
5
10
25
50
75
100
0.51
0.58
0.73
0.87
0.93
0.96

Fig. 2b

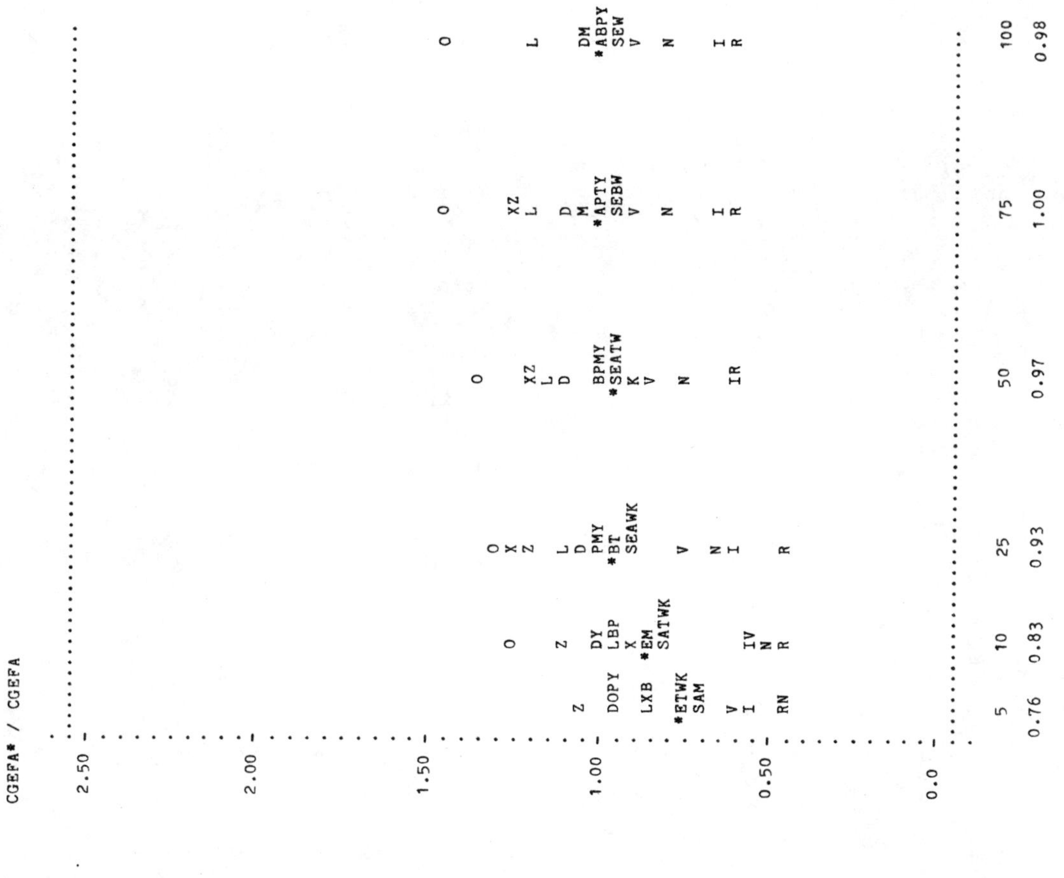

Fig. 3a

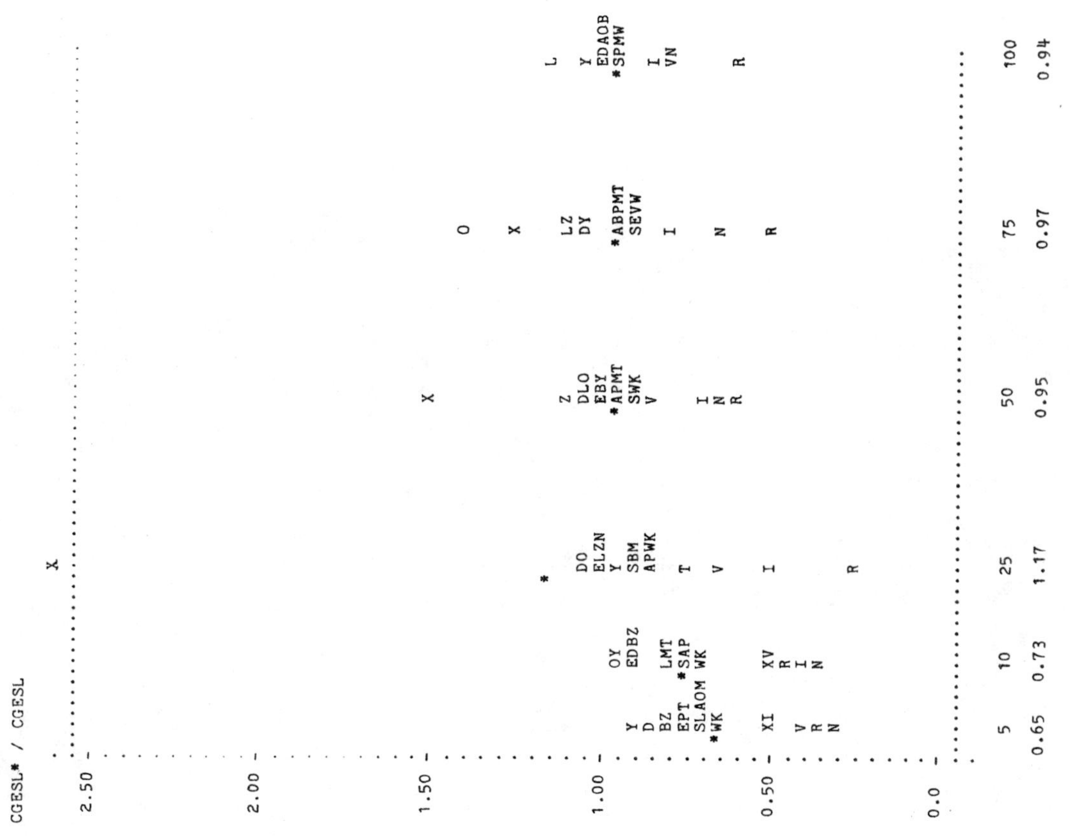

Fig. 3b

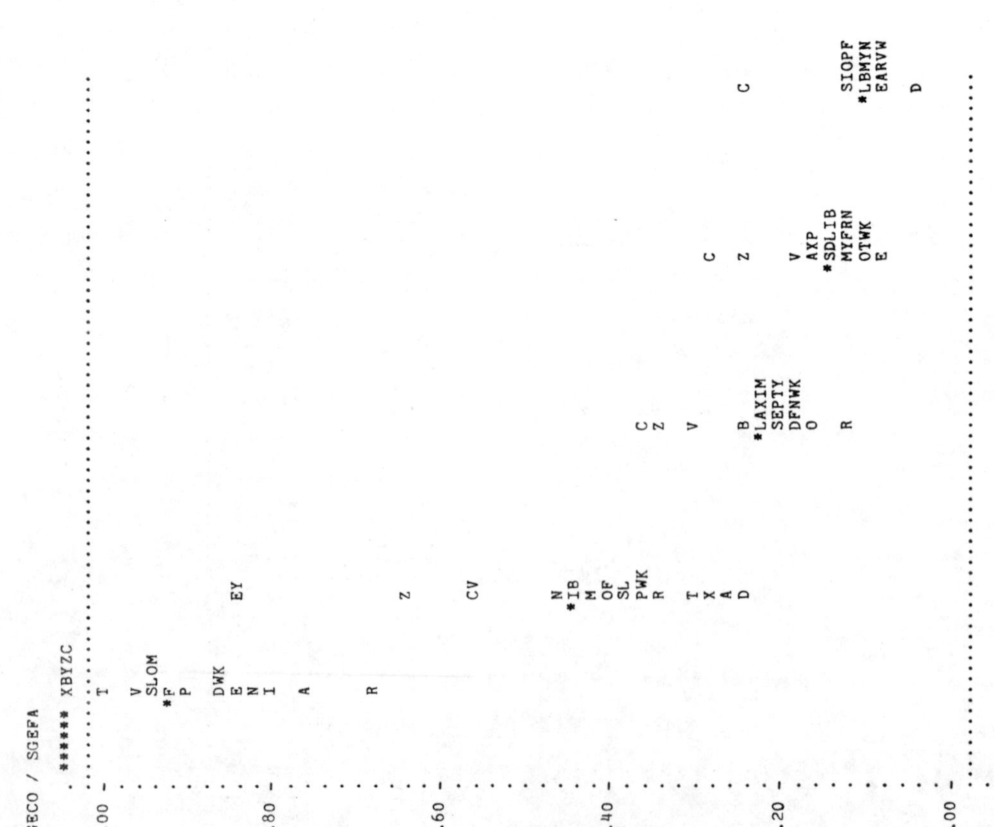
SGECO / SGEFA
2.00
1.80
1.60
1.40
1.20
1.00
5 10 25 50 75 100
2.76 1.92 1.44 1.22 1.15 1.11

Fig. 4a

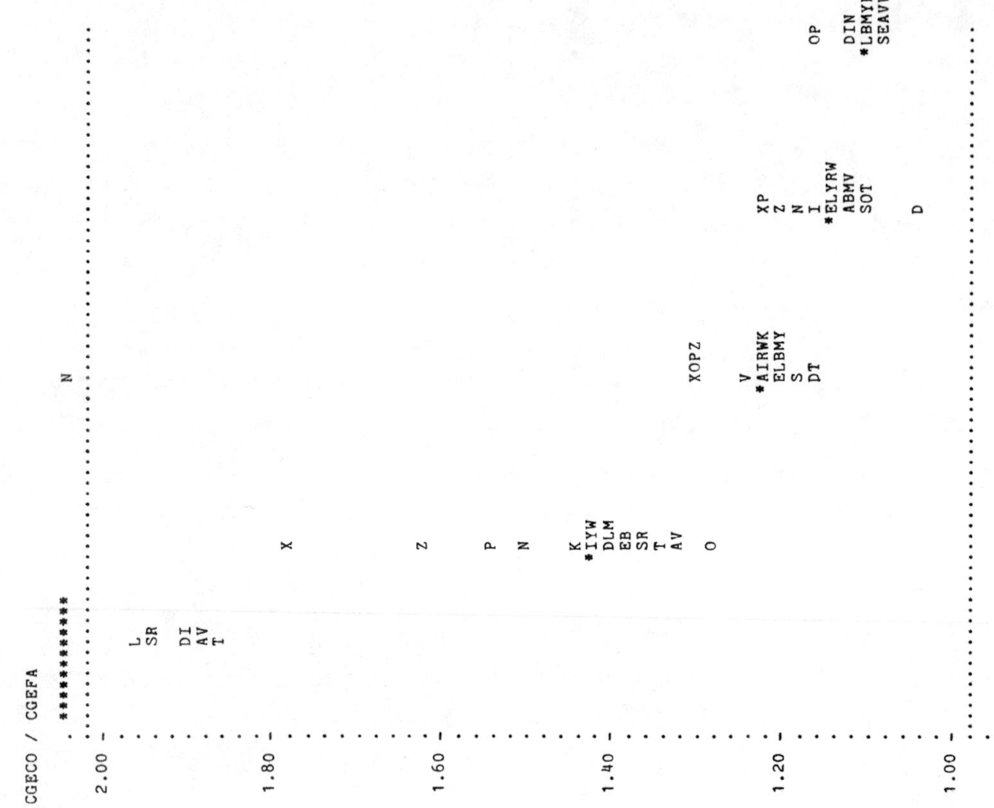
CGECO / CGEFA
2.00
1.80
1.60
1.40
1.20
1.00
5 10 25 50 75 100
3.02 2.07 1.43 1.22 1.14 1.11

Fig. 4b

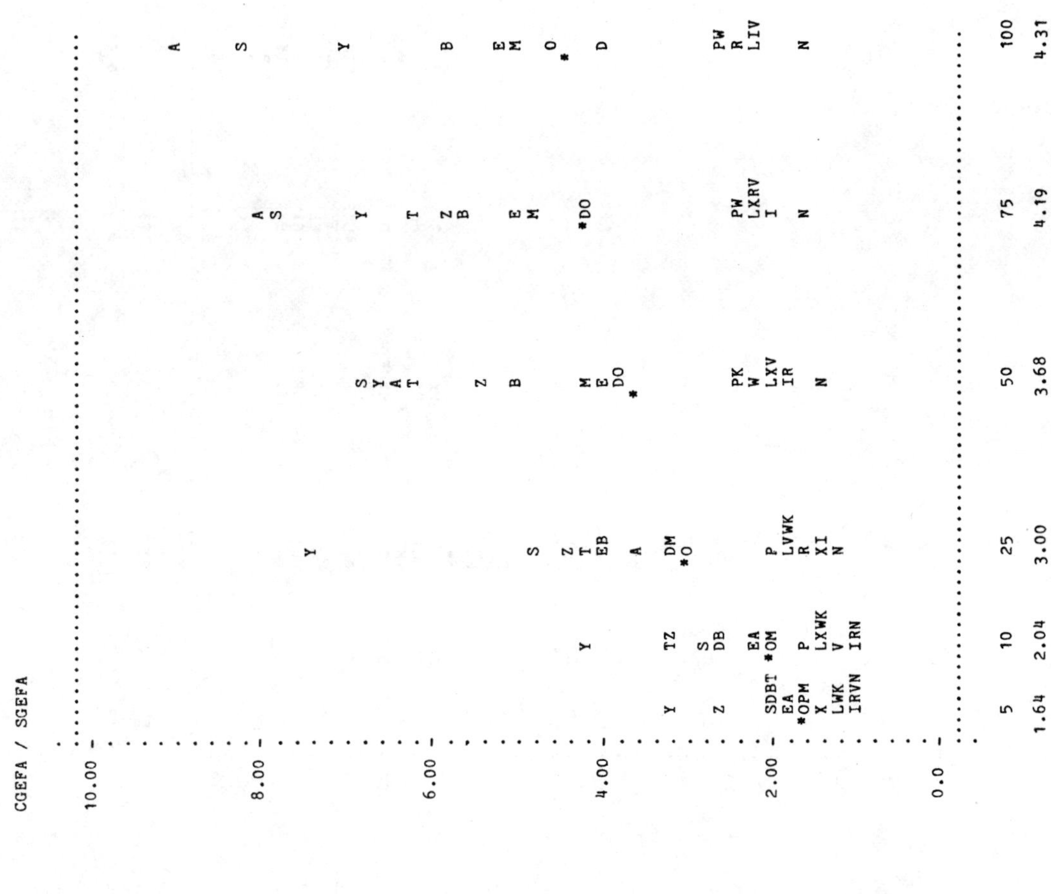
CGEFA / SGEFA
10.00
8.00
6.00
4.00
2.00
0.0
5 10 25 50 75 100
1.64 2.04 3.00 3.68 4.19 4.31

Fig. 5a

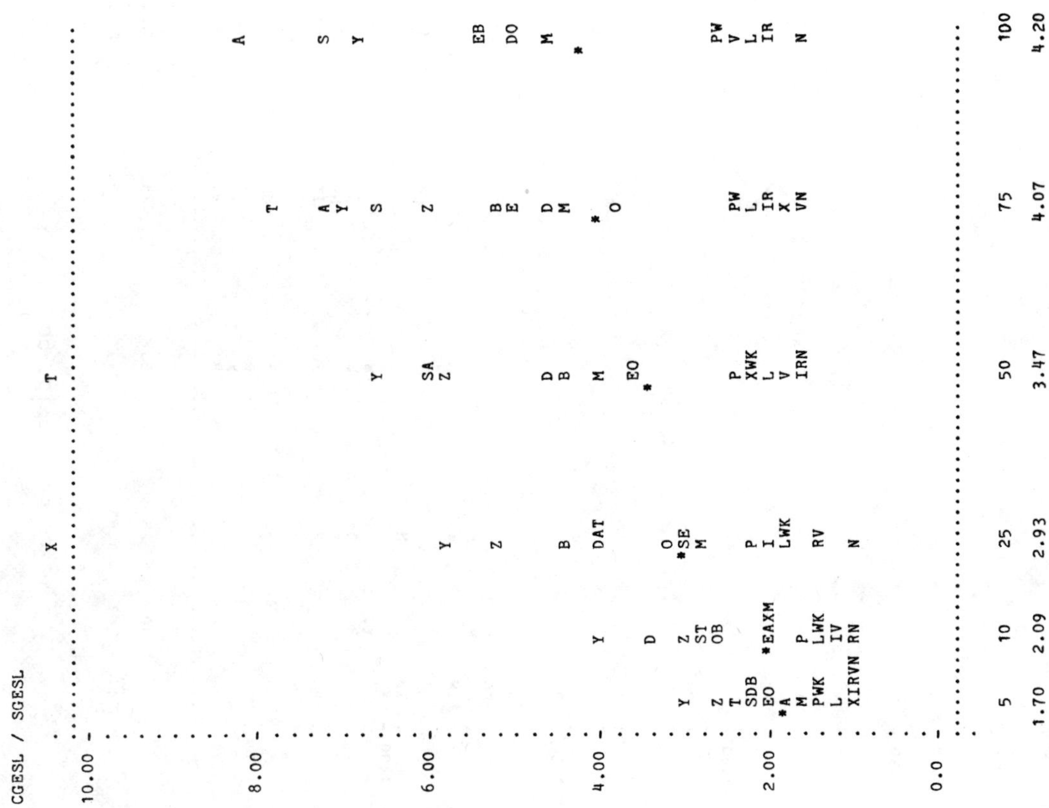
CGESL / SGESL
10.00
8.00
6.00
4.00
2.00
0.0
5 10 25 50 75 100
1.70 2.09 2.93 3.47 4.07 4.20

Fig. 5b

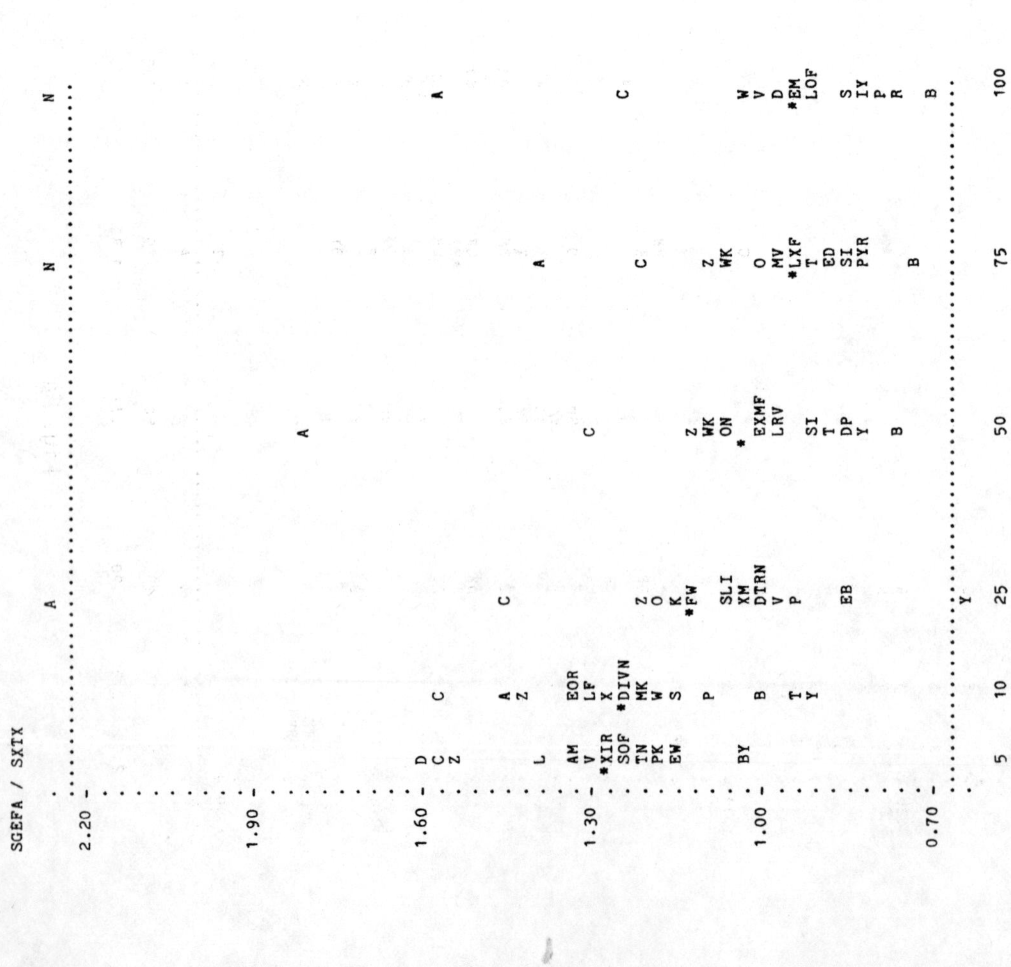
SGEFA / SXTX
2.20
1.90
1.60
1.30
1.00
0.70
5
10
25
50
75
100
1.27
1.23
1.11
1.02
0.95
0.94

Fig. 6a

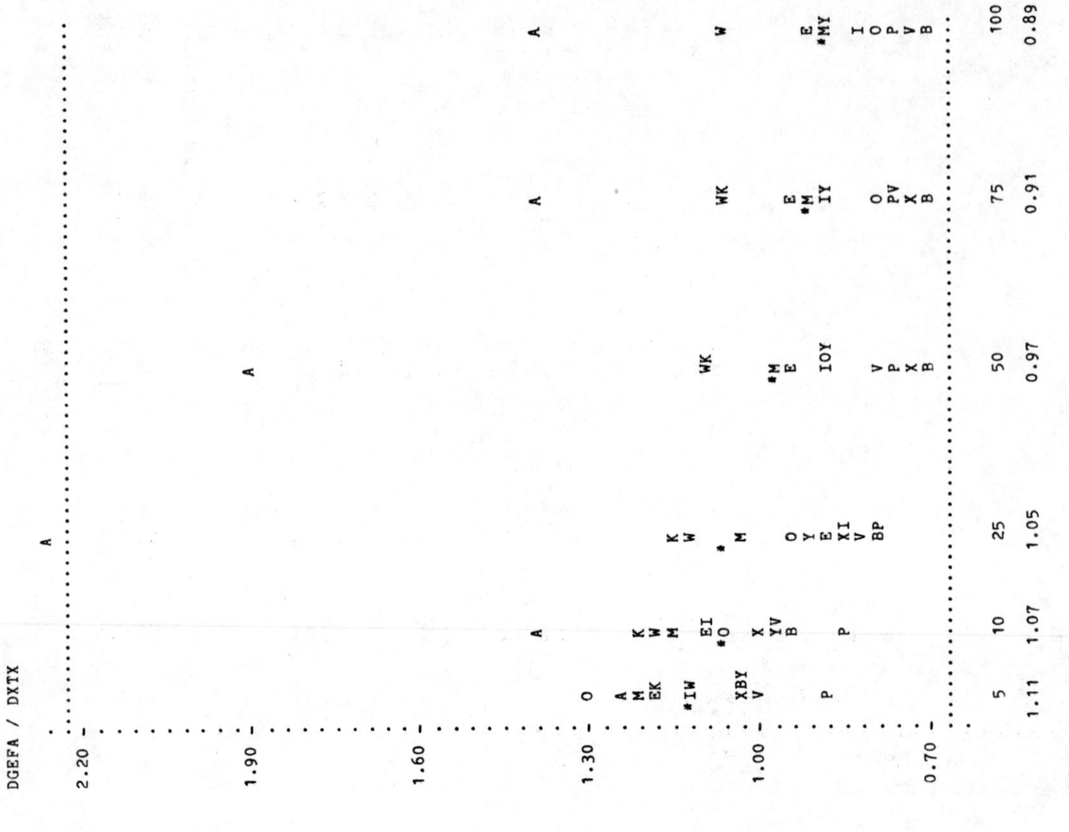
DGEFA / DXTX
2.20
1.90
1.60
1.30
1.00
0.70
5
10
25
50
75
100
1.11
1.07
1.05
0.97
0.91
0.89

Fig. 6b

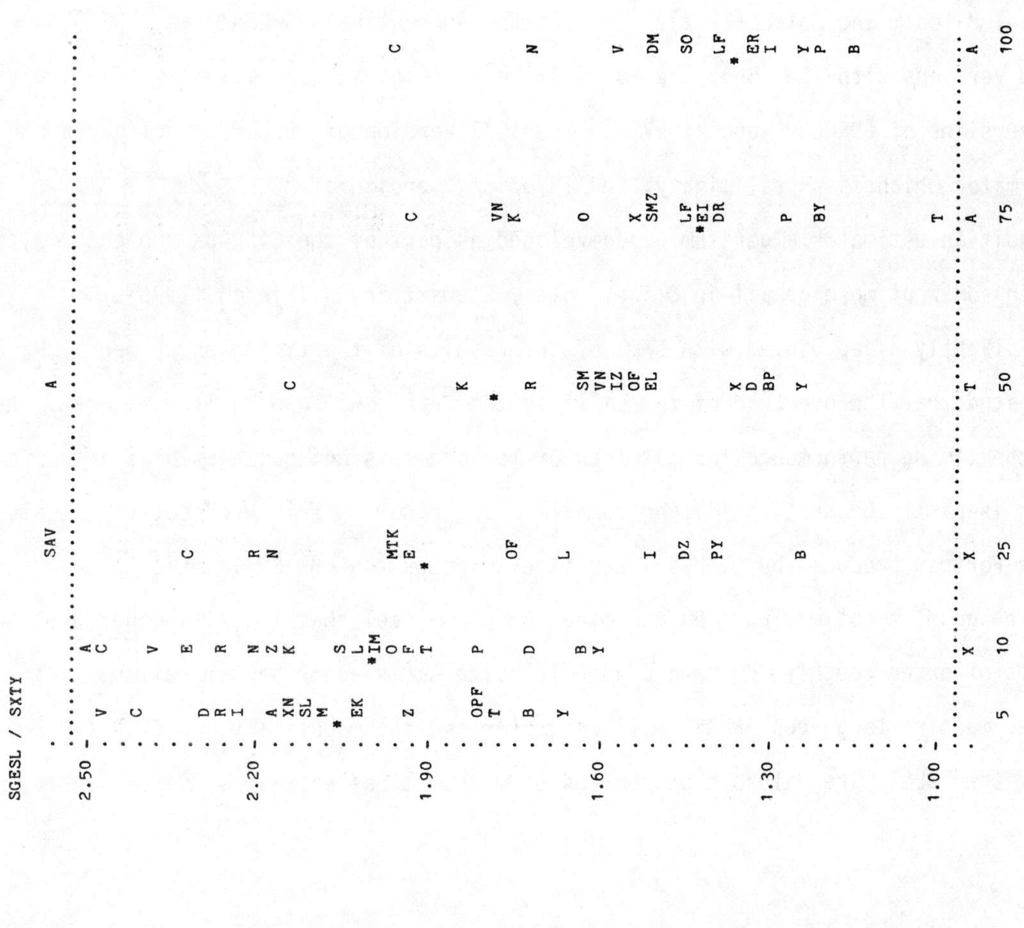
SGESL / SXTY
SAV
2.50
2.20
1.90
1.60
1.30
1.00
5 10 25 50 75 100
2.05 2.00 1.90 1.77 1.43 1.36

Fig. 7a

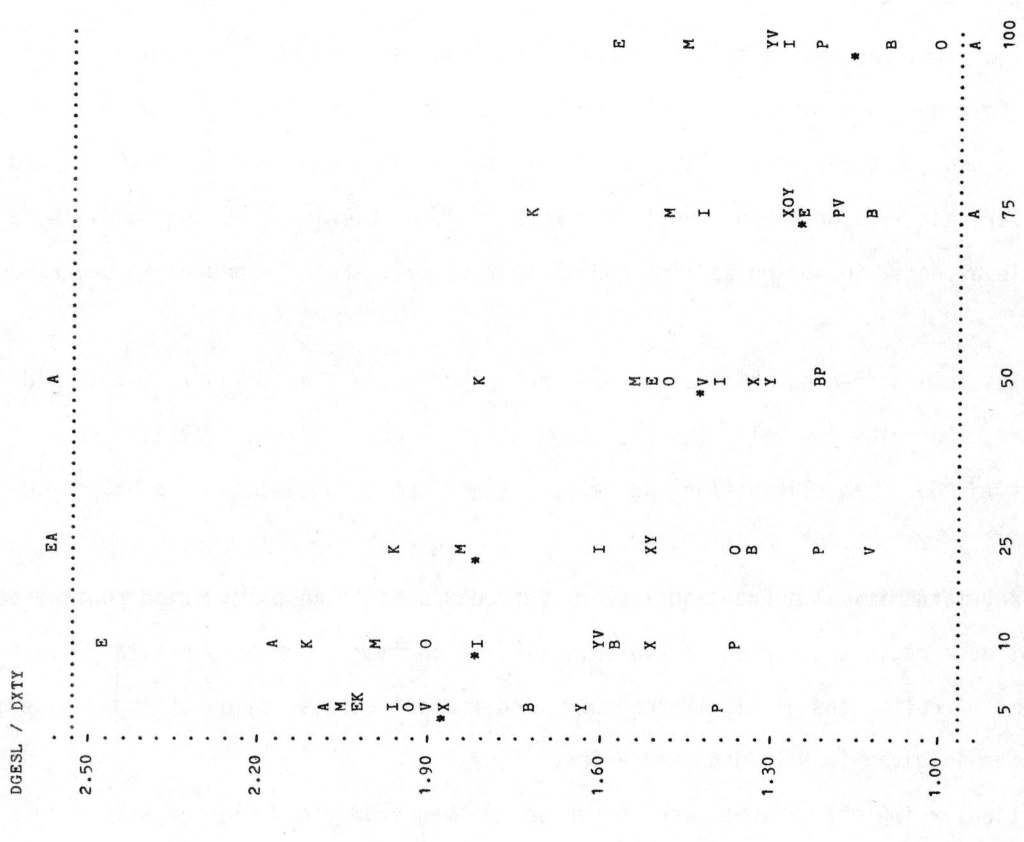
DGESL / DXTY
EA
2.50
2.20
1.90
1.60
1.30
1.00
5 10 25 50 75 100
1.87 1.82 1.80 1.42 1.25 1.15

Fig. 7b

7. Notes and References

As an algorithm, Gaussian elimination was known long before Gauss. A 3 by 3 example occurs in a Chinese manuscript over 2000 years old and Gauss himself refers to the method as commonly known. However, its error properties, including the effects of pivoting and condition, were not well understood until the work of J. H. Wilkinson around 1960. Some fairly subtle aspects, including scaling and element growth, are not completely understood today.

Three books which discuss elimination and include proofs of the inequalities quoted in section 6 are: Forsythe and Moler (1967), Stewart (1973) and Wilkinson (1963). Many of the variants of Gaussian elimination and related algorithms are discussed in Householder (1964).

Almost any mathematical subroutine library includes a Gaussian elimination routine and so we cannot even begin to discuss or evaluate all the software currently available for this problem. A collection of Algol procedures and a succinct discussion of their numerical properties is given in Wilkinson and Reinsch (1971).

The particular implementations used here have evolved from the series of subroutines called DECOMP and SOLVE which are included in Forsythe and Moler (1967), Moler (1972) and Forsythe, Malcolm and Moler (1977). In fact the subroutines SGEFA* and SGESL* , that is the versions with the BLAS replaced by in-line loops, are virtually identical to the later versions of DECOMP and SOLVE . The 1977 version of DECOMP includes a condition estimator which is a preliminary, and inferior, version of SGECO .

The condition estimator algorithm was developed as part of the LINPACK project. It is described in somewhat more detail in Cline, Moler, Stewart and Wilkinson (1979).

We are slightly disappointed with some of the results of the timing experiment. We had not anticipated that the overhead of the calls to the BLAS would be quite so great. As a result, the timing performance for matrices of low order is not quite as good as we would like. This is partly because optimizing compilers are becoming fairly effective and also because the Fortran produced by TAMPR when it eliminates the BLAS is exactly what the compilers are good at optimizing. On the other hand, we feel that the timing performance for matrices of order roughly 50 and higher is quite satisfactory and more important. Furthermore, machine languages BLAS will be faster and the modularity and clarity made possible by the BLAS are valuable properties of mathematical software. Consequently, we have decided to keep the BLAS . Anyone who has a large number of small systems of equations to solve quickly is welcome to contact the LINPACK project about obtaining a version without them.

Versions of the BLAS written in Fortran with the view of leading to efficient object code on many machines were also developed as part of the LINPACK project. The idea of unrolling loops is not new, but as far as we know, this is the first time it had been pursued in a high-level language; see Dongarra and Hinds (1978).

Chapter 2: Band Matrices

Subroutines: SGBCO, SGBFA, SGBSL, SGBDI

1. Overview

Purpose. The LINPACK subroutines in this chapter operate on general nonsymmetric band matrices. The operations performed include the triangular factorization of matrices, the estimation of the matrix condition number, the solution of simultaneous linear equations and the calculation of determinants.

Background. A band matrix is a matrix whose nonzero elements are all fairly near the main diagonal, specifically $a_{ij} = 0$ if $i-j > m_\ell$ or $j-i > m_u$. The integers m_ℓ and m_u are called the lower and upper band widths and $m = m_\ell + m_u + 1$ is the total band width. The subroutines for band matrices use less time and storage than the subroutines for full matrices if $2m_\ell + m_u < n$. Numerically, when the same matrix is input to the two sets of subroutines, the computed results are identical, but the elements are stored in different locations.

Tridiagonal matrices are the special case $m_\ell = m_u = 1$. They can be handled by the subroutines in this chapter, but the special subroutines in Chapter 7 are more efficient.

Let A be a real or complex band matrix of order n . There is an upper triangular band matrix U and a matrix L which is the product of elementary lower triangular band matrices and permutation matrices such that $A = LU$. This factorization can be used to solve linear equations $Ax = b$ by solving successively $L(Ux) = b$ and to compute the determinant of A as $\det(L)\cdot\det(U)$. If needed the inverse of A can also be obtained.

The condition number $\kappa(A)$ is a quantity which measures the sensitivity of the solution x to errors in the matrix A and the right hand side b . If the relative error in A is of size ε , then the resulting relative error in x can be as large as $\kappa(A)\varepsilon$. Errors in A can arise in many ways. In particular, the effect of the roundoff error introduced by the subroutines in this chapter can usually be assessed by taking ε to be a small multiple of the rounding unit.

It is possible to efficiently compute a quantity RCOND which is an estimate of the reciprocal condition, $1/\kappa(A)$. If RCOND is approximately 10^{-d} then the elements of x can usually be expected to have d fewer significant figures of accuracy than the elements of A . Consequently, if RCOND is so small that in floating point arithmetic it is negligible compared to 1.0 , then x may have no significant figures. On most computers, this condition may be tested by the logical expression

$$1.0 + \text{RCOND .EQ. } 1.0 \ .$$

When this expression is true, the matrix can be considered to be "singular to working precision." As a special case, if exact singularity is detected, RCOND may be set to 0.0 .

If A is badly scaled, then the interpretation of RCOND is more delicate. For a detailed discussion of RCOND , including the consequences of unusual scaling in A and errors in b , see Chapter 1, sections 4 and 6.

2. Usage

When Gaussian elimination is performed on a band matrix, the pivoting causes the introduction of nonzero elements outside the band. If m_ℓ and m_u are the lower and upper band widths of the original matrix, then its two triangular factors have band widths m_ℓ and $m_\ell + m_u$ and storage must be provided for the extra m_ℓ diagonals. This is illustrated by the following example with $n = 9$, $m_\ell = 2$ and $m_u = 3$. The original matirx is

11	12	13	14	0	0	0	0	0
21	22	23	24	25	0	0	0	0
31	32	33	34	35	36	0	0	0
0	42	43	44	45	46	47	0	0
0	0	53	54	55	56	57	58	0
0	0	0	64	65	66	67	68	69
0	0	0	0	75	76	77	78	79
0	0	0	0	0	86	87	88	89
0	0	0	0	0	0	97	98	99

The band storage requires $2m_\ell + m_u + 1 = 8$ rows arranged as follows. The * indicates elements which are never referenced, but for which the space must be provided. The + indicates elements which may be filled in during the elimination.

*	*	*	*	*	+	+	+	+
*	*	*	*	+	+	+	+	+
*	*	*	14	25	36	47	58	69
*	*	13	24	35	46	57	68	79
*	12	23	34	45	56	67	78	89
11	22	33	44	55	66	77	88	99
21	32	43	54	65	76	87	98	*
31	42	53	64	75	86	97	*	*

The elements in position (i,j) of the original matrix is stored in position (k,j) of the band array where $k = i-j+m$ and $m = m_\ell + m_u + 1$. The following program segment will transfer a band matrix from conventional full matrix storage in A to band storage in ABD.

```
      M = ML + MU + 1
      DO 20 J = 1, N
         I1 = MAX0(1, J-MU)
         I2 = MIN0(N, J+ML)
         DO 10 I = I1, I2
            K = I - J + M
            ABD(K,J) = A(I,J)
   10    CONTINUE
   20 CONTINUE
```

Single precision, general band matrices. The four subroutines for single precision, general band matrices are SGBCO , SGBFA , SGBSL , and SGBDI . Ordinarily, SGBCO or SGBFA will be called once to factor a particular matrix and then SGBSL and SGBDI will be called to apply the factorization as many times as needed.

SGBCO uses Gaussian elimination with partial pivoting to compute the LU factorization of a band matrix and then estimates its condition. The calling sequence is

CALL SGBCO(ABD,LDA,N,ML,MU,IPVT,RCOND,Z) .

On entry,

ABD is a doubly subscripted array with dimension (LDA,N) which contains the band of the matrix A whose factorization is to be computed. The columns of A are stored in the columns of ABD and the diagonals of A are stored in rows ML + 1 through 2*ML + MU + 1 of ABD . The first ML rows are used for work space and output.

LDA is the leading dimension of the array ABD , which must satisfy $LDA \geq 2*ML + MU + 1$.

N is the order of A and the number of elements in the vectors IPUT and Z.

ML is the number of diagonals below the main diagonal in the band, which must satisfy $0 \leq ML < N$.

MU is the number of diagonals above the main diagonal in the band, which must satisfy $0 \leq MU < N$ and preferably should satisfy $ML \leq MU$.

On return,

ABD contains in its first ML + MU + 1 rows an upper triangular band matrix U and in its next ML rows the multipliers necessary to construct a matrix L so that A = LU . The ML + MU by ML + MU upper left triangle and the

ML by ML lower right triangle are never referenced.

IPVT is a singly subscripted integer array of dimension N which contains the pivot information necessary to construct the permutations in L . Specifically, IPVT(K) is the index of the K-th pivot row.

RCOND is an estimate of the reciprocal condition, $1/\kappa(A)$. If RCOND is so small that the logical expression 1.0 + RCOND .EQ. 1.0 is true, then A can usually be regarded as singular to working precision. If RCOND is exactly zero, then SGBSL will divide by zero.

Z is a singly subscripted array of dimension N used for work space. If A is close to a singular matrix, then Z will contain an approximate null vector in the sense that $\|Az\| = \text{RCOND}\cdot\|A\|\cdot\|z\|$ (see Section 4).

SGBFA should be used in place of SGBCO if the condition estimate is not needed. The calling sequence is

```
CALL SGBFA(ABD,LDA,N,ML,MU,IPVT,INFO)
```

On entry,

ABD is a doubly subscripted array with dimension (LDA,N) which contains the band of the matrix A whose factorization is to be computed. The columns of A are stored in the columns of ABD and the diagonals of A are stored in rows ML + 1 through 2*ML + MU + 1 of ABD . The first ML rows are used for work space and output.

LDA is the leading dimension of the array ABD , which must satisfy LDA $\geq$ 2*ML + MU + 1 .

N is the order of A and the number of elements in the vector IPVT .

ML is the number of diagonals below the main diagonal in the band, which must satisfy $0 \leq \text{ML} < \text{N}$.

MU is the number of diagonals above the main diagonal in the band, which must satisfy $0 \leq \text{MU} < \text{N}$ and preferably should satisfy $\text{ML} \leq \text{MU}$.

On return,

ABD contains in its first ML + MU + 1 rows an upper triangular band matrix U and in its next ML rows the multipliers necessary to construct a matrix L so that A = LU . The ML + MU by ML + MU upper left triangle and the ML by ML lower right triangle are never referenced.

IPVT is a singly subscripted integer array of dimension N which contains the pivot information necessary to construct the permutations in L . Specifically, IPVT(K) is the index of the K-th pivot row.

INFO is an integer returned by SGBFA which, if it is 0 , indicates that SGBSL can be safely used. If INFO = K ≠ 0 , then SGBSL will divide by U(K,K) = 0.0 . If U has several zero diagonal elements, K will be the index of the last one. Although a nonzero INFO technically indicates singularity, RCOND is a more reliable indicator.

SGBCO is usually called first to factor the matrix and estimate its condition. The actual factorization is done by SGBFA which can be called in place of SGBCO if the condition estimate is not needed. The time required by SGBCO is roughly (1 + 6/ML) times the time required by SGBFA .

Since any matrix has an LU factorization, there is no error return from SGBCO or SGBFA . However, the factors can be singular and consequently unusable by SGBSL . Either RCOND or INFO should be tested before calling SGBSL .

SGBSL uses the LU factorization of a band matrix A to solve linear systems of the form

$$Ax = b$$

or

$$A^T x = b$$

where A^T is the transpose of A . The calling sequence is

```
CALL SGBSL(ABD,LDA,N,ML,MU,IPVT,B,JOB) .
```

On entry,

ABD is a doubly subscripted array with dimension (LDA,N) which contains the factorization computed by SGBCO or SGBFA . It is not changed by SGBSL .

LDA is the leading dimension of the array ABD .

N is the order of the matrix A and the number of elements in the vectors B and IPVT .

ML is the number of diagonals below the main diagonal.

MU is the number of diagonals above the main diagonal.

IPVT is a singly subscripted integer array of dimension N which contains the pivot information from SGBCO or SGBFA .

B is a singly subscripted array of dimension N which contains the right hand side b of a system of simultaneous linear equations $Ax = b$ or $A^Tx = b$.

JOB indicates what is to be computed. If JOB is 0 , the system $Ax = b$ is solved and if JOB is nonzero, the system $A^Tx = b$ is solved.

On return,

B contains the solution, x .

If the upper triangular factor of A has a zero element on the diagonal (a situation that will cause INFO ≠ 0 in SGBFA or RCOND = 0.0 in SGBCO), a division by zero will occur in SGBSL . Technically this means that the matrix A is singular, but it is often caused by incorrect setting of LDA or other improper use of the subroutines.

SGBDI uses the LU factorization of a matrix to compute its determinant. The calling sequence is

```
CALL SGBDI(ABD,LDA,N,ML,MU,IPVT,DET) .
```

On entry,

ABD is a doubly subscripted array with dimension (LDA,N) which contains the factorization computed by SGBCO or SGBFA . It is not changed by SGBDI .

LDA is the leading dimension of the array ABD .

N is the order of the matrix A and the number of elements in the vector IPVT.

ML is the number of diagonals below the main diagonal.

MU is the number of diagonals above the main diagonal.

IPVT is a singly subscripted integer array of dimension N which contains the pivot information from SGBCO or SGBFA .

On return,

DET is a singly subscripted array with 2 elements which contains the determinant of A in the form det(A) = DET(1)*10.0**DET(2) , although this expression may underflow or overflow if evaluated. DET(1) is normalized so that

$1.0 \le |DET(1)| < 10.0$ or $DET(1) = 0.0$. DET(2) contains an integer stored as a real number.

No direct provision is made for computing the inverse of a band matrix because the inverse is usually a full n by n matrix which cannot be stored in the band storage. Moreover, calculations formulated in terms of matrix inverses are invariably more efficient when expressed in terms of the solution of sets of linear equations. However, an example in section 3 shows how the inverse can be obtained using SGBSL .

Double precision, general band matrices. The calling sequences of the double precision, general band subroutines DGBCO , DGBFA , DGBSL and DGBDI are the same as those of the corresponding single precision "S" subroutines except that A , B , RCOND , DET and Z are DOUBLE PRECISION variables.

Complex, general band matrices. The calling sequences of the complex, general band subroutines CGBCO , CGBFA , CGBSL and CGBDI are the same as those of the corresponding single precision "S" subroutines except that A , B , DET and Z are COMPLEX variables, RCOND is a REAL variable and the system solved by CGBSL when JOB is nonzero involves the complex conjugate transpose of A .

Double precision complex, general band matrices. In those computing systems where they are available, the calling sequences of the double precision complex, general band subroutines ZGBCO , ZGBFA , ZGBSL and ZGBDI are the same as those of the corresponding single precision "S" subroutines except that A , B , DET and Z are COMPLEX*16 varibles, RCOND is a DOUBLE PRECISION variable and the system solved by ZGBSL when JOB is nonzero involves the complex conjugate transpose of A .

3. Examples

The first example is a complete program which factors a pentadiagonal matrix, tests for near singularity, and then solves a single system of linear equations. The system is

$$\begin{bmatrix} 11 & 12 & 13 & & & & & \\ 21 & 22 & 23 & 24 & & 0 & & \\ 31 & 32 & 33 & 34 & 35 & & & \\ & \cdot & \cdot & \cdot & \cdot & \cdot & & \\ & & \cdot & \cdot & \cdot & \cdot & \cdot & \\ & 0 & & 86 & 87 & 88 & 89 & \\ & & & & 97 & 98 & 99 & \end{bmatrix} x = \begin{bmatrix} 1 \\ 1 \\ 1 \\ \cdot \\ \cdot \\ 1 \\ 1 \end{bmatrix}$$

```
      REAL ABD(7,9),B(9),Z(9),RCOND,T
      INTEGER IPVT(9)
      DATA LDA /7/
      N = 9
      ML = 2
      MU = 2
      M = ML + MU + 1
      DO 20 J = 1, N
         I1 = MAX0(1, J-MU)
         I2 = MIN0(N, J+ML)
         DO 10 I = I1, I2
            K = I - J + M
            ABD(K,J) = 10 * I + J
   10    CONTINUE
   20 CONTINUE
C
      CALL SGBCO(ABD,LDA,N,ML,MU,IPVT,RCOND,Z)
      WRITE(6,30) RCOND
   30 FORMAT(9H RCOND = , E15.5)
      T = 1.0 + RCOND
      IF (T .EQ. 1.0) GO TO 90
C
      DO 40 I = 1, N
         B(I) = 1.0
   40 CONTINUE
      CALL SGBSL(ABD,LDA,N,ML,MU,IPVT,B,0)
      DO 50 I = 1, N
         WRITE(6,60) B(I)
   50 CONTINUE
   60 FORMAT(F15.6)
      STOP
C
   90 WRITE(6,99)
   99 FORMAT(40H MATRIX IS SINGULAR TO WORKING PRECISION)
      STOP
      END
```

The next segment finds the inverse of a pentadiagonal matrix of order 50 by successively solving $Ax_j = e_j$ where e_j is the j-th column of the identify and x_j is the j-th column of A^{-1}. Note that different dimensions are used for ABD and AINV. This program is primarily for illustration; its actual use should be avoided whenever possible.

```
      DIMENSION ABD(7,50),AINV(50,50),IPVT(50)
      DATA LDA/7/, M/5/, M2/2/
      N = 50
      DO 15 J = 1, N
         I1 = MAX0(1, J-M2)
         I2 = MIN0(N, J+M2)
         DO 10 I = I1, I2
            K = I - J + M
            ABD(K,J) = (I,J)-th element of A
   10    CONTINUE
   15 CONTINUE
      CALL SGBFA(ABD,LDA,N,M2,M2,IPVT,INFO)
      IF (INFO .NE. 0) GO TO . . .
      DO 30 J = 1, N
         DO 20 I = 1, N
            AINV(I,J) = 0.0
   20    CONTINUE
         AINV(J,J) = 1.0
         CALL SGBSL(ABD,LDA,N,M2,M2,IPVT,AINV(1,J),0)
   30 CONTINUE
         .
         .
         .
```

4. Programming Details

The algorithms employed by the subroutines for band matrices are essentially the same as those employed by the subroutines for full matrices. Only the storage arrangement and the ranges of the DO-loops are different. Except for the operations on zeros, the two sets of routines do the same arithmetic operations in the same order. Thus anyone attempting to understand the band subroutines in detail is advised to first study the full subroutines.

SGBFA

The principal integer variables have the following meanings:

K	index of the pivot column.
L	index in the band structure of the pivot row.
IPVT(K)	index in the full structure of the pivot row.
M	row index in the band structure of the diagonal elements.
JZ	column index of the last nonzero element in the last active row.
JU	column index of the last nonzero element of the pivot row.
J	column index during elimination.

MM index in the band structure of the K-th row.

LM number of nonzero elements below the diagonal in the K-th column.

The following example, taken from section 2, illustrates how these variables are used. It has N = 8 , MU = 3 and ML = 2 .

	K ↓				JU ↓	JZ ↓			
	*	*	*	*	*	0_1	+	+	+
	*	*	*	*	0_0	0_1	+	+	+
	*	*	*	14	$\underline{25}$	36	47	58	69
	*	*	13	$\underline{24}$	35	46	57	68	79
	*	12	$\underline{23}$	34	45	56	67	78	89
M →	11	$\underline{22}$	33	44	55	66	77	88	99
LM { MM ↗	$\underline{21}$	32	43	54	65	76	87	98	*
LM { L ↗	31	42	53	64	75	86	97	*	*

Elements labeled with integers are input and the integers indicate their position in the original matrix. Elements labeled * are never referenced, elements labeled + are the auxiliary storage that is filled in by the pivoting. The element shown as 0_0 is set to zero before the elimination begins. The situation during the first step of the elimination, that is K = 1 , is shown. The diagonal pointer remains at M = 6 throughout. With JZ = 6 , the elements shown as 0_1 are set to zero. The pivot search involves the LM+1 = 2+1 = 3 nonzero elements in the first column. Suppose that the second of these, labeled 21, is the largest and is chosen as pivot. Then the underlined elements constitute the pivot row and so L = 7 , IPVT(1) = 2 and JU = 5 . The elimination involves the column index J = 2,...,5 and the two row pointers, MM = 5,...,2 and L = 6,...,3 . The underlined elements are exchanged with the elements directly above them. This causes one element of fill-in, in the position labeled 0_0 . Note that the two 0_1's would have been filled in if 31 had been chosen as pivot. Later values of K will lead to the remaining +'s being zeroed and then possibly overwritten with nonzeros.

<u>SGBCO and SGBSL</u>

These are versions of SGECO and SGESL , modified to handle the band storage. It is assumed that complete fill-in has occurred during the factorization so that the upper triangular factor U has ML + MU diagonals above the main diagonal even though, for some matrices, portions of these diagonals may be zero. The variable LM contains the length of the vectors processed in the inner loop, that is by SAXPY and SDOT . For the systems involving U or U^T , LM usually has the value ML+MU , except near the bottom of U where the vectors become shorter. For the systems involving L or L^T , LM usually has the value ML , except near the top of L where the vectors become shorter.

SGBDI

The inverse of a band matrix is usually a full matrix which cannot be stored in the band storage. Consequently, SGBDI does not compute the inverse. It consists merely of the determinant part of SGEDI .

5. Performance

Accuracy. In Chapter 1, section 6, the following roundoff error bounds for computations involving full matrices are discussed:

$$\|A-LU\| \le \rho_n \|A\| \varepsilon_M$$
$$\|Ax-b\| \le \sigma_n \|A\| \, \|x\| \varepsilon_M$$
$$\|x-x_*\| \le \sigma_n \kappa(A) \|x\| \varepsilon_M \ .$$

These bounds apply as well to band matrices. It is possible to obtain smaller growth coefficients ρ_n and σ_n that reflect the band structure, but we will not do so here because these bounds are rarely used in any quantitative way.

For any particular problem, the actual roundoff error, as opposed to the above roundoff error bounds, is the same for the full and band routines.

Timing. To obtain a rough estimate for the execution time required by a particular subroutine on a particular computer, let μ be the time required by that computer to execute the following Fortran statement once

```
Y(I) = Y(I) + T*X(I)   .
```

This involves one floating-point multiplication, one floating-point addition, a few one-dimensional indexing operations, and a few storage references. Let n be the order of the band matrix and let m_ℓ and m_u be the lower and upper band widths. Assume $m_\ell \le m_u$.

The time for SGBFA depends upon the amount of pivoting required. Let m_u' be an unknown quantity somewhere in the range

$$m_u \le m_u' \le \min(m_\ell + m_u, n) \ .$$

If the matrix is diagonally dominant, no pivoting will be needed and so $m_u' = m_u$. Otherwise pivoting will usually be required and so $m_u' = m_\ell + m_u$, unless this is greater than

n . The operation counts predict an execution time of

$$\left(nm_\ell m_{u'} - \frac{1}{2} m_\ell m_{u'}^2 - \frac{1}{6} m_\ell^3\right)\mu \ .$$

The last two terms in this estimate come from the "end effects" near the bottom of the band. In the common situation where m_ℓ and m_u are both much smaller than n , the predicted time is somewhere between

$$nm_\ell m_u \quad \text{and} \quad nm_\ell(m_\ell+m_u)$$

depending upon how much pivoting is done. Note that the estimate is a linear function of the order of the matrix and a quadratic function of the band width.

The time for SGBSL does not depend upon the amount of pivoting required. Let $m_{u''} = \min(m_\ell+m_u, n)$. The operation counts predict an execution time of

$$\left(nm_\ell + nm_{u''} - \frac{1}{2} m_\ell^2 - \frac{1}{2} m_{u''}^2\right)\mu \ .$$

If m_ℓ and m_u are both much smaller than n , the predicted time is

$$n(2m_\ell+m_u)\mu \ .$$

Note that this is linear in both the order and the band width.

The estimated time for SGBCO , if m and m_u are much smaller than n , is the time for SGBFA plus $n(8m_\ell+3m_u)$.

To summarize and simplify, assume that pivoting is required and that $m_\ell = m_u = m \ll n$. Then estimates for the execution times can be obtained from the following table. The estimates may be quite inaccurate for very small m , small n , or m nearly equal to n .

Subroutine	Time
SGBCO	$(2nm^2 + 11nm)\mu$
SGBFA	$2nm^2\mu$
SGBSL	$3nm\mu$

Estimates for the execution times of the double precision and complex subroutines can be obtained by changing μ appropriately.

Chapter 3: Positive Definite Matrices

Subroutines: SPOCO, SPOFA, SPOSL, SPODI, and
SPPCO, SPPFA, SPPSL, SPPDI

1. Overview

Purpose. The LINPACK subroutines in this chapter operate on symmetric positive definite full matrices stored in singly or doubly subscripted arrays. The computing costs in terms of both time and storage are about half the corresponding costs for nonsymmetric matrices. The operations performed include the triangular factorization of matrices, the estimation of matrix condition, the solution of simultaneous linear equations and the calculation of determinants and inverses.

Operations on band matrices, nonsymmetric matrices, symmetric matrices which are not positive definite, tridiagonal matrices and rectangular matrices are covered in other chapters.

Mathematical background. A real matrix A is positive definite if and only if it is symmetric, that is $A = A^T$, and the quadratic form x^TAx is positive for all nonzero vectors x . Since the latter condition is difficult to check directly, it is usually replaced by other conditions in practice. For example, A is positive definite if and only if $A = B^TB$ for some rectangular matrix B with linearly independent columns.

If it is not known whether a particular symmetric matrix is positive definite, then the subroutines in Chapter 5 should be used.

A complex matrix A is positive definite if and only if it is Hermitian, that is if A is equal to its complex conjugate transpose A^H , and x^HAx is positive for all nonzero complex vectors x . A complex symmetric matrix, i.e. one equal to its transpose without conjugation, must be handled by the subroutines in Chapter 5.

Let A be a real or complex positive definite matrix. There is an upper triangular matrix R so that $A = R^TR$ if A is real or $A = R^HR$ if A is complex. Such a factorization can be used to estimate the condition number of A , to solve simultaneous linear equations involving A , and to compute the determinant and inverse of A .

The upper triangle of a symmetric matrix can be stored in a singly subscripted array with $n(n+1)/2$ elements, thereby saving almost half the usual storage. Such an arrangement is called packed storage. The subroutines which operate on positive definite matrices in packed storage produce identical numerical results and usually require about the same execution time as the subroutines for conventional storage.

The condition number $\kappa(A)$ is a quantity which measures the sensitivity of the solution x to errors in the matrix A and the right hand side b . If the relative error in A is of size ε , then the resulting relative error in x can be as large as $\kappa(A)\varepsilon$. Errors in A can arise in many ways. In particular, the effect of the roundoff error introduced by the subroutines in this chapter can usually be assessed by taking ε to be a small multiple of the rounding unit.

It is possible to efficiently compute a quantity RCOND which is an estimate of the reciprocal condition, $1/\kappa(A)$. If RCOND is approximately 10^{-d} then the elements of x can usually be expected to have d fewer significant figures of accuracy than the elements of A . Consequently, if RCOND is so small that in floating point arithmetic it is negligible compared to 1.0 , then x may have no significant figures. On most computers, this condition may be tested by the logical expression

1.0 + RCOND .EQ. 1.0 .

When this expression is true, the matrix can be considered to be "singular to working precision." As a special case, if exact singularity is detected, RCOND may be set to 0.0 .

If A is badly scaled, then the interpretation of RCOND is more delicate. For a detailed discussion of RCOND , including the consequences of unusual scaling in A and errors in b , see Chapter 1, sections 4 and 6.

2. Usage

Single precision, positive definite matrices. The four subroutines for single precision, positive definite matrices are SPOCO , SPOFA , SPOSL , and SPODI . Ordinarily, SPOCO or SPOFA will be called once to factor a particular matrix and then SPOSL and SPODI will be called to apply the factorization as many times as needed.

SPOCO uses the Cholesky algorithm to compute the R^TR factorization of a matrix and then estimates its condition. The calling sequence is

CALL SPOCO(A,LDA,N,RCOND,Z,INFO) .

On entry,

A is a doubly subscripted array with dimension (LDA,N) which contains the symmetric matrix whose factorization is to be computed. Only the upper triangle, including the diagonal, are used.

LDA is the leading dimension of the array A .

N is the order of the matrix A and the number of elements in the vector Z .

On return,

A contains in its upper triangle an upper triangular matrix R so that $A = R^TR$. The strict lower triangle is unchanged. The factorization is not complete if INFO is not zero.

RCOND is an estimate of the reciprocal condition, $1/\kappa(A)$. If RCOND is so small that the logical expression 1.0 + RCOND .EQ. 1.0 is true, then A can usually be regarded as singular to working precision. RCOND is unchanged from its input value if INFO is not zero.

Z is a singly subscripted array of dimension N used for work space. If A is close to a singular matrix, then Z will contain an approximate null vector in the sense that $\|Az\| = \text{RCOND}\cdot\|A\|\cdot\|z\|$.

INFO is an integer used to indicate an error condition. INFO is set to 0 if A is found to be positive definite and was successfully factored. INFO is set to $K > 0$ if the leading submatrix of order K is found not to be positive definite, possibly because of rounding error.

SPOFA should be used in place of SPOCO if the condition estimate is not needed. The calling sequence is

```
CALL SPOFA(A,LDA,N,INFO) .
```

On entry,

A is a doubly subscripted array with dimension (LDA,N) which contains the symmetric matrix whose factorization is to be computed. Only the upper triangle, including the diagonal, is used.

LDA is the leading dimension of the array A .

N is the order of the matrix A .

On return,

A contains in its upper triangle an upper triangular matrix R so that $A = R^TR$. The strict lower triangle is unchanged. The factorization is not complete if INFO is not zero.

INFO is an integer used to indicate an error condition. INFO is set to 0 if A is found to be positive definite and was successfully factored. INFO is set to $K > 0$ if the leading submatrix of order K is found not to be positive definite, possibly because of rounding error.

SPOCO is usually called first to factor the matrix and estimate its condition. The actual factorization is done by SPOFA which can be called in place of SPOCO if the condition estimate is not needed. The time required by SPOCO is roughly $(1 + 18/N)$ times the time required by SPOFA. Thus when N = 18, SPOCO costs twice as much as SPOFA, but when N = 180, SPOCO costs 10 percent more.

SPOSL uses the R^TR factorization of a matrix A to solve symmetric linear systems of equations, $Ax = b$. It should not be used if SPOCO or SPOFA has set INFO to a nonzero value. The calling sequence is

```
CALL SPOSL(A,LDA,N,B) .
```

On entry,

A is a doubly subscripted array with dimension (LDA,N) which contains the factorization computed by SPOCO or SPOFA. It is not changed by SPOSL.

LDA is the leading dimension of the array A.

N is the order of the matrix A and the number of elements in the vector B.

B is a singly subscripted array of dimension N which contains the right hand side b of a system of simultaneous linear equations $Ax = b$.

On return,

B contains the solution, x.

SPODI uses the R^TR factorization of a matrix to compute its determinant and inverse. However, many calculations formulated in terms of matrix inverses can be reformulated in terms of the solution of sets of linear equations. The reformulated versions often require less time and produce more accurate results. Several examples are included in section 3. SPODI should not be used if SPOCO or SPOFA has set INFO to a nonzero value. The calling sequence is

```
CALL SPODI(A,LDA,N,DET,JOB) .
```

On entry,

A is a doubly subscripted array with dimension (LDA,N) which contains the factorization computed by SPOCO or SPOFA.

LDA is the leading dimension of the array A .

N is the order of the matrix A .

JOB indicates what is to be computed. If JOB is 11 then both the determinant and inverse are computed. If JOB is 1 only the inverse is computed. If JOB is 10 only the determinant is computed.

On return,

A contains the upper triangle of the inverse of the original matrix if requested. If the units digit of JOB is zero, then A is unchanged.

DET is a singly subscripted array with 2 elements which contains the determinant of A in the form det(A) = DET(1)*10.0**DET(2) , although this expression may underflow or overflow if evaluated. DET(1) is normalized so that $1.0 \leq |DET(1)| < 10.0$ or DET(1) = 0.0 . DET(2) contains an integer stored as a real number. If the tens digit of JOB is zero, then DET is not referenced.

SPODI can also be used with the QR factorization computed by SQRDC . In this case, SPODI computes the determinant and/or inverse of X^TX where X is the rectangular matrix input to SQRDC . This approach avoids the actual formation of X^TX . In terms of the parameters for SQRDC , the calling sequence of SPODI is

```
CALL SPODI(X,LDX,P,DET,JOB) .
```

On entry,

X is a doubly subscripted array of dimension (LDX,P) containing in its upper triangle the factor R output by SQRDC . The elements of X below the diagonal are not referenced.

LDX is the leading dimension of the array X .

P is the number of columns of X and the order of X^TX .

JOB indicates what is to be computed. If JOB is 11 then both the determinant and inverse are computed. If JOB is 1 only the inverse is computed. If JOB is 10 only the determinant is computed.

On return,

X contains the upper triangle of the inverse of X^TX if requested. If the units digit of JOB is zero, then X is unchanged.

DET is a singly subscripted array with 2 elements which contains the determinant of X^TX , stored as described above.

Packed storage. The calling sequences of the four subroutines for single precision, positive definite matrices stored in packed form are:

```
CALL SPPCO(AP,N,RCOND,Z,INFO)
CALL SPPFA(AP,N,INFO)
CALL SPPSL(AP,N,B)
CALL SPPDI(AP,N,DET,JOB)
```

The only difference in usage between the packed storage "PP" subroutines and the full storage "PO" subroutines is in the storage of the matrix. The following program segment will transfer the upper triangle of a symmetric matrix from conventional full matrix storage in A to packed storage in the singly subscripted array AP . In practice, A(I,J) is usually replaced by the direct calculation of the I,J-th element.

```
      K = 0
      DO 20 J = 1, N
         DO 10 I = 1, J
            K = K + 1
            AP(K) = A(I,J)
   10    CONTINUE
   20 CONTINUE
```

This stores the columns of the upper triangle (which are the same as the rows of the lower triangle) sequentially in the N*(N+1)/2 elements of a singly subscripted array. Since there are no doubly subscripted arrays in these subroutines, there is no need for the parameter LDA . The parameters N , RCOND , Z , INFO , B , DET and JOB have exactly the same meanings as they do for the SPO subroutines.

There are no numerical differences whatsoever between the results produced by the SPO and SPP subroutines. The execution time will usually be about the same because both sets of subroutines use the BLAS for their inner loops.

Double precision, positive definite matrices. The calling sequences of the double precision positive definite subroutines DPOCO , DPOFA , DPOSL , DPODI , DPPCO , DPPFA , DPPSL and DPPDI are the same as those of the corresponding single precision "S" subroutines except that A , AP , B , RCOND , DET and Z are DOUBLE PRECISION variables.

Complex, positive definite matrices. The calling sequences of the complex positive definite subroutines CPOCO , CPOFA , CPOSL , CPODI , CPPCO , CPPFA , CPPSL and

CPPDI are the same as those of the corresponding single precision "S" subroutines except that A , AP , B and Z are COMPLEX variables and DET and RCOND are REAL variables.

Double precision complex positive definite matrices. In those computing systems where they are available, the calling sequences of the double precision complex positive definite subroutines APOCO , ZPOFA , ZPOSL , ZPODI , ZPPCO , ZPPFA , ZPPSL and SPPDI are the same as those of the corresponding single precision "S" subroutines except that A , AP , B and Z are COMPLEX*16 variables, and DET and RCOND are DOUBLE PRECISION variables.

3. Examples

The following program segments illustrate the use of the single precision subroutines for positive definite matrices. Examples showing the use of the "D" , "C" and "Z" subroutines could be obtained by changing the subroutine names and type declarations.

The first program factors a matrix, tests for positive definiteness and for near singularity and then solves a single system Ax = b . Note that only the upper triangle of the symmetric matrix is generated.

```
      REAL A(50,50),B(50),Z(50),T,RCOND
      DATA LDA/50/
      N = ...
      DO 20 J = 1, N
         DO 10 I = 1, J
            A(I,J) = ...
10       CONTINUE
20    CONTINUE
      CALL SPOCO(A,LDA,N,RCOND,Z,INFO)
      IF (INFO .NE. 0) GO TO 80
      T = 1.0 + RCOND
      IF(T .EQ. 1.0) GO TO 90
      DO 30 I = 1, N
         B(I) = ...
30    CONTINUE
      CALL SPOSL(A,LDA,N,B)
      DO 40 I = 1, N
         WRITE(..., ...) B(I)
40    CONTINUE
      STOP
80    WRITE(..., 89)
89    FORMAT(32H MATRIX IS NOT POSITIVE DEFINITE)
      STOP
```

```
90 WRITE(..., 99)
99 FORMAT(40H MATRIX IS SINGULAR TO WORKING PRECISION)
   STOP
   END
```

The following program generates an approximation to the Hilbert matrix, $a_{i,j} = 1/(i+j-1)$, in packed storage, finds the determinant and inverse, prints out the determinant in a simulated E format that allows for a four-digit exponent, and then prints out the lower triangle of the computed inverse.

```
   REAL AP(55),DET(2)
   N = 10
   K = 0
   DO 20 I = 1, N
      DO 10 J = 1, I
         K = K + 1
         AP(K) = 1.0/FLOAT(I+J-1)
10    CONTINUE
20 CONTINUE
   CALL SPPFA(AP,N,INFO)
   IF(INFO .NE. 0) STOP
   CALL SPPDI(AP,N,DET,11)
   K = INT(DET(2))
   WRITE(...,30) DET(1),K
30 FORMAT(15H DETERMINANT = , F20.15, 1HE, I5)
   WRITE(...,40)
40 FORMAT(11H INVERSE = )
   K = 1
   DO 50 I = 1, N
      L = K + I - 1
      WRITE(...,60) (AP(J), J = K, L)
      K = L + 1
50 CONTINUE
60 FORMAT(10F13.0)
   STOP
   END
```

This program segment replaces C, a matrix with L columns, by $A^{-1}C$ where A is a positive definite matrix. It does not explicitly form A^{-1}.

```
      N = ...
      DO 20 J = 1, N
         DO 10 I = 1, J
            A(I,J) = ...
   10    CONTINUE
   20 CONTINUE
      CALL SPOCO(A,LDA,N,RCOND,Z,INFO)
      IF(INFO .NE. 0) GO TO ...
      T = 1.0 + RCOND
      IF(T .EQ. 1.0) GO TO ...
      DO 30 J = 1, L
         CALL SPOSL(A,LDA,N,C(1,J))
   30 CONTINUE
```

The following segment forms $D = C^TA^{-1}C$ where A is N by N positive definite and C is N by L . It uses the positive definite factorizer, SPOFA , the triangular solver STRSL (see Chapter 6) and the inner product SDOT . The calculation is based on the fact that since $A = R^TR$ then $D = (R^{-T}C)^T(R^{-T}C)$.

```
      CALL SPOFA(A,LDA,N,INFO)
      IF(INFO .NE. 0) GO TO ...
      DO 10 J = 1, L
         CALL STRSL(A,LDA,N,C(1,J),11,INFO)
   10 CONTINUE
      DO 30 J = 1, L
         DO 20 I = 1, J
            D(I,J) = SDOT(N,C(1,I),1,C(1,J),1)
            D(J,I) = D(I,J)
   20    CONTINUE
   30 CONTINUE
```

4. Algorithms

The factorization. The Cholesky algorithm is used to factor a real symmetric or complex Hermitian positive definite matrix. For real matrices, the equation

$$A = R^TR$$

or for complex matrices, the equation

$$A = R^HR$$

where R^H is the complex conjugate transpose of R , together with the requirements that R be upper triangular and have (real) positive diagonal entries uniquely determines all the elements of R . They can be computed in the natural order beginning with $r_{1,1}$ and continuing through the columns of R to $r_{n,n}$. The algorithm is

$$
\begin{array}{l}
\underline{\text{for}}\ j = 1,\ldots,n\ \underline{\text{do}} \\
\quad \underline{\text{for}}\ k = 1,\ldots,j-1\ \underline{\text{do}} \\
\qquad r_{k,j} = \left(a_{k,j} - \sum_{i=1}^{k-1} \bar{r}_{i,k} r_{i,j}\right) / r_{k,k}; \\
\quad r_{j,j} = \left(a_{j,j} - \sum_{k=1}^{j-1} |r_{i,j}|^2\right)^{1/2} \\
\underline{\text{end}}\ j
\end{array}
$$

The calculation of a diagonal element $r_{j,j}$ requires the square root of a quantity which is positive if and only if the leading j by j submatrix of A is positive definite. Since a matrix is positive definite if and only if all of its leading submatrices are positive definite, the algorithm will require the square root of a nonpositive quantity and hence fail if and only if A is not positive definite.

There is a modification of the Cholesky algorithm which produces a factorization of the form $A = R^T DR$ where D is diagonal and R has ones on its diagonal. The modified algorithm does not require square roots, and hence is slightly faster, but the unmodified algorithm is used in this chapter of LINPACK to retain compatibility with the QR decomposition of rectangular matrices and to simplify many applications.

<u>The condition estimate</u>. The definition of matrix condition number and the description of an algorithm for estimating it are included in section 4 of Chapter 1. The discussion also applies to this chapter if U is replaced by R and L by R^T . However, since SGEFA and SPOFA produce different factorizations, SGECO and SPOCO may produce different estimates of the condition of the same positive definite matrix.

<u>Solving linear systems</u>. With the factorization $A = R^H R$ the linear system $Ax = b$ is equivalent to the two triangular systems, $R^H y = b$ and $Rx = y$. The algorithm thus involves two stages. The first stage solves $R^H y = b$. A column oriented algorithm produces the components of y in the order $y_1, y_2, \ldots, y_n$. The computation of each component involves the inner product of a column of R with the portion of y already computed. The second stage solves $Rx = y$. A column oriented algorithm produces the components of x in the order $x_n, \ldots, x_2, x_1$. When x_k has been computed, then x_k times the k-th column of R is subtracted from y to give an equation for the remaining components of x . The intermediate solution y overwrites b and the final solution x overwrites y.

```
for k = 1,...,n do
    b_k ← (b_k - Σ_{i=1}^{k-1} r̄_{i,k} b_i) / r_{k,k}
end k
    (b now contains y)
for k = n,...,1 do
    b_k ← b_k / r_{k,k};
    for i = 1,...,k-1 do
        b_i ← b_i - b_k r_{i,k}
end k
    (b now contains x)
```

If the steps involved in computing the inner products were written out, the two stages would be seen to involve the same amounts of work.

Determinant. The factorization $A = R^H R$ (with real elements on the diagonal of R) allows the determinant $\det(A)$ to be computed from

$$\det(A) = \prod_{k=1}^{n} r_{k,k}^2 \; .$$

Inverse. The factorization $A = R^H R$ allows the inverse to be computed from

$$A^{-1} = R^{-1}(R^{-1})^H \; .$$

The first stage involves the formation of R^{-1} in place of R using a column oriented algorithm. Let $S = R^{-1}$, let R_{k-1} be the leading $k-1$ by $k-1$ submatrix of R, let r_k be the vector consisting of the first $k-1$ components of the k-th column of R and let S_{k-1} and s_k be the corresponding parts of S. Then

$$\begin{bmatrix} R_{k-1} & r_k \\ 0 & r_{k,k} \end{bmatrix} \begin{bmatrix} S_{k-1} & s_k \\ 0 & s_{k,k} \end{bmatrix} = \begin{bmatrix} I_{k-1} & 0 \\ 0 & 1 \end{bmatrix} .$$

Consequently,

$$s_{k,k} = 1/r_{k,k}$$
$$s_k = -s_{k,k} S_{k-1} r_k$$

The product $S_{k-1} r_k$ is computed as a linear combination of the columns of S_{k-1}, taking advantage of the triangularity. The second stage involves the formation of the upper half of $A^{-1} = SS^H$ in place of S. The computation is based on

$$\begin{bmatrix} S_{j-1} & s_j \\ 0 & s_{j,j} \end{bmatrix} \begin{bmatrix} S_{j-1}^H & 0 \\ s_j^H & s_{j,j} \end{bmatrix} = \begin{bmatrix} S_{j-1}S_{j-1}^H + s_j s_j^H & s_{j,j} s_j \\ s_{j,j} s_j^H & s_{j,j}^2 \end{bmatrix} .$$

Once $S_{j-1}S_{j-1}^H$ has been formed in place of S_{j-1}, the matrix $S_jS_j^H$ can be obtained by adding multiples of s_j to the earlier columns and then multiplying the entire j-th column (that is s_j together with $s_{j,j}$) by $s_{j,j}$.

The complete algorithm for generating A^{-1} from R follows. When implemented, the elements $a_{i,j}$ of $S = R^{-1}$ overwrite the elements $r_{i,j}$ of R in the upper triangle of A and then the elements $a_{i,j}$ of the upper half of A^{-1} overwrite the $s_{i,j}$.

```
for k = 1,...,n do
    s[k,k] = 1/r[k,k];
    for i = 1,...,k-1 do
        s[i,k] = -s[k,k]·r[i,k];
        for j = k+1,...,n do
            s[k,j] = 0;
            for i = 1,...,k do
                s[i,j] ← s[i,j] + r[k,j]·s[i,k];
        end j
end k
for j = 1,...,n do
    for k = 1,...,j-1 do
        for i = 1,...,k do
            a[i,k] ← a[i,k] + s[k,j]·s[i,j]
    end k;
    for i = 1,...,j do
        a[i,j] = s[j,j]·s[i,j]
end j
```

Relationship with the QR decomposition. Subroutine SPODI can also be used with the decomposition of a rectangular matrix produced by SQRDC (see Chapter 9). In this case, the original matrix is called X, it has n rows and p columns, and SQRDC produces an orthogonal Q (in factored form) and an upper triangular matrix R so that $X = QR$. If the p by p matrix $A = X^TX$ were to be formed and factored by SPOFA, the result would be an upper triangular matrix $\tilde{R}$ with

$$\tilde{R}^T\tilde{R} = X^TX = R^TQ^TQR = R^TR .$$

It follows that $\tilde{R} = R$, except possibly for the signs of the rows (or for complex multipliers of modulus one). However, formation of X^TX with finite precision arithmetic may result in an undesirable loss of accuracy. Consequently the triangular factor R obtained by SQRDC directly from X is often preferable to the one that would be obtained by SPOFA from X^TX.

The p by p matrix $A^{-1} = (X^TX)^{-1}$ is useful in least squares calculations. It can be produced by SPODI directly from R (the orthogonal factor Q is not involved). In other words, SQRDC followed by SPODI produces $(X^TX)^{-1}$ without the formation of X^TX itself. (The determinant of X^TX can also be obtained, although it is of questionable utility.)

5. Programming Details

SPOFA

A Cholesky algorithm involving columns and upper triangles employs inner, rather than outer, products and so the main loop in SPOFA uses SDOT, rather than SAXPY. In some computing environments this may improve efficiency because, although SDOT and SAXPY involve the same number of floating point operations, the intermediate results of SDOT may be stored in fast arithmetic registers instead of possibly slower main memory.

An example of a nontrivial program transformation possible with TAMPR is provided by CPOFA and SPOFA. The complex version includes the following statements involving the complex matrix A and a real internal variable S :

```
IF (S .LE. 0.0 .OR. AIMAG(A(J,J)) .NE. 0.0) GO TO 40
A(J,J) = CMPLX(SQRT(S),0.0)
```

The first statement checks for positive definiteness and also checks that the input matrix has a real diagonal, which it must if it is Hermitian. The second statement produces real, positive diagonal elements in the factor R. The rules used by TAMPR to transform programs from complex to real arithmetic include the following:

```
AIMAG(expression) → 0.0
0.0 .NE. 0.0 → .FALSE.
boolean .OR. .FALSE. → boolean
CMPLX(expression, 0.0) → expression
```

These rules lead to the following statements in the real version:

```
IF (S .LE. 0.0) GO TO 40
A(J,J) = SQRT(S)
```

SPOCO

The calculation of $\|A\|$ is complicated by the requirement that only the upper triangle of the symmetric matrix be used and the desire to access the elements one column at a time. SASUM can be used to compute norms of the portions of the columns in the upper triangle, but the remaining elements must be obtained from other columns using symmetry. The vector Z is used here as a work vector to accumulate the norms of the columns.

The estimation of $\|A^{-1}\|$ involves the solution of four successive triangular systems, the first and third involving R^T and the second and fourth involving R. The elements of the special right hand side are determined during the solution of the first triangular system. The program is very similar to SGECO with U replaced by R and L replaced by R^T. In particular, both programs use SSCAL to rescale and thereby avoid overflow.

<u>SPOSL</u>

The column orientation implies that SDOT is involved in the solution of $R^Ty = b$ and that SAXPY is involved in the solution of $Rx = y$.

If the user fails to check for nonzero INFO after SPOCO or SPOFA and thereby uses SPOSL incorrectly, it may divide by zero or produce meaningless results with no further error indication.

<u>SPODI</u>

The algorithm for computing $(R^TR)^{-1}$ in place involves multiplication of columns by scalars and addition of scalar multiples of columns to other columns. These are accomplished by SSCAL and SAXPY, respectively.

Division by zero may occur in SPODI if it is incorrectly called after a nonzero INFO. It may also occur in CPODI if the Fortran compiler improperly computes the reciprocal of $x+iy$ by $(x-iy)/(x^2+y^2)$.

<u>SPPCO, SPPFA, SPPSL, SPPDI</u>

The subroutines for packed symmetric matrices are virtually identical to the subroutines for full symmetric matrices. The one-dimensional subscripting is accomplished with three additional internal integer variables, JJ, KK and KJ. The packed array elements AP(JJ), AP(KK) and AP(KJ) correspond to A(J,J), A(K,K) and A(K,J), respectively. Note that AP(KK+1) then corresponds to A(1,K+1).

If the same matrix is stored in full form and processed by an SPO subroutine and stored in packed form and processed by an SPP subroutine, the two subroutines will perform identical sequences of floating point operations. Only the subscripting operations will differ.

6. Performance

Accuracy. The Cholesky factorization has very satisfactory numerical properties. The quantitative results of the error analysis can be expressed in terms of the computer rounding unit ε_M and the vector and matrix norms defined in Chapter 1, section 4. Let A be the symmetric, positive definite matrix of floating point numbers actually input to SPOFA or SPOCO and let R be the resulting factor. Let b be the vector input to SPOSL and let x be the resulting solution. Let X be the approximate inverse computed by SPODI . If A is nonsingular, let $x_* = A^{-1}b$. Then it is possible to prove that there are coefficients ρ_n and σ_n depending upon n , but not upon A , so that

$$\|A-R^TR\| \leq \rho_n \|A\| \varepsilon_M$$

$$\|Ax-b\| \leq \sigma_n \|A\| \, \|x\| \varepsilon_M$$

$$\|x-x_*\| \leq \sigma_n \kappa(A) \|x\| \varepsilon_M$$

$$\|AX-I\| \leq \sigma_n \|A\| \, \|X\| \varepsilon_M \; .$$

These inequalities have the same form as those given in Chapter 1 for the nonsymmetric problem. The major theoretical difference is that in this situation the growth coefficients ρ_n and σ_n are of size n^2 rather than 2^n . Moreover, even the n^2 results in part from a factor of n introduced in summarizing many inequalities involving individual elements by a single inequality involving norms.

Although no extensive experiments have been carried out, we expect that in practice with almost all matrices A , the above inequalities will hold with ρ_n and σ_n replaced by coefficients of order unity.

Timing. To obtain a rough estimate for the execution time required by a particular subroutine on a particular computer, let ν be the time required by that computer to execute the following Fortran statement once

```
S = S + X(I)*Y(I) .
```

This involves one floating point multiplication, one floating point addition, a few one-dimensional indexing operations, and a few storage references. On some computers, the variable S may be saved in an arithmetic register and so ν may be somewhat smaller than the quantity μ used in Chapter 1. Let n be the order of the matrix involved. Then estimates for the execution times can be obtained from the following table. The estimates may be quite inaccurate for small n , say $n \leq 10$.

Subroutine	Time
SPOCO, SPPCO	$(1/6\ n^3 + 3\ n^2)\nu$
SPOFA, SPPFA	$1/6\ n^3\nu$
SPOSL, SPPSL	$n^2\nu$
SPODI, SPPDI (for A^{-1})	$1/3\ n^3\nu$

7. Notes and References

Andre-Louis Cholesky (1875-1918) was a French military officer involved in geodesy and surveying in Crete and North Africa just before World War I. He developed the method now named after him to compute solutions to the normal equations for some least squares data fitting problems arising in geodesy. His work was posthumously published on his behalf in 1924 by a fellow officer, Benoit, in the Bulletin geodesique.

Although the square-root-free lower triangular factorization $A = LDL^T$ is commonly used today, we have found that the cost of the square roots in the factorization and the extra divisions in the solution is insignificant compared to the convenience of working with RR^T. The distinction between R and L is, of course, largely a matter of notation.

The error analysis summarized briefly in section 6 is given in Stewart (1973) and Wilkinson (1963).

A collection of Algol procedures and a succinct discussion of their numerical properties is given in Wilkinson and Reinsch (1971).

Chapter 4: Positive Definite Band Matrices

Subroutines: SPBCO, SPBFA, SPBSL, SPBDI

1. Overview

Purpose. The LINPACK subroutines in this chapter operate on symmetric positive definite band matrices. The operations performed include the triangular factorization of matrices, the estimation of matrix condition, the solution of simultaneous linear equations and the calculation of determinants.

Background. A real matrix A is positive definite if it is symmetric, that is $A = A^T$, and if the quadratic form x^TAx is positive for all nonzero real vectors x. Since the latter condition is difficult to check directly, it is usually replaced by other conditions in practice. For example, A is positive definite if $A = B^TB$ for some rectangular matrix B with linearly independent columns. A complex matrix A is positive definite if it is Hermitian, that is if A is equal to its complex conjugate transpose A^H, and if x^HAx is positive for all nonzero complex vectors x.

A positive definite band matrix is a positive definite matrix whose nonzero elements are all fairly near the main diagonal, specifically $a_{ij} = 0$ if $|i-j| > m$. The integer m is called the half band width and $2m+1$ is the total band width. The subroutines for positive definite band matrices use less storage than the subroutines for positive definite full matrices if $m < n/2$ and use less time if $m < n/\sqrt{3}$. Numerically, when the same matrix is input to the two sets of subroutines, the computed results are identical, but the elements are stored in different locations.

Tridiagonal matrices are the special case $m = 1$. They can be handled by the subroutines in this chapter, but the special subroutines in Chapter 7 are more efficient.

Let A be a real or complex positive definite band matrix. There is an upper triangular band matrix R so that $A = R^TR$ if A is real or $A = R^HR$ if A is complex. Such a factorization can be used to estimate the condition number of A, to solve simultaneous linear equations involving A, and to compute the determinant of A. If needed, the inverse of A can also be obtained.

The condition number $\kappa(A)$ is a quantity which measures the sensitivity of the solution x to errors in the matrix A and the right hand side b. If the relative error in A is of size ε, then the resulting relative error in x can be as large as $\kappa(A)\varepsilon$.

Errors in A can arise in many ways. In particular, the effect of the roundoff error introduced by the subroutines in this chapter can usually be assessed by taking ε to be a small multiple of the rounding unit.

It is possible to efficiently compute a quantity RCOND which is an estimate of the reciprocal condition, $1/\kappa(A)$. If RCOND is approximately 10^{-d} then the elements of x can usually be expected to have d fewer significant figures of accuracy than the elements of A . Consequently, if RCOND is so small that in floating point arithmetic it is negligible compared to 1.0 , then x may have no significant figures. On most computers, this condition may be tested by the logical expression

1.0 + RCOND .EQ. 1.0 .

When this expression is true, the matrix can be considered to be "singular to working precision." As a special case, if exact singularity is detected, RCOND may be set to 0.0 .

If A is badly scaled, then the interpretation of RCOND is more delicate. For a detailed discussion of RCOND , including the consequences of unusual scaling in A and errors in b , see Chapter 1, sections 4 and 6.

2. Usage

The following example illustrates the storage of positive definite band matrices. The original matrix is

11	12	13	0	0	0	0
12	22	23	24	0	0	0
13	23	33	34	35	0	0
0	24	34	44	45	46	0
0	0	35	45	55	56	57
0	0	0	46	56	66	67
0	0	0	0	57	67	77

Its order is n = 7 and its half band width is m = 2 . The band storage is

*	*	13	24	35	46	57
*	12	23	34	45	56	67
11	22	33	44	55	66	77

The *'s denote elements in the m by m triangle at the upper left which are not used.

The following program segment will transfer the m+1 diagonals in the upper triangle of a symmetric band matrix from conventional storage in A to band storage in ABD . In practice, A(I,J) is usually replaced by the direct calculation of the I,J-th element.

```
         M = half band width
         DO 20 J = 1, N
            I1 = MAX0(1, J-M)
            DO 10 I = I1, J
               K = I-J+M+1
               ABD(K,J) = A(I,J)
      10    CONTINUE
      20 CONTINUE
```

Single precision, positive definite band matrices. The four subroutines for single precision, positive definite matrices are SPBCO , SPBFA , SPBSL , and SPBDI . Ordinarily, SPBCO or SPBFA will be called once to factor a particular matrix and then SPBSL and SPBDI will be called to apply the factorization as many times as needed.

SPBCO uses the Cholesky algorithm to compute the R^TR factorization of a band matrix and then estimates its condition. The calling sequence is

CALL SPBCO(ABD,LDA,N,M,RCOND,Z,INFO) .

On entry,

ABD is a doubly subscripted array with dimension (LDA,N) which contains the band of a symmetric matrix whose factorization is to be computed. The columns of the upper triangle of A are stored in the columns of ABD and the diagonals of the upper triangle of A are stored in the rows of ABD .

LDA is the leading dimension of the array ABD , which must satisfy LDA $\geq$ M+1 .

N is the order of the matrix A and the number of elements in the vector Z .

M is the number of diagonals above the main diagonal in the band, which must satisfy $0 \leq M < N$.

On return,

ABD contains the band of an upper triangular matrix R so that $A = R^TR$. The factorization is not complete if INFO is not zero.

RCOND is an estimate of the reciprocal condition, $1/\kappa(A)$. If RCOND is so small that the logical expression 1.0 + RCOND .EQ. 1.0 is true, then A can usually be regarded as singular to working precision. RCOND is unchanged from its input value if INFO is not zero.

Z is a singly subscripted array of dimension N used for work space. If A is close to a singular matrix, then Z will contain an approximate null vector in the sense that $\|Az\| = RCOND \cdot \|A\| \cdot \|z\|$.

INFO is an integer used to indicate an error condition. INFO is set to 0 if A is found to be positive definite and was successfully factored. INFO is set to $K > 0$ if the leading submatrix of order K is not positive definite.

SPBFA should be used in place of SPBCO if the condition estimate is not needed. The calling sequence is

```
CALL SPBFA(ABD,LDA,N,M,INFO) .
```

On entry,

ABD is a doubly subscripted array with dimension (LDA,N) which contains the band of a symmetric matrix whose factorization is to be computed. The columns of the upper triangle of A are stored in the columns of ABD and the diagonals of the upper triangle of A are stored in the rows of ABD .

LDA is the leading dimension of the array ABD , which must satisfy $LDA \geq M+1$.

N is the order of the matrix A .

M is the number of diagonals above the main diagonal in the band, which must satisfy $0 \leq M < N$.

On return,

ABD contains the band of an upper triangular matrix R so that $A = R^T R$. The factorization is not complete if INFO is not zero.

INFO is an integer used to indicate an error condition. INFO is set to 0 if A is found to be positive definite and was successfully factored. INFO is set to $K > 0$ if the leading submatrix of order K is not positive definite.

SPBCO is usually called first to factor the matrix and estimate its condition. The actual factorization is done by SPBFA which can be called in place of SPBCO if the condition estimate is not needed. The time required by SPBCO is roughly $(1 + 12/M)$ times the time required by SPBFA .

SPBSL uses the $R^T R$ factorization of a band matrix A to solve symmetric linear systems of equations, $Ax = b$. It should not be used if SPBCO or SPBFA has set INFO to a nonzero value. The calling sequence is

```
CALL SPBSL(ABD,LDA,N,M,B) .
```

On entry,

ABD is a doubly subscripted array with dimension (LDA,N) which contains the factorization computed by SPBCO or SPBFA . It is not changed by SPBSL .

LDA is the leading dimension of the array ABD .

N is the order of the matrix A and the number of elements in the vector B .

M is the half band width.

B is a singly subscripted array of dimension N which contains the right hand side b of a system of simultaneous linear equations Ax = b .

On return,

B contains the solution, x .

SPBDI uses the R^TR factorization of a matrix to compute its determinant. The calling sequence is

CALL SPBDI(ABD,LDA,N,M,DET) .

On entry,

ABD is a doubly subscripted array with dimension (LDA,N) which contains the factorization computed by SPBCO or SPBFA . It is not changed by SPBDI .

LDA is the leading dimension of the array ABD .

N is the order of the matrix A .

M is the half band width.

On return,

DET is a singly subscripted array with 2 elements which contains the determinant of A in the form det(A) = DET(1)*10.0**DET(2) , although this expression may underflow or overflow if evaluated. DET(1) is normalized so that $1.0 \leq |DET(1)| < 10.0$ or DET(1) = 0.0 . DET(2) contains an integer stored as a real number.

No direct provision is made for computing the inverse of a band matrix because the inverse is usually a full n by n matrix which cannot be stored in the band storage. Moreover, calculations formulated in terms of matrix inverses are invariably more efficient when expressed in terms of the solution of sets of linear equations. However, an example in section 3 shows how the inverse can be obtained using SPBSL .

Double precision, positive definite band matrices. The calling sequences of the double precision positive definite band subroutines DPBCO , DPBFA , DPBSL , and DPBDI are the same as those of the corresponding single precision "S" subroutines except that ABD , B , RCOND , DET and Z are DOUBLE PRECISION variables.

Complex, positive definite band matrices. The calling sequences of the complex positive definite band subroutines CPBCO , CPBFA , CPBSL , and CPBDI are the same as those of the corresponding single precision "S" subroutines except that ABD , B and Z are COMPLEX variables and DET and RCOND are REAL variables.

Double precision complex positive definite band matrices. In those computing systems where they are available, the calling sequences of the double precision complex positive definite band subroutines ZPBCO , ZPBFA , ZPBSL and ZPBDI are the same as those of the corresponding single precision "S" subroutines except that ABD , B and Z are COMPLEX*16 variables, and DET and RCOND are DOUBLE PRECISION variables.

3. Example

This example factors a positive definite pentadiagonal matrix, tests for near singularity, and then finds the inverse by successively solving $Ax_j = e_j$, $j = 1,\ldots,n$. Note that different dimensions are used for ABD and AINV . This example is primarily for illustration; its actual use should be avoided whenever possible.

```
      DIMENSION ABD(3,50),AINV(50,50),Z (50)
      DATA LDA/3/
      N = ...
      M = 2
      DO 20 J = 1, N
         I1 = MAXO(1, J-M)
         DO 10 I = I1, J
            K = I-J+M+1
            ABD(K,J) = (I,J)-th element of A
   10    CONTINUE
   20 CONTINUE
      CALL SPBCO(ABD,LDA,N,M,RCOND,Z,INFO)
      IF (INFO .NE. 0) GO TO ...
      T = 1.0 + RCOND
      IF (T .EQ. 1.0) GO TO ...
      DO 40 J = 1, N
         DO 30 I = 1, N
            AINV(I,J) = 0.0
   30    CONTINUE
         AINV(J,J) = 1.0
```

```
      CALL SPBSL(ABD,LDA,N,M,AINV(1,J))
   40 CONTINUE
         :
```

4. Programming Details

The algorithms employed by the subroutines for positive definite band matrices are essentially the same as those employed by the subroutines for full positive definite matrices. Only the storage arrangement and the ranges of the DO-loops are different. Except for the operations on zeros, the two sets of routines do the same arithmetic operations in the same order.

SPBFA

No pivoting is required so there is no fill-in and no extra storage space required. The index J has the same meaning in SPOFA and SPBFA ; it is the index of the column in A which is overwritten by the corresponding column of R . In both subroutines, J goes from 1 to N . The index K has two roles in SPOFA . It is a row index within the J-th column and, because of the symmetry, it is also the column index of the elements used in determining R(K,J) . In SPBFA , two variables must be used for these two roles; they are called JK and K , respectively. The lower limit on the K-loop is MU which is equal to 1 except when J < M , and so the J-th column has fewer than M nonzero elements above the diagonal (M is the input half band width). The dot product involved in computing the element of R whose indices in the band structure are K and J involves K-MU elements (that is K-1 , except for small J). The indices of the first elements of the two columns involved in the dot product are (IK,JK) and (MU,J) . In the full matrix, these would correspond to (J-M,K) and (J-M,J) , respectively.

SPBCO and SPBSL

These are versions of SPOCO and SPOSL , modified to handle the band storage. The additional indices are LM , LA and LB . LM is the number of terms involved in each call to SDOT or SAXPY . It is usually equal to M , except when a "short" column near the beginning of the band matrix is involved. LA and LB are the starting indices in the pertinent column of A and in the right hand side.

SPBDI

The inverse of a band matrix is usually a full matrix which cannot be stored in the band storage. Consequently, SPBDI does not compute the inverse. It consists merely of the determinant part of SPODI .

5. Performance

Timing. To obtain a rough estimate for the execution time required by a particular subroutine on a particular computer, let ν be the time required by that computer to execute the following Fortran statement once.

```
S = S + X(I)*Y(I)
```

Let n be the order of the matrix involved and let m be its half band width. Then estimates for the execution times can be obtained from the following table. The estimates may be quite inaccurate for small n or very small m.

Subroutine	Time
SPBCO	$(1/2\ nm^2 - 1/3\ m^3 + 6nm - 3m^2)\nu$
SPBFA	$(1/2\ nm^2 - 1/3\ m^3)\nu$
SPBSL	$(2nm - m^2)\nu$

Chapter 5: Symmetric Indefinite Matrices

Subroutines: SSICO, SSIFA, SSISL, SSIDI, CHICO, CHIFA, CHISL, CHIDI, SSPCO, SSPFA, SSPSL, SSPDI, CHPCO, CHPFA, CHPSL, CHPDI

1. Overview

Purpose. The LINPACK subroutines in this chapter operate on full real symmetric matrices, full complex Hermitian matrices, and full complex symmetric matrices, which are stored in singly or doubly subscripted arrays. The computing costs in terms of both time and storage are about half the corresponding costs for nonsymmetric matrices. The subroutines will operate on full real symmetric and full complex Hermitian matrices which are positive definite but at a small increase in time over the subroutines in Chapter 3. The operations performed include the triangular factorization of matrices, the estimation of the matrix condition number, the solution of simultaneous linear equations, and the calculation of determinants, inverses and inertia. (Note: Inertia is not defined for complex symmetric matrices.)

Operations on nonsymmetric matrices, symmetric positive definite matrices, tridiagonal matrices, and rectangular matrices are covered in other chapters. Symmetric indefinite band matrices should employ the general band subroutines in Chapters 2 and 7.

Background. A matrix A is symmetric if $A = A^T$ ($a_{ij} = a_{ji}$ for all i,j) and is Hermitian if $A = A^H$ ($a_{ij} = \bar{a}_{ji}$ for all i,j). The eigenvalues of a real symmetric or complex Hermitian matrix are all real; a complex symmetric matrix does not, in general, have all real eigenvalues. The inertia of a real symmetric or complex Hermitian matrix A is the triple (π,ν,ζ), where π, ν and ζ are, respectively, the number of positive, negative and zero eigenvalues of A, counted with multiplicities. Then the rank of A is $\pi+\nu$ and the signature of A is $\pi-\nu$. The inertia of a real symmetric (complex Hermitian) matrix A is a complete set of invariants of A under congruence transformations, $A \rightarrow S^TAS$ ($A \rightarrow S^HAS$), where S is real (complex) and nonsingular. The terms inertia and signature are usually not defined for complex symmetric matrices.

A real symmetric or complex Hermitian matrix of order n is positive definite (positive semi-definite, negative definite, negative semi-definite) if all its eigenvalues are positive (non-negative, negative, non-positive), i.e., if $\pi = n$ ($\nu = 0$, $\nu = n$, $\pi = 0$). A real symmetric or complex Hermitian matrix is indefinite if it has at least one positive and at least one negative eigenvalue, i.e., if $\pi > 0$ and $\nu > 0$. We shall consider all complex symmetric matrices (which are not actually real) to be indefinite.

Equivalently, a real symmetric matrix is positive definite (positive semi-definite, negative definite, negative semi-definite) if $x^TAx > 0$ (≥ 0, < 0, ≤ 0) for all nonzero real x and is indefinite if $x^TAx > 0$ and $y^TAy < 0$ for some real x and y; a complex Hermitian matrix is positive definite (positive semi-definite, negative definite, negative semi-definite) if $x^HAx > 0$ (≥ 0, < 0, ≤ 0) for all nonzero complex x and is indefinite if $x^HAx > 0$ and $y^HAy < 0$ for some complex x and y.

Let A be a real or complex symmetric matrix or a complex Hermitian matrix. Then there is a block diagonal matrix D with blocks of order 1 or 2 and a matrix U which is the product of elementary unit upper triangular and permutation matrices such that $A = UDU^T$ with $D = D^T$ if $A = A^T$ or $A = UDU^H$ with $D = D^H$ if $A = A^H$ is Hermitian. Such a factorization can be used to solve simultaneous linear equations, $Ax = b$, by solving $U(D(U^Tx)) = b$ if $A = A^T$ or $U(D(U^Hx)) = b$ if $A = A^H$; to compute the determinant as $\det A = \det D$; to compute the inverse of A as $A^{-1} = (U^{-1})^T D^{-1} U^{-1}$ if $A = A^T$ or $A^{-1} = (U^{-1})^H D^{-1} U^{-1}$ if $A = A^H$; and to compute the inertia of A if A is real symmetric or complex Hermitian. For the details of this algorithm, see Section 4; for the details of its performance on symmetric matrices, see Section 6; and for a discussion of factoring symmetric matrices, see Section 7.

The condition number $\kappa(A)$ is a quantity which measures the sensitivity of the solution x to errors in the matrix A and the right hand side b. If the relative error in A is of size ε, then the resulting relative error in x can be as large as $\kappa(A)\varepsilon$. Errors in A can arise in many ways. In particular, the effect of the roundoff error introduced by the subroutines in this chapter can usually be assessed by taking ε to be a small multiple of the rounding unit.

The condition number $\kappa(A)$ can be computed exactly, as shown in Section 3, but it is costly to obtain since it requires the computation of A^{-1}. A quantity RCOND, which is an estimate of the reciprocal condition $1/\kappa(A)$, can, however, be computed efficiently. If RCOND is approximately 10^{-d}, then the elements of x can usually be expected to have d fewer significant figures of accuracy than the elements of A. Consequently, if RCOND is so small that in floating point arithmetic it is negligible compared to 1.0, then x may have no significant figures. On most computers, this condition may be tested by the logical expression

```
1.0 + RCOND .EQ. 1.0 .
```

When this expression is true, the matrix can be considered to be "singular to working precision." As a special case, if exact singularity is detected, RCOND is set to 0.0 .

If A is badly scaled, then the interpretation of RCOND is more delicate. For a detailed discussion of RCOND , including the consequences of unusual scaling in A and errors in b , see the Introduction and Chapter 1, Section 4.

A symmetric or Hermitian matrix can be stored in a singly subscripted array with n(n+1)/2 elements, thereby saving almost half the usual storage. Such an arrangement is called packed storage. The subroutines which use packed storage produce identical numerical results and usually require about the same execution time as the subroutines for conventional storage.

2. Usage

Real Hermitian matrices are actually real symmetric, so there are no subroutines beginning with SHI , SHP , DHI , or DHP ; instead they begin SSI , SSP , DSI , and DSP .

Single precision, real symmetric matrices. The four subroutines for single precision, real symmetric matrices are SSICO , SSIFA , SSISL , and SSIDI . Ordinarily, SSICO or SSIFA is called once to factor the matrix, and then SSISL or SSIDI can be called to apply the factorization as many times as needed. Fortran naming conventions with regard to type are observed.

SSICO computes the symmetric indefinite factorization of a matrix ($A = UDU^T$) and estimates its (reciprocal) condition number. The calling sequence is

```
CALL SSICO(A,LDA,N,KPVT,RCOND,Z) .
```

On entry,

A — is a doubly subscripted array with dimension (LDA,N) which contains the symmetric matrix whose factorization is to be computed. Only the upper triangle (including the diagonal) is used.

LDA — is the leading dimension of the array A .

N — is the order of the matrix A and the number of elements in the vectors KPVT and Z .

On return,

A contains in its upper triangle (including its diagonal) the information necessary to construct a matrix U and block diagonal matrix D so that $A = UDU^T$.

KPVT is a singly subscripted integer array of dimension N which contains the pivot information necessary to construct the permutations in U . Specifically, KPVT(K) is the index of the K-th pivot row and column.

RCOND is an estimate of the reciprocal condition, $1/\kappa(A)$. If RCOND is so small that the logical expression 1.0 + RCOND .EQ. 1.0 is true, then A can usually be regarded as singular to working precision. (RCOND = 0.0 if exact singularity is detected or the estimate underflows.)

Z is a singly subscripted array of dimension N used for work space. If A is close to a singular matrix, then Z will contain an approximate null vector z in the sense that $\|Az\| = \text{RCOND}\cdot\|A\|\cdot\|z\|$.

SSIFA should be used in place of SSICO if the condition estimate is not needed. The calling sequence is

CALL SSIFA(A,LDA,N,KPVT,INFO) .

On entry,

A is a doubly subscripted array with dimension (LDA,N) which contains the symmetric matrix whose factorization is to be computed. Only the upper triangle (including the diagonal) is used.

LDA is the leading dimension of the array A .

N is the order of the matrix A and the number of elements in the vector KPVT .

On return,

A contains in its upper triangle (including its diagonal) the information necessary to construct a matrix U and block diagonal matrix D so that $A = UDU^T$.

KPVT is a singly subscripted integer array of dimension N which contains the pivot information necessary to construct the permutations in U . Specifically, KPVT(K) is the index of the K-th pivot row and column.

INFO is an integer returned by SSIFA which, if it is 0 , indicates that SSISL or SSIDI can be safely used. If INFO = K $\neq$ 0 , then SSISL and the inversion part of SSIDI will divide by zero. All 2 by 2 diagonal blocks of D are nonsingular; if D has several singular 1 by 1 diagonal blocks, K will be the index of the one nearest the top. Although a nonzero INFO technically indicates singularity, RCOND is a more reliable indicator.

SSICO is usually called first to factor the matrix and estimate its condition. The actual factorization is done by SSIFA , which can be called directly in place of SSICO if the condition estimate is not needed.

Since any symmetric matrix has a UDU^T factorization, there is no error return from SSICO or SSIFA . However, the factors can be singular and consequently unusable by SSISL and the inversion part of SSIDI . Either RCOND or INFO should be tested before calling SSISL or SSIDI .

SSISL uses the UDU^T factorization of a symmetric matrix A to solve a symmetric linear system of equations, Ax = b . It should not be used if SSICO has set RCOND = 0.0 or if SSIFA has set INFO to a nonzero value. The calling sequence is

```
CALL SSISL(A,LDA,N,KPVT,B) .
```

On entry,

A is a doubly subscripted array with dimension (LDA,N) which contains information from the factorization computed by SSICO or SSIFA . It is not changed by SSISL .

LDA is the leading dimension of the array A .

N is the order of the matrix A and the number of elements in the vectors B and KPVT .

KPVT is a singly subscripted integer array of dimension N which contains the pivot information from SSICO or SSIFA .

B is a singly subscripted array of dimension N which contains the right hand side b of the system of simultaneous linear equations Ax = b .

On return,

B contains the solution, x .

If the factor D of $A = UDU^T$ has a singular diagonal block (a situation that will set INFO $\neq$ 0 in SSIFA or RCOND = 0.0 in SSICO), a division by zero will be attempted in SSISL . Technically this means that the matrix A is singular, but it may be caused by incorrect setting of LDA or other improper use of the subroutines.

SSIDI uses the UDU^T factorization of a real symmetric matrix to compute its inertia, determinant, and inverse. Note, however, that many calculations formulated in terms of matrix inverses can be reformulated in terms of the solution of sets of linear equations. The reformulated versions usually require less time and produce more accurate results. Several examples are included in Section 3. The calling sequence is

CALL SSIDI(A,LDA,N,KPVT,DET,INERT,WORK,JOB) .

On entry,

A is a doubly subscripted array with dimension (LDA,N) which contains information from the factorization computed by SSICO or SSIFA .

LDA is the leading dimension of the array A .

N is the order of the matrix A and the number of elements in the vectors KPVT and WORK .

KPVT is a singly subscripted integer array of dimension N which contains the pivot information from SSICO or SSIFA .

WORK is a singly subscripted array of dimension N used for work space. WORK is referenced only if the inverse is computed.

JOB indicates what is to be computed, by the digits of its decimal expansion ABC , where the inertia is computed if A $\neq$ 0 , the determinant is computed if B $\neq$ 0, and the inverse is computed if C $\neq$ 0 . Thus, if JOB is

111 then the inertia, determinant, and inverse are computed;

110 then the inertia and determinant are computed;

101 then the inertia and inverse are computed;

100 then only the inertia is computed;

11 then the determinant and inverse are computed;

10 then only the determinant is computed;

1 then only the inverse is computed.

The inverse should not be requested if SSICO has set RCOND = 0.0 or if

SSIFA has set INFO to a nonzero value.

On return,

A contains the upper triangle of the inverse of the original matrix in its upper triangle, if requested. If the units digit of JOB is zero, then A is unchanged.

DET is a singly subscripted array with 2 elements which contains the determinant of A in the form det(A) = DET(1)*10.0**INT(DET(2)) , although this expression may underflow or overflow if evaluated. DET(1) is normalized so that $1.0 \leq |DET(1)| < 10.0$ or DET(1) = 0.0 . DET(2) contains an integer stored as a real number. If the tens digit of JOB is zero, then DET is not referenced.

INERT is a singly subscripted array with 3 elements which contains the inertia of A . INERT(1) , INERT(2) and INERT(3) are the number of positive, negative and zero eigenvalues of A , respectively. If the hundreds digit of JOB is zero, then INERT is not referenced.

Packed storage. The calling sequence of the four subroutines for single precision, real symmetric matrices stored in packed form are:

```
CALL SSPCO(AP,N,KPVT,RCOND,Z)
CALL SSPFA(AP,N,KPVT,INFO)
CALL SSPSL(AP,N,KPVT,B)
CALL SSPDI(AP,N,KPVT,DET,INERT,WORK,JOB) .
```

The only difference between the packed storage "SSP" subroutines and the full storage "SSI" subroutines is the storage of the matrix. The following program segment will transfer the upper triangle of a symmetric matrix from conventional full matrix storage in A to packed storage in the singly subscripted array AP .

```
      K = 0
      DO 20 J = 1, N
         DO 10 I = 1, J
            K = K + 1
            AP(K) = A(I,J)
   10    CONTINUE
   20 CONTINUE
```

This stores the columns of the upper triangle of the two-dimensional array (which are the same as the rows of the lower triangle) sequentially in the N*(N+1)/2 elements of a singly subscripted array; the corresponding subscript is K = I + J(J-1)/2 . Since there are no doubly subscripted arrays in the packed subroutines, there is no need for the parameter LDA . The parameters N , KPVT , RCOND , Z , INFO , B , DET , INERT , WORK and JOB are exactly the same as for the SSI subroutines.

There are no numerical differences whatsoever between the results produced by the "SSI" and "SSP" subroutines. The execution times will usually be about the same because both sets of subroutines use the BLAS for their inner loops.

Double precision, real symmetric matrices. The calling sequences of the double precision, real symmetric subroutines DSICO , DSIFA , DSISL , DSIDI , DSPCO , DSPFA , DSPSL and DSPDI are the same as those of the corresponding single precision "SS" subroutines except that A, AP , B , RCOND , DET , WORK and Z are DOUBLE PRECISION variables.

Single precision, complex Hermitian matrices. The calling sequences of the single precision, complex Hermitian subroutines CHICO , CHIFA , CHISL , CHIDI , CHPCO , CHPFA , CHPSL and CHPDI are the same as those of the corresponding single precision "SS" subroutines except that A , AP , B , WORK and Z are COMPLEX variables. (DET and RCOND are still REAL variables.)

Double precision, complex Hermitian matrices. In those computing systems where they are available, the calling sequences of the double precision, complex Hermitian subroutines ZHICO , ZHIFA , ZHISL , ZHIDI , ZHPCO , ZHPFA , ZHPSL and ZHPDI are the same as those of the corresponding single precision "SS" subroutines except that A , AP , B , WORK and Z are COMPLEX*16 variables, and DET and RCOND are DOUBLE PRECISION variables.

Single precision, complex symmetric matrices. The calling sequences of the single precision, complex symmetric subroutines CSICO , CSIFA , CSISL , CSPCO , CSPFA , and CSPSL are the same as those of the corresponding "SS" subroutines except that A , AP , B and Z are COMPLEX variables. (RCOND is still a REAL variable.)

The calling sequences for CSIDI and CSPDI do not have the parameter INERT since inertia is not defined for complex symmetric matrices. Here JOB consists of at most 2 digits; DET and WORK are COMPLEX variables.

```
CALL CSIDI(A,LDA,N,KPVT,DET,WORK,JOB)

CALL CSPDI(AP,N,KPVT,DET,WORK,JOB)
```

JOB indicates what is to be computed. Thus, if JOB is 11 , then both the determinant and inverse are computed. If JOB is 10 , only the determinant is computed. If JOB is 1 , only the inverse is computed. The inverse should not be computed if CSICO (CSPCO) has set RCOND = 0.0 or if CSIFA (CSPFA) has set INFO to a nonzero value.

Double precision, complex symmetric matrices. In those computing systems where they are available, the calling sequences of the double precision, complex symmetric subroutines ZSICO , ZSIFA , ZSISL , ZSIDI , ZSPCO , ZSPFA , ZSPSL and ZSPDI are the same as those of the corresponding single precision "CS" subroutines except that A , AP , B , WORK , Z and DET are COMPLEX*16 variables, and RCOND is a DOUBLE PRECISION variable.

3. Examples

The following program segments illustrate the use of the single precision subroutines for real symmetric matrices. Examples showing the use of "D" , "C" and "Z" subroutines could be obtained by changing the subroutine names and type declarations (except that there is no parameter INERT for CSIDI , CSPDI , ZSIDI , and ZSPDI).

The first program segment factors a matrix, tests for near singularity, and then solves a single system Ax = b and computes the inertia of A . Note that only the upper triangle of the symmetric matrix is generated.

```
      REAL A(50,50),B(50),WORK(50),Z(50),DET(2),T,RCOND
      INTEGER KPVT(50),INERT(3)
      DATA LDA/50/
      N = ...
      DO 20 J = 1, N
         DO 10 I = 1, J
            A(I,J) = ...
   10    CONTINUE
   20 CONTINUE
      CALL SSICO(A,LDA,N,KPVT,RCOND,Z)
      T = 1.0 + RCOND
      IF(T .EQ. 1.0) GO TO 90
      DO 30 I = 1, N
         B(I) = ...
   30 CONTINUE
      CALL SSISL(A,LDA,N,KPVT,B)
      DO 40 I = 1, N
         WRITE(..., ...) B(I)
   40 CONTINUE
      CALL SSIDI(A,LDA,N,KPVT,DET,INERT,WORK,100)
```

```
      DO 50 L = 1, 3
         WRITE(..., ...) INERT(L)
   50 CONTINUE
      STOP
   90 WRITE(..., 99)
   99 FORMAT(40H MATRIX IS SINGULAR TO WORKING PRECISION)
      STOP
      END
```

The following program segment generates an approximation to a modified Hilbert matrix, $a_{i,j} = 1/(i+j-\tau)$, in packed storage; finds the inertia, determinant, and inverse; prints out the determinant in a simulated E format that allows for a four-digit exponent; and then prints out the upper triangle of the computed inverse.

```
      REAL AP(55),DET(2),WORK(10),TAU
      INTEGER KPVT(10),INERT(3)
      TAU = 3.5
      N = 10
      K = 0
      DO 20 J = 1, N
         DO 10 I = 1, J
            K = K + 1
            AP(K) = 1.0/FLOAT(I+J-TAU)
   10    CONTINUE
   20 CONTINUE
      CALL SSPFA(AP,N,KPVT,INFO)
      IF(INFO .NE. 0) STOP
      CALL SSPDI(AP,N,KPVT,DET,INERT,WORK,111)
      WRITE(..., 30)(INERT(L),L=1,3)
   30 FORMAT(10H INERTIA = , 3I4)
      K = INT(DET(2))
      WRITE(..., 40) DET(1),K
   40 FORMAT(14H DETERMINANT = , F20.15, 1HE, I4)
      WRITE(..., 50)
   50 FORMAT(10H INVERSE = )
      K = 1
      DO 60 I = 1, N
         L = K + I - 1
         WRITE(..., 70) (AP(J), J = K, L)
         K = L + 1
   60 CONTINUE
   70 FORMAT(10G12.6)
      STOP
      END
```

The next program segment replaces C , a matrix with L columns, by $A^{-1}C$ without explicitly forming A^{-1} .

```
      CALL SSIFA(A,LDA,N,KPVT,INFO)
      IF (INFO .NE. 0) GO TO ...
      DO 10 J = 1, L
         CALL SSISL(A,LDA,N,KPVT,C(1,J))
   10 CONTINUE
```

The next program segment replaces C , a matrix with L rows, by CA^{-1} without explicitly forming A^{-1} . Since this involves the rows rather than the columns of C , the device used in the previous example is not applicable.

```
      CALL SSIFA(A,LDA,N,KPVT,INFO)
      IF (INFO .NE. 0) GO TO ...
      DO 30 I = 1, L
         DO 10 J = 1, N
            B(J) = C(I,J)
   10    CONTINUE
         CALL SSISL(A,LDA,N,KPVT,B)
         DO 20 J = 1, N
            C(I,J) = B(J)
   20    CONTINUE
   30 CONTINUE
```

The next program segment prints out the estimated condition number COND and the determinant of a matrix. The determinant is printed in a simulated E format that allows for a four-digit exponent and avoids underflow/overflow difficulties.

```
      CALL SSICO(A,LDA,N,KPVT,RCOND,Z)
      IF (RCOND .EQ. 0.0) GO TO ...
      COND = 1.0/RCOND
      CALL SSIDI(A,LDA,N,KPVT,DET,INERT,WORK,10)
      K = INT(DET(2))
      WRITE(..., 10) COND,DET(1),K
   10 FORMAT(13H CONDITION = , E15.5/15H DETERMINANT = , F20.15, 1HE, I4)
```

The next example illustrates how the actual condition number $\kappa(A)$ of a matrix A might be computed by forming the matrix inverse; $\kappa(A)$ is denoted by CONDA here.

```
      ANORM = 0.0
      DO 10 J = 1, N
         ANORM = AMAX1(ANORM, SASUM(J,A(1,J),1) + SASUM(N-J,A(J,J+1),LDA))
   10 CONTINUE
      CALL SSIFA(A,LDA,N,KPVT,INFO)
      IF (INFO .NE. 0) GO TO ...
```

```
      CALL SSIDI(A,LDA,N,KPVT,DET,INERT,WORK,1)
      AINORM = 0.0
      DO 20 J = 1, N
         AINORM = AMAX1(AINORM,SASUM(J,A(1,J),1) + SASUM(N-J,A(J,J+1),LDA))
   20 CONTINUE
      CONDA = ANORM*AINORM
```

(The Basic Linear Algebra Subprogram

SASUM(J,A(1,J),1) computes $\sum_{I=1}^{J} |A(I,J)|$

and

SASUM(N-J,A(J,J+1),LDA) computes $\sum_{I=J+1}^{N} |A(J,I)|$.)

4. Algorithmic Details

The diagonal pivoting factorization. The algorithm used here to factor a symmetric or Hermitian matrix is a generalization of Lagrange's method for reducing a quadratic form to a diagonal form; it corresponds to block symmetric Gaussian elimination. The symmetric case will be discussed here; the Hermitian case follows by replacing T (transpose) by H (conjugate transpose) throughout.

Let A be an n by n (real or complex) symmetric matrix. The factorization subroutines generate a nonsingular matrix U^{-1} of the form

$$U^{-1} = U_1P_1 \cdots U_nP_n$$

and a block diagonal matrix $D = D^T$ with 1 by 1 or 2 by 2 diagonal blocks such that

$$U^{-1}A(U^{-1})^T = D \ .$$

Each P_k is either the identity or a permutation matrix obtained by interchanging two columns of the identity. Each U_k is a block "elementary eliminator" which differs from the identity at most by elements above the diagonal in s columns, where s is 1 or 2 , i.e.,

$$U_k = \left[\begin{array}{c|c|c} I_{k-s} & m_k & 0 \\ \hline 0 & I_s & 0 \\ \hline 0 & 0 & I_{n-k} \end{array}\right] ,$$

where I_j is the j by j identity $(j = k-s,s,n-k)$ and m_k is $k-s$ by s . The elements of m_k , called multipliers, are chosen to introduce zeros into the corresponding positions of the matrix. The permutation P_k is chosen so that the s by s pivot will provide numerical stability.

The calculation of $U^{-1}A(U^{-1})^T$ is accomplished by carrying out permutations and eliminations on the upper triangle of A (including the diagonal), rather than by actual multiplication of the matrices U^{-1} , A , and $(U^{-1})^T$. Neither U nor U^{-1} is formed explicitly, but rather the multipliers are stored above the diagonal in the array originally containing A , the upper triangle of the corresponding symmetric s by s diagonal block pivot d_k is stored in the upper triangle of the location corresponding to I_s in U_k , and the index which specifies the permutation is stored in the pivot vector element KPVT(K) . If no permutation occurs, then KPVT(K) = K .

When a 2 by 2 pivot is employed at step k , then step k-1 is skipped and $P_{k-1} = I$, $U_{k-1} = I$, and KPVT(K-1) = KPVT(K) = the negative of the index which specifies the permutation.

The factorization uses $|z| \equiv \text{CABS1}(z) \equiv |\text{real}(z)| + |\text{imag}(z)|$ instead of the modulus of z , because CABS1 can be computed more rapidly than the conventional modulus, and yet it has all the necessary numerical properties.

The factorization algorithm can be described as follows. In order to preserve column orientation, the factorization is obtained by working from the last column to the first. Thus, the factorization loop parameter k goes backwards from n to 1 in steps of 1 or 2. In the following, let $\alpha \equiv (1 + \sqrt{17})/8 \doteq 0.6404$ (a fixed, machine-independent parameter).

When the loop parameter has the value k , then the matrix is in the form

$$\left[\begin{array}{c|c} A_k & 0 \\ \hline 0 & D_k \end{array}\right] ,$$

where $A_k = A_k^T$ is k by k and $D_k = D_k^T$ is (n-k) by (n-k) and block diagonal with blocks of order 1 or 2. A permutation matrix P_k and a resulting s by s pivot d_k , with s = 1 or 2, are then determined as follows:

(1) determine $\lambda_k = |(A_k)_{rk}| \equiv \max_{1 \le j \le k-1} |(A_k)_{jk}|$, the largest off-diagonal element in the last column of A_k ;

(2) if $|(A_k)_{kk}| \geq \alpha\lambda_k$

(2.1) then $P_k = I$ and s = 1 ;

(2.2) else determine $\sigma_k = \max\left\{\max_{r+1 \le j \le k} |(A_k)_{rj}| , \max_{1 \le j \le r-1} |(A_k)_{jr}|\right\}$, the largest off-diagonal element in the r-th column of A_k ; now there are 3 cases:

(2.2.1) if $|(A_k)_{kk}|\sigma_k \geq \alpha\lambda_k^2$, then $P_k = I$ and s = 1 ;

(2.2.2) if $|(A_k)_{rr}| \geq \alpha\sigma_k$, then P_k is the matrix obtained by interchanging the rth and k^{th} columns of I and $s = 1$;

(2.2.3) otherwise, P_k is the matrix obtained by interchanging the rth and $k\text{-}1^{st}$ columns of I and $s = 2$.

Let $\tilde{A}_k = P_k A_k P_k \equiv \left[\begin{array}{cc|c} B_k & a_k & \\ a_k^T & d_k & 0 \\ \hline 0 & & D_k \end{array}\right]$, where d_k is s by s with $s = 1$ or 2 , B_k is (k-s) by (k-s) and a_k is k-s by s. If A is nonsingular, then the above conditions ensure that d_k^{-1} exists and is not too large.

The multipliers are determined by solving

$$m_k d_k = -a_k \,.$$

This involves simply dividing by d_k if $s = 1$ or solving $k-2$ systems of order 2 if $s = 2$.

The elimination step yields

$$U_k A_k U_k^T = \left[\begin{array}{cc|c} I_{k-s} & m_k & \\ 0 & I_s & 0 \\ \hline 0 & & I_{n-k} \end{array}\right] \left[\begin{array}{cc|c} B_k & a_k & \\ a_k^T & d_k & 0 \\ \hline 0 & & D_k \end{array}\right] \left[\begin{array}{cc|c} I_{k-s} & 0 & \\ m_k^T & I_s & 0 \\ \hline 0 & & I_{n-k} \end{array}\right]$$

$$= \left[\begin{array}{cc|c} B_k - m_k d_k m_k^T & 0 & \\ 0 & d_k & 0 \\ \hline 0 & & D_k \end{array}\right].$$

If $s = 2$, set $P_{k-1} = I$ and $U_{k-1} = I$. To iterate the loop, let

$$A_{k-s} \equiv B_k - m_k d_k m_k^T \,,$$

let

$$D_{k-s} \equiv \left[\begin{array}{c|c} d_k & 0 \\ \hline 0 & D_k \end{array}\right],$$

and decrease k by s.

The final factorization can be written

$$U_1 P_1 \ldots U_n P_n A P_n U_n^T \ldots P_1 U_1^T = D$$

or

$$A = UDU^T \,,$$

where

$$U = P_n U_n^{-1} \ldots P_1 U_1^{-1}$$

and

$$U_k^{-1} = \left[\begin{array}{c|c|c} I_{k-s} & -m_k & 0 \\ \hline 0 & I_s & 0 \\ \hline 0 & 0 & I_{n-k} \end{array}\right]$$

with $s = 1$ or 2 .

Note that a singular d_k does not indicate failure of the factorization but simply that the factor D is singular and cannot be used for solving linear systems or computing A^{-1} .

The condition estimate. RCOND is computed in a manner similar to that described in Chapter 1, Section 4. The outline of the process is:

compute $\|A\|$,

factor $A = UDU^T$,

solve $UDw = e$,

solve $U^T y = w$,

solve $UDv = y$,

solve $U^T z = v$,

$\text{RCOND} = \|y\|/(\|A\|\,\|z\|)$.

The elements of the vector e are determined for $k = n-1,\ldots,1$ by

$$e_k = \text{sign}\left(\sum_{j=k+1}^{n} (U^{-1})_{kj} e_j\right) ,$$

where $e_n = 1$.

Solving linear systems. Given the factorization $A = UDU^T$, solving the linear system $Ax = b$ is equivalent to solving $DU^T x = U^{-1} b$, i.e.,

$$DU_1^{-T} P_1 \ldots U_n^{-T} P_n x = U_1 P_1 \ldots U_n P_n b .$$

This requires n^2+2n multiplications (and divisions) and $n^2 - \frac{1}{2}n$ additions if A is n by n.

The inertia. For real symmetric and complex Hermitian matrices A , the inertia of A is the same as the inertia of D since U is nonsingular. When a 2 by 2 block occurs in D , conditions (1)-(2.2.3) above ensure that the determinant of that 2 by 2 block is negative and hence that it has one positive and negative eigenvalue. Let D have p blocks of order 1 and q blocks of order 2 , with $p+2q = n$. If the p blocks of order 1 have β positive, γ negative, and ζ zero elements, then A has $\pi = \beta+q$ positive, $\nu = \gamma+q$ negative, and ζ zero eigenvalues.

The determinant. Since $\det U = \pm 1$, $\det A = \det D$. In order to prevent overflow, the determinant of a 2 by 2 block is computed as follows:

(i) if A is real symmetric, $\det\begin{bmatrix} a & b \\ b & c \end{bmatrix} = \left[\frac{ac}{|b|} - |b|\right]|b|$, where $|b| = \mathrm{ABS}(b)$;

(ii) if A is complex symmetric, $\det\begin{bmatrix} a & b \\ b & c \end{bmatrix} = \left[\frac{ac}{b} - b\right]b$;

(iii) if A is complex Hermitian, $\det\begin{bmatrix} a & b \\ \bar{b} & c \end{bmatrix} = \left[\frac{ac}{|b|} - |b|\right]|b|$, where $|b| \equiv \sqrt{b\bar{b}} = \sqrt{\mathrm{real}(b)^2 + \mathrm{imag}(b)^2}$. (Note that it is necessary to use CABS rather than CABS1 here.)

Inversion in place. The inverse can be constructed as

$$A^{-1} = U^{-T}D^{-1}U^{-1} = P_nU_n^{-T}\ldots P_1U_1^{-T}D^{-1}U_1P_1\ldots U_nP_n \ .$$

The loop parameter k goes from 1 to n . When the loop parameter has the value k , the leading k by k submatrix contains

$$\begin{bmatrix} C_{k-s} & m_k \\ m_k^T & d_k \end{bmatrix},$$

where d_k is s by s, s = 1 or 2, and $C_{k-s} \equiv A_{k-s}^{-1}$ (only the upper triangle is actually stored). Then

(i) form d_k^{-1} ;

(ii) form $\tilde{C}_k \equiv \begin{bmatrix} I_{k-s} & 0 \\ m_k^T & I_s \end{bmatrix}\begin{bmatrix} C_{k-s} & 0 \\ 0 & d_k^{-1} \end{bmatrix}\begin{bmatrix} I_{k-s} & m_k \\ 0 & I_s \end{bmatrix} = \begin{bmatrix} C_{k-s} & C_{k-s}m_k \\ m_k^TC_{k-s} & d_k^{-1} + m_k^TC_km_k \end{bmatrix}$;

(iii) form $C_k = P_k\tilde{C}_kP_k$.

Finally, $A^{-1} = C_n$. The product $C_{k-s}m_k$ is formed using only half of C_{k-s} and a column-oriented algorithm; this is done by an appropriate combination of CDOTC and CAXPY BLAS.

In order to prevent overflow, the inverse of a 2 by 2 diagonal block is computed as follows:

(i) if A is real symmetric, then $\begin{bmatrix} a & b \\ b & c \end{bmatrix}^{-1} = \frac{1}{|b|\left(\frac{a}{|b|}\cdot\frac{c}{|b|} - 1\right)}\begin{bmatrix} c/|b| & -b/|b| \\ -b/|b| & a/|b| \end{bmatrix}$, where $|b| = \mathrm{ABS}(b)$;

(ii) if A is complex symmetric, then $\begin{bmatrix} a & b \\ b & c \end{bmatrix}^{-1} = \frac{1}{b\left(\frac{a}{b}\cdot\frac{c}{b} - 1\right)}\begin{bmatrix} c/b & -1 \\ -1 & a/b \end{bmatrix}$;

(iii) if A is complex Hermitian, then $\begin{bmatrix} a & b \\ \bar{b} & c \end{bmatrix}^{-1} = \dfrac{1}{|b|\left(\frac{a}{|b|}\cdot\frac{c}{|b|}-1\right)}\begin{bmatrix} c/|b| & -b/|b| \\ -\bar{b}/|b| & a/|b| \end{bmatrix}$,

where $|b| \equiv \sqrt{b\bar{b}}$ = CABS(b) = $\sqrt{\text{real}(b)^2 + \text{imag}(b)^2}$. (Note that it is necessary to use CABS rather than CABS1 here.)

Conditions (1)-(2.2.3) above guarantee that any 2 by 2 diagonal block will have nonzero determinant. When A is real symmetric or complex Hermitian, the determinant is always negative.

Computing the inverse from the factorization requires an additional $\frac{1}{3}n^3$ multiplications and $\frac{1}{3}n^3$ additions for an n by n matrix.

5. Programming Details

CHIFA, CHPFA

Since $A = A^H$, the diagonal of A is actually real. Although A is stored in a complex array, the diagonal being real is preserved under rounding errors by setting

```
A(J,J) = CMPLX(REAL(A(J,J)),0.0E0)
```

whenever A(J,J) has been changed in a computation. This prevents the introduction of unnecessary rounding errors and allows the computation of the inertia in CHIDI .

CSIDI, CSPDI

Complex symmetric matrices do not necessarily have real eigenvalues, e.g., $A = \begin{bmatrix} i & 0 \\ 0 & -i \end{bmatrix}$ or $\begin{bmatrix} 1 & i \\ i & 2 \end{bmatrix}$, and inertia is usually not defined for complex symmetric matrices; thus, CSIDI and CSPDI do not have the parameter INERT .

Since the diagonal of a complex symmetric matrix may be complex, the diagonal elements of the reduced matrices must be computed using complex arithmetic in CSIFA and CSPFA (unlike in CHIFA and CHPFA , in which the diagonal elements are always real in theory and hence their imaginary parts may be set to zero). Thus, if an element from a 1 by 1 diagonal block from CSIFA or CSPFA were $1+10^{-10}i$, one could not be certain whether this element corresponded to a complex eigenvalue or to a real eigenvalue with the 10^{-10} having been introduced as a rounding error. Hence, the computation of inertia for complex symmetric matrices is not attempted.

6. Performance

If A is n by n, then the diagonal pivoting factorization requires at most

$\frac{1}{6}n^3 + \frac{3}{4}n^2 + \frac{7}{3}n$ multiplications (and divisions),

$\frac{1}{6}n^3 + \frac{1}{4}n^2 + \frac{7}{6}n$ additions, and

$\frac{1}{2}n^2 + \frac{3}{2}n$ storage (n^2+n if A is stored as a two-dimensional array);

it requires $\geq \frac{1}{2}n^2$ but $\leq n^2-1$ comparisons.

The condition number $\kappa(A) \equiv \|A\| \|A^{-1}\|$ can be computed as shown in Section 3; this requires the computation of A^{-1} ; if A is n by n, forming A^{-1} requires an additional $\frac{1}{3}n^3$ multiplications and $\frac{1}{3}n^3$ additions; then $\kappa(A)$ requires another $2n^2$ additions. The computation of the estimate RCOND requires $2n^2$ multiplications and $3n^2$ additions after the factorization has been obtained. Hence, if A^{-1} is being computed anyway, then $\kappa(A)$ can be computed cheaply; if A^{-1} is not needed, then $\kappa(A)$ is expensive to compute, but RCOND can be obtained cheaply.

The importance of the condition number is due to its effect on perturbations. When solving systems of linear equations, $Ax = b$, a relative perturbation in A or b may cause the relative error in the solution to be magnified by $\kappa(A)$:

(i) if $Ax = b$ and $Ay = b+f$, then

$$\frac{\|x-y\|}{\|x\|} \leq \kappa(A) \frac{\|f\|}{\|b\|} \quad \text{and} \quad \frac{\|x-y\|}{\|y\|} \leq \kappa(A) \frac{\|f\|}{\|b+f\|} \ ;$$

(ii) if $Ax = b$ and $(A+E)z = b$, then

$$\frac{\|x-z\|}{\|x\|} \leq \left(\frac{\kappa(A)}{1 - \kappa(A) \frac{\|E\|}{\|A\|}} \right) \frac{\|E\|}{\|A\|} \doteq \kappa(A) \frac{\|E\|}{\|A\|} \quad \text{and} \quad \frac{\|x-y\|}{\|y\|} \leq \kappa(A) \frac{\|E\|}{\|A\|} \ ;$$

and

(iii) if $Ax = b$ and $(A+E)w = b+f$, then

$$\frac{\|x-w\|}{\|x\|} \leq \left(\frac{\kappa(A)}{1 - \kappa(A) \frac{\|E\|}{\|A\|}} \right) \left(\frac{\|E\|}{\|A\|} + \frac{\|b\|}{\|f\|} \right) \doteq \kappa(A) \left(\frac{\|E\|}{\|A\|} + \frac{\|b\|}{\|f\|} \right) ;$$

(provided $\kappa(A) \frac{\|E\|}{\|A\|} < 1$ above).

Thus, relative perturbations in A and b of size ε may cause relative perturbations in x of size $\varepsilon\kappa(A) \doteq \varepsilon/\text{RCOND}$.

A similar situation holds when computing inverses. Since

$$\frac{\|(A+E)^{-1} - A^{-1}\|}{\|(A+E)^{-1}\|} \leq \kappa(A) \frac{\|E\|}{\|A\|} \ ,$$

a relative perturbation in A of size ε may cause a relative perturbation in the inverse of size $\varepsilon\kappa(A) \doteq \varepsilon/\text{RCOND}$.

Furthermore, associated with failure of a factorization algorithm in exact arithmetic is instability in finite precision arithmetic. We say that a factorization algorithm is <u>stable</u> if, for every matrix A , the computed factors of A , say F_1, F_2 and F_3, are the exact factors of a matrix close to A , i.e., instead of obtaining $A = F_1F_2F_3$, we have $F_1F_2F_3 = A+E$, where E is small compared to A . We would like $|E_{ij}/A_{ij}|$ to be small for each nonzero A_{ij} ; however, one usually settles for the requirement that $\|E\|/\|A\|$ be small for some norm $\|\cdot\|$. Thus, a stable factorization algorithm provides the factors of a matrix A+E , which is a small perturbation of A . However, as seen above, any such relative perturbation may be magnified by $\kappa(A)$ when solving linear systems or computing inverses.

A rounding error analysis shows that the computed factors U and D produced by the diagonal pivoting factorization are the exact factors of A+E , where

$$\|E\|_\infty \equiv \max_i \sum_{j=1}^{n} |E_{ij}| < \beta^{-t}(7.9n^2 + 21.6n)g(A)$$

on a machine using t digit, base β arithmetic; g(A) is the largest element (in modulus) in all the reduced matrices; and

$$g(A) \leq (2.57)^{n-1} \max_{i,j}|A_{ij}| < (2.57)^{n-1}\|A\|_\infty .$$

This exponential growth may seem alarming at first glance, but the important fact established by the error analysis is that the reduced matrices cannot grow abruptly from step to step. No example is yet known for which significant element growth occurs at every step of the factorization. For further discussion see Section 7.

7. Notes and References

In the following, in general, only the symmetric case will be discussed; the Hermitian case follows by replacing T (transpose) by H (complex conjugate transpose) throughout.

When A is symmetric, we may always neglect the symmetry of A and use triangular factorization, A = LU , where L is a product of elementary unit lower triangular and permutation matrices and U is upper triangular. If A is n by n, this requires $n^3/3$ multiplications, $n^3/3$ additions, $n^2/2$ comparisons, and n^2 storage (the lower order terms have been suppressed). Then Ax = b can be solved by solving Ly = b for y and Ux = y for x , which requires an additional n^2 multiplications and n^2 additions to obtain x .

Can we take advantage of the symmetry of A to solve $Ax = b$ in $n^3/6$ multiplications, $n^3/6$ additions and $n^2/2$ storage?

There are several well-known factorizations of symmetric matrices, e.g.,

(1) the orthogonal (or spectral) decomposition, $A = O\Lambda O^T$, where O is orthogonal and Λ is diagonal [Wilkinson, 1965]; the diagonal elements of Λ are the eigenvalues of A;

(2) the symmetric triangular factorization, $A = \tilde{U}\tilde{D}\tilde{U}^T$, where $\tilde{U}$ is unit upper triangular and $\tilde{D}$ is diagonal [Wilkinson, 1965];

(3) the Cholesky factorization, $A = R^TR$, where R is upper triangular [Wilkinson, 1965];

(4) the tridiagonal factorization, $A = \hat{U}T\hat{U}^T$, where $\hat{U}$ is a product of elementary unit upper triangular and permutation matrices and T is symmetric and tridiagonal [Aasen, 1971]; and

(5) the diagonal pivoting factorization, $A = UDU^T$, where U is a product of elementary unit upper triangular and permutation matrices and D is symmetric block diagonal with blocks of order 1 or 2 [Bunch, 1971; Bunch and Parlett, 1971; Bunch and Kaufman, 1977]. This factorization is a generalization of Lagrange's method for reducing quadratic forms to diagonal forms [Mirsky, 1955].

The orthogonal factorization (1) is more costly than the triangular factorization, $A = LU$, and we shall not consider it further.

Each factorization (2)-(5) requires $\frac{1}{6}n^3$ multiplications and $\frac{1}{6}n^3$ additions. As we shall see, factorizations (4) and (5) exist for every symmetric matrix, but (2) and (3) may not.

The symmetric triangular factorization (2), $A = \tilde{U}\tilde{D}\tilde{U}^T$, does not exist for every symmetric matrix A, e.g., $A = \begin{bmatrix} 0 & 1 \\ 1 & 1 \end{bmatrix}$. Even if we generalize the factorization to allow $\tilde{U}$ to be a product of elementary unit upper triangular and permutations, the factorization may not exist, e.g., $A = \begin{bmatrix} 0 & 1 \\ 1 & 0 \end{bmatrix}$.

But if A is also positive definite or negative definite, then the $\tilde{U}\tilde{D}\tilde{U}^T$ factorization of A, with unit upper triangular $\tilde{U}$, always exists. If A is positive definite, then the diagonal elements of $\tilde{D}$ are positive and $A = R^TR$, where R is $\tilde{D}^{\frac{1}{2}}\tilde{U}^T$; this is the Cholesky decomposition. On the other hand, if $A = R^TR$ exists, where R is upper triangular, then A is positive semi-definite. Even if we generalize the Cholesky factorization to $A = R^TSR$, where R is upper triangular and S is a diagonal matrix with diagonal elements from $\{-1,0,1\}$, the factorization may not exist for all symmetric A , e.g., let $A = \begin{bmatrix} 0 & 1 \\ 1 & 0 \end{bmatrix}$.

We shall now show that factorizations (2) and (3) are unstable. Let $A = \begin{bmatrix} \varepsilon & 1 \\ 1 & \varepsilon \end{bmatrix}$, where $0 < \varepsilon < 1$. Then factorization (2) gives

$$A = \tilde{U}\tilde{D}\tilde{U}^T , \quad \text{where} \quad \tilde{D} = \begin{bmatrix} \varepsilon - \frac{1}{\varepsilon} & 0 \\ 0 & \varepsilon \end{bmatrix} \quad \text{and} \quad \tilde{U} = \begin{bmatrix} 1 & 1/\varepsilon \\ 0 & 1 \end{bmatrix} .$$

However, if ε is small enough (e.g., $\varepsilon = 10^{-5}$ in nine decimal digit arithmetic), then the finite precision operation $\varepsilon - 1/\varepsilon$ yields $-1/\varepsilon$. Thus, the computed $\tilde{D}$ is $\tilde{D}_C = \begin{bmatrix} -\frac{1}{\varepsilon} & 0 \\ 0 & \varepsilon \end{bmatrix}$. But $\tilde{U}\tilde{D}_C\tilde{U}^T = \begin{bmatrix} 0 & 1 \\ 1 & \varepsilon \end{bmatrix} = A+E$ implies $E = \begin{bmatrix} -\varepsilon & 0 \\ 0 & 0 \end{bmatrix}$. Thus $|E_{11}/A_{11}| = 1$.

Since $A = \begin{bmatrix} \varepsilon & 1 \\ 1 & \varepsilon \end{bmatrix}$ does not have a Cholesky factorization (over the reals), we shall seek the factorization $A = R^TSR$, where R is upper triangular and S is a diagonal matrix with diagonal elements from $\{-1,0,1\}$. Then $S = \begin{bmatrix} 1 & 0 \\ 0 & -1 \end{bmatrix}$ and $R = \begin{bmatrix} \varepsilon^{\frac{1}{2}} & \varepsilon^{-\frac{1}{2}} \\ 0 & (\frac{1}{\varepsilon} - \varepsilon)^{\frac{1}{2}} \end{bmatrix}$. Once again, if ε is small enough, we obtain the computed R as $R_C = \begin{bmatrix} \varepsilon^{\frac{1}{2}} & \varepsilon^{-\frac{1}{2}} \\ 0 & \varepsilon^{-\frac{1}{2}} \end{bmatrix}$. Then $R_C^TSR_C = \begin{bmatrix} \varepsilon & 1 \\ 1 & 0 \end{bmatrix} = A+E$ implies $E = \begin{bmatrix} 0 & 0 \\ 0 & -\varepsilon \end{bmatrix}$ and $|E_{22}/A_{22}| = 1$.

For further examples, see Bunch and Parlett [1971].

The performances of the tridiagonal factorization (4) and the diagonal pivoting factorization (5) are comparable. Both are stable. The tridiagonal factorization requires $\frac{1}{2}n^2$ comparisons and has

$$g(A) < 2 \cdot 4^{n-2} \max_{i,j} |A_{ij}| ,$$

where $g(A)$ is the largest element (in modulus) in all the reduced matrices. (Such large growth does not occur in practice.) The diagonal pivoting factorization (5) has the advantage over (4) of providing also the inertia of a real symmetric or complex Hermitian matrix from inspection of the factor D .

Factorization (5) has two versions:

(i) a complete pivoting version (analogous to Gaussian elimination with complete pivoting) requiring $\geq \frac{1}{12} n^3$ but $\leq \frac{1}{6} n^3$ comparisons and has

$$g(A) < 3nf(n)\max_{i,j}|A_{ij}| ,$$

where $f(n) = \left(\prod_{k=2}^{n} k^{\frac{1}{k-1}}\right)^{\frac{1}{2}} < 2n^{\frac{1}{4}\log n}$. (Note that $g(A) < \sqrt{n}\, f(n) \max_{i,j}|A_{ij}|$ for Gaussian elimination with complete pivoting.)

(ii) a partial pivoting version (analogous to Gaussian elimination with partial pivoting) requiring $\geq \frac{1}{2}n^2$ but $\leq n^2-1$ comparisons and has

$$g(A) < (2.57)^{n-1} \max_{i,j}|A_{ij}| .$$

(Note that $g(A) < 2^{n-1}\max_{i,j}|A_{ij}|$ for Gaussian elimination with partial pivoting.) However, since such large element growth does not occur in practice for the diagonal pivoting factorization with partial pivoting (as it analogously does not for Gaussian elimination with partial pivoting), the factorization subroutines in Chapter 5 use the diagonal pivoting factorization with partial pivoting.

A detailed discussion of the diagonal pivoting factorization can be found in Bunch [1971], Bunch and Parlett [1971], and Bunch and Kaufman [1977]. An Algol version of the algorithm is in Bunch, Kaufman, and Parlett [1976]. A comparison of various algorithms for solving symmetric indefinite systems of equations can be found in Barwell and George [1976].

Chapter 6: Triangular Matrices

Subroutines: STRCO, STRSL, STRDI

1. Overview

Purpose. The LINPACK subroutines in this chapter operate on upper or lower triangular matrices. The operations performed include the estimation of the matrix condition number, the solution of simultaneous linear equations, and the calculation of determinants and inverses.

Background. An upper triangular matrix T has $t_{ij} = 0$ if $i > j$. A lower triangular matrix T has $t_{ij} = 0$ if $i < j$. Such matrices may arise as primary data, or may result from some of the LINPACK factorizations and decompositions. The subroutines in this chapter reference only the relevant triangular portion of the storage array. The remainder of the array need not contain zeros and so may be used to store other information.

The condition number of a matrix is a quantity which measures the sensitivity of the solution of simultaneous linear equations to errors in the matrix. For more details, see Chapter 1.

2. Usage

Single precision, triangular matrices. The three subroutines for single precision, triangular matrices are STRCO , STRSL and STRDI . Any can be used independently of the others.

STRCO estimates the condition of an upper or lower triangular matrix and finds an approximate null vector if the matrix is nearly singular. The calling sequence is

```
CALL STRCO(T,LDT,N,RCOND,Z,JOB) .
```

On entry,

T is a doubly subscripted array with dimension (LDT,N) which contains the triangular matrix. Only the elements on and either above or below the diagonal (see JOB) are referenced and none of the elements are altered.

LDT is the leading dimension of the array T .

N is the order of the triangular matrix and the number of elements in the vector Z.

JOB = 0 if the lower triangular part of T is to be used.

= nonzero if the upper triangular part of T is to be used.

On return,

RCOND is an estimate of the reciprocal condition, $1/\kappa(T)$. If RCOND is so small that the logical expression 1.0 + RCOND .EQ. 1.0 is true, then T can usually be regarded as singular to working precision. RCOND will be zero if any of the diagonal elements of T are zero, or if the estimate underflows.

Z is a singly subscripted array of N elements used for work space. If T is close to a singular matrix, then Z will contain an approximate null vector in the sense that $\|Tz\| = \text{RCOND}\cdot\|T\|\cdot\|z\|$.

STRSL solves triangular linear systems of the form

$$Tx = b$$

or

$$T^T x = b$$

where T^T is the transpose of T . The calling sequence is

CALL STRSL(T,LDT,N,B,JOB,INFO) .

On entry,

T is a doubly subscripted array with dimension (LDT,N) which contains the triangular matrix. Only the elements on and either above or below the diagonal (see JOB) are referenced and none of the elements are altered.

LDT is the leading dimension of the array T .

N is the order of the triangular matrix and the number of elements in the vector B.

B is a singly subscripted array of N elements which contains the right hand side of the system.

JOB specifies what kind of system is to be solved. If JOB is

00 solve $Tx = b$, T lower triangular,

01 solve $Tx = b$, T upper triangular,

10 solve $T^T x = b$, T lower triangular,

11 solve $T^T x = b$, T upper triangular.

On return,

B contains the solution x if T is nonsingular. Otherwise B is unaltered.

INFO is zero if T is nonsingular. Otherwise INFO contains the index of the first zero diagonal entry of T .

STRDI computes the determinant and/or the inverse of an upper or lower triangular matrix. The calling sequence is

```
CALL STRDI(T,LDT,N,DET,JOB,INFO) .
```

On entry,

T is a doubly subscripted array with dimension (LDT,N) which contains the triangular matrix. Only the elements on and either above or below the diagonal (see JOB) are used.

LDT is the leading dimension of the array T .

N is the order of the triangular matrix.

JOB indicates what is to be computed. It is a three digit decimal integer where the units digit indicates whether the matrix is upper or lower triangular, the tens digit indicates if the inverse is to be computed and the hundreds digit indicates if the determinant is to be computed. Specifically,

- 010 indicates no determinant, inverse of lower triangular,
- 011 indicates no determinant, inverse of upper triangular,
- 100 indicates determinant only,
- 110 indicates determinant and inverse of lower triangular,
- 111 indicates determinant and inverse of upper triangular.

On return,

T contains the inverse if requested and if INFO is zero. If the tens digit of JOB is zero, T is unaltered.

DET is a singly subscripted array with 2 elements which contains the determinant of T in the form det(T) = DET(1)*10.0**DET(2) , although this expression may underflow or overflow if evaluated. DET(1) is normalized so that $1.0 \le |DET(1)| < 10.0$ or DET(1) = 0.0 . DET(2) contains an integer stored as a real number. If the hundreds digits of JOB is zero, then DET is not referenced.

INFO is zero if T is nonsingular. Otherwise INFO contains the index of the first zero diagonal entry of T . INFO is unchanged if the inverse is not requested.

Double precision, triangular matrices. The calling sequences of the double precision, triangular subroutines DTRCO , DTRSL and DTRDI are the same as those of STRCO , STRSL and STRDI except that T, B , RCOND , DET , and Z are DOUBLE PRECISION variables.

Complex, triangular matrices. The calling sequences of the complex triangular subroutines CTRCO , CTRSL and CTRDI are the same as those of STRCO , STRSL and STRDI except that T, B , DET and Z are COMPLEX variables, RCOND is a real variable and the system solved by CTRSL when JOB is 10 or 11 involves the complex conjugate transpose of T .

Double precision complex, triangular matrices. In those computing systems where they are available, the calling sequences of the double precision complex, triangular subroutines ZTRCO , ZTRSL and ZTRDI are the same as those of STRCO , STRSL and STRDI except that T, B , DET and Z are COMPLEX*16 variables, RCOND is a DOUBLE PRECISION variable and the system solved by ZTRSL when JOB is 10 or 11 involves the complex conjugate transpose of T .

Chapter 7: Tridiagonal Matrices

Subroutines, SGTSL, SPTSL

1. Overview

Purpose. The LINPACK subroutines in this chapter solve simultaneous linear equations involving general tridiagonal matrices and symmetric positive definite tridiagonal matrices.

Background. A tridiagonal matrix is a matrix whose nonzero elements are found only on the diagonal, subdiagonal, and superdiagonal of the matrix, specifically $a_{ij} = 0$ if $|i-j| > 1$. The tridiagonal matrix is a special case of the band matrix described in Chapter 2.

2. Usage

Single precision, general tridiagonal matrices. The subroutine for single precision general tridiagonal matrices is SGTSL . SGTSL uses Gaussian elimination with partial pivoting to factor a tridiagonal matrix and simultaneously solve a system of linear equations. The factorization is not saved.

The calling sequence is

```
CALL SGTSL(N,C,D,E,B,INFO)
```

The parameters have the following meanings.

N — is the order of the tridiagonal matrix and the number of elements in the vectors C , D , E , and B .

C — is a singly subscripted array used to hold the subdiagonal of the tridiagonal matrix in positions C(2) through C(N) . On return, C is destroyed.

D — is a singly subscripted array used to hold the diagonal of the tridiagonal matrix. On return, D is destroyed.

E — is a singly subscripted array used to hold the superdiagonal of the tridiagonal matrix in positions E(1) through E(N-1) . On return E is destroyed.

B — is a singly subscripted array used to hold the right hand side of a system of simultaneous linear equations. On return, it contains the solution.

INFO — is an integer returned which, if it is 0 , indicates that the solution has been found. If INFO ≠ 0 , then INFO is the index of a zero pivot element detected during the factorization. The factorization is stopped when a zero pivot is found.

<u>Single precision, symmetric positive definite tridiagonal matrices</u>. The subroutine for single precision symmetric positive definite tridiagonal matrices is SPTSL . SPTSL performs a decomposition of the matrix and solves a linear system of equations. Subroutine SPTSL uses a form of decomposition which is fast, but the routine does not check the input matrix for positive definiteness.

The calling sequence is

```
CALL SPTSL(N,D,E,B)
```

The parameters have the following meanings.

N is the order of the tridiagonal matrix and the number of elements in the vectors D , E and B .

D is a singly subscripted array used to hold the diagonal of the tridiagonal matrix. On return, D is destroyed.

E is a singly subscripted array used to hold the super diagonal elements of the symmetric tridiagonal matrix in positions E(1) through E(N-1) . On return, E is destroyed.

B is a singly subscripted array used to hold the right hand side of the system of simultaneous linear equations. On return, it contains the solution.

The factorization and the solution of equations are performed together in this subroutine. This subroutine should only be used when the input matrix is symmetric and positive definite. But caution is necessary since the subroutine does not detect error conditions. If the matrix is singular a division by zero may occur. If the matrix is not positive definite the solution returned may be inaccurate.

<u>Double precision, tridiagonal matrices</u>. The calling sequences of the double precision, tridiagonal solver subroutines DGTSL and DPTSL are the same as those of the corresponding single precision "S" subroutines except that C , D , E , and B are DOUBLE PRECISION variables.

<u>Complex, tridiagonal matrices</u>. The calling sequences of the complex, tridiagonal solver subroutines CGTSL and CPTSL are the same as those of the corresponding single precision "S" subroutines except that C , D , E , and B are COMPLEX variables.

<u>Double precision complex, tridiagonal matrices</u>. In those computing systems where they are available, the calling sequences of the double precision complex tridiagonal subroutines

ZGTSL and ZPTSL are the same as those of the corresponding single precision "S" subroutines except that C , D , E , and B are COMPLEX*16 variables.

3. Examples

The following program segments illustrate the use of the single precision subroutines for general tridiagonal matrices and for symmetric positive definite tridiagonal matrices. Examples showing the use of the "D" , "C" , and "Z" subroutines could be obtained by changing the subroutine name and type declarations.

The first program solves a general tridiagonal system.

```
      REAL C(50), D(50), E(50), B(50)
      N = ...
      NM1 = N - 1
      D(1) = ...
      E(1) = ...
      B(1) = ...
      DO 10 I = 2, NM1
         C(I) = ...
         D(I) = ...
         E(I) = ...
         B(I) = ...
   10 CONTINUE
      C(N) = ...
      D(N) = ...
      B(N) = ...
      CALL SGTSL(N,C,D,E,B,INFO)
      IF ( INFO .NE. 0 ) GO TO 30
      DO 20 I = 1, N
         WRITE(..., ...) B(I)
   20 CONTINUE
      STOP
   30 WRITE(...,99) INFO
   99 FORMAT(44H MATRIX SINGULAR, ZERO PIVOT DETECTED AT ROW,I5)
      STOP
      END
```

The next program segment solves a symmetric positive definite tridiagonal system.

```
      REAL D(50), E(50), B(50)
      N = ...
      NM1 = N - 1
      DO 10 I = 1, NM1
         D(I) = ...
```

```
      E(I) = ...
      B(I) = ...
10 CONTINUE
   D(N) = ...
   B(N) = ...
   CALL SPTSL(N,D,E,B)
   DO 20 I = 1, N
      WRITE(..., ...) B(I)
20 CONTINUE
   STOP
   END
```

4. Algorithms

The factorization and solution for general tridiagonal systems. The algorithm used to factor and solve a general tridiagonal matrix is a version of Gaussian elimination with partial pivoting and simple back substitution. The method of factorization is the same as that in Chapter 1 except that the L_k matrices generated during the elimination are applied to the right hand side, B , as they are generated and are not saved.

The original tridiagonal matrix is destroyed; the arrays C , D , E after execution of the algorithm contain the U matrix from the LU decomposition generated during the factorization.

The factorization and solution for symmetric positive definite tridiagonal systems. The algorithm used to factor and solve a symmetric positive definite tridiagonal matrix is based on Gaussian elimination, but with no pivoting. The algorithm starts the elimination of elements off the diagonal at both the top subdiagonal and the bottom superdiagonal simultaneously, and proceeds until the elimination meets in the middle. The back substitution then starts from the middle and works outward to the top and bottom of the matrix simultaneously.

A description of the algorithm follows.

KB = n-1;

for K = 1,..., $\lfloor (n-1)/2 \rfloor$ do

$T \leftarrow e_K/d_K$;

$d_{K+1} \leftarrow d_{K+1} - T * e_K$;

$b_{K+1} \leftarrow b_{K+1} - T * b_K$;

$T \leftarrow e_{KB}/d_{KB+1}$;

```
        d_KB ← d_KB - T * e_KB;
        b_KB ← b_KB - T * b_KB+1;
        KB = KB-1;
    end K
    KP1 = ⌊(n-1)/2⌋ + 1;
    if mod(N,2) = 0 then
    do
        Apply one more step of elimination to
        KP1 row and increment KP1.
    end
    b_KP1 = b_KP1/d_KP1;
    K = ⌊(n-1)/2⌋ - 1;
    Ke = KP1 + K;
    for KF = KP1,...,KE do
        b_K ← (b_K - e_K * b_K+1)/d_K;
        b_KF+1 ← (b_KF+1 - e_KF * b_KF)/d_KF+1;
        K = K-1
    end KF
    if mod(N,2) = 0 then
        b_1 ← (b_1 - e_1 * b_2)/d_1;
```

The elimination can be thought of as proceeding as follows:

```
before the first step     after the second step     after the last step
xx                        xx                        xx
xxx                       0xx                       0xx
 xxx                       0xx                        ...
  xxx                       xxx                        ...
   ...                       ...                        ...
    ...                       ...                        0xx
     ...                       ...                        0x0
      xxx                       xxx                        xx0
       xxx                       xx0                        ...
        xx                        xx0                        ...
                                   xx                         ...
                                                               xx0
                                                                xx
```

This method has advantages over a straightforward elimination process. The program is faster since the loop overhead is reduced by a factor of two.

5. Notes and References

The algorithm for solving general tridiagonal systems is quite standard. The positive definite algorithm in this chapter is slightly unusual in the way the reduction is carried out. This algorithm was originally motivated by trying to solve such systems as fast as possible. Because of the two-way nature of the algorithm, systems can be solved up to 25% faster than conventional algorithms. Although the techniques used here were independently discovered, they have been known for some time (private communications, J. H. Wilkinson).

Chapter 8: The Cholesky Decomposition

Subroutine: SCHDC

1. Overview

Purpose. SCHDC is a subroutine to compute the Cholesky decomposition of a positive definite matrix. A pivoting option allows the user to estimate the condition of a positive definite matrix or determine the rank of a positive semidefinite matrix.

The Cholesky decomposition. Let A be a symmetric matrix of order p. Then A is positive definite if $x^TAx > 0$ for every nonzero vector x. If A is positive definite, A can be factored uniquely in the form

$$A = R^TR$$

where R is an upper triangular matrix with positive diagonal elements. This is the Cholesky decomposition of A, and R is its Cholesky factor.

A knowledge of the Cholesky factorization of A enables one to solve systems of the form

$$Ab = c \tag{1.1}$$

by first solving

$$R^Tw = c$$

and then

$$Rb = w .$$

These systems may be solved via two calls to the LINPACK routine STRSL or by a single call to SPOSL .

If A and R are partitioned in the forms

$$A = \begin{bmatrix} A_{11} & A_{12} \\ A_{21} & A_{22} \end{bmatrix}, \quad R = \begin{bmatrix} R_{11} & R_{12} \\ 0 & R_{22} \end{bmatrix}, \tag{1.2}$$

where A_{11} and R_{11} are of order k, then

$$A_{11} = R_{11}^TR_{11} ,$$

so that R_{11} is the Cholesky factor of the leading principal submatrix A_{11} of A. Thus a knowledge of the Cholesky decomposition of an entire matrix A enables one to solve linear systems involving any leading principal submatrix of A.

Least squares. Positive definite systems arise naturally in least squares problems. Let X be an n by p matrix with linearly independent columns, and let y be an n-vector.

Consider the problem of determining a p-vector b such that

$$\rho^2 = \|y-Xb\|^2 \tag{1.3}$$

is minimized. Here $\|\cdot\|$ denotes the Euclidean vector norm defined by $\|y\|^2 = \Sigma y_i^2$. It is well known that the solution b satisfies the system of normal equations

$$(X^TX)b = X^Ty . \tag{1.4}$$

Since the columns of X are independent, X^TX can be shown to be positive definite. Hence, if we set

$$A = X^TX , \quad c = X^Ty ,$$

the system (1.4) reduces to (1.1), and the Cholesky decomposition of X^TX can be used to solve the least squares problem.

In Chapter 9 we shall present an alternative way of solving least squares problems by means of the QR decomposition. The question of whether to form and solve the normal equations or to compute the QR decomposition is too complicated to treat in full detail in this guide. The basic tradeoff is between the superior numerical properties of the QR decomposition and the greater speed with which the normal equations can be formed. On computers with a short floating-point word, solution via the QR decomposition is probably preferable; with a long word, the speed of forming the normal equations will generally make it more attractive. However, the reader is warned that there are other tradeoffs, and that decisions must be made on a problem-to-problem basis.

Once the normal equations have been formed and decomposed, it is easy to delete a terminal set of columns from the problem. Specifically, let

$$X = (X_1, X_2) ,$$

where X_1 has k columns, and consider the problem of choosing $b^{(1)}$ to minimize

$$\rho_1^2 = \|y-X_1b^{(1)}\|^2 . \tag{1.5}$$

If we partition

$$c = \begin{bmatrix} c_1 \\ c_2 \end{bmatrix} ,$$

where c_1 is a k-vector, then the normal equations for this problem become

$$A_{11}b^{(1)} = c_1 , \tag{1.6}$$

where A_{11} is the leading principal submatrix of A of order k [cf. (1.2)]. From the above observations, it is not necessary to compute a Cholesky factorization to solve (1.6) for $b^{(1)}$.

The Cholesky decomposition can be used to solve least squares problems in a slightly different way that lends itself to subsequent manipulation of the decomposition (see Chapter 10). Consider the augmented matrix

$$\tilde{X} = (X, y)$$

and the corresponding cross product matrix

$$\tilde{A} = \tilde{X}^T\tilde{X} = \begin{bmatrix} A & c \\ c^T & y^Ty \end{bmatrix} .$$

Let $\tilde{R}$ be the Cholesky factor of $\tilde{A}$. Then $\tilde{R}$ has the form

$$\tilde{R} = \begin{bmatrix} R & z \\ 0 & \rho \end{bmatrix} ,$$

where R is the Cholesky factor of A. It can be shown that ρ^2 is the residual sum of squares in (1.3) and that

$$z = R^{-T}c ,$$

so that the least squares solution satisfies

$$Rb = z$$

and can be computed, say, by a single call to STRSL. If z is partitioned in the form

$$z = \begin{bmatrix} z_1 \\ z_2 \end{bmatrix} ,$$

the solution $b^{(1)}$ of the truncated problem (1.5) is given by

$$R_{11}b^{(1)} = z_1 ,$$

and the residual sum of squares by

$$\rho_1^2 = \rho^2 + \|z_2\|^2 .$$

Pivoting. A matrix A is positive semi-definite if $x^TAx \geq 0$ whenever x is nonzero. A positive semi-definite matrix need not have a unique Cholesky decomposition; however, its rows and columns can be rearranged so that it does. Specifically, there is a permutation matrix E (i.e. an identity matrix with its columns permuted) such that

(1.7a) $$E^TAE = R^TR$$

where R is an upper triangular matrix of the form

(1.7b) $$R = \begin{bmatrix} R_{11} & R_{12} \\ 0 & 0 \end{bmatrix} .$$

Here R_{11} is of order k and has positive diagonal elements. It follows that k is the rank of A. It should be noted that E is not unique, although once it has been specified, the decomposition (1.7) is unique.

SCHDC provides a pivoting option to compute a decomposition of the form (1.7). During the computation of the reduction, rows and columns of A are interchanged in order to make the leading diagonal elements of R large. Specifically, the strategy results in a matrix R that satisfies

$$r_{kk}^2 \geq \sum_{i=k}^{j} r_{ij}^2 \quad (j = k,k+1,\ldots,n) .$$

It follows that if $r_{kk} = 0$ then R is zero on and below its k-th row.

An important application of pivoting in the Cholesky decomposition is to least squares problems in which the columns of X are linearly dependent. If $A = X^TX$ has the decomposition (1.7) and XE is partitioned in the form

$$XE = (X_1,X_2) ,$$

where X_1 has k columns, then it can be shown that the columns of X_1 are independent and

$$X_2 = X_1R_{11}^{-1}R_{12} ,$$

so that the columns of X_2 are linear combinations of the columns of X_1. The solution vector $b^{(1)}$ corresponding to these columns can be computed by partitioning

$$E^Tc = \begin{bmatrix} c_1' \\ c_2' \end{bmatrix}$$

and solving $(R_{11}^TR_{11})b^{(1)} = c_1'$. Note that the components of $b_1^{(1)}$ computed in this way will correspond to the columns of X_1, which in general will be scattered throughout the original matrix X (cf. section 3).

It may happen that one will want to force some columns of X into a least squares fit. To accommodate this need, the pivoting option allows one to specify diagonals of A that are to be moved to the leading positions and frozen there during the reduction. Likewise, if one is working with the augmented matrix $\tilde{A}$, it is important that the last diagonal not be moved, and this is also provided for in SCHDC .

In practice one will not compute diagonal elements of R that are exactly zero, and one is faced with the problem of deciding when a diagonal element is negligible. We recommend the following strategy. First estimate the errors in the elements of the matrix A (if A is known exactly, take the error in a_{ij} to be a small multiple of $a_{ij} \cdot \varepsilon_M$, where ε_M is the rounding unit for the computer in question). Then scale the rows and columns of A so that the error estimates are approximately equal to a common value ε, and consider r_{jj} to be negligible if $r_{jj}^2 < \varepsilon$. For further justification of this strategy see the introduction to this guide.

Estimation of condition. The spectral norm of a matrix A is the number

$$\|A\| = \sup_{\|x\|=1} \|Ax\| .$$

If A is nonsingular, the condition number of A is

$$\kappa(A) = \|A\| \, \|A^{-1}\| .$$

The importance of the condition number is that it allows the assessment of the accuracy of the solution of (1.1). Specifically, if E is an error matrix with $\|A^{-1}\| \, \|E\| < 1$, then A+E is nonsingular. If

$$(A+E)\bar{b} = c$$

then

(1.8) $$\frac{\|b-\bar{b}\|}{\|\bar{b}\|} \leq \kappa(A) \frac{\|E\|}{\|A\|}$$

so that κ measures how much a relative error in A is magnified in the solution. It is important to realize that the bound (1.8) may be unrealistic unless A has been scaled as described above.

If the pivoting option in SCHDC has been exercised with the input array JPVT initialized to zero, the condition number of A can be estimated from the output by

(1.9) $$\kappa \cong (A(1,1)/A(P,P))**2$$

provided INFO = P . This is always an underestimate, usually by a factor of two or three, and never, in our experience, by a factor greater than ten. (However, see section 6.)

Relation to SPOFA. The main reason for prefering SCHDC to the routines of Chapter 3 is the pivoting option. If pivoting is not needed, the subroutine SPOFA will compute the Cholesky decomposition of a positive definite matrix A and SPOCO will estimate its condition. SPOSL may be used with the output of any of the routines SPOFA , SPOCO , or SCHDC .

2. Usage

The calling sequence for SCHDC is

```
CALL SCHDC(A,LDA,P,WORK,JPVT,JOB,INFO) .
```

On entry,

A — is a doubly subscripted real array of dimension (LDA,P) containing the symmetric matrix A whose Cholesky decomposition is to be computed. Only the upper half of A need be stored. The lower part of the array A is not referenced.

LDA is the leading dimension of the array A .

P is an integer containing the order of the matrix A .

WORK is a singly subscripted real array of dimension P used as a work array.

JPVT is a singly subscripted integer array of dimension P that controls the pivoting, if it has been requested. The K-th diagonal element of A is placed in one of three classes:

if JPVT(K) > 0 , A(K,K) is an initial element;

if JPVT(K) = 0 , A(K,K) is a free element;

if JPVT(K) < 0 , A(K,K) is a final element.

Before the decomposition is computed, initial elements are moved to the leading part of A and final elements to the trailing part of A . During the reduction only rows and columns corresponding to free elements are moved. JPVT is not referenced if JOB = 0 .

JOB is an integer that initiates column pivoting. If JOB = 0 pivoting is not done; if JOB = 1 , it is.

On return,

A contains in its upper half the Cholesky factor of the matrix A as it has been permuted by pivoting.

JPVT If pivoting was requested, JPVT(J) contains the index of the diagonal element of A that was moved into the J-th position.

INFO contains the index of the last positive diagonal element of the Cholesky factor.

For positive definite matrices, INFO = P is the normal return. For pivoting with positive semi-definite matrices, INFO will in general be less than P . However, INFO may be greater than the rank of A , since rounding error can cause an otherwise zero element to become positive. Indefinite systems will always cause INFO to be less than P .

In the double precision routine DCHDC , all real parameters become double precision; in the complex routine CCHDC , they become complex.

3. Examples

In the following examples we assume the following specifications:

```
      INTEGER LDA,P,JPVT(P)
      REAL A(LDA,P),C(P),W(P),WORK(P)
```

Here LDA $\geq$ P .

1. SCHDC may be used with the pivoting option to estimate the condition of a positive definite matrix A . What is produced by SCHDC in this case is the Cholesky factorization R^TR of E^TAE , where E is the permutation matrix corresponding to the array JPVT and satisfies $E^TE = I$. Thus to solve the linear system

$$Ab = c \tag{3.1}$$

one must write it in the form

$$R^TR(E^Tb) = E^Tc$$

and form successively

$$u = E^Tc \ ,$$

$$v = (R^TR)^{-1}u \ ,$$

$$b = Ev \ .$$

The subroutine SPOSL will calculate v from u . The problem of calculating E^Tc and Ev from the information contained in JPVT is rather tricky. The following subroutine PERMUT will do the job.

```
      SUBROUTINE PERMUT(X,P,K,JOB)
      INTEGER P,K(P),JOB
      REAL X(P)
C
C     PERMUT REARRANGES THE ELEMENTS OF THE
C     ARRAY X AS SPECIFIED BY THE PERMUTATION
C     K(1),K(2),...,K(P) OF THE INTEGERS 1,2,...,P.
C
C     ON RETURN
C
C        IF JOB.EQ.0, X(K(I)) IS MOVED TO X(I) FOR I=1,2,...,P.
C
C        IF JOB.NE.0, X(I) IS MOVED TO X(K(I)) FOR I=1,2,...,P.
C
C     AUTHOR :  YIH LING, UNIVERSITY OF MARYLAND, 8/31/78
C
      INTEGER I,J,N
      REAL T
C
      IF (P .EQ. 1) RETURN
      DO 10 I=1,P
         K(I) = -K(I)
   10 CONTINUE
      IF (JOB .NE. 0) GO TO 60
C
C        FORWARD PERMUTATION
C
         DO 50 I=1,P
            IF (K(I) .GT. 0) GO TO 40
               J = I
               K(J) = -K(J)
```

```
                  N = K(J)
   20             CONTINUE
                     IF (K(N) .GT. 0) GO TO 30
                     T = X(J)
                     X(J) = X(N)
                     X(N) = T
                     K(N) = -K(N)
                     J = N
                     N = K(N)
                  GO TO 20
   30             CONTINUE
   40          CONTINUE
   50       CONTINUE
         GO TO 100
   60 CONTINUE
C
C        BACKWARD PERMUTATION
C
            DO 90 I=1,P
               IF (K(I) .GT. 0) GO TO 80
               K(I) = -K(I)
               J = K(I)
   70          CONTINUE
               IF (J .EQ. I) GO TO 80
                  T = X(I)
                  X(I) = X(J)
                  X(J) = T
                  K(J) = -K(J)
                  J = K(J)
                  GO TO 70
   80          CONTINUE
   90       CONTINUE
  100 CONTINUE
      RETURN
      END
```

PERMUT , SCHDC , and SPOSL are used in the following sequence of code which estimates the reciprocal of the condition number of the positive definite matrix A and solves the system (3.1), overwriting C with the solution.

```
      DO 10 I=1,P
         JPVT(I) = 0
   10 CONTINUE
      CALL SCHDC(A,LDA,P,WORK,JPVT,1,INFO)
      IF(INFO .NE. P) STOP
      RCOND = (A(P,P)/A(1,1))**2
      CALL PERMUT(C,P,JPVT,0)
      CALL SPOSL(A,LDA,P,C)
      CALL PERMUT(C,P,JPVT,1)
```

2. In some statistical applications, it is necessary to have the matrix A^{-1} . The upper half of this matrix can be obtained from the output of SCHDC by executing the call

SPODI(A,LDA,P,DUM,1) .

(See Chapter 3 for the documentation of SPODI .) However, it is important to realize that many calculations that seemingly require A^{-1} can be done directly from R . For example, suppose one needs to compute the quadratic form

$$s = w^T A^{-1} w .$$

Since $A^{-1} = R^{-1}R^{-T}$, s can be written in the form $w^T R^{-1} R^{-T} w = (R^{-T}w)^T (R^{-T}w)$, or

$$s = \|R^{-T}w\|^2 .$$

Hence, once A has been reduced, s can be computed by the following sequence:

```
      CALL STRSL(A,LDA,P,W,11)
      S = 0.
      DO 10 J=1,P
         S = S + W(J)**2
   10 CONTINUE
```

4. Algorithmic Details

The CHDC programs are the only LINPACK subroutines where the implementation in complex arithmetic presents any difficulties. The problem is keeping track of when to conjugate quantities in the face of a storage scheme that represents both a_{ij} $(i \leq j)$ and its complementary element $a_{ji} = \bar{a}_{ij}$ by a_{ij} alone. For this reason, we shall describe the algorithm for a Hermitian positive-definite matrix A of order p .

In order to obtain information necessary for pivoting, the Cholesky factorization is computed by an elimination scheme that is a slight variant of Gaussian elimination (by contrast the POFA routines compute the Cholesky factorizations of the successive leading principal submatrices of A). For the first step set $A_1 = A$. We shall determine a vector

$$r_1^H = (r_{11}, r_{12}, \ldots, r_{1p})$$

such that

$$A_1 - r_1 r_1^H = \begin{bmatrix} 0 & 0 \\ 0 & A_2 \end{bmatrix} \tag{4.1}$$

where A_2 is of order $p-1$.

From (4.1) it is easily seen that

$$a_{11}^{(1)} - \bar{r}_{11} r_{11} = 0 .$$

Since A_1 is positive definite, $a_{11}^{(1)} > 0$ and we may take

$$r_{11} = \sqrt{a_{11}^{(1)}} > 0 . \tag{4.2}$$

The other elements of r_1 are uniquely determined by the equation

$$a_{1j} - r_{11} r_{1j} = 0 \quad (j=2,\ldots,p)$$

in the form

$$r_{1j} = a_{1j}/r_{11} \quad (j=2,\ldots,p) . \tag{4.3}$$

Finally,

$$a_{ij}^{(2)} = a_{ij}^{(1)} - \bar{r}_{1i} r_{1j}$$

(4.4) $$= a_{ij}^{(1)} - \frac{a_{i1}^{(1)} a_{1j}^{(1)}}{a_{11}^{(1)}} \qquad (i,j=2,\ldots,p) \ .$$

From the second expression in (4.4) it is seen that A_2 is just the submatrix that would be obtained by applying Gaussian elimination to A, and thus A_2 is also positive definite. Hence we may repeat the process by determining a vector

$$r_2^H = (r_{22},\ldots,r_{2p})$$

such that

$$A_2 - r_2 r_2^H = \begin{bmatrix} 0 & 0 \\ 0 & A_3 \end{bmatrix}$$

where A_3 is of order $p-2$. In terms of the original matrix,

$$A - \begin{bmatrix} r_{11} & 0 \\ \bar{r}_{12} & r_{22} \\ \vdots & \vdots \\ \bar{r}_{1p} & \bar{r}_{2p} \end{bmatrix} \begin{bmatrix} r_{11} & r_{12} \cdots r_{1p} \\ 0 & r_{22} \cdots r_{2p} \end{bmatrix} = \begin{bmatrix} 0 & 0 \\ 0 & A_3 \end{bmatrix} .$$

The process can be continued to build up row-by-row an upper triangular matrix R such that

$$A - R^H R = 0 ,$$

from which it follows that R is the Cholesky factor of A.

The formulas for the general step are similar to (4.2), (4.3), and (4.4):

$$r_{kk} = \sqrt{a_{kk}^{(k)}} ,$$

$$r_{kj} = a_{kj}^{(k)} / r_{kk} \quad (j=k+1,\ldots,p) ,$$

$$a_{ij}^{(k+1)} = a_{ij}^{(k)} - \bar{r}_{ki} r_{kj} \quad (i,j=k+1,\ldots,p) .$$

In an implementation where only the upper half of A is stored in an array, it is natural to overwrite a_{kj} with r_{kj} and $a_{ij}^{(k)}$ by $a_{ij}^{(k+1)}$. However, this makes it impossible to generate A_{k+1} without repeatedly traversing the k-th row of the array in order to obtain the elements of r_{kj}. We can circumvent this difficulty by temporarily storing $r_{kk},\ldots,r_{kp}$ in a work array t. This leads to the following algorithm.

(4.5)

1 : <u>loop</u> <u>for</u> $k := 1$ <u>to</u> p

1.1 : $a_{kk} := \mathrm{sqrt}(a_{kk});$

1.2 : $t_k := a_{kk}$;

1.3 : <u>loop</u> <u>for</u> $j := k+1$ <u>to</u> p

1.3.1 : $a_{kj} := a_{kj}/t_k;$

1.3.2 : $t_j := \bar{a}_{kj};$

1.3.3 : $a_{ij} := a_{ij} - t_i a_{kj}$ $(i:=k+1,\ldots,j);$

1.3 : <u>end</u> <u>loop</u>;

1 : <u>end</u> <u>loop</u>;

Pivoting is incorporated into the algorithm in the following way. At the k-th stage, a diagonal element $a_{\ell\ell}^{(k)}$ $(\ell \geq k)$ is selected and rows and columns k and ℓ of A_k are permuted so that $a_{\ell\ell}^{(k)}$ is moved into the k-th diagonal position. This amounts to replacing A_k by $\bar{P}_k A_k \bar{P}_k$, where $\bar{P}_k$ is the permutation matrix obtained by interchanging columns k and ℓ of the identity matrix of order $p-k+1$.

To see what this means in terms of the original matrix A , note that by the k-th step we shall have determined a $(k-1)\mathrm{x}p$ matrix R_k such that

$$A - R_k^H R_k = \begin{bmatrix} 0 & 0 \\ 0 & A_k \end{bmatrix}.$$

Hence if we set $P_k = \mathrm{diag}(I_{k-1}, \bar{P}_k)$, we have

$$P_k A P_k - (R_k P_k)^H (R_k P_k) = \begin{bmatrix} 0 & 0 \\ 0 & \bar{P}_k A_k \bar{P}_k \end{bmatrix}.$$

This says that if we interchange columns k and ℓ of R_k , the effect of pivoting is the same as if the pivoting had been performed on A before applying the algorithm. It follows that the final effect of all the pivoting is to compute the Cholesky factorization of $P_{p-1} \cdots P_1 A P_1 \cdots P_{p-1}$.

Since the k-th and ℓ-th columns of R_k are stored over the corresponding columns of A_k in the array, the permutation of R_k can be done along with the permutation of A_k simply by regarding the entire array as a symmetric matrix. Since the lower part of the array is not stored, the actual interchanging cannot proceed by exchanging rows and then columns. Rather one must interchange elements as illustrated below for $p=8$, $k=3$, $\ell=6$ (elements with corresponding numbers are exchanged with one another).

x	x	1	x	x	1	x	x
	x	2	x	x	2	x	x
		3	4	5	x	6	7
			x	x	4	x	x
				x	5	x	x
					3	6	7
						x	x
							x

A general algorithm for accomplishing the interchange is the following (here ":=:" is the interchange operator).

(4.6)

1 : a_{ik} :=: $a_{i\ell}$ $(i:=1,\ldots,k-1)$;

2 : a_{kk} :=: $a_{\ell\ell}$;

3 : $a_{k\ell} := \bar{a}_{k\ell}$;

4 : <u>loop</u> <u>for</u> $j := k+1$ <u>to</u> $\ell-1$

4.1 : $t := \bar{a}_{kj}$;

4.2 : $a_{kj} := \bar{a}_{j\ell}$;

4.3 : $a_{j\ell} := t$;

4 : <u>end</u> <u>loop</u>;

5 : a_{kj} :=: $a_{\ell j}$ $(j:=k+1,\ldots,p)$;

Note the way complex quantities must be conjugated.

The design of SCHDC does not allow complete freedom of pivoting, since some diagonal elements are frozen into place. If a diagonal element is free, it is exchanged with the largest free diagonal element.

5. Programming Details

The CHDC subroutines are for the most part a straightforward implementation of the algorithm described in the last section. The major difference is that the pivoting operations represented by statements 4 and 5 of (4.6) are incorporated into (4.5) in order to avoid making an extra pass over the matrix.

In outline, SCHDC goes as follows:

1 : arrange the pivot elements as specified by JPVT ;

2 : <u>loop</u> <u>for</u> K := 1 <u>to</u> P

2.1 : determine index of the next pivot element;

2.2 : return with INFO = K-1 if the pivot element is not positive;

2.3 : begin the interchange;

2.4 : perform the reduction step, interchanging along the way;

2 : end loop;

The following is an elaboration of this outline.

1. This is done in two steps. First initial elements are moved to the beginning, then final elements are moved to the end. The variables PL and PU are set so that the free elements, if any, are A(PL,PL),...,A(PU,PU) . JPVT is set so that JPVT(K) is the element of the original matrix occupying position K .

2. There are only P-1 steps in the reduction; however, the test in 2.2 must be performed when K = P .

2.1. MAXL is the index. If A(K,K) is frozen, MAXL = K . Otherwise MAXL is set so that A(MAXL,MAXL) is the largest of the free elements.

2.2. If A(MAXL,MAXL) ≤ 0 , the reduction cannot be continued.

2.3. This part effects steps 1, 2, and 3 in (4.6). In addition, JPVT is updated.

2.4. This part is a merging of (4.5) and steps 4 and 5 of (4.6).

6. Performance

Operation counts. SCHDC requires approximately $p^3/6$ floating point multiplications and as many additions. The indexing and looping overhead are proportional, so that the time required to decompose a matrix will tend to increase as p^3 for large p . For p small, certainly for $p \leq 5$, other overhead dominates the calculation.

The work involved in pivoting is proportional to p^2 and, consequently, becomes insignificant as p increases. However, for small values of p , the overhead can be significant.

Effects of rounding error. If A is positive definite and not too ill-conditioned (say $10p\varepsilon_M < 1/\kappa(A)$) , then the reduction will go through to completion, and the computed factor R will satisfy

$$R^TR = A+E , \tag{6.1}$$

where the elements of E satisfy

$$|e_{ij}| \leq \mu \cdot p \cdot \max\{|a_{ij}|\}\varepsilon_M \tag{6.2}$$

for some factor μ of order unity.

The application of the algorithm to semidefinite matrices has not been analyzed; however, if pivoting is used to compute the decomposition (1.7), it is to be expected that the computed R will satisfy (6.2), provided R_{11} is not too ill-conditioned.

Condition estimation. If the pivoting option is used on the positive definite matrix A , (1.9) provides an estimate of the condition number of A . This number is always an underestimate; however, numerical experiments suggest that it is unlikely to underestimate κ by more than a factor of ten. The estimate appears to be better when the eigenvalues $\lambda_1 \geq \lambda_2 \geq \dots \geq \lambda_p$ of A are clustered into two groups, one near λ_1 and the other near λ_p . An exception to the above statements occurs when r_{pp} is approximately $\sqrt{\varepsilon_M}\, r_{11}$ or less, in which case the computed A(P,P) can be expected to consist entirely of rounding error and cannot be used to estimate κ ; however, in this case κ is certainly of order greater than $1/\varepsilon_M$.

7. Notes and References

The Cholesky decomposition has long been used to solve linear systems, especially in statistical applications, where it is known as the square root method [cf. Dwyer (1945)]. Our use of p for the order of A comes from the notation of regression analysis, in which n is usually reserved for the number of rows in the least squares matrix and p refers to the number of columns [cf. Seber (1977)].

The factorization $A = R^TR$ is related to the LU factorizations of Chapter 1 as follows. Let $D = \mathrm{diag}(r_{11}^2, r_{22}^2, \dots, r_{pp}^2)$, and $\bar{R} = D^{-\frac{1}{2}}R$, so that $\bar{R}$ has ones on its diagonal. Then the decomposition A = LU computed, say by SGEFA , is formally equivalent to $A = \bar{R}^T(D^{\frac{1}{2}}R)$, so that $L = \bar{R}^T$ and $U = D^{\frac{1}{2}}R$. A different variant can be obtained by writing $A = \bar{R}^TD\bar{R}$. This form of the factorization, which is usually written $A = LDL^T$, is in wide use, nominally because it can be computed without square roots. We have stayed with the original form in order to make the output consistent with that of SQRDC . A complete discussion of these variants and their relation to Gaussian elimination is given by Householder (1964).

Although the algorithm used by SPOFA appears different from the one here, they actually perform the same arithmetic operations in a different order. Hence the two algorithms have the same numerical properties. However, the algorithm adopted here enables one to check the relative sizes of candidates for r_{kk} without having to compute them, which is necessary for pivoting.

It should be noted that the array JPVT returned by SCHDC is a different animal than the array IPVT returned by SGEFA and related subroutines. The latter contains n integers recording the interchanges made in the course of the reduction. On the other hand, JPVT(K) contains the index of the diagonal element that finally ends up in position K . This is the natural choice for users who subsequently expect to use SCHEX (Ch. 10) to reorder the decomposition, since to keep track of where things are, one has only to perform an equivalent reordering of the elements of JPVT .

The question of whether or not to use the normal equations in solving least squares problems has surfaced only recently, since the alternative method of orthogonal triangularization is relatively new [Golub (1965)]. Some discussion may be found in Golub and Wilkinson (1966) and Stewart (1974); however, the subject is tricky, and informed men of good will can disagree, even in a specific application.

However R is obtained, whether from X^TX or X , it is seldom necessary in least squares and regression problems to go on and compute $A^{-1} = (R^TR)^{-1}$. This has already been illustrated in section 3 for the computation of $w^TA^{-1}w$. Other examples are given by Golub and Styan (1973), some of whose algorithms are implemented in the programs of Chapter 10.

The rounding-error analysis for the Cholesky algorithm parallels that of Gaussian elimination, which can be found in the books by Wilkinson (1963,1965) and Stewart (1974). The fact that A is positive definite makes the algorithm unconditionally stable, since the elements cannot grow in the reduction. There is no published error analysis for the semi-definite case; however, Moler and Stewart (1978) give an analysis of the case when A is a projection (i.e. $A^2 = A$), which is important because the rows of R form an orthonormal basis for the column space of A .

The relation of the condition number of A to the accuracy of solutions of perturbed systems is now classical, and proofs can be found in almost any elementary numerical analysis text that treats numerical linear algebra.

Chapter 9: The QR Decomposition

Subroutines: SQRDC, SQRSL

1. Overview

Purpose. The subroutines of this chapter compute the QR decomposition of a matrix X and apply it to compute coordinate transformations, projections, and least squares solutions. A pivoting option allows the user to detect dependencies among the columns of X.

The QR Decomposition. Let X be an n by p matrix. Then there is an orthogonal matrix Q such that Q^TX is zero below its diagonal. For convenience we shall assume that $n \geq p$ (for the case $n < p$, see the end of this section). Then Q^TX can be written in the form

(1.1) $$Q^TX = \begin{bmatrix} R \\ 0 \end{bmatrix}$$

where R is upper triangular.

If we partition $Q = (Q_1, Q_2)$ where Q_1 has p columns, then

(1.2) $$X = Q_1R .$$

This shows that if X is of rank p, the columns of Q_1 form an orthonormal basis for the space spanned by the columns of X. The matrix

$$P_X = Q_1Q_1^T$$

is the orthogonal projection onto the column space of X. The matrix

$$P_X^{\perp} = Q_2Q_2^T$$

is the projection onto the orthogonal complement of X.

If X is partitioned in the form

$$X = (X_1, X_2) ,$$

where X_1 has k columns, and R is partitioned in the form

$$R = \begin{bmatrix} R_{11} & R_{12} \\ 0 & R_{22} \end{bmatrix} ,$$

where R_{11} is $k\times k$, then

$$Q^TX_1 = R_{11}$$

so that Q and R_{11} comprise the QR decomposition of X_1. If $Q_1 = (Q_1^{(1)}, Q_2^{(1)})$ is partitioned conformally with X, then the columns of $Q_1^{(1)}$ are an orthonormal basis for the column space of X_1, from which projections can be computed. This truncated QR decomposition, which can be had at no cost after the full QR decomposition has been computed, is useful in applications. The subroutine SQRSL allows the user to access this decomposition.

The QR decomposition and the Cholesky decomposition (cf. Chapter 8) are closely related. From (1.1) and the fact that Q is orthogonal, it follows that

$$X^TX = R^TR .$$

Thus, if R is chosen to have positive diagonal elements, it is a Cholesky factor of X^TX. If X has linearly independent columns, X^TX is positive definite and R is unique, along with $Q_1 = XR^{-1}$ (cf. (1.2)). The matrix R_{11} is the Cholesky factor of $X_1^TX_1$, which is the leading principal submatrix of order k of X^TX.

Least squares. The QR decomposition can be used to solve least squares problems involving X. Given an n-vector y, consider the problem of determining a p-vector b such that

$$\rho^2 \equiv \|y-Xb\|^2 = \min . \tag{1.3}$$

Here, $\|r\|$ is the Euclidean vector norm defined by $\|r\|^2 = \Sigma r_i^2$. If X has linearly independent columns, then R is nonsingular, and it can be shown that

$$b = R^{-1}Q_1^Ty . \tag{1.4}$$

Hence, if we set

$$z = Q_1^Ty$$

we can compute b by solving the system

$$Rb = z . \tag{1.5}$$

At the solution, the residual vector

$$r = y-Xb$$

is the projection of y onto the orthogonal complement of the column space of X. From (1.2) it follows that

$$r = P_X^{\perp}y = Q_2Q_2^Ty .$$

Hence, if we set

$$s = Q_2^Ty ,$$

then

$$r = Q_2s ,$$

and the residual sum of squares ρ^2 is given by

$$\rho^2 = \|r\|^2 = \|Q_2s\|^2 = \|s\|^2 .$$

The solution of the truncated problem of minimizing

$$\rho_1^2 = \|y-X_1b^{(1)}\|^2$$

is given by

$$b^{(1)} = R_{11}^{-1}Q_1^{(1)T}y \equiv R_{11}^{-1}z ,$$

where Q_1 has been partitioned in the form

$$Q_1 = (Q_1^{(1)},Q_2^{(1)}) ,$$

and likewise

$$z^T = (z_1^T,z_2^T) .$$

The residual sum of squares is given by

$$\rho_1^2 = \|Q_2^Ty\|^2 + \|Q_2^{(1)T}y\|^2 \equiv \|s\|^2 + \|z_2\|^2 .$$

Thus a knowledge of the QR factorization enables one to solve least squares problems with any terminal set of columns deleted.

If we compute the QR decomposition of the augmented matrix

$$\tilde{X} = (X,y) ,$$

then the triangular part can be shown to have the form

$$\tilde{R} = \begin{bmatrix} R & z \\ 0 & \rho \end{bmatrix} .$$

This provides an alternate way of computing z and ρ -- namely compute the QR decomposition of $\tilde{X}$.

<u>Pivoting</u>. If X has rank $k < p$, then X does not have a unique QR decomposition. However, there is a permutation matrix E (i.e., an identity matrix with its columns permuted) such that if XE is partitioned in the form

$$XE = (X_1,X_2) ,$$

where X_1 has k columns, then the columns of X_1 are linearly independent. It can be shown that the triangular part of the QR decomposition has the form

$$Q_1^TXE = R = \begin{bmatrix} R_{11} & R_{12} \\ 0 & 0 \end{bmatrix}$$

where R_{11} and R_{12} are unique. Moreover,

$$X_2 = X_1R_{11}^{-1}R_{12} ,$$

which expresses the remaining columns of XE as linear combinations of the columns of X_1.

We can obtain a solution $b^{(1)}$ of the least squares problem involving X_1 in the usual way by truncating the QR decomposition of XE . It should be noted that the individual components of $b^{(1)}$ are associated with the corresponding columns of XE which may be spread out through the original matrix X .

The subroutine SQRDC provides an option to permute the columns of X so that the initial columns of XE are independent. The pivoting is done while the decomposition is being computed, and the strategy for selecting columns results in a matrix R that satisfies

$$r_{kk}^2 \geq \sum_{i=k}^{j} r_{ij}^2 \qquad (j = k,k+1,\ldots,p) .$$

It then follows that if r_{kk} is zero, rows k through p are also zero.

It may happen that one will want to force some columns of X into a least squares fit. To accommodate this need, the pivoting option allows one to specify columns of X that are to be moved to the leading positions and frozen there during the reduction. Likewise if one is working with the augmented matrix $\tilde{X}$, it is important that the last diagonal not be moved, and this is also provided for in SCHDC .

In practice one will not compute diagonal elements of R that are exactly zero, and one is faced with the problem of deciding when a diagonal element is negligible. We recommend the following stragegy. First, estimate the errors in the matrix X . (If X is known exactly, take the error in x_{ij} to be a small multiple of $x_{ij} \cdot \varepsilon_M$, where ε_H is the rounding unit for the computer in question.) Then scale the rows and columns of X so that the error estimates are approximately equal to a common value ε (N.B. in least squares applications, row scaling may represent an impermissible change of model). Then consider r_{jj} to be negligible if $r_{jj} < \varepsilon$. For further discussion of this strategy, see the introduction to this guide.

<u>The pseudo-inverse</u>. If X has full rank p , then the pseudo-inverse (also called the Moore-Penrose generalized inverse) of X is given by the expression

$$X^{\dagger} = R^{-1}Q_1^T .$$

From (1.4) it follows, that $X^{\dagger}y$ is the least squares solution of the problem (1.3). We warn the user that although the pseudo-inverse occurs frequently in the literature of various fields, there is seldom any need to compute it explicitly. For example, if one is solving least squares problems, one can solve (1.5) directly without going to the added expense of computing $X^{\dagger}$.

A discussion of the pseudo-inverse for matrices of less than full rank is given in Chapter 11.

<u>Estimation of condition</u>. The spectral norm of a matrix X is the number

$$\|X\| = \sup_{\|x\|=1} \|Xx\| .$$

If X is of full rank p , then the condition number of X is

$$\kappa(X) = \|X\| \|X^{+}\| .$$

The importance of the condition number is that it allows the assessment of the accuracy of least squares solutions. Specifically, let E be an error matrix satisfying $\|X^{+}\| \; \|E\| < 1/5$. Then X+E is of full rank. Let b be the solution of the least squares problem (1.3) and let $\bar{b}$ be the solution of the same problem with X replaced by S+E. Then

$$\text{(1.6)} \qquad \frac{\|b-\bar{b}\|}{\|b\|} \le 1.6\left[\kappa(X) + \kappa^{2}(X)\frac{\|r\|}{\|X\|\,\|b\|}\right]\frac{\|E\|}{\|X\|} .$$

(As E approaches zero, the constant 1.6 may be reduced, ultimately approaching one.) We stress that this bound may be unrealistic unless X has been scaled as described above so that the elements of E are approximately equal.

When the pivoting option in SQRDC has been taken with the input array JPVT initialized to zero, the condition of X can be estimated from the output by

$$\text{(1.7)} \qquad \kappa \cong X(1,1)/X(P,P) .$$

This is always an underestimate, usually by a factor of two or three and never, in our experience, by a factor greater than ten (however, see section 6).

The case $n < p$. When $n < p$, the QR decomposition assumes the form

$$\text{(1.8)} \qquad Q^{T}X = (R \;\; S)$$

where R is a p by p upper triangular matrix. If the first p columns are linearly independent, then the decomposition is unique.

The pivoting option allows one to isolate a set of linearly independent columns. Specifically, what is produced by SQRDC is a permutation E such that

$$\text{(1.9)} \qquad Q^{T}XE = (R \;\; S)$$

The pivoting will force R to be nonsingular if X has a set of linearly independent columns, and in this case the first p columns of XE will also form a nonsingular matrix.

A decomposition of the form (1.8) can be used to solve underdetermined systems of the form

$$Xb = y .$$

In fact, a solution is given by

$$b = E\begin{bmatrix} R^{-1}Q^{T}y \\ 0 \end{bmatrix} .$$

Organization. SQRDC does not compute Q explicitly, since the storage required to retain Q is prohibitive when n is large. Instead, SQRDC computes Q as the product of $m = \min\{p,n-1\}$ Householder transformations. Specifically, transformations $H_1, H_2, \ldots, H_m$

are determined so that

$$H_m \cdots H_2 H_1 X = \begin{cases} [R \;\; S], & \text{if } n \le p \\ \begin{bmatrix} R \\ 0 \end{bmatrix}, & \text{if } n > p . \end{cases}$$

The transformations are stored where zeros are introduced in X , plus one auxiliary m-vector, and R and S are generated in situ in X . The truncated decomposition is obtained in SQRSL by working only with $H_1, \ldots, H_k$.

Although for most applications it is not necessary to know the form of the transformations, or even that Q is represented as a product of them, a few applications that go beyond the capabilities of SQRSL may require that the user manipulate the transformations explicitly. For details, see sections 4 and 5.

2. Usage

SQRDC and SQRSL will normally be used together, SQRDC to compute the QR decomposition of an n by p matrix X and SQRSL to apply the part of the decomposition corresponding to the first $k \le \min\{n,p\}$ columns.

The calling sequence for SQRDC is

```
CALL SQRDC(X,LDX,N,P,QRAUX,JPVT,WORK,JOB)
```

On entry,

X — is a doubly subscripted array of dimension (LDX,P) containing the n by p matrix X whose QR decomposition is to be computed.

LDX — is the leading dimension of the array X .

N — is the number of rows of the matrix X .

P — is the number of columns of the matrix X .

JPVT — is a singly subscripted integer array of dimension P that controls the pivoting, if it has been requested. The K-th column X(K) of X is placed in one of three classes:

if JPVT(K) > 0 , X(K) is an initial column;

if JPVT(K) = 0 , X(K) is a free column;

if JPVT(K) < 0 , X(K) is a final column.

Before the decomposition is computed, initial columns are moved to the leading part of X and final columns to the trailing part of X . During the reduction, only free columns are moved. JPVT is not referenced if JOB is zero.

WORK is a singly subscripted array of dimension P that is used as a work array. WORK is not referenced if JOB = 0 .

JOB is an integer that initiates column pivoting. If JOB = 0 , pivoting is not done. If JOB = 1 , pivoting is done.

On return,

X contains in its upper triangle the upper triangular matrix R of the QR factorization. Below its diagonal, X contains information from which the orthogonal part of the decomposition can be recovered.

QRAUX is a singly subscripted array of dimension P that contains further information required to recover the orthogonal part of the decomposition.

JPVT JPVT(J) contains the index of the column that was moved into column J , provided pivoting has been requested. Thus on return, SQRDC will have computed the QR decomposition, not of X , but of the matrix whose columns are $X_{JPVT(1)},\ldots,X_{JPVT(P)}$.

SQRSL manipulates a truncated decomposition. For $k \leq \min\{n,p\}$, let X_k denote the matrix obtained from X by interchanging its columns as specified by JPVT and then taking the first k columns of the result. Then the output of SQRDC provides a QR decomposition of X_k , and SQRSL manipulates it to compute coordinate transformations, projections, and least squares solutions.

The calling sequence for SQRSL is

```
CALL SQRSL(X,LDX,N,K,QRAUX,Y,QY,QTY,B,RSD,XB,JOB,INFO)
```

On entry,

X is the output array from SQRDC .

LDX is the leading dimension of the array X .

N is the number of rows of X .

K is the number of columns of the matrix X_k described above.

QRAUX is the auxiliary output from SQRDC .

Y is a singly subscripted array of dimension at least N containing the N-vector to be manipulated by SQRSL .

JOB is a parameter that determines what is to be computed. JOB has the decimal expansion ABCDE , where

if $A \neq 0$	QY	is to be computed
if B,C,D, or $E \neq 0$	QTY	is to be computed
if $C \neq 0$	B	is to be computed
if $D \neq 0$	RSD	is to be computed
if $E \neq 0$	XB	is to be computed.

Note that a request to compute B , RSD , or XB automatically triggers the computation of QTY , for which storage must be provided in the calling sequence.

On return, if the computation has been requested by JOB ,

QY is a singly subscripted array of dimension N that contains the vector Qy .

QTY is a singly subscripted array of dimension N that contains the vector Q^Ty .

B is a singly subscripted array of dimension P that contains the solution of the least squares problem of minimizing $\|y-X_kb\|$. Note that the j-th component of B refers to the j-th column of X_k which corresponds to the $JPVT_j$ column of the original matrix X .

RSD is a singly subscripted array of dimension N that contains the residual vector $y-X_kb$. This is also the orthogonal projection of y onto the orthogonal complement of the column space of X .

XB is a singly subscripted array of dimension N that contains the least squares approximation Xb . It is also the projection of y onto the column space of X .

INFO is zero unless the computation of B has been requested and R is exactly singular. In this case, INFO is the index of the first zero diagonal element of R and B is left unaltered.

The parameters QY , QTY , B , RSD , and XB are not referenced if their computation is not requested, and in this case can be replaced by dummy variables in the calling program. To save storage, the user may in some cases use the same array for different parameters in the calling sequence. A frequently occurring example is when one wishes to compute any of

B , RSD , or XB and does not need Y or QTY . In this case one may identify Y , QTY , and one of B , RSD , or XB , while providing separate arrays for anything else that is to be computed. Thus the calling sequence

```
CALL SQRSL(X,LDX,N,K,QRAUX,Y,DUM,Y,B,Y,DUM,110,INFO)
```

will result in the computation of B and RSD , with RSD overwriting Y . More generally, each item in the following list contains groups of permissible identifications for a single calling sequence.

1. (Y,QTY,B) (RSD) (XB) (QY)
2. (Y,QTY,RSD) (B) (XB) (QY)
3. (Y,QTY,XB) (B) (RSD) (QY)
4. (Y,QY) (QTY,B) (RSD) (XB)
5. (Y,QY) (QTY,RSD) (B) (XB)
6. (Y,QY) (QTY,XB) (B) (RSD)

In any group the value returned in the array allocated to the group corresponds to the last member of the group.

In the double precision programs DQRDC and DQRSL all real arrays become double precision arrays. In the complex programs CQRDC and CQRSL all real arrays become complex arrays.

3. Examples

In the examples below, the following declarations are assumed.

```
REAL X(LDX,P), QRAUX(P), Y(N), RSD(N), B(P), U(P), W(P)
```

where LDX $\geq$ N .

1. The most important application of the programs SQRDC and SQRSL is to the least squares problem of finding a vector b to minimize

$$\|y-Xb\|^2 ,$$

where $\|z\|^2 = \Sigma z_i^2$. This can be accomplished in two statements as follows.

```
CALL SQRDC(X,LDX,N,P,QRAUX,JDUM,DUM,0)
CALL SQRSL(X,LDX,N,P,QRAUX,Y,DUM,RSD,B,RSD,DUM,110,INFO)
```

The residual vector y-Xb is returned in the array RSD . The computation of b requires the computation of $Q^T y$ as an intermediate vector; however, the array RSD is used to hold this vector.

The user should test INFO after executing the above sequence. If it is not zero, a diagonal element of R is zero, and the solution is not correct. This can mean that there are dependencies in the columns of X , in which case the program in Example 3 may be applicable. However, it is frequently the result of a programming blunder, such as the improper setting of LDX .

In some statistical applications it is necessary to have the matrix $(X^TX)^{-1}$. The upper half of this symmetric matrix can be obtained in the upper triangle of X by executing the call

```
CALL SPODI(X,LDX,P,DUM,1)
```

(See Chapter 3 for the documentation of SPODI .) Since this statement changes the upper triangle of X , further calls to SQRSL to compute B will not work; an alternative is to transfer the upper triangle of X to another array C and then call SPODI as above with C replacing X .

It is important to note that many calculations that seemingly involve $(X^TX)^{-1}$ can be done directly from R . For example, suppose one needs to compute the quadratic form

$$s = w^T(X^TX)^{-1}w .$$

Since $(X^TX)^{-1} = R^{-1}R^{-T}$, s can be written in the form

$$s = \|R^{-T}w\|^2 .$$

Hence, once X has been reduced, s can be computed by the following sequence:

```
      CALL STRSL(X,LDX,P,W,11)
      S = 0.
      DO 10 J = 1, P
         S = S + W(J)**2
   10 CONTINUE
```

2. Since SQRDC overwrites the matrix X with quantities required by SQRSL , the user who needs the elements of X for later reference must save them elsewhere. In many applications, however, all that the user requires is to compute the product $y = Xu$ for an arbitrary vector u . Since for $n \geq p$

$$Xu = Q\begin{bmatrix} R \\ 0 \end{bmatrix}u = Q\begin{bmatrix} Ru \\ 0 \end{bmatrix}$$

and since R is explicitly available in the upper part of X , this product may be calculated in the following manner.

```
      DO 10 I = 1, N
         Y(I) = 0.
   10 CONTINUE
      DO 30 J = 1, P
         DO 20 I = 1, J
            Y(I) = Y(I) + X(I,J)*U(J)
   20    CONTINUE
   30 CONTINUE
      CALL SQRSL(X,LDX,N,P,QRAUX,Y,Y,DUM,DUM,DUM,DUM,10000,INFO)
```

3. In section 1 we described how pivoting can be used to detect dependencies among the columns of X. The following routine SQRST (ST for solve with tolerance) calculates the QR decomposition with pivoting of a matrix X and tests the diagonal elements against a user-supplied tolerance, tol. Specifically the first integer k is determined for which

$$|r_{k+1,k+1}| \le \text{tol}\cdot|r_{11}| .$$

Then SQRSL is called to perform a truncated fit of the first k columns of the permuted X to an input vector y. The coefficient vector of this fit is unscrambled to correspond to the original columns of X, and the coefficients corresponding to unused columns are set to zero. When $n < p$, the routine solves underdetermined systems.

The results of SQRST depend very much on how the problem is scaled. If the strategy suggested in the introduction is followed, the user will scale X so that the estimated errors in the elements are approximately equal to a common value ε. Then tol should be taken to be larger than $\sqrt{n}\,\varepsilon$ divided by the norm of the largest column of X. With this value of tol, satisfactorily stable solutions will be obtained when $|r_{kk}|$ is significantly greater than $\text{tol}\cdot|r_{11}|$. As $|r_{kk}|$ approaches $\text{tol}\cdot|r_{11}|$, the solutions grow progressively more sensitive to the errors in X.

```
      SUBROUTINE SQRST(X,LDX,N,P,Y,TOL,B,RSD,K,JPVT,QRAUX,WORK)
      INTEGER LDX,N,P,K,JPVT(1)
      REAL X(LDX,1),Y(1),TOL,B(1),RSD(1),QRAUX(1),WORK (1)
C
C     SQRST IS A SUBROUTINE TO COMPUTE LEAST SQUARES SOLUTIONS
C     TO THE SYSTEM
C
C     (1)               X * B = Y,
C
C     WHICH MAY BE EITHER UNDER-DETERMINED OR OVER-DETERMINED.
C     THE USER MAY SUPPLY A TOLERANCE TO LIMIT THE COLUMNS OF
C     X USED IN COMPUTING THE SOLUTION.  IN EFFECT, A SET OF
C     COLUMNS WITH A CONDITION NUMBER APPROXIMATELY BOUNDED BY
C     1/TOL IS USED, THE OTHER COMPONENTS OF B BEING SET TO ZERO.
C
C     ON ENTRY
C
```

```
C        X     REAL(LDX,P), WHERE LDX.GE.N
C              X CONTAINS THE NXP COEFFICIENT MATRIX OF
C              THE SYSTEM (1), X IS DESTROYED BY SQRST.
C
C        LDX   INTEGER
C              LDX IS THE LEADING DIMENSION OF THE ARRAY X.
C
C        N     INTEGER
C              N IS THE NUMBER OF ROWS OF THE MATRIX X.
C
C        P     INTEGER
C              P IS THE NUMBER OF COLUMNS OF THE MATRIX X.
C
C        Y     REAL(N)
C              Y CONTAINS THE RIGHT HAND SIDE OF THE SYSTEM (1).
C
C        TOL   REAL
C              TOL IS THE NONNEGATIVE TOLERANCE USED TO
C              DETERMINE THE SUBSET OF COLUMNS OF X INCLUDED
C              IN THE SOLUTION.  IF TOL IS ZERO, A FULL
C              COMPLEMENT OF MIN(N,P) COLUMNS IS USED.
C
C        JPVT  INTEGER(P)
C              JPVT IS AN ARRAY USED BY SQRDC.
C
C        QRAUX REAL(P)
C              QRAUX IS AN ARRAY USED BY SQRDC AND SQRSL.
C
C        WORK  REAL(P)
C              WORK IS A WORK ARRAY USED BY SQRDC.
C
C     ON RETURN
C
C        X     X CONTAINS THE OUTPUT ARRAY FROM SQRDC.
C
C        B     REAL(P)
C              B CONTAINS THE SOLUTION VECTOR. COMPONENTS
C              CORRESPONDING TO COLUMNS NOT USED ARE SET TO ZERO.
C
C        RSD   REAL(N)
C              RSD CONTAINS THE RESIDUAL VECTOR Y-X*B.
C
C        K     INTEGER
C              K CONTAINS THE NUMBER OF COLUMNS USED IN THE
C              SOLUTION.
C
C        JPVT  CONTAINS THE PIVOT INFORMATION FROM SQRDC.
C
C        QRAUX CONTAINS THE ARRAY OUTPUT BY SQRDC.
C
C     ON RETURN THE ARRAYS X, JPVT AND QRAUX CONTAIN THE
C     USUAL OUTPUT FROM SQRDC, SO THAT THE QR DECOMPOSITION
C     OF X WITH PIVOTING IS FULLY AVAILABLE TO THE USER.
C     IN PARTICULAR, COLUMNS JPVT(1), JPVT(2),...,JPVT(K)
C     WERE USED IN THE SOLUTION, AND THE CONDITION NUMBER
C     ASSOCIATED WITH THOSE COLUMNS IS ESTIMATED BY
C     ABS(X(1,1)/X(K,K)).
C
C     SQRST USES THE LINPACK SUBROUTINES SQRDC AND SQRSL.
C
C     INTERNAL VARIABLES.
C
      INTEGER INFO,J,KK,M
      REAL T
C
```

```
C     INITIALIZE JPVT SO THAT ALL COLUMNS ARE FREE.
C
      DO 10 J=1,P
         JPVT(J) = 0
   10 CONTINUE
C
C     REDUCE X
C
      CALL SQRDC(X,LDX,N,P,QRAUX,JPVT,WORK,1)
C
C     DETERMINE WHICH COLUMNS TO USE.
C
      K = 0
      M = MIN0(N,P)
      DO 20 KK=1,M
         IF (ABS(X(KK,KK)) .LE. TOL*ABS(X(1,1))) GO TO 30
         K = KK
   20 CONTINUE
   30 CONTINUE
C
C     SOLVE THE TRUNCATED LEAST SQUARES PROBLEM.
C
      IF (K .NE. 0)
     1   CALL SQRSL(X,LDX,N,K,QRAUX,Y,RSD,RSD,B,RSD,RSD,110,INFO)
C
C     SET THE UNUSED COMPONENTS OF B TO ZERO AND INITIALIZE JPVT
C     FOR UNSCRAMBLING
C
      DO 40 J=1,P
         JPVT(J) = -JPVT(J)
         IF (J .GT. K) B(J) = 0.
   40 CONTINUE
C
C     UNSCRAMBLE THE SOLUTION.
C
      DO 70 J=1,P
         IF (JPVT(J) .GT. 0) GO TO 70
         K = -JPVT(J)
         JPVT(J) = K
   50    CONTINUE
            IF (K .EQ. J) GO TO 60
            T = B(J)
            B(J) = B(K)
            B(K) = T
            JPVT(K) = -JPVT(K)
            K = JPVT(K)
         GO TO 50
   60    CONTINUE
   70 CONTINUE
      RETURN
      END
```

4. Algorithmic Details

In this section we assume that $n > p$. The modifications required for $n \leq p$ are described at the end of the section

The reduction. As was mentioned in section 1, SQRDC generates an orthogonal matrix Q of the form

$$Q = H_1 H_2 \dots H_p$$

such that

$$Q^T X = \begin{bmatrix} R \\ 0 \end{bmatrix}, \tag{4.1}$$

where R is upper triangular. Each matrix H_ℓ is a Householder transformation of the form

$$H_\ell = I - \frac{u_\ell u_\ell^T}{\rho_\ell} \tag{4.2}$$

where the first $\ell-1$ components of u_ℓ are zero. Each H_ℓ is chosen to introduce zeros into the last $n-\ell$ components of the ℓ-th column of X.

For the moment we shall focus on the course of the reduction, leaving the details of how the Householder transformations are computed and applied for later. Initially X has the form illustrated below for $n = 5$ and $p = 3$:

$$X = \begin{bmatrix} x & x & x \\ (x) & x & x \\ (x) & x & x \\ (x) & x & x \\ (x) & x & x \end{bmatrix}. \tag{4.3}$$

The Householder transformation H_1 is determined so that the product of H_1 and the first column of X is zero in the last $n-1$ components. When this transformation is applied to X it has the effect of introducing zeros into the elements circled in (4.3). Thus $H_1 X$ has the form

$$H_1 X = \begin{bmatrix} r_{11} & r_{12} & r_{13} \\ 0 & x & x \\ 0 & (x) & x \\ 0 & (x) & x \\ 0 & (x) & x \end{bmatrix}. \tag{4.4}$$

The matrix H_2 is now chosen to introduce zeros into the elements circled in (4.4). Because the first component of the vector u_2 that determines H_2 is zero (cf. (4.2)), the components labeled r and 0 are undisturbed by the application of H_2 to $H_1 X$, and the result is

$$\text{(4.5)}\qquad \begin{bmatrix} r_{11} & r_{12} & r_{13} \\ 0 & r_{22} & r_{23} \\ 0 & 0 & x \\ 0 & 0 & \textcircled{x} \\ 0 & 0 & \textcircled{x} \end{bmatrix}$$

Finally H_3 is chosen to introduce zeros into the elements circled in (4.5). Again elements labeled r and 0 are not disturbed. The final result is

$$\text{(4.6)}\qquad H_3H_2H_1X = \begin{bmatrix} r_{11} & r_{12} & r_{13} \\ 0 & r_{22} & r_{23} \\ 0 & 0 & r_{33} \\ 0 & 0 & 0 \\ 0 & 0 & 0 \end{bmatrix}$$

The right hand side of (4.6) has the same form as the right hand side of (4.1). Since each H_ℓ is orthogonal, so is the product $H_3H_2H_1$. Thus the required reduction is finished.

To complete the description of the algorithm we must show how the Householder transformations are generated and how they are applied to the matrix X . For simplicity we describe this only for the first step of the reduction, the other steps being similar.

Let x denote the first column of X . We must choose u_1 and ρ_1 in (4.2) so that

$$H_1x = \tau e_1 ,$$

where, since H_1 is orthogonal, $\tau = \pm\|x\|$. We take

$$\text{(4.7)}\qquad u_1 = e_1 + \frac{x}{\sigma\|x\|} ,$$

where $\sigma = \pm 1$ according as the first component of x is nonnegative or not. Letting ξ denote the first component of x , we take

$$\rho_1 = 1 + \frac{\xi}{\sigma\|x\|} .$$

Note that ρ_1 is just the first component of u_1 , and because of the choice of σ no cancellation can take place when it is calculated. It is now a simple calculation to verify that

$$H_1x = \left(I - \frac{u_1u_1^T}{\rho_1}\right)x = x - \frac{\left(e_1 + \frac{x}{\sigma\|x\|}\right)\left(e_1 + \frac{x}{\sigma\|x\|}\right)^T x}{1 + \frac{\xi}{\sigma\|x\|}} = x - \frac{\left(e_1 + \frac{x}{\sigma\|x\|}\right)\left(\xi + \sigma\|x\|\right)}{1 + \frac{\xi}{\sigma\|x\|}}$$

$$= x - \frac{(\sigma\|x\|e_1 + x)(\xi + \sigma\|x\|)}{\sigma\|x\| + \xi} = -\sigma\|x\|e_1 .$$

It follows that

$$\tau = -\sigma\|x\| \ .$$

We apply the transformation columnwise. Let

$$X = (x_1, x_2, \ldots, x_p) \ .$$

Then

$$H_1 X = (H_1 x_1, H_1 x_2, \ldots, H_1 x_p) \ .$$

The calculation of $H_1 x_1$ is handled specially, since all its components but the first are zero. This component, r_{11}, is $-\sigma\|x_1\|$. To calculate $H_1 x_j$ for $j > 1$, we write

$$H_1 x_j = \left(I - \frac{u_1 u_1^T}{\rho_1}\right) x_j = x_j - \left(\frac{u_1^T x_j}{\rho_1}\right) u_1 \ .$$

This leads to the following sequence of computations:

$$1: \quad t := u_1^T x_j / \rho_1;$$

$$2: \quad x_j := x_j - t u_1;$$

The Householder transformation H_1 is entirely determined by the vector u_1. For future use the last $n-1$ components of u_1 can be stored in the locations that were zeroed by H_1. The first component, which is also ρ_1, must be stored elsewhere.

When x is zero, the transformation may be skipped. This case can be recorded for future use by setting the first component ρ_1 of u_1 to zero (in all other cases $\rho_1 \geq 1$).

Incorporation of column pivoting. In the description of the orthogonal reduction given above, the ℓ-th step can be viewed as performing a first step on the $(n-\ell+1)$ by $(p-\ell+1)$ matrix in the southeast corner of X -- call it $X^{(\ell)}$. For technical reasons described in section 1, it is sometimes desirable to bring the column of largest norm to the front of $X^{(\ell)}$ before proceeding with the reduction, a technique which is called pivoting. This can easily be done by computing the norms of the columns of $X^{(\ell)}$, finding the one of largest norm and interchanging it with the ℓ-th column. However, the repeated computation of norms will increase the arithmetic work in computing the decomposition by a factor of 1.5 . An alternative is to compute the norms of the columns of X initially and update these values as the decomposition proceeds. However, some care must be taken to avoid numerical problems.

In outline the technique goes as follows. Let

$$X^{(\ell)} = \left(x_\ell^{(\ell)}, x_{\ell+1}^{(\ell)}, \ldots, x_p^{(\ell)}\right) \ .$$

Then if $\tilde{H}_\ell$ is the $(n-\ell+1)$ by $(n-\ell+1)$ trailing submatrix of the ℓ-th Householder transformation,

$$\tilde{H}_\ell X^{(\ell)} = \begin{pmatrix} r_{\ell\ell} & r_{\ell,\ell+1} & \cdots & r_{\ell,p} \\ 0 & x_{\ell+1}^{(\ell+1)} & \cdots & x_p^{(\ell+1)} \end{pmatrix} .$$

Since $\tilde{H}_\ell$ is orthogonal

$$\|x_j^{(\ell)}\|^2 = \left\| \begin{pmatrix} r_{\ell j} \\ x_j^{(\ell+1)} \end{pmatrix} \right\|^2 = |r_{\ell j}|^2 + \|x_j^{(\ell+1)}\|^2$$

or

(4.8)
$$\|x_j^{(\ell+1)}\| = \left(\|x_j^{(\ell)}\|^2 - |r_{\ell j}|^2\right)^{1/2} .$$

This formula allows us to compute one set of norms from the preceding.

There are two difficulties with this formula. First, if $\|x_j^{(\ell)}\|^2$ overflows or underflows, it will fail. This problem can easily be managed by writing the formula (4.8) in the form

(4.9)
$$\|x_j^{(\ell+1)}\| = \|x_j^{(\ell)}\| \left[1 - \left(\frac{|r_{\ell j}|}{\|x_j^{(\ell)}\|} \right)^2 \right]^{1/2} .$$

Since $|r_{\ell j}| \leq \|x_j^{(\ell)}\|$, this formula cannot generate an overflow, and any underflowing quantity will be insignificant in comparison to one.

The second difficulty is that rounding error severely limits the applicability of (4.9). If the term $(|r_{\ell j}|/\|x_j^{(\ell)}\|)^2$ agrees with 1 to almost all its significant figures, say to within some modest multiple of the rounding unit ε_M , then the computed value of $\|x_j^{(\ell+1)}\|$ will be of the order $\varepsilon_M^{1/2}\|x_j^{(\ell)}\|$ no matter how small the actual value is. A more detailed analysis shows that if

(4.10)
$$\lambda \|x_j^{(\ell+1)}\| \leq \varepsilon_M^{1/2} \|x_j^{(1)}\| ,$$

where $\lambda \leq 1$ is a constant of order unity, then $\|x_j^{(\ell+1)}\|$ will be inaccurately computed by the repeated application of (4.9). Thus, whenever (4.10) is satisfied we must recompute $\|x_j^{(\ell+1)}\|$. Combining (4.9) and (4.10), we see that we wish to recompute $\|x_j^{(\ell+1)}\|$ whenever

$$\lambda \frac{\|x_j^{(\ell)}\|}{\|x_j^{(1)}\|} \left[1 - \left(\frac{|r_{\ell j}|}{\|x_j^{(\ell)}\|} \right)^2 \right]^{1/2} \leq \varepsilon_M^{1/2} .$$

This procedure has the disadvantage that it requires an additional array of dimension p to hold the accurately calculated norms for later comparisons. In SQRDC we have taken

$\lambda^2 = .05$. Note that this means that the norms may be computed to as little as one significant decimal digit, and hence in close cases rounding error may cause the pivot order to vary.

Application of the decomposition to a vector. The subroutine SQRSL applies the QR decomposition to a vector y to compute a number of quantities (cf. the discussion in section 1). The decomposition actually used is not that of the original matrix X but of the matrix

$$X_k = (x_{jpvt(1)}, x_{jpvt(2)}, \ldots, x_{jpvt(k)})$$

where $k \le \min\{n,p\}$ is a parameter specified by the user (when pivoting is not done, X_k consists of the first k columns of X). The orthogonal part of this decomposition is given by

$$Q = H_1 H_2 \ldots H_k \ .$$

1. Qy is computed in the form

$$Qy = H_1 H_2 \ldots H_k y$$

where the Householder transformations $H_1, \ldots, H_k$ are applied as described above.

2. $Q^T y$ is computed in the form

$$Q^T y = H_k H_{k-1} \ldots H_1 y \ .$$

This vector must be computed in order to compute all the other quantities. For future reference let $Q = (Q_1, Q_2)$, where Q_1 has k columns, and let

$$Q^T y = \begin{bmatrix} Q_1^T y \\ Q_2^T y \end{bmatrix} = \begin{bmatrix} z \\ s \end{bmatrix} .$$

3. The least squares solution $b = R^{-1} Q_1^T y$ is computed as the solution of the triangular system

(4.11) $$Rb = z \ .$$

4. The least squares residual $y - Xb = Q_2 Q_2^T y$ is computed in the form

(4.12) $$r = H_1 H_2 \ldots H_k \begin{bmatrix} 0 \\ s \end{bmatrix} .$$

The vector r is also the projection onto the orthogonal complement of the column space of X .

5. The least squares approximation $Xb = Q_1 Q_1^T y$ is computed in the form

(4.13) $$Xb = H_1 H_2 \ldots H_k \begin{bmatrix} z \\ 0 \end{bmatrix} .$$

The vector Xb is also the projection onto the column space of X .

The case $n \le p$. This case differs from the case $n > p$ in that only n-1 transformations are performed in the reduction.

Modifications for complex arithmetic. The only modification of the algorithm that complex arithmetic entails is that σ in (4.7) should be defined by

$$\sigma = \begin{cases} \frac{\xi}{|\xi|} & \text{if} \quad \xi \ne 0 \\ 1 & \text{if} \quad \xi = 0 \end{cases} .$$

5. Programming Details

SQRDC. In outline, SQRDC proceeds as follows.

1 : *if* JOB ≠ 0 *then*

1.1 : exchange the columns of X for which JPVT(J) > 0 to the front of the array;

1.2 : exchange the columns for which JPVT(J) < 0 to the end of the array;

1 : *end if*;

2 : compute the norms of the free columns, storing the values in WORK and QRAUX;

3 : *loop for* L:=1 *to* min{N,P}

3.1 : *if* column L is free *then*

3.1.1 : from among the free columns locate the one of largest norm and exchange it with column L;

3.1 : *end if*;

3.2 : *if* L≠N *then*

3.2.1 : compute the Householder transformation for column L;

3.2.2 : apply the transformation to columns L+1,L+2,...,P, updating the norms of the columns;

3.2.3 : save the vector determining the transformation;

3.2.4 : compute r_{LL} and place it in X(L,L);

3.2 : *end if*;

3 : *end loop*;

The following is an elaboration on the above outline.

1. At the end of this section the columns that are to be frozen are moved to the beginning or end of X as specified by JPVT and their order is recorded in JPVT . The

integers PL and PU are set so that the free columns, which can be moved during pivoting, are columns PL,PL+1,...,PU .

2. As these norms are updated, WORK will contain the old norm and QRAUX will contain the updated norm.

3. This is the main loop for the reduction. At most min{N-1,P} transformations will be performed in the reduction; however, when P > N , an extra pass is required to pivot on the N-th column.

3.1. Columns PL,PL+1,...,PU are the free ones. When an interchange is performed the entire column of the array is moved. This insures that in the final decomposition the columns of R will be properly positioned. The entries in JPVT , QRAUX and WORK are also interchanged.

3.2.1. The Householder transformation is generated as described in section 4. The (N-L+1)-vector u that determines the transformation is stored in X(L,L),X(L+1,L),..., X(N,L), so that it can be conveniently applied to the remaining columns. A zero column causes QRAUX to be set to zero and 3.2.2 to be skipped.

3.2.2. The algorithms for applying the transformation and updating the norms are described in section 4.

3.2.3. The first component of u , which is in X(L,L) is placed in QRAUX(L) for use by SQRSL . The other components of u remain in the array X .

3.2.4. The value of r_{LL} is computed and stored where it belongs in X(L,L) .

SQRSL. In outline, SQRSL goes as follows.

```
1   : determine from the parameter JOB what is to be computed;
2   : if N=1 then
2.1 :   compute the required quantities;
2.2 :   return;
2   : end if;
3   : if QY or QTY are to be computed then move Y into QY and QTY as
          required;
3   : end if;
4   : if required, compute QY;
5   : if required, compute QTY;
6   : if B, RSD, or XB are to be computed then initialize B, RSD, and XB
          from QTY as required;
```

6 : end if;

7 : if required, compute B;

8 : if required, compute RSD;

9 : if required, compute XB;

The following is an elaboration of the above outline.

1. JOB is decoded as described in section 2. The logical variables CQY , CQTY , CB , CRSD , and CXB are set to true if the corresponding parameters are to be computed.

2. The case N=1 requires enough special handling to warrant a section of its own.

3. The quantities QY and QTY will be computed by multiplying the Householder transformations into Y , which at this time is moved to QY and QTY . The move must be done for both arrays before the transformations can be applied to either, since if, say, QY shares an array with Y in the calling sequence, any operation on QY will change Y .

4,5. The vectors QY and QTY are computed by multiplying by the Householder transformations stored in the lower part of X and in QRAUX . To apply the L-th transformation, the value of X(L,L) is saved and QRAUX(L) is placed in X(L,L) so that the vector that determines the transformation is in X(L,L),X(L+1,L),...,X(N,L) . The transformation is then applied in the usual way, after which X(L,L) is restored to its original value.

6. B , RSD , and XB are computed from pieces of QTY . For reasons similar to those in step 3, all the arrays must be initialized simultaneously.

7. B is computed by solving the system (4.11).

8,9. RSD and XB are computed in the same loop, since they require the same sequence of transformations.

6. Performance

Operation counts. An elementary operation count shows that when $n \geq p$, SQRDC requires approximately

$$np^2 - \frac{p^3}{3}$$

multiplications and the same number of additions. When $n \leq p$, SQRDC requires

$$n^2p - \frac{n^3}{3}$$

multiplications and likewise the same number of additions. Indexing and looping overhead are proportional to these approximations so that as n and p increase they accurately reflect the order of growth in the work.

The multiplication count for SQRSL depends on what is computed:

QY QTY	$(2n-k)k$,
RSD XB	$2(2n-k)k$,
B	$(2n-k)k + \frac{1}{2}k^2$.

Here $k \leq \min\{n,p\}$ is the number of columns of X involved in the computation. The number of additions is approximately the same.

<u>Timings</u>. Extensive timing runs have been made on SQRDC and SQRSL . The execution times vary widely from machine to machine and from compiler to compiler on a given machine. In order to simplify this mass of raw data, we present not the times, but their ratios to the time required by a simple process of comparable magnitude (e.g. a matrix multiplication of appropriate order). This process dramatically reduces the variation across machines and systems.* The price to be paid is that the user cannot obtain actual execution times from these data, only an idea of how much more it will cost him to do the computation in question than another, conceptually simpler computation. However, we feel that the user who needs actual execution times should measure them himself, since minor changes in a computer system can have a great effect on the times.

When $n \geq p$ the natural process with which to compare SQRDC applied to the n by p matrix X is the formation of the upper half of X^TX , which has $np^2/2$ multiplication count and represents an alternative approach to solving least squares problems. When $n < p$, we compare the time for a QR decomposition with the time to compute the (i,j)-elements of X^TX for $i = 1,\ldots,n$ and $j = i,\ldots,p$, which is a process of comparable order. The elements of X^TX are computed element by element using a BLAS dot-product subroutine. The results are presented in Table 1, whose entries have the following format.

	$\dfrac{r_n}{s_r}$	
r_e		r_u

*Machines designed to perform vector operations with high efficiency are exceptional in that they tend to give higher ratios than their more pedestrian counterparts. For this reason, we have excluded them from the summary below. For a fuller discussion of this phenomenon, see Chapter 1.

where

r_n is the average of the ratios,

r_e is the smallest ratio,

r_u is the largest ratio,

s_r is the standard deviation of the ratios.

The results suggest that on the average it takes between 1½ and 2½ as much time to reduce X as to form X^TX. The ratios are less for $n < p$ and do not vary much $(1.5 \leq r_n \leq 1.9)$. For $n > p$, the ratios are largest when p is small.

It is somewhat difficult to design a valid measure for the effects of pivoting on times, since these will vary according to the problem being solved. In tests run on random matrices, the pivoting option increased the average (across machines) execution times by a factor of between 1.1 and 1.8. In general the factor becomes smaller for increasing n and, when $p \leq n$, for increasing p.

There are too many optional computations in SQRSL to conveniently summarize them here. Accordingly we have chosen to present ratios for computing the residual vector, which is also the projection of y onto the orthogonal complement of the column space of X. The times are compared with the times required to compute X^Ty, again using a BLAS dot-product subroutine.

The results are summarized in Table 2, in which the entries have the same format as in Table 1. Only results for $p < n$ are given, since for $p \geq n$ the computation is no more than an elaborate way of calculating a zero vector. The results show that a residual computation requires between 3 and 5 times the amount of time as the computation of X^Ty, the lower ratios obtaining for n and p large. Computation of XB will require about the same amount of time; computation of QY and QTY about half the time. It is important to note that these times are often insignificant compared to the cost of the original reduction.

Effects of rounding error. The effects of rounding are best described in terms of the Frobenius matrix norm defined by

$$\|X\|_F^2 = \sum_{i,j} x_{ij}^2 .$$

Let R denote the computed triangular factor. Then it can be shown that there is an orthogonal matrix $Q = (Q_1, Q_2)$, with Q_1 $n \times \min\{n,p\}$, such that

$$X + E = Q_1 R_1 . \tag{6.1}$$

Table 1

(QR decomposition)/(X^TX)

n \ p	5	10	25	50	75	100
5	2.3 2.0 2.6 .20	1.9 1.6 2.3 .17	1.8 1.5 2.1 .16	1.7 1.3 2.0 .17	1.7 1.4 2.0 .15	1.7 1.4 2.0 .15
10	2.5 2.1 3.0 .26	2.1 1.8 2.6 .21	1.8 1.5 2.1 .17	1.7 1.4 2.0 .17	1.8 1.4 2.2 2.2	1.7 1.4 2.0 .20
25	2.5 2.0 3.2 .28	2.3 2.0 2.8 .23	1.8 1.2 2.2 .23	1.6 1.4 1.9 .16	1.6 1.3 1.9 .17	1.6 1.3 1.8 .17
50	2.5 2.0 3.2 .28	2.3 1.9 2.9 .25	2.0 1.8 2.4 .17	1.7 1.4 1.9 .13	1.5 1.2 1.7 .13	1.5 1.2 1.7 .15
75	2.5 2.2 3.4 .32	2.3 1.7 2.8 .26	2.1 1.8 2.4 .14	1.8 1.6 2.1 .12	1.6 1.4 1.8 .12	1.5 1.2 1.6 .12
100	2.4 2.0 3.0 .26	2.3 1.8 3.0 .30	2.1 1.8 2.4 .16	1.9 1.6 2.0 .12	1.7 1.5 1.9 .11	1.6 1.3 1.7 .10

Table 2

(RESID)/(X^Ty)

n \ p	5	10	25	50	75	100
5						
10	5.1 4.2 5.6 .41					
25	4.8 4.3 5.4 .37	4.4 3.6 5.7 .45				
50	4.9 3.6 5.5 .48	4.5 3.7 5.5 .45	3.8 3.2 4.4 .33			
75	4.6 3.6 5.3 .40	4.4 3.6 5.1 .39	4.0 3.4 4.8 .32	3.2 2.7 3.8 .25		
100	4.7 4.2 5.4 .38	4.4 3.8 5.3 .41	4.0 3.5 4.5 .30	3.5 3.2 3.8 .18	3.0 2.7 3.5 .25	

The matrix E satisfies

$$\frac{\|E\|_F}{\|X\|_F} \leq \phi(n,p)\varepsilon_M ,$$

where $\phi(n,p)$ is used generically in this section for a slowly growing function of n and p (n^2p^2 is too large), and ε_M is the rounding unit for the computer in question. Thus SQRDC computes the QR decomposition of a slightly perturbed matrix X .

The same stability properties extend to SQRSL . Namely, the computed vectors QY , QTY , RSD , and XB satisfy

$$QY = Q(y+h_1) ,$$
$$QTY = Q^T(y+h_2) ,$$
$$RESID = Q_2Q_2^T(y+h_3) ,$$
$$XB = Q_1Q_1^T(y+h_4) ,$$

where Q is the same orthogonal matrix as above and

$$\frac{\|h_i\|_F}{\|y\|_F} \leq \phi(n,p)\varepsilon_M \qquad (i = 1,2,3,4) .$$

Finally, the computed solution b of the least squares problem (1.3) actually minimizes

$$\|y-(X+F)b\|_2$$

where

$$\frac{\|F\|_F}{\|X\|_F} \leq \phi(n,p)\varepsilon_M .$$

Unfortunately, the matrix F is not the same as E in (6.1).

Condition estimation. If the pivoting option is used in SQRDC , the condition of X can be estimated from (1.7). This number is always an underestimate; however, numerical experiments suggest that it is unlikely to underestimate κ by a factor of more than ten. The estimate appears to be better when the singular values $\sigma_1 \geq \sigma_2 \geq \cdots \geq \sigma_p$ of X (see Chapter 11) are clustered in two groups, one near σ_1 and the other near σ_p . An exception to the above statements occurs when r_{pp} is approximately $\varepsilon_M r_{11}$, in which case the computed X(P,P) can be expected to consist entirely of rounding error and cannot be used to compute κ ; however, in this case κ is certainly greater than about $1/\varepsilon_M$.

7. Notes and References

The transformations that the algorithms of this section are based on originated with Householder (1958), at least as a computational tool. They have been variously known as Householder transformations, elementary Hermitian matrices, and elementary reflectors.

Golub (1965) was the first to describe in detail how to use Householder transformations to solve least squares problems and, in conjunction with Businger (1965), publish a program. SQRDC is a lineal descendant of this work. In designing it we have departed from the usual notation of numerical analysts, in which the least squares problem is written

$$\text{minimize } \|b-Ax\| ,$$

where A is $m \times n$. Instead we have adopted a notation commonly used by statisticians [cf. Seber (1977)].

The scaling of the vector u defining a Householder transformation can be done in various ways [cf. (4.2)]. The one adopted here appears to be new and has the advantage that ρ is the first component of u and does not have to be stored separately. The criterion for recomputing column norms is also new, although Lawson and Hanson (1974) do something quite similar in their least squares codes.

It should be noted that the array JPVT returned by SQRDC is a different animal than the array IPVT returned by SGEFA and related subroutines. The latter contains $n-1$ integers recording the interchanges made in the course of the reduction. On the other hand, JPVT(K) contains the index of the diagonal element that finally ends up in position K. This is the natural choice for users who subsequently expect to use SCHEX (Chapter 10) to reorder the decomposition, since to keep track of where things are one has only to perform an equivalent reordering of the elements of JPVT. Incidentally, the pivoting strategies of SQRDC and SCHDC are essentially identical; except for rounding errors they will produce the same sequence of pivots when applied respectively to X and to X^TX.

Mathematically, the columns of Q_1 are the vectors that would have been obtained if one had applied the Gram-Schmidt orthogonalization to the columns of X. Numerically, the vectors produced by the process can be far from orthogonal; however, Björck (1967a) has shown that a variant, the so-called modified Gram-Schmidt method, can be used successfully to solve least squares problems. If one is willing to do some extra work, orthogonality can be preserved by a reorthogonalization process [Wilkinson (1963), Daniel et al. (1976)]. All told, a well designed set of programs based on the Gram-Schmidt process could be a reasonable alternative to the programs of this chapter.

The method of iterative refinement for linear systems, which was discussed in Chapter 1, can be extended to improve the accuracy of least squares solutions. The technique has been described and analyzed in a series of papers by Björck (1967b, 1968) and Björck and Golub (1967).

The question of whether or not to use the normal equations in solving least squares problems has surfaced only recently, since the method of orthogonal triangularization is relatively new. Some discussion may be found in Golub and Wilkinson (1966) and Stewart (1974); however, the subject is tricky, and informed men of good will can disagree, even in a specific application.

However R is obtained, whether from X^TX or X, it is seldom necessary in least squares and regression problems to go on and compute $A^{-1} = (R^TR)^{-1}$. This has already been illustrated in section 3 for the computation of $w^TA^{-1}w$. Other examples are given by Golub and Styan (1973), some of whose algorithms are implemented in the programs of Chapter 10. Incidentally, one reason that SQRSL does not return an unscrambled solution b corresponding to the original matrix X is that in many applications it is more important that the components of b correspond to the columns of R.

The basic rounding error analyses for orthogonal triangularization are given by Wilkinson (1965a, 1965b) and extended slightly by Stewart (1974) to cover least squares solutions. A formal analysis of the computation of projections does not seem to have been published; however, it is a relatively trivial consequence of the works cited above.

The bound (1.6) relating the perturbation in a least squares solution to perturbations in X is a simplification of the bound given by Stewart (1977a) in a survey of the perturbation theory for generalized inverses, least squares, and projections.

Chapter 10: Updating QR & Cholesky Decompositions

Subroutines: SCHUD, SCHDD, SCHEX

1. Overview

Purpose. The programs in this chapter efficiently recompute the Cholesky factor of a matrix A after A has been modified by the addition of a symmetric rank-one matrix, by the subtraction of a symmetric rank-one matrix, or the symmetric permutation of the rows and columns of A. These programs can also be used to update the triangular part of the QR decomposition of a matrix X when X is modified respectively by the addition of a row, by the deletion of a row, or by the permutation of its columns.

Background. Let A be a positive definite matrix of order p. Then A has a Cholesky factorization of the form

$$A = R^T R$$

where R is an upper triangular matrix. This factorization, which has many important applications, can be computed by the LINPACK subroutines SPOFA, SPOCO, and SCHDC.

In some applications, A is modified in a simple manner to form a new matrix $\tilde{A}$ whose Cholesky factorization is needed. If one simply forms $\tilde{A}$ and computes its Cholesky factor $\tilde{R}$ in the usual way, it will require an amount of work proportional to p^3. However, if the Cholesky factorization of A has already been computed, it may be possible to compute $\tilde{R}$ directly from R with less work. This process is generally referred to as updating a Cholesky decomposition. The subroutines SCHUD, SCHDD, and SCHEX allow the user to update a Cholesky decomposition for three important kinds of modifications.

1. The addition of a positive semidefinite rank-one matrix (SCHUD). Here $\tilde{A}$ has the form

   $$\tilde{A} = A + xx^T$$

   where x is a p-vector. This specific kind of modification is also called updating (as opposed to the generic use of the term above).

2. The subtraction of a positive semidefinite rank-one matrix (SCHDD). Here $\tilde{A}$ has the form

   $$\tilde{A} = A - xx^T$$

   where x is a p-vector. This modification is called downdating to distinguish it from updating as used in 1. It is important to realize that downdating problems can be quite ill-conditioned. In the first place, it may happen that $\tilde{A}$ is not positive definite, in which case it does not have a Cholesky factorization. Even when $\tilde{A}$ is positive definite, $\tilde{R}$ may be inaccurately computed if the modification comes near to reducing the rank of A .

3. The symmetric permutation of the rows and columns of A (SCHEX). Here

$$\tilde{A} = E^T A E$$

where E is a permutation matrix (i.e. an identity matrix with its columns permuted). Two types of permutations are provided for: a right circular shift in which rows and columns

$$1,\ldots,k-1,k,k+1,\ldots,\ell,\ell+1,\ldots,p$$

are permuted to

$$1,\ldots,k-1,\ell,k,k+1,\ldots,\ell-1,\ell+1,\ldots,p;$$

a left circular shift in which rows and columns

$$1,\ldots,k-1,k,\ldots,\ell-1,\ell,\ell+1,\ldots,p$$

are permuted to

$$1,\ldots,k-1,k+1,\ldots,\ell,k,\ell+1,\ldots,p.$$

An important application of the updating routines is the efficient solution of least squares problems that are modifications of an original problem. Specifically, given an n by p matrix X and an n-vector y , we wish to determine a p-vector b such that

$$\rho^2 = \|y-Xb\|^2 \tag{1.1}$$

is minimized (here $\|\cdot\|$ is the usual Euclidean vector norm). In Chapter 8 it was shown that this problem can be solved by forming the matrix

$$(X,y)^T(X,y) = \begin{bmatrix} A & c \\ c^T & \delta \end{bmatrix}$$

and computing its Cholesky factor

$$\begin{bmatrix} R & z \\ 0 & \rho \end{bmatrix}. \tag{1.2}$$

Then $Rb = z$ and ρ^2 is the residual sum of squares in (1.1).

If we have computed the factor (1.2), then the updating routines can be applied to it so that the new factor does not have to be recomputed. Each subroutine corresponds to a specific modification of the original least squares problem.

1. SCHUD. This gives the factor

$$\begin{bmatrix} \tilde{R} & \tilde{z} \\ 0 & \tilde{\rho} \end{bmatrix}$$

corresponding to the augmented least squares problem with the matrices

$$\tilde{X} = \begin{bmatrix} X \\ x^T \end{bmatrix}, \quad \tilde{y} = \begin{bmatrix} y \\ \eta \end{bmatrix};$$

i.e. a least squares problem with a row added.

2. SCHDD. If X and y have the form

$$X = \begin{bmatrix} \tilde{X} \\ x^T \end{bmatrix}, \quad y = \begin{bmatrix} \tilde{y} \\ \eta \end{bmatrix},$$

then SCHDD computes the factor corresponding to $\tilde{X}$ and $\tilde{y}$; i.e. a least squares problem with a row removed.

3. SCHEX. This gives the factor corresponding to the matrix

$$\tilde{X} = XE ;$$

i.e. to a least squares problem with its columns permuted. Thus SCHEX can be used to move columns of X into the final positions in the array so that they may be removed from the problem, as described in Chapters 8 and 9.

Note that the matrix (1.2) is the triangular part of the QR factorization of (X,y) . Consequently, the routines of this chapter can also be regarded as updating the triangular part of a QR factorization.

Organization. The subroutines perform the updating by determining a sequence of orthogonal transformations, called plane rotations, that relate $\tilde{R}$ to R . These transformations are then used to determine $\tilde{z}$ and $\tilde{\rho}$. This makes it possible for the user to update several vectors z and corresponding values of ρ at a time. Information that will allow the user to recover the transformations is returned by the subroutines.

2. Usage

SCHUD updates the Cholesky factorization $A = R^TR$ of a positive definite matrix A to produce the Cholesky factorization $\tilde{R}^T\tilde{R}$ of $A + xx^T$, where x is a vector. Specifically, given an upper triangular matrix R of order p , p-vectors x and z and a scalar y , SCHUD determines an orthogonal matrix U and a scalar $\tilde{\zeta}$ such that

$$U \begin{bmatrix} R & z \\ x^T & y \end{bmatrix} = \begin{bmatrix} \tilde{R} & \tilde{z} \\ 0 & \tilde{\zeta} \end{bmatrix},$$

where $\tilde{R}$ is upper triangular. A residual norm ρ associated with z is updated according to the formula $\tilde{\rho} = \sqrt{\rho^2 + \tilde{\zeta}^2}$. There are provisions for updating more than one pair (z,ρ) -- or none at all.

The matrix U is determined as the product $U_p \ldots U_1$ of plane rotations, where U_i

acts in the (i,p+1)-plane (see section 4 for details).

The calling sequence for SCHUD is

```
CALL SCHUD(R,LDR,P,X,Z,LDZ,NZ,Y,RHO,C,S)
```

On entry,

R is a doubly subscripted array of dimension (LDR,P) that contains the upper triangular matrix to be updated. The elements below the diagonal of R are not referenced by SCHUD .

LDR is the leading dimension of the array R .

P is an integer containing the order of the matrix R .

X is a singly subscripted array of dimension P that contains the row vector to be added to R . X is not altered by SCHUD .

Z is a doubly subscripted array with dimensions (LDZ,NZ) that contains NZ columns of p-vectors which are to be updated with R .

LDZ is the leading dimension of the array Z .

NZ is the number of vectors in Z . If NZ is zero, Z , Y , and RHO are not referenced.

Y is a singly subscripted array of dimension NZ containing the scalars for updating with Z . Y is not altered by SCHUD .

RHO is a singly subscripted array of dimension NZ that contains residual norms to be updated with Z . If RHO(J) < 0 , RHO(J) is not referenced.

C is a singly subscripted array of dimension P .

S is a singly subscripted array of dimension P .

On return,

R
Z
RHO contain the updated quantities.

C contains the cosines of the transforming rotations.

S contains the sines of the transforming rotations.

SCHDD downdates the Cholesky factorization $A = R^TR$ of a positive definite matrix A to produce the Cholesky factorization $\tilde{R}^T\tilde{R}$ of $A - xx^T$, where x is a vector. Specifically, given an upper triangular matrix R of order p , p-vectors x and z and a scalar y, SCHDD attempts to determine an orthogonal matrix U and a scalar ζ such that

$$U\begin{bmatrix} R & z \\ 0 & \zeta \end{bmatrix} = \begin{bmatrix} \tilde{R} & \tilde{z} \\ x^T & y \end{bmatrix}$$

where $\tilde{R}$ is upper triangular. A residual norm ρ associated with z is downdated according to the formula $\tilde{\rho} = \sqrt{\rho^2 - \zeta^2}$, if this is possible. There are provisions for downdating more than one pair (z, ρ) -- or none at all.

The matrix U is determined as the product $U_1 \ldots U_p$ of plane rotations, where U_i acts in the $(p+1, i)$ plane (see section 4 for details).

The calling sequence for SCHDD is

```
CALL SCHDD(R,LDR,P,X,Z,LDZ,NZ,Y,RHO,C,S,INFO)
```

On entry,

R — is a doubly subscripted array of dimension (LDR,P) that contains the upper triangular matrix to be downdated. The elements of R lying below the diagonal are not referenced by SCHDD .

LDR — is the leading dimension of the array R .

P — is an integer containing the order of the matrix R .

X — is a singly subscripted array of dimension P that contains the row vector to be removed from R . X is not altered by SCHDD .

Z — is a doubly subscripted array with dimensions (LDZ,NZ) that contains NZ columns of p-vectors which are to be downdated with R .

LDZ — is the leading dimension of the array Z .

NZ — is the number of vectors in Z . If NZ is zero, Z , Y , and RHO are not referenced.

Y — is a singly subscripted array of dimension NZ containing the scalars for downdating Z . Y is not altered by SCHDD .

RHO — is a singly subscripted array of dimension NZ containing the residual norms to be downdated.

C — is a singly subscripted array of dimension P .

S — is a singly subscripted array of dimension P .

On return,

R
Z
RHO
contain the downdated quantities, provided they could be computed (see INFO).

C contains the cosines of the transforming rotations.

S contains the sines of the transforming rotations.

INFO is zero if the downdating was successful. If R could not be downdated, INFO = -1 , and all quantities remain unaltered. If any RHO(J) could not be downdated, INFO = 1 . The RHO(J)'s that could not be downdated are set to -1.

SCHEX updates the Cholesky factorization of a positive definite matrix A after symmetric permutation of its rows and columns. Two types of permutations may be specified: a right circular shift among rows and columns k through ℓ , and a left circular shift among rows and columns k through ℓ. The updating transformation is written as the product $U_{\ell-k} \cdots U_2 U_1$ of plane rotations, which are returned by SCHEX . At the user's option, the transformations are multiplied to a set of vectors z .

The right circular shift corresponds to the permutation

$$1,\ldots,k-1,\ell,k,\ldots,\ell-1,\ell+1,\ldots,p \ .$$

The rotations U_i are in the $(\ell-i,\ell-i+1)$ plane.

The left circular shift corresponds to the permutation

$$1,\ldots,k-1,k+1,\ldots,\ell,k,\ell+1,\ldots,p \ .$$

The rotations U_i are in the $(k+i-1,k+i)$ plane.

The calling sequence for SCHEX is

```
CALL SCHEX(R,LDR,P,K,L,Z,LDZ,NZ,C,S,JOB) .
```

On entry,

R is a doubly subscripted array of dimension (LDR,P) that is to be updated. The elements below the diagonal of R are not referenced.

LDR is the leading dimension of the array R .

P is an integer containing the order of the matrix R .

K is the first column of R to be altered.

L is the last column of R to be altered. L must be strictly greater than K .

Z is a doubly subscripted array with dimensions (LDZ,NZ) whose columns contain NZ p-vectors that are to be transformed along with R .

LDZ is the leading dimension of the array Z .

NZ is the number of vectors in Z . The array Z is not referenced if NZ = 0 .

C is a singly subscripted array of dimension L .

S is a singly subscripted array of dimension L .

JOB selects which kind of shift will be performed as follows:

JOB = 1 , right circular shift,
JOB = 2 , left circular shift.

On return,

R
Z contain the updated quantities.

C contains the L-K cosines of the transforming rotations.

S contains the L-K sines of the transforming rotations.

Double precision programs. In the double precision routines, all the parameters in the calling sequence that are typed real become double precision.

Complex programs. In the complex routines all parameters in the calling sequence that are typed real become complex, with the exception of RHO and C , which remain real.

3. Examples

In the examples below the following specifications are assumed:

```
REAL R(LDR,P),B(P),C(P),S(P),X(P),Z(P),RHO,Y
```

where LDR $\geq$ P .

The first example shows how SCHUD may be used to solve a very large least squares problem. The first step is to initialize R , Z , and RHO to zero.

```
      RHO = 0.
      DO 20 J = 1, P
         Z(J) = 0.
         DO 10 I = 1, J
            R(I,J) = 0.
   10    CONTINUE
   20 CONTINUE
```

The next step is to use SCHUD to form R , Z , and RHO by adding X and y a row at a time. Here we assume that we have available a subroutine GETXY that generates the next row of the least squares matrix and the corresponding component of y .

```
      DO 30 I = 1, N
         CALL GETXY(X,Y)
         CALL SCHUD(R,LDR,P,X,Z,P,1,Y,RHO,C,S)
   30 CONTINUE
```

In this example we are processing only one vector y ; however, if there are more, they should be processed at this time, since otherwise the reduction of X will have to be entirely redone.

The last step is to generate the least squares solution $b = R^{-1}z$. This can be done by a call to STRSL , which will overwrite z by b . However, because z contains important information, we prefer to save it.

```
      DO 40 J = 1, P
         B(J) = Z(J)
   40 CONTINUE
      CALL STRSL(R,LDR,P,B,1,INFO)
```

The next example shows that SCHEX can be used to interchange two columns without disturbing the others. This is done by two calls: a right shift that puts column ℓ in column k followed by a left shift that puts column k (now in position $k+1$) into column ℓ and restores the other columns.

```
      CALL SCHEX(R,LDR,P,K,L,Z,P,1,C,S,1)
      IF (K+1 .NE. L)
     *   CALL SCHEX(R,LDR,P,K+1,L,Z,P,1,C,S,2)
```

The last example concerns the test of the hypothesis $b_k = 0$, where $k < p$. Under the usual statistical hypotheses, the quantity $(n-p)z_p^2/\rho^2$ is an F statistic that can be used to test the hypotheses $b_p = 0$. Thus to test the hypotheses $b_k = 0$, we need only move it to the last place. This gives the following sequence:

```
      CALL SCHEX(R,LDR,P,K,P,Z,P,1,C,S,1)
      F = FLOAT(N-P)*(Z(P)/RHO)**2
      CALL SCHEX(R,LDR,P,K,P,Z,P,1,C,S,2)
```

The last call to SCHEX restores the columns to their original order. Alternatively, the user can just remember the new order, say by recording it in an integer array.

4. Algorithmic Details

Plane rotations. The algorithms of this section are all implemented by a class of orthogonal transformations variously called plane rotations, Givens rotations, or Givens transformations. Accordingly, we start with a description of these transformations.

A plane rotation in the (i,j)-plane is a matrix of the form

$$U_{ij} = \begin{array}{c} \\ i \\ \\ j \\ \\ \end{array} \overset{\begin{array}{ccccc} & i & & j & \end{array}}{\begin{bmatrix} I & 0 & 0 & 0 & 0 \\ 0 & c & 0 & s & 0 \\ 0 & 0 & I & 0 & 0 \\ 0 & -s & 0 & c & 0 \\ 0 & 0 & 0 & 0 & I \end{bmatrix}},$$

where

(4.1) $$c^2 + s^2 = 1 .$$

Because of (4.1), we can write $c = \cos\phi$ and $s = \sin\phi$ for some angle ϕ. Geometrically, U_{ij} is a rotation counterclockwise through ϕ in the plane with the i-th unit vector as its x-axis and the j-th unit vector as its y-axis.

Computationally, plane rotations have two attractive features. First, a plane rotation is inexpensive to apply to a vector. In fact, if $w = U_{ij}v$, then

(4.2) $$\begin{aligned} w_i &= cv_i + sv_j , \\ w_j &= cv_j - sv_i , \\ w_k &= v_k \ (k \neq i,j) . \end{aligned}$$

Thus a plane rotation may be multiplied into a vector at a cost of two additions and four multiplications.

The second feature is that U_{ij} can be chosen to introduce a zero into the j-th component of a vector. If in (4.2) we set

$$c = \frac{v_i}{\sqrt{v_i^2+v_j^2}} , \qquad s = \frac{v_j}{\sqrt{v_i^2+v_j^2}} ,$$

then

$$\begin{aligned} w_i &= \sqrt{v_i^2+v_j^2} , \\ w_j &= 0 . \end{aligned}$$

Thus a sequence of rotations may be chosen to introduce zeros into a matrix; but not arbitrarily, since later rotations may destroy zeros introduced earlier.

Plane rotations may also be defined over the complex field, in which case the working 2 by 2 submatrix has the form

(4.3) $$\begin{bmatrix} c & s \\ -\bar{s} & c \end{bmatrix} .$$

The following algorithm generates a complex rotation of the form (4.3) such that

$$\begin{bmatrix} c & s \\ -\bar{s} & c \end{bmatrix}\begin{bmatrix} a \\ b \end{bmatrix} = \begin{bmatrix} \nu \\ 0 \end{bmatrix}.$$

Note that the resulting c is real, which saves operations when the rotation is applied.

```
if |a| = 0 then
  c := 0;
  s := 1;
  ν := b;
else
  σ = |a| + |b|;
  δ = σ(|a/σ|^2+|b/σ|^2)^(1/2);
  α = a/|a|;
  c = |a|/δ;
  s = αb̄/δ;
  ν = αδ;
end if;
```

The computation of δ has been arranged to avoid overflows and destructive underflows.

Basic relations. In all the algorithms of this section we start with the Cholesky factorization

$$\begin{bmatrix} A & c \\ c^T & \delta \end{bmatrix} = \begin{bmatrix} R^T & 0 \\ z^T & \rho \end{bmatrix}\begin{bmatrix} R & z \\ 0 & \rho \end{bmatrix}$$

and wish to obtain the factorization

$$\begin{bmatrix} \tilde{A} & \tilde{c} \\ \tilde{c}^T & \tilde{\delta} \end{bmatrix} = \begin{bmatrix} \tilde{R}^T & 0 \\ \tilde{z}^T & \tilde{\rho} \end{bmatrix}\begin{bmatrix} \tilde{R} & \tilde{z} \\ 0 & \tilde{\rho} \end{bmatrix}, \tag{4.4}$$

where $\tilde{A}$, $\tilde{c}$, and $\tilde{\delta}$ are the modified quantities. It follows from (4.4) that to show that any of the algorithms work, all we need show is that the quantities $\tilde{R}$, $\tilde{z}$, and $\tilde{\rho}$ produced by it satisfy

(4.5)

1. $\tilde{R}^T\tilde{R} = \tilde{A}$
2. $\tilde{R}^T\tilde{z} = \tilde{c}$
3. $\tilde{z}^T\tilde{z} + \tilde{\rho}^2 = \tilde{\delta}$.

Adding xx^T (SCHUD). In this case we have

$$\begin{bmatrix} \tilde{A} & \tilde{c} \\ \tilde{c}^T & \tilde{\delta} \end{bmatrix} = \begin{bmatrix} A & c \\ c^T & \delta \end{bmatrix} + \begin{bmatrix} x \\ \eta \end{bmatrix}\begin{bmatrix} x^T & \eta \end{bmatrix}$$

so that

$$\tilde{A} = A + xx^T$$

$$\tilde{c} = c + \eta x$$

$$\tilde{\delta} = \delta + \eta^2 .$$

To update the factorization we shall construct an orthogonal matrix U such that

$$U\begin{bmatrix} R & z \\ x^T & \eta \end{bmatrix} = \begin{bmatrix} \tilde{R} & \tilde{z} \\ 0 & \tilde{\delta} \end{bmatrix}$$

where R is upper triangular. We then define

$$\tilde{\rho}^2 = \rho^2 + \tilde{\delta}^2 .$$

To see that this will work, note that because U is orthogonal

$$\begin{bmatrix} R^T & x \\ z^T & \eta \end{bmatrix}\begin{bmatrix} R & z \\ x^T & \eta \end{bmatrix} = \begin{bmatrix} \tilde{R}^T & 0 \\ \tilde{z}^T & \tilde{\delta} \end{bmatrix}\begin{bmatrix} \tilde{R} & \tilde{z} \\ 0 & \tilde{\delta} \end{bmatrix}$$

Hence

1. $\tilde{R}^T\tilde{R} = R^TR+xx^T = A+xx^T = \tilde{A}$
2. $\tilde{R}^T\tilde{z} = R^Tz+\eta x = c+\eta x = \tilde{c}$
3. $\tilde{z}^T\tilde{z}+\tilde{\rho}^2 = \tilde{z}^T\tilde{z}+\tilde{\delta}^2+\rho^2 = z^Tz+\eta^2+\rho^2 = \delta+\eta^2 = \tilde{\delta}$.

Thus the basic relations (4.5) are satisfied, and $\tilde{R}$, $\tilde{z}$, and $\tilde{\rho}$ are the desired quantities.

The matrix U is computed as the product $U_p \ldots U_1$, where U_i is a rotation in the $(i,p+1)$-plane. Specifically consider the matrix

$$\begin{bmatrix} R \\ x^T \end{bmatrix}$$

illustrated here for $p = 4$:

$$\begin{bmatrix} r & r & r & r \\ 0 & r & r & r \\ 0 & 0 & r & r \\ 0 & 0 & 0 & r \\ (x) & x & x & x \end{bmatrix}$$

The rotation U_1 in the (1,5)-plane is determined to introduce a zero in the element circled above. After its application the matrix has the form

$$\begin{bmatrix} \tilde{r} & \tilde{r} & \tilde{r} & \tilde{r} \\ 0 & r & r & r \\ 0 & 0 & r & r \\ 0 & 0 & 0 & r \\ 0 & (x) & x & x \end{bmatrix}$$

The rotation U_2 in the (2,5)-plane is determined to introduce a zero into the (5,2)-element, and so on:

$$\begin{bmatrix} \tilde{r} & \tilde{r} & \tilde{r} & \tilde{r} \\ 0 & r & r & r \\ 0 & 0 & r & r \\ 0 & 0 & 0 & r \\ 0 & x & x & x \end{bmatrix} \xrightarrow{U_2} \begin{bmatrix} \tilde{r} & \tilde{r} & \tilde{r} & \tilde{r} \\ 0 & \tilde{r} & \tilde{r} & \tilde{r} \\ 0 & 0 & r & r \\ 0 & 0 & 0 & r \\ 0 & 0 & x & x \end{bmatrix} \xrightarrow{U_3} \begin{bmatrix} \tilde{r} & \tilde{r} & \tilde{r} & \tilde{r} \\ 0 & \tilde{r} & \tilde{r} & \tilde{r} \\ 0 & 0 & \tilde{r} & \tilde{r} \\ 0 & 0 & 0 & r \\ 0 & 0 & 0 & x \end{bmatrix} \xrightarrow{U_4} \begin{bmatrix} \tilde{r} & \tilde{r} & \tilde{r} & \tilde{r} \\ 0 & \tilde{r} & \tilde{r} & \tilde{r} \\ 0 & 0 & \tilde{r} & \tilde{r} \\ 0 & 0 & 0 & \tilde{r} \\ 0 & 0 & 0 & 0 \end{bmatrix} .$$

The rotations are multiplied into $(z^T,\eta)^T$, so that at the end

$$\begin{bmatrix} \tilde{z} \\ \tilde{\zeta} \end{bmatrix} = U_p U_{p-1} \cdots U_1 \begin{bmatrix} z \\ \eta \end{bmatrix} .$$

<u>Subtracting xx^T (SCHDD)</u>. In this case we have

$$\begin{bmatrix} \tilde{A} & \tilde{c} \\ \tilde{c}^T & \tilde{\delta} \end{bmatrix} = \begin{bmatrix} A & c \\ c^T & \delta \end{bmatrix} - \begin{bmatrix} x \\ \eta \end{bmatrix} \begin{bmatrix} x^T & \eta \end{bmatrix}$$

so that

$$\tilde{A} = A - xx^T$$

$$\tilde{c} = c - \eta x$$

$$\tilde{\delta} = \delta - \eta^2 .$$

To downdate the factorization we shall construct an orthogonal matrix U and a scalar ζ such that

$$U \begin{bmatrix} R & z \\ 0 & \zeta \end{bmatrix} = \begin{bmatrix} \tilde{R} & \tilde{z} \\ x^T & \eta \end{bmatrix} ,$$

where $\tilde{R}$ is upper triangular. If $\zeta \leq \rho$, we set

(4.6) $$\tilde{\rho} = \sqrt{\rho^2 - \zeta^2} .$$

To see that this will work, note that

(4.7) $$\begin{bmatrix} R^T & 0 \\ z^T & \zeta \end{bmatrix} \begin{bmatrix} R & z \\ 0 & \zeta \end{bmatrix} = \begin{bmatrix} \tilde{R}^T & x \\ \tilde{z}^T & \eta \end{bmatrix} \begin{bmatrix} \tilde{R} & \tilde{z} \\ x^T & \eta \end{bmatrix} .$$

We must now verify that the conditions (4.5) are satisfied.

1. From (4.7), $R^TR = \tilde{R}^T\tilde{R} + xx^T$. Hence
$$\tilde{R}^T\tilde{R} = R^TR - xx^T = A - xx^T = \tilde{A} .$$

2. From (4.7), $R^Tz = \tilde{R}^T\tilde{z} + \eta x$. Hence
$$\tilde{R}^T\tilde{z} = R^Tz - \eta x = c - \eta x = \tilde{c} .$$

3. From (4.7), $z^Tz + \zeta^2 = \tilde{z}^T\tilde{z} + \eta^2$. Hence from (4.6)
$$\tilde{z}^T\tilde{z} + \tilde{\rho}^2 = z^Tz + \zeta^2 - \eta^2 + \tilde{\rho}^2$$
$$= z^Tz + \rho^2 - \eta^2 = \delta - \eta^2 = \tilde{\delta} .$$

The calculation of U is done as follows:

1: solve the system $R^T a = x$;

2: <u>if</u> $\|a\|_2 \geq 1$ <u>then</u> quit;

3: $\alpha := \sqrt{1-\|a\|_2^2}$;

4: determine rotations $U_1, U_2, \ldots, U_p$, with U_i in the (p+1,i)-plane so that

$$U_1 U_2 \ldots U_p \begin{bmatrix} a \\ \alpha \end{bmatrix} = \begin{bmatrix} 0 \\ 1 \end{bmatrix}; \tag{4.8}$$

5: form

$$\begin{bmatrix} \tilde{R} \\ \tilde{x}^T \end{bmatrix} = U_1 U_2 \ldots U_p \begin{bmatrix} R \\ 0 \end{bmatrix}; \tag{4.9}$$

In order to justify this algorithm, we must show three things. First, it must be established that $\|a\| < 1$ is a necessary condition for the downdating to be possible (that it is sufficient will be established by the fact that the algorithm works). Second, we must show how to compute the transformations in step 4. Finally, we must show that the calculation in step 5 yields an upper triangular $\tilde{R}$ with $\tilde{x} = x$.

We first show that if $\|a\| > 1$, then $A - xx^T$ is not positive definite. We have

$$A - xx^T = R^T R - xx^T = R^T(I-aa^T)R .$$

Now if $\|a\| \geq 1$, $I - aa^T$ has the nonpositive eigenvalue $1 - \|a\|^2$, and $R^T(I-aa^T)R$ is not positive definite.

The following sequence illustrates for $p = 3$ the order in which zeros are introduced in step 4.

$$\begin{bmatrix} a \\ a \\ a \\ \alpha \end{bmatrix} \xrightarrow{U_3} \begin{bmatrix} a \\ a \\ 0 \\ \alpha \end{bmatrix} \xrightarrow{U_2} \begin{bmatrix} a \\ 0 \\ 0 \\ \alpha \end{bmatrix} \xrightarrow{U_1} \begin{bmatrix} 0 \\ 0 \\ 0 \\ \alpha \end{bmatrix} .$$

The final value of α must be unity, since

$$\left\| U_1 U_2 \ldots U_p \begin{bmatrix} a \\ \alpha \end{bmatrix} \right\|_2 = \left\| \begin{bmatrix} a \\ \alpha \end{bmatrix} \right\|_2 = 1 .$$

The fact that $\tilde{R}$ is upper triangular follows from the structure of the rotations U_i . In particular if r_j and $\tilde{r}_j$ denote the j-th columns of R and $\tilde{R}$, then because the last $p-j$ elements of r_j are zero:

$$\begin{bmatrix} r_j \\ x_j \end{bmatrix} = U_1 \ldots U_p \begin{bmatrix} r_j \\ 0 \end{bmatrix} = U_1 \ldots U_j \begin{bmatrix} r_j \\ 0 \end{bmatrix}, \tag{4.10}$$

and the remaining rotations leave the zero elements in positions $j+1, \ldots, p$ undisturbed. That $\tilde{x} = x$ follows from (4.9) and (4.10). Specifically, since $U = U_1 \ldots U_p$ is orthogonal.

$$x = (R^T\ 0)\begin{bmatrix} a \\ \alpha \end{bmatrix} = (R^T\ 0)U^TU\begin{bmatrix} a \\ \alpha \end{bmatrix}$$

$$= (\tilde{R}^T\ \tilde{x})\begin{bmatrix} 0 \\ 1 \end{bmatrix} = \tilde{x}\ .$$

We cannot determine z and ρ, as we did in the updating algorithm, by multiplying by U, since they occur on opposite sides of equation (4.6). Instead we apply the following algorithm:

(4.11)

$\zeta_1 := \eta;$

<u>loop</u> <u>for</u> $i = 1,2,\ldots,p$

  $\tilde{z}_i := (z_i - s_i\zeta_i)/c_i;$

  $\zeta_{i+1} := c_i\zeta_i - s_i\tilde{z}_i;$

<u>end</u> <u>loop</u>;

$\zeta := \zeta_{p+1};$

Here c_i and s_i are the sines and cosines that determine U_i.

This algorithm is well defined, since $\alpha > 0$ implies that all the c_i are nonzero. To see that it produces the required quantities, note that the formulas inside the loop are equivalent to

$$U_i^T\begin{bmatrix} \tilde{z}_1 \\ \vdots \\ \tilde{z}_{i-1} \\ \tilde{z}_i \\ \vdots \\ z_p \\ \zeta_i \end{bmatrix} = \begin{bmatrix} \tilde{z}_1 \\ \vdots \\ \tilde{z}_{i-1} \\ z_i \\ \vdots \\ z_p \\ \zeta_{i+1} \end{bmatrix}.$$

Hence

$$U_p^T \cdots U_1^T\begin{bmatrix} \tilde{z} \\ \eta \end{bmatrix} = \begin{bmatrix} z \\ \zeta \end{bmatrix},$$

as required.

<u>Permutations (SCHEX)</u>. In this case we have

$$\begin{bmatrix} \tilde{A} & \tilde{c} \\ \tilde{c}^T & \tilde{\delta} \end{bmatrix} = \begin{bmatrix} E^TAE & E^Tc \\ c^TE & \delta \end{bmatrix}$$

so that

$$\tilde{A} = E^TAE$$

$$\tilde{c} = E^Tc$$

$$\tilde{\delta} = \delta\ .$$

To update the factorization we shall compute an orthogonal transformation U such that

$$\begin{bmatrix} U & 0 \\ 0 & 1 \end{bmatrix}\begin{bmatrix} RE & z \\ 0 & \rho \end{bmatrix} = \begin{bmatrix} \tilde{R} & \tilde{z} \\ 0 & \rho \end{bmatrix},$$

where $\tilde{R}$ is upper triangular.

To see that this works, note that

$$\begin{bmatrix} E^TR^T & 0 \\ z^T & \rho \end{bmatrix}\begin{bmatrix} RE & z \\ 0 & \rho \end{bmatrix} = \begin{bmatrix} \tilde{R}^T & 0 \\ \tilde{z}^T & \rho \end{bmatrix}\begin{bmatrix} \tilde{R} & \tilde{z} \\ 0 & \rho \end{bmatrix}.$$

Hence

1. $\tilde{R}^T\tilde{R} = E^TR^TRE = E^TAE = \tilde{A}$.
2. $\tilde{R}^T\tilde{z} = E^TR^Tz = E^Tc = \tilde{c}$.
3. $\tilde{z}^T\tilde{z}+\rho^2 = z^Tz+\rho^2 = \delta = \tilde{\delta}$.

Thus the basic relations (4.5) are satisfied. Note that ρ is not changed by the updating.

Two kinds of permutations are treated here. A right circular shift among columns k through ℓ and a left circular shift among columns k through ℓ. In both cases the algorithms will be sufficiently well illustrated for the case $p = 6$, $k = 2$, and $\ell = 5$.

For the right circular shift, the matrix RE assumes the form

$$\begin{bmatrix} x & x & x & x & x & x \\ 0 & x & x & x & x & x \\ 0 & x^3 & 0^3 & x & x & x \\ 0 & x^2 & 0 & 0^2 & x & x \\ 0 & x^1 & 0 & 0 & 0^1 & x \\ 0 & 0 & 0 & 0 & 0 & x \end{bmatrix} \tag{4.12}$$

To reduce RE to triangular form, the elements x^i are successively annihilated by rotations U_i in the $(\ell-i,\ell-i+1)$-plane. The application of U_i introduces a nonzero element on the diagonal at the position labeled 0^i; however, the final matrix $\tilde{R}$ is upper triangular. The rotations are multiplied into z to yield $\tilde{z}$.

For the left circular shift, the matrix RE assumes the form

$$\begin{bmatrix} x & x & x & x & x & x \\ 0 & x & x & x & x & x \\ 0 & x^1 & x & x & 0 & x \\ 0 & 0 & x^2 & x & 0 & x \\ 0 & 0 & 0 & x^3 & 0 & x \\ 0 & 0 & 0 & 0 & 0 & x \end{bmatrix} \tag{4.13}$$

To reduce RE to triangular form, the elements labeled x^i are successively annihilated by rotations U_i in the $(k+i-1,k+i)$-plane. The final matrix $\tilde{R}$ is upper triangular. The rotations are multiplied into z to yield $\tilde{z}$.

5. Programming Details

In implementing the algorithms of the last section, we have been guided by two considerations: first to access the array R by columns and second to avoid referencing elements below the diagonal of R . These constraints, especially the first, have complicated the programs somewhat. In particular, the user is required to provide storage via the calling sequence for the sines and cosines that determine the transformations (but note that the downdating algorithm requires that the rotations be saved, no matter how it is implemented).

SCHUD. In outline SCHUD goes as follows:

```
1   : loop for j := 1,2,...,p
1.1 :    apply U_1,U_2,...,U_{j-1} to column j;
1.2 :    determine U_j;
1   : end loop;
2   : loop for j := 1,2,...,NZ
2.1 :    apply U_1,U_2,...,U_p to (z_j^T,y_j)^T;
2.2 :    update ρ_j;
2   : end loop;
```

The following is an elaboration of this outline:

1. The index j points to the column of R being processed.

1.1. This is skipped when $j = 1$. During the application of the rotations, the component x_j of x^T is stored and modified in XJ .

1.2. The BLAS subroutine SROTG determines the j-th rotation as the one annihilating XJ in the pair (R(J,J),XJ) .

2. If NZ is zero, this section of code is skipped.

2.1. The value of y is stored in ZETA for updating. At the end ZETA contains $\tilde{\zeta}$.

2.2. This updating is not done if $\rho < 0$. Special care is taken to handle overflows and underflows.

SCHDD. In outline SCHDD goes as follows:

```
1   : solve the triangular system R^T a = x;
2   : if ||a|| ≥ 1 then
2.1 :    INFO := -1;
2.2 :    return;
```

2 : <u>end</u> <u>if</u>;
3 : $\alpha = \sqrt{1-\|a\|^2}$;
4 : reduce $(a^T,\alpha)^T$;
5 : <u>loop</u> <u>for</u> j := 1,2,...,p
5.1 :   apply the rotations to $(r_j^T,0)^T$;
5 : <u>end</u> <u>loop</u>;
6 : <u>loop</u> <u>for</u> j := 1,2,...,NZ
6.1 :   apply the rotations to z_j and ζ;
6.2 :   <u>if</u> $\rho_j < \zeta$ <u>then</u>
6.2.1:   INFO := 1;
6.2.2: ρ_j := -1;
6.2 :   <u>else</u>
6.2.3: $\rho_j := \sqrt{\rho_j^2-\zeta^2}$;
6.2 :   <u>end</u> <u>if</u>;
6 : <u>end</u> <u>loop</u>;

The following is an elaboration of this outline.

<u>1</u>. The solution is accumulated in the array S .

<u>2</u>. If $\|a\| \geq 1$, then $R^TR - xx^T$ is indefinite, and the downdate cannot be effected.

<u>3,4</u>. The reduction of $(a^T,\alpha)^T$ to $(0,1)^T$ is described in section 4. Because the final vector must be nonnegative, the subroutine SROTG is not used to generate the rotations. The cosines and sines are stored in S and C .

<u>5</u>. As is indicated by (4.10), only the first j rotations need be applied to r_j . The (p+1)-element is represented by XX .

<u>6</u>. This is skipped if NZ = 0 .

<u>6.1</u>. This is done according to (4.11). The ζ_j's are accumulated in ZETA , which is initialized to Y(J) .

<u>6.2</u>. The downdating of the residual norm cannot be done if $\rho_j < \zeta$. In this case INFO is set to unity and RHO(J) to -1 , so that the user will know which were the offending pairs (z,η) . Otherwise, ρ is downdated, with the usual precautions being taken against overflows and destructive underflows.

<u>SCHEX</u>. The permuted forms (4.12) and (4.13) have elements below the diagonal of R . In order to avoid referencing any subdiagonal element of the array in which R is stored,

these elements are saved in the array S until they are needed. We will consider the two kinds of shifts separately.

The right circular shift consists of four stages:

1 : reorder the columns;

2 : calculate the rotations;

3 : <u>loop</u> for j := k+1,p

3.1 : apply the rotations to column j of R;

3 : <u>end</u> <u>loop</u>;

4 : apply the rotations to z;

1. In reordering the columns, the elements $r_{1\ell}, r_{2\ell}, \ldots, r_{\ell\ell}$ are moved into $s_\ell, s_{\ell-1}, \ldots, s_1$ respectively. The columns are then shifted right, and the elements $s_\ell, s_{\ell-1}, \ldots, s_{\ell-k+2}$ are moved into $r_{1k}, r_{2k}, \ldots, r_{k-1,k}$. This leaves the elements that determine $U_1, U_2, \ldots, U_{\ell-k}$ in $s_1, s_2, \ldots, s_{\ell-k}$.

2. The rotations are determined in a straightforward manner by SROTG .

3. For $j < \ell$, only rotations $U_{\ell-j+1}, U_{\ell-j+2}, \ldots, U_{\ell-k}$ must be applied. Thereafter all the rotations must be applied.

4. This is not done if NZ = 0 .

The left circular shift differs from the right in that the rotations $U_1, U_2, \ldots, U_{j-k}$ be applied to column j before U_{j-k+1} can be determined. The outline is as follows:

1 : rearrange the columns;

2 : <u>loop</u> <u>for</u> j := k,k+1,...,p

2.1 : <u>if</u> j > k <u>then</u> apply the rotations to r_j; <u>fi</u>;

2.2 : <u>if</u> $j < \ell$ <u>then</u> determine $U_{j-k+\ell}$; <u>fi</u>;

2 : <u>end</u> <u>loop</u>;

3 : apply the rotations to z;

1. The array S is used as temporary storage during the rearrangement. At the end the subdiagonal elements occupy positions S(1),...,S(L-K) .

2. The index variable points to the column being processed.

2.1. If $k < j < \ell$ then only rotations $U_1, U_2, \ldots, U_{j-k+1}$ are applied.

3. This is not done if NZ = 0 .

6. Performance

Operation counts. The following operation counts are asymptotically correct for increasing p. They do not include indexing and looping overhead, which can account for a considerable fraction of the total execution time. However, this overhead is proportional to the number of floating point operations, so that the operation counts accurately reflect the order of the growth in work with increasing p.

We have also included the number of plane rotations generated by the algorithms. Although the work due to generating plane rotations is asymptotically negligible, for smaller values of p -- certainly for $p \leq 10$ -- it is significant.

The operation counts for SCHUD are:

$2p^2$ floating-point multiplications,

p^2 floating-point additions,

p rotation generations.

Each vector z updated by SCHUD requires

$4p$ floating-point multiplications,

$2p$ floating-point additions.

The operation counts for SCHDD are

$\frac{5}{2}p^2$ floating-point multiplications,

$\frac{3}{2}p^2$ floating-point additions,

p rotation generations.

Each vector z downdated by SCHDD requires

$3p$ floating-point multiplications,

p floating-point divisions,

$2p$ floating-point additions.

The operation counts for SCHEX depend on k and ℓ, which determine which columns are shifted, and they do not depend on JOB . They are

$4\left[p - \frac{1}{2}(\ell+k)\right](\ell-k)$ floating-point multiplications,

$4\left[p - \frac{1}{2}(\ell+k)\right](\ell-k)$ floating-point additions,

$\ell-k$ rotation generations.

Each vector z updated by SCHEX requires

$4(\ell-k)$ floating-point multiplications,

$2(\ell-k)$ floating-point additions.

<u>Timings</u>. Extensive timing runs have been made on SCHUD , SCHDD , and SCHEX . The execution times vary widely from machine to machine and from compiler to compiler on a given machine. In order to simplify this mass of raw data, we present not the times, but their ratios to the time required by a simple process of comparable magnitude (e.g. a matrix multiplication of appropriate order). This process dramatically reduces the variation across machines and systems.* The price to be paid is that the user cannot obtain actual execution times from these data, only an idea of how much more it will cost him to do the computation in question than another conceptually simpler computation. However, we feel that the user who needs actual execution times should measure them himself, since minor changes in a computer system can have a great effect on the times.

The standard of comparison for the routines of this chapter is the time required to compute $A + xx^T$. This has a p^2 multiplication count, which is of the same order as the operation counts given above.

The ratios for SCHUD are summarized in Table 1. In addition to means of ratios across machines, we give their standard deviations in parentheses. The ratios decrease from about 5.8 for $p = 5$ to 2.3 for $p = 100$. We have also included ratios for NZ = 10 , to give some idea of the marginal cost of updating individual vectors. The relative increment decreases strongly with increasing p .

Table 2 presents the mean ratios for SCHDD . As might be expected from the operation counts, the ratios are higher; otherwise, SCHDD behaves much like SCHUD .

The mean ratios for SCHEX are given in Table 3. These will, of course, vary with k and ℓ , and here we give ratios for $k = 1$, $\ell = p$ and $k \cong p/3$, $\ell \cong 2p/3$, the latter being regarded as a "typical" use of SCHEX . The ratios decrease, as expected, with increasing p .

<u>The effects of rounding error</u>. Since the subroutines of this section may be applied repeatedly to a single matrix, it is important to have an idea of how rounding errors accumulate. The interpretation of the results of rounding-error analyses depends on whether one is concerned with the Cholesky decomposition of A or one is manipulating the

---

*Machines designed to perform vector operations with high efficiency are exceptional in that they tend to give higher ratios than their more pedestrian counterparts. For this reason, we have excluded them from the summary below. For a fuller discussion of this phenomenon, see Chapter 1.

Table 1
(SCHUD)/$(A+xx^T)$

NZ \ p	5	10	25	50	75	100
0	5.6 (1.8)	3.8 (1.3)	2.6 (1.3)	2.2 (1.4)	2.0 (1.3)	2.0 (1.4)
10	15.5 (3.9)	7.9 (2.2)	4.2 (1.9)	2.9 (1.9)	2.5 (1.6)	2.4 (1.7)

Table 2
(SCHDD)/$(A+xx^T)$

NZ \ p	5	10	25	50	75	100
0	7.5 (2.1)	5.1 (1.6)	3.3 (1.4)	3.2 (1.6)	2.6 (1.5)	2.6 (1.7)
10	16.3 (5.4)	8.9 (3.0)	4.9 (2.3)	3.6 (2.2)	3.1 (1.9)	2.9 (2.0)

Table 3
(SCHEX)/$(A+xx^T)$

Right Circular Shift

p	5	10	25	50	75	100
$k = 1$ $\ell = p$	6.3 (1.7)	4.6 (1.2)	3.5 (.96)	3.0 (.93)	2.7 (.82)	2.6 (.76)
$k = \frac{1}{3}p$ $\ell = \frac{2}{3}p$	3.5 (1.1)	2.2 (.57)	1.3 (.36)	1.1 (.32)	.95 (.28)	.90 (.24)

Left Circular Shift

p	5	10	25	50	75	100
$k = 1$ $\ell = p$	6.3 (1.9)	4.6 (1.3)	3.5 (1.0)	2.9 (.96)	2.7 (.84)	2.6 (.73)
$k = \frac{1}{3}p$ $\ell = \frac{2}{3}p$	3.7 (1.2)	2.2 (.63)	1.3 (3.7)	1.1 (.33)	.93 (.33)	.90 (.30)

QR factorization of a matrix X . In what follows, $\tilde{R}$ and $\bar{R}$ denote respectively exact and computed matrices after the update with a similar convention for $\tilde{A} = \tilde{R}^T\tilde{R}$, $\phi(p)$ is used generically for a slowly growing function of p (e.g. p^2); and ε_M is the rounding unit for the computer in question.

For SCHUD and SCHEX the computed value $\bar{R}$ satisfies

$$\bar{A} \equiv \bar{R}^T\bar{R} = \tilde{A}+E$$

where

$$\frac{\|E\|_2}{\|\tilde{A}\|_2} \le \phi(p)\cdot\varepsilon_M .$$

Thus the computed Cholesky factor is the Cholesky factor of a matrix near $\tilde{A}$. It follows that rounding errors will accumulate rather slowly over repeated applications of the algorithm.

For SCHDD the error matrix E satisfies

$$\frac{\|E\|_2}{\|\tilde{A}\|_2} \le \phi(p)\,\frac{\|A\|_2}{\|\tilde{A}\|_2}\cdot\varepsilon_M .$$

This result is not as nice; for if $\tilde{A}$ is appreciably smaller than A , the matrix $\bar{A}$ can be quite inaccurate.

If SCHUD and SCHEX are used to update the triangular part of the QR factorization of a matrix, it can be shown that there is an orthogonal matrix Q such that

$$Q^T(\tilde{X}+E) = \begin{bmatrix} \bar{R} \\ 0 \end{bmatrix},$$

where

$$\frac{\|E\|_2}{\|X\|_2} \le \phi(p)\cdot\varepsilon_M .$$

Thus $\bar{R}$ is the triangular part of the QR factorization of a slight perturbation of $\tilde{X}$.

There is no nice backward error analysis for the use of SCHDD to remove a row from X . The best we can say is that $\bar{R}$ is very near the result that would be obtained by removing x^T+e^T from X , where

$$\frac{\|e\|_2}{\|x\|_2} \le \phi(p)\cdot\varepsilon_M .$$

Unfortunately, this does not imply that $\bar{R}$ is stably computed. Even worse, if $\kappa(\bar{R})$ is of order $1/\sqrt{\varepsilon_M}$ or bigger, the downdating algorithm may fail entirely. We stress that these limitations are intrinsic to the problem; no other algorithm can be expected to do better.

7. Notes and References

The idea of updating goes back at least to the early days of linear programming, where the object in question was the inverse of the matrix of active constraints (see [Dantzig, 1963]). The numerical difficulties entailed by working with the inverse led Bartels (1971) to propose that the LU factorization be updated instead. Further extensions of this idea have been investigated in works by Gill, Golub, Murray, and Saunders (1974), Gill, Murray, and Saunders (1975), Lawson and Hanson (1974), and Daniel, Gragg, Kaufman, and Stewart (1976), to name a few.

The updating algorithm used here is due to Golub (1965). The downdating algorithm is due to Saunders (1972), with slight extensions to accommodate the downdating of least squares problems. The specific algorithm for updating after permutations is new; however, the basic ideas may be found in Daniel et al. (1976).

The subroutines of this section are particularly useful in dealing with least squares problems having too many rows to fit in the high speed memory of the computer, since for many applications all that is required is that R, z, and ρ be known. In particular, Golub and Styan (1973) show how updating routines can be used in a variety of statistical applications.

Because of the close connection between the Cholesky factorization and the QR factorization, the algorithms of this chapter may be regarded as updating half of the QR factorization. A serious omission is our failure to provide LINPACK subroutines in the spirit of Daniel, et al. (1976) to update the entire QR factorization. Such subroutines, though more expensive in storage and operations, would allow the user to downdate stably and have easy access to the individual elements of projections.

The rounding-error analyses of SCHUD and SCHEX are simple extensions of results that have already appeared in the literature (e.g. [Wilkinson, 1965]). Stewart (1977b) has given a detailed rounding-error analysis of the algorithms in SCHDD.

Chapter 11: The Singular Value Decomposition

Subroutine: SSVDC

1. Overview

Purpose. SSVDC is a subroutine to compute the singular value decomposition of a real n by p matrix X.

Background. Let X be a real n by p matrix. Then there is an n by n orthogonal matrix U and a p by p orthogonal matrix V such that U^TXV assumes one of the two following forms:

$$(1.1)\qquad \begin{aligned} &1.\quad U^TXV = \begin{bmatrix} \Sigma \\ 0 \end{bmatrix} \quad \text{if } n \geq p , \\ &2.\quad U^TXV = [\Sigma\ 0] \quad \text{if } n \leq p . \end{aligned}$$

Here

$$\Sigma = \operatorname{diag}(\sigma_1,\sigma_2,\ldots,\sigma_m) ,$$

where $m = \min\{n,p\}$, and

$$\sigma_1 \geq \sigma_2 \geq \cdots \geq \sigma_m \geq 0 .$$

The decomposition (1.1) is called the singular value decomposition of X. The scalars $\sigma_1,\sigma_2,\ldots,\sigma_m$ are the singular values of X. The columns of U are the left singular vectors of X and the columns of V are the right singular vectors of X.

When $n >> p$, it is impractical to store all the matrix U. However, if we partition U in the form

$$U = (U_1,U_2) ,$$

where U_1 has p columns, then

$$X = U_1\Sigma V^T .$$

This decomposition will be called the singular value factorization of the matrix X, and in many applications it is all that is needed. When $n \geq p$, SSVDC allows for the computation of this factorization instead of the complete decomposition.

For definiteness, we shall assume that $n \geq p$ in the rest of this section, the extensions to the case $n < p$ being trivial.

Rank determination. If X is of rank $k < p$, then the singular values of X satisfy

$$\sigma_1 \geq \cdots \geq \sigma_k > \sigma_{k+1} = \cdots = \sigma_p = 0 .$$

Conversely, if $\sigma_k \neq 0$ and $\sigma_{k+1} = \ldots = \sigma_p = 0$, then X is of rank k. Thus the singular value decomposition can be used to determine the rank of a matrix.

In practice one will seldom compute singular values that are exactly zero, and one is left with the problem of deciding when a singular value is near enough to zero to be negligible. Since the singular values of X change under different scalings of the rows and columns of X, it is important that X be scaled properly before its singular value decomposition is computed. We suggest the following strategy (for more details see the introduction to this guide).

First estimate the errors in the elements of the matrix X (if X is known exactly, take the error in x_{ij} to be a small multiple of $x_{ij} \cdot \varepsilon_M$, where ε_M is the rounding unit for the computer in question). Scale the rows and columns of X so that the error estimates are approximately equal to a common value ε. Then consider σ_j to be negligible if $\sigma_j < \varepsilon$. (N.b. in least squares problems, row scaling may represent an impermissible change of model.)

Projections. If X has rank k and we partition U_1 in the form

$$U_1 = (U_1^{(1)}, U_2^{(1)}) ,$$

where $U_1^{(1)}$ is n by k, then the columns of $U_1^{(1)}$ form an orthonormal basis for the column space of X. Consequently, the orthogonal projection onto the column space of X is given by

$$P_X = U_1^{(1)} U_1^{(1)T} . \tag{1.2}$$

The projection onto the orthogonal complement is given by

$$P_X^{\perp} = (U_2^{(1)}, U_2)(U_2^{(1)}, U_2)^T . \tag{1.3}$$

Likewise if V is partitioned in the form

$$V = (V_1, V_2)$$

where V_1 is p by k, then the columns of V_1 form an orthonormal basis for the row space of X. Consequently, the orthogonal projection onto the row space of X is given by

$$R_X = V_1 V_1^T$$

and the complementary projection by

$$R_X^{\perp} = V_2 V_2^T .$$

Least squares. The singular value decomposition can be used to compute solutions to the least squares problem of determining a vector b such that

$$\rho = \|y-Xb\| \tag{1.4}$$

is minimized (here $\|\cdot\|$ denotes the usual Euclidean vector norm). Specifically, let X be of rank k and let U and V be partitioned as above. Let Σ be partitioned in the form

$$\Sigma = \mathrm{diag}(\Sigma_1, \Sigma_2) ,$$

where Σ_1 is k by k. Then the general form of a solution to the least squares problem is

$$b_w = V_1\Sigma_1^{-1}U_1^{(1)T}y + V_2w \tag{1.5}$$

where w is arbitrary. Of all solutions, b_0 is the one for which $\|b_w\|$ is smallest.

Since the vector Xb is given by

$$Xb = P_Xy$$

and the residual vector $r = y-Xb$ is given by

$$r = P_X^{\perp}y ,$$

these quantities can be computed directly from the singular value decomposition via (1.2) and (1.3).

The pseudo-inverse. If X is of rank k, the pseudo-inverse of X is the matrix

$$X^{\dagger} = V_1\Sigma_1^{-1}U_1^{(1)T} .$$

From (1.5) it is seen that for any vector y, $X^{\dagger}y$ is the minimum norm solution of the least squares problem (1.4). We warn the user that although the pseudo-inverse occurs frequently in the literature of various fields, there is seldom any need to compute it explicitly. For example, least squares solutions are better computed directly from (1.5).

Condition numbers. If X is judged to be of rank k, it is natural to solve least squares problems involving X by setting the last $p-k$ singular values to zero -- that is by applying (1.5) with $w = 0$. The question then arises of how a solution so computed varies with perturbations in X. The question can be answered in terms of the condition number

$$\kappa_k(X) = \sigma_1/\sigma_k .$$

Let $\|\cdot\|$ denote the spectral matrix norm defined by

$$\|X\| = \sup_{\|x\|=1} \|Xx\| .$$

Let E be a perturbation of X satisfying

$$\sigma_k \geq 10\|E\| > \|E\| > \sigma_{k+1} .$$

Let b_0 be the solution computed from (1.5) and let $\bar{b}_0$ be the solution computed analogously for X+E . Then

$$\frac{\|b_0-\bar{b}_0\|}{\|b_0\|} \leq 9\left[\kappa_k(X) + \kappa_k^2(X)\frac{\|r\|}{\|X\|\,\|b_0\|}\right]\frac{\|E\|}{\|X\|} , \tag{1.6}$$

where r denotes the residual $r = y-Xb_0$. We stress that this bound may be unrealistic unless X has been scaled as described above so that the elements of E are approximately equal.

2. Usage

The calling sequence for SSVDC is

CALL SSVDC(X,LDX,N,P,S,E,U,LDU,V,LDV,WORK,JOB,INFO)

On entry

X is a doubly subscripted array of dimension (LDX,P) containing the n by p matrix X whose singular value decomposition is to be computed.

LDX is the leading dimension of the array X .

N is the number of rows of the matrix X .

P is an integer containing the number of columns of the matrix X .

LDU is the leading dimension of U .

LDV is the leading dimension of V .

WORK is a work array of dimension at least N .

JOB is an integer that controls the computation of the singular vectors. It has the decimal expansion AB with the following meaning:

A = 0 do not compute the left singular vectors;

A = 1 compute all n left singular vectors;

A > 1 compute the first min{n,p} left singular vectors (i.e. the singular value factorization described in section 1);

B = 0 do not compute the right singular vectors;

B > 0 compute the right singular vectors.

On return

S is an array of dimension min{N+1,P} that ordinarily contains the singular values of X arranged in descending order of magnitude. However, see the discussion of INFO for exceptions.

E — is an array of dimension P that ordinarily contains zeros. However, see the discussion of INFO for exceptions.

U — is an array of dimension (LDU,M) where M=N if JOB $\le$ 11 and M = min{N,P} if JOB $\ge$ 20. U contains the left singular vectors if their computation has been requested. Whenever the request would allow the vectors to be stored in X (N $\le$ P or JOB $\ge$ 20), U may be identified with X in the calling sequence. U is not referenced if the computation of left singular vectors has not been requested.

V — is an array of dimension (LDV,P) that contains the right singular vectors if their computation has been requested. If N $\ge$ P , then V may be identified with X in the calling sequence. V is not referenced if the computation of right singular vectors has not been requested.

INFO — The singular values S(INFO+1),S(INFO+2),...,S(M) , where M=MIN(N,P) are correct. Thus if INFØ=0 , all the singular values have been computed correctly. Otherwise the singular values of X are those of the upper bidiagonal matrix with S as its diagonal and E as its super diagonal.

At most one of the arrays U and V may be identified with X in the calling sequence.

3. Examples

In the examples below the following specifications are assumed.

```
DIMENSION X(25,15),U(20,20),V(15,15),S(25),E(25),QRAUX(25),WORK(25)
LDX = 25
LDU = 20
LDV = 15
```

1. The following calling sequence computes the singular values of a 15 by 10 matrix contained in the array X . The left singular vectors are returned in the array U , and the right singular vectors overwrite X .

```
CALL SSVDC(X,LDX,15,10,S,E,U,LDU,X,LDX,WORK,11,INFO)
```

2. The following calling sequence computes the singular values of a 20 by 9 matrix contained in the array X . The first nine left singular vectors overwrite X .

```
CALL SSVDC(X,LDX,20,9,S,E,X,LDX,DUM,IDUM,WORK,20,INFO)
```

3. In some applications where $n >> p$, it is only required to compute the right singular vectors. In this case the LINPACK subroutine SQRDC should be used to reduce X initially to triangular form R. Since the right singular vectors of X and R are the same, one can then compute them from the smaller matrix R. Code for this computation might go as follows for a N by P matrix contained in X.

```
      CALL SQRDC(X,LDX,N,P,QRAUX,IDUM,DUM,0)
      DO 20 I=1,P
         DO 10 J=I,P
            V(J,I)=0.
            V(I,J)=X(I,J)
   10    CONTINUE
   20 CONTINUE
      CALL SSVDC(V,LDV,P,P,S,E,DUM,IDUM,V,LDV,WORK,01,INFO)
```

It should be noted that after this calculation the arrays X and QRAUX contain information required by SQRSL to solve least squares problems and perform other manipulations involving the column space of X ; for further information see the documentation for SQRDC and SQRSL .

4. Algorithmic Details

SSVDC reduces the matrix X to diagonal form by a sequence of orthogonal equivalence transformations of the form

$$X := U^T X V .$$

The reduction is divided into two distinct parts. In the first part, X is reduced to a bidiagonal form illustrated below for $n=6$ and $p=4$:

$$\begin{bmatrix} x & x & 0 & 0 \\ 0 & x & x & 0 \\ 0 & 0 & x & x \\ 0 & 0 & 0 & x \\ 0 & 0 & 0 & 0 \\ 0 & 0 & 0 & 0 \end{bmatrix}$$

The second part consists of the iterative reduction of the bidiagonal form to diagonal form by a variant of the QR algorithm.

Reduction to bidiagonal form. The reduction to bidiagonal form is accomplished by means of Householder transformations. The details of generating and applying Householder transformations are discussed in the documentation for the programs SQRDC and SQRSL . Here we will outline the steps that lead to the bidiagonal form, for the case $n=6$ and $p=5$.

Initially X has the form

$$
\begin{bmatrix}
x & x & x & x & x \\
\textcircled{x} & x & x & x & x \\
\textcircled{x} & x & x & x & x \\
\textcircled{x} & x & x & x & x \\
\textcircled{x} & x & x & x & x \\
\textcircled{x} & x & x & x & x
\end{bmatrix} . \tag{4.1}
$$

A Householder transformation U_1 is chosen so that premultiplying it into X introduces zeros into the elements circled in (4.1). Thus U_1X has the form

$$
\begin{bmatrix}
x & x & \textcircled{x} & \textcircled{x} & \textcircled{x} \\
0 & x & x & x & x \\
0 & x & x & x & x \\
0 & x & x & x & x \\
0 & x & x & x & x \\
0 & x & x & x & x
\end{bmatrix} . \tag{4.2}
$$

Next a Householder transformation V_1 is chosen so that postmultiplying it to X introduces zeros into the elements circled in (4.2). Thus U_1XV_1 has the form

$$
\begin{bmatrix}
x & x & 0 & 0 & 0 \\
0 & x & x & \textcircled{x} & \textcircled{x} \\
0 & \textcircled{x} & x & x & x \\
0 & \textcircled{x} & x & x & x \\
0 & \textcircled{x} & x & x & x \\
0 & \textcircled{x} & x & x & x
\end{bmatrix} .
$$

Now U_2 is chosen to introduce zeros into the second column as indicated above; then V_2 is chosen to introduce zeros into the second row. The process continues with alternate pre- and postmultiplications to produce a sequence of matrices of the form

$$\begin{bmatrix} x & x & 0 & 0 & 0 \\ 0 & x & x & 0 & 0 \\ 0 & 0 & x & x & x \\ 0 & 0 & x & x & x \\ 0 & 0 & x & x & x \\ 0 & 0 & x & x & x \end{bmatrix} \rightarrow \begin{bmatrix} x & x & 0 & 0 & 0 \\ 0 & x & x & 0 & 0 \\ 0 & 0 & x & x & 0 \\ 0 & 0 & 0 & x & x \\ 0 & 0 & 0 & x & x \\ 0 & 0 & 0 & x & x \end{bmatrix} \rightarrow \begin{bmatrix} x & x & 0 & 0 & 0 \\ 0 & x & x & 0 & 0 \\ 0 & 0 & x & x & 0 \\ 0 & 0 & 0 & x & x \\ 0 & 0 & 0 & 0 & x \\ 0 & 0 & 0 & 0 & x \end{bmatrix} \rightarrow \begin{bmatrix} x & x & 0 & 0 & 0 \\ 0 & x & x & 0 & 0 \\ 0 & 0 & x & x & 0 \\ 0 & 0 & 0 & x & x \\ 0 & 0 & 0 & 0 & x \\ 0 & 0 & 0 & 0 & 0 \end{bmatrix}$$

If $p > n$, then the final matrix will have the form illustrated below for $n=4$ and $p=6$:

$$\begin{bmatrix} x & x & 0 & 0 & 0 & 0 \\ 0 & x & x & 0 & 0 & 0 \\ 0 & 0 & x & x & 0 & 0 \\ 0 & 0 & 0 & x & x & 0 \end{bmatrix} . \tag{4.3}$$

In general the final bidiagonal matrix is generated in the form

$$U_k \ldots U_2 U_1 X V_1 V_2 \ldots V_\ell$$

where $k = \min\{p,n-1\}$ and $\ell = \min\{n,p-2\}$. Since the information that determines a Householder transformation of order i may be stored in i locations, the transformations U_i and V_i may be stored in the array X, provided the elements of the bidiagonal matrix are moved to other arrays as they are generated. After the process has been completed, the transformations

$$\tilde{U} = U_1 U_2 \ldots U_k ,$$

$$\tilde{V} = V_1 V_2 \ldots V_\ell ,$$

may be explicitly calculated, so that $\tilde{U}^T X \tilde{V}$ is the final bidiagonal form.

The products of X and the V_i are calculated in a slightly unusual way in order to make the algorithm column oriented. Specifically, a typical transformation V has the form

$$I - \rho v v^T$$

where ρ is a scalar and v is a vector. If X is partitioned in the form $X = (x_1, x_2, \ldots, x_p)$, then

$$XV = X - \rho X v v^T = X - w v^T$$

where $w = \rho X v = \rho(v_1 x_1 + v_2 x_2 + \ldots + v_p x_p)$. Thus the column oriented algorithm for computing XV goes as follows:

$$1 : w := \rho(v_1x_1+v_2x_2+\ldots+v_px_p)$$
$$2 : x_j := x_j - v_jw \ (j=1,2,\ldots,p)$$

<u>The QR algorithm for singular values</u>. If $n \geq p$, the reduction to bidiagonal form results in a square bidiagonal matrix of order p whose singular values are those of the original matrix X. When $n < p$, the resulting bidiagonal matrix is n by $(n+1)$ (cf. (4.3)); however, by appending a row of zeros one can obtain a bidiagonal matrix of order $n+1$ whose singular values are those of X with an extra singular value of zero. Thus the problem is reduced to that of finding the singular values of a square, bidiagonal matrix of order, say, m. Denote this matrix by B, its diagonal elements by s_i $(i=1,2,\ldots,m)$, and its superdiagonal elements by e_i $(i=1,2,\ldots,m-1)$. Thus B has the form

$$B = \begin{bmatrix} s_1 & e_1 & & & \\ & s_2 & e_2 & & 0 \\ & & \ddots & \ddots & \\ & 0 & & s_{m-1} & e_{m-1} \\ & & & & s_m \end{bmatrix}.$$

Since the squares of the singular values of B are the eigenvalues of the symmetric tridiagonal matrix $C = B^TB$, the singular values of B may in principle be calculated by using the implicitly shifted QR algorithm to find the eigenvalues of C. This algorithm has been described and analyzed in detail elsewhere. Here we only outline the method and its properties in sufficient detail to justify the algorithm we actually use.

The QR algorithm begins with a shift κ, which is computed from the 2 by 2 trailing principal submatrix of C. A plane rotation V_{12} in the (1,2)-plane is determined so that

$$(4.4) \qquad (c_{11}-\kappa, c_{21}, 0, \ldots, 0)V_{12} = (g, 0, 0, \ldots, 0)$$

where $g = \sqrt{(c_{11}-\kappa)^2+c_{21}^2}$ (for more on plane rotations see the documentation of the LINPACK subroutines SCHUD, SCHDD, and SCHEX). The matrix $V_{12}^TCV_{12}$ has the form

$$\begin{bmatrix} x & x & \textcircled{x} & 0 & 0 & 0 \\ x & x & x & 0 & 0 & 0 \\ \textcircled{x} & x & x & x & 0 & 0 \\ 0 & 0 & x & x & x & 0 \\ 0 & 0 & 0 & x & x & x \\ 0 & 0 & 0 & 0 & x & x \end{bmatrix}.$$

A rotation V_{23} in the (2,3) plane is now chosen so that $V_{23}^T V_{12}^T C V_{12} V_{23}$ has the form

$$\begin{bmatrix} x & x & 0 & 0 & 0 & 0 \\ x & x & x & (x) & 0 & 0 \\ 0 & x & x & x & 0 & 0 \\ 0 & (x) & x & x & x & 0 \\ 0 & 0 & 0 & x & x & x \\ 0 & 0 & 0 & 0 & x & x \end{bmatrix},$$

i.e. so that the nonzero element off the tridiagonal is moved from the (3,1) position to the (4,2) position. This process is continued to give plane rotations $V_{12}, V_{23}, \ldots, V_{m-1,m}$ such that

$$C' = V_{m-1,m}^T \cdots V_{23}^T V_{12}^T C V_{12} V_{23} \cdots V_{m-1,m} \tag{4.5}$$

is tridiagonal. If none of the subdiagonal elements of C are zero, the product $V_{12} V_{23} \cdots V_{m-1,m}$ is uniquely determined by V_{12} and the fact that C' is tridiagonal.

Thus the QR algorithm produces a sequence of orthogonally similar, tridiagonal matrices. If the shift is properly chosen, the element $c_{n,n-1}$ will rapidly approach zero, and hence $c_{n,n}$ will approach an eigenvalue. Moreover, the other subdiagonal elements will generally tend to converge slowly to zero, so that on a large problem some may become negligible and cause the problem to break up into two smaller ones.

There are two reasons for not computing the singular value decomposition by forming C and applying the QR algorithm. The first is that the squaring of the singular values that occurs when one passes from B to C may cause a loss of accuracy in the smallest singular values, since these become much smaller in comparison to the largest one. Second, the QR algorithm provides only the eigenvectors of $C = B^T B$, i.e. only the right singular vectors of B. To compute the left singular vectors, one must find the eigenvectors of BB^T. To circumvent these difficulties, we shall use an algorithm in which the explicit formation of $B^T B$ is avoided.

The algorithm is based on the following observation. Suppose the rotation V_{12} is determined as described above, and that we can determine plane rotations $V_{23}, \ldots, V_{m-1,m}$ and $U_{12}^T, U_{23}^T, \ldots, U_{m-1,m}^T$ such that

$$B' = U_{m-1,m}^T \cdots U_{23}^T U_{12}^T B V_{12} V_{23} \cdots V_{m-1,m} \tag{4.6}$$

is bidiagonal. Then

$$B'^T B' = V_{m-1,m}^T \cdots V_{23}^T V_{12}^T C V_{12} V_{23} \cdots V_{m-1,m}$$

is tridiagonal. Hence by the above observation on the uniqueness of the product $V_{12} V_{23} \cdots V_{m,m-1}$, the matrix $B'^T B'$ is the matrix C' of (4.5). Thus we can effect a QR step by manipulating only the matrix B.

The actual reduction implied by (4.6) goes as follows. We are initially given V_{12}. The matrix BV_{12} has the form

$$\begin{bmatrix} x & x & 0 & 0 & 0 \\ \textcircled{x} & x & x & 0 & 0 \\ 0 & 0 & x & x & 0 \\ 0 & 0 & 0 & x & x \\ 0 & 0 & 0 & 0 & x \end{bmatrix} .$$

A rotation U_{12}^T in the (1,2)-plane is chosen to annihilate the element circled above. The matrix $U_{12}^T BV_{12}$ then has the form

$$\begin{bmatrix} x & x & \textcircled{x} & 0 & 0 \\ 0 & x & x & 0 & 0 \\ 0 & 0 & x & x & 0 \\ 0 & 0 & 0 & x & x \\ 0 & 0 & 0 & 0 & x \end{bmatrix} .$$

A rotation V_{23} in the (2,3) plane is chosen to annihilate the element circled above, giving a matrix $U_{12}^T BV_{12}V_{23}$ of the form

$$\begin{bmatrix} x & x & 0 & 0 \\ 0 & x & x & 0 \\ 0 & \textcircled{x} & x & x \\ 0 & 0 & x & x \\ 0 & 0 & 0 & x \end{bmatrix}$$

The general algorithm proceeds as above, alternately annihilating elements below the diagonal and above the superdiagonal as indicated below.

$$\begin{bmatrix} x & x & x^2 & 0 & 0 \\ x^1 & x & x & x^4 & 0 \\ 0 & x^3 & x & x & x^6 \\ 0 & 0 & x^5 & x & x \\ 0 & 0 & 0 & x^7 & x \end{bmatrix}$$

Each element annihilated introduces its successor, which is in turn annihilated.

We turn now to some of the important questions that must be answered before we can realize this outline as a working algorithm.

<u>Determination of the initial transformation</u>. Ordinarily the shift κ for the QR algorithm is determined as the eigenvalue of

$$\begin{bmatrix} c_{m-1,m-1} & c_{m-1,m} \\ c_{m,m-1} & c_{mm} \end{bmatrix}$$

that lies nearest c_{mm}. The formulas simplify somewhat if we choose κ from the eigenvalues of the trailing 2 by 2 submatrix of BB^T. Accordingly κ is chosen as the eigenvalue of

$$\begin{bmatrix} s_{m-1}^2 + e_{m-1}^2 & s_m e_{m-1} \\ s_m e_{m-1} & s_m^2 \end{bmatrix}$$

that lies closest to s_m^2. This number can readily be computed via the quadratic formula as follows:

$$\text{(4.7)} \qquad \begin{aligned} &1:\ b := \left[(s_{m-1}+s_m)(s_{m-1}-s_m)+e_{m-1}^2\right]/2\ ; \\ &2:\ c := (s_m e_{m-1})^2\ ; \\ &3:\ d := \text{sign}(b)\sqrt{b^2+c}\ ; \\ &4:\ \kappa := s_m^2 - c(b+d)^{-1}\ ; \end{aligned}$$

The rotation V_{12} can then be determined as described above (cf. (4.4)).

Tests for negligibility. The convergence theory for the QR algorithm implies that the element e_{m-1} should converge rapidly to zero, and the other elements e_ℓ may converge more slowly to zero. Thus it is necessary to decide when a super-diagonal element is negligible. We have chosen a very conservative criterion: e_ℓ is negligible if

$$\text{(4.8)} \qquad |e_\ell| \le \varepsilon_M(|s_{\ell+1}| + |s_\ell|)$$

where ε_M is the rounding unit for the computer in question.

Convergence and deflation. When e_{m-1} is judged negligible, s_m can be accepted as an approximate singular value. The iteration can then proceed with the leading principal submatrix of B of order m-1, which contains the remaining singular values of B.

Splitting. With moderately large problems, it is probable that at some point an off-diagonal element e_ℓ ($\ell < m-1$) will be judged negligible. This case does not represent convergence; however, the singular values of B are just those of its ℓ by ℓ leading principal submatrix and its $(m-\ell)$ by $(m-\ell)$ trailing principal submatrix. It is possible for the algorithm to find the singular values of each of these submatrices separately, at considerable savings in work when the left or right singular vectors are to be computed. SSVDC computes the singular values of the trailing submatrix first.

Zero singular values. In principle, zero singular values must manifest themselves by zero diagonal entries in B. In practice, they will cause negligible values of the s_ℓ to appear. Here we call s_ℓ negligible if

$$|s_\ell| \le \varepsilon_M(|e_{\ell-1}|+|e_\ell|)\ .$$

When such a negligible diagonal element is present, the problem can be reduced in one of two ways.

The first applies when for $\ell < m$ the element s_ℓ is negligible. If s_ℓ is set to zero, there results a matrix of the form illustrated below for $m=5$ and $\ell=2$:

$$\begin{bmatrix} x & x & 0 & 0 & 0 \\ 0 & 0 & \textcircled{x} & 0 & 0 \\ 0 & 0 & x & x & 0 \\ 0 & 0 & 0 & x & x \\ 0 & 0 & 0 & 0 & x \end{bmatrix} .$$

In this case a rotation U_{23}^T in the (2,3)-plane is chosen to annihilate e_2 . The resulting matrix has the form

$$\begin{bmatrix} x & x & 0 & 0 & 0 \\ 0 & 0 & 0 & \textcircled{x} & 0 \\ 0 & 0 & x & x & 0 \\ 0 & 0 & 0 & x & x \\ 0 & 0 & 0 & 0 & x \end{bmatrix} .$$

Next a rotation U_{24}^T in the (2,4)-plane is chosen to annihilate the circled element, which results in a matrix of the form

$$\begin{bmatrix} x & x & 0 & 0 & 0 \\ 0 & 0 & 0 & 0 & \textcircled{x} \\ 0 & 0 & x & x & 0 \\ 0 & 0 & 0 & x & x \\ 0 & 0 & 0 & 0 & x \end{bmatrix} .$$

Finally a rotation U_{25}^T in the (2,5)-plane annihilates the circled element and restores the matrix to bidiagonal form. However, the element e_2 (or in general e_ℓ) is zero, and the problem splits as described above.

The second reduction applies when $s_m = 0$. It is sufficiently well illustrated for $m = 4$, in which case the matrix has the form

$$\begin{bmatrix} x & x & 0 & 0 \\ 0 & x & x & 0 \\ 0 & 0 & x & \textcircled{x} \\ 0 & 0 & 0 & 0 \end{bmatrix} .$$

A rotation V_{34} in the (3,4)-plane is chosen so that the circled element is annihilated. The resulting matrix BV_{34} hss the form

$$\begin{bmatrix} x & x & 0 & 0 \\ 0 & x & x & (x) \\ 0 & 0 & x & 0 \\ 0 & 0 & 0 & 0 \end{bmatrix}$$

Next a rotation V_{24} in the (2,4)-plane is chosen to annihilate the circled element, giving a matrix of the form

$$\begin{bmatrix} x & x & 0 & (x) \\ 0 & x & x & 0 \\ 0 & 0 & x & 0 \\ 0 & 0 & 0 & 0 \end{bmatrix}$$

Finally a rotation in the (1,4)-plane annihilates the circled element and restores bidiagonality. The resulting matrix has $e_{m-1} = 0$, so that $s_m = 0$ will be accepted as a singular value.

Computation of the singular vectors. As we mentioned earlier, the transformations that reduce X to bidiagonal form can be saved and multiplied together to give explicitly the orthogonal matrices $\tilde{U}$ and $\tilde{V}$ that reduce X to bidiagonal form. To complete the computation of the singular vectors, all one must do is postmultiply the rotations labeled U and V into $\tilde{U}$ and $\tilde{V}$, which can be done as they are generated. Note that the fact that we are postmultiplying by rotations insures that the arrays U and V will be manipulated by column operations.

Modifications for complex matrices. The reduction to bidiagonal form requires the manipulation of complex Householder transformations, which are discussed in the documentation for SQRDC and SQRSL .

The resulting bidiagonal matrix will in general have complex entries; however, they may be made real in the following manner. Multiply the first row of B (i.e. s_1 and e_1) by a scalar $\bar{u}_1$ of absolute value unity that makes s_1 real. Multiply the second column of the resulting matrix (i.e. e_1 and s_2) by a scalar v_1 of absolute value unity that makes e_1 real. Multiply the second row of the resulting matrix by a factor $\bar{u}_2$ of absolute value unity that makes s_2 real, and continue in the obvious way. The matrix

$\text{diag}(\bar{u}_1,\bar{u}_2,\ldots,\bar{u}_m)\ B\ \text{diag}(v_1,v_2,\ldots,v_{m-1})$ will have real entries. Of course, when singular vectors are desired, these transformations must be accumulated in $\tilde{U}$ and $\tilde{V}$, which here amounts only to multiplying the i-th column of $\tilde{U}$ by u_i and the i-th column of $\tilde{V}$ by v_i.

Because the matrix B is real, the iterative reduction to diagonal form goes exactly as described above. However, since the rotations that must be accumulated in the complex matrices $\tilde{U}$ and $\tilde{V}$ are real, there are considerable savings in arithmetic operations over the accumulation of complex rotations.

5. Programming Details

In outline SSVDC is organized as follows:

```
        1         :  initialize;
        2         :  reduce to bidiagonal form;
        3         :  set up the bidiagonal matrix of order M;
        4         :  if required, initialize U and V;
       (5         :  transform the elements of S and E so that they are real;)
        6         :  loop # M:=M,M-1,...,0 #
        6.1       :    if all singular values have been found # M=0 # then leave 6; fi;
        6.2       :    if ITER > MAXIT then leave 6; fi;
        6.3       :    determine the value of KASE and L;
        6.4       :    branch to case KASE of 4;
        6.4.1     :      case 1 deflate negligible S(M); end case 1;
        6.4.2     :      case 2 split at negligible S(L); end case 2;
        6.4.3     :      case 3 # QR step #
        6.4.3.1   :        calculate the shift;
        6.4.3.2   :        perform the QR step;
        6.4.3.3   :        ITER = ITER+1;
        6.4.3     :      end case 3;
        6.4.4     :      case 4 # convergence #
        6.4.4.1   :        make the singular value positive and order it;
        6.4.4.2   :        ITER := 0; M := M-1;
        6.4.4     :      end case 4;
        6.4       :    end branch;
        6         :  end loop;
```

What follows here is an elaboration of this outline.

<u>1</u>. The parameter MAXIT, which controls the maximum number of iterations for any singular value, is set to 30. The parameters WANTU and WANTV are set to true according as JOB indicates that U or V is to be computed. NCU is set to the number of columns

of U to be computed (either N or P).

2. The reduction to bidiagonal form is described in Section 4. Some special features of this section of code are:

1) NCT is the number of columns to be reduced and NRT is the number of rows to be reduced.

2) During the premultiplication of a left transformation, the elements necessary to compute the next right transformation are collected in the unused part of the array E . This avoids an extra sweep across the matrix.

3) The postmultiplication of a right transformation as described in Section 4 requires that the vector $w = \rho Xv$ be accumulated. This is done in the array WORK .

4) The diagonal and superdiagonal entries of the bidiagonal matrix are stored in S and E as they are computed.

5) If U is to be computed, the vectors determining the left transformation are stored in the array U for subsequent back multiplication. The same goes for V .

3. If $N \geq P$, the bidiagonal matrix is of order $M = P$. If $N < P$, an extra row of zeros is added to make the order $M = N + 1$ (the spurious zero singular value is immediately removed at step 6.4.1).

4. The multiplications of the transformations that determine the initial U and V are performed <u>in situ</u>.

5. This step is only done for complex matrices.

6. This loop is effectively on the order M of the bidiagonal matrix, which is decreased each time a singular value is found. Throughout this loop, all transformations on the bidiagonal matrix are accumulated in the arrays U and V as specified by the parameter JOB .

6.1. This is the normal exit.

6.2. This is an error exit. INFO is set to M to indicate which singular values have converged.

6.3. In this section two passes are made backwards through the bidiagonal matrix, one to find negligible superdiagonal elements and the other to find negligible diagonal elements. In the tests no explicit use is made of the rounding unit ε_M . Instead the tests are based on the observation that for nonnegative floating point numbers

$$f\ell(a+b) = b \iff a \leq \varepsilon_M b \ .$$

At the end of this section the integers KASE and L have been set as follows (n.b. E(0) is assumed always to be negligible).

KASE = 1 S(M) and E(M-1) are negligible.

KASE = 2 S(L) is negligible, E(L),...,E(M-1) are not negligible, and $L < M$.

KASE = 3 E(L) is negligible, E(L+1),...,E(M-1) are not negligible, and $L < M-1$.

KASE = 4 E(M-1) is negligible.

6.4. The branch to the various cases is accomplished by means of a computed GO TO .

6.4.1. If KASE = 1 , S(M) is negligible and a zero is introduced into E(M-1) as described in section 4.

6.4.2. If KASE = 2 , S(L) , $L \neq M$, is negligible, and a zero is introduced into E(L) as described in section 4.

6.4.3. If KASE = 3 , a QR step must be performed on the submatrix subtended by S(L+1),...,S(M) . This section is divided into two parts: the computation of the initial transformation and the QR step proper.

6.4.3.1. The initial transformation is determined by (4.4) and (4.7), which depend on S(L+1), E(L+1), S(M-1), E(M-1), and S(M). To avoid overflows and destructive underflows, these quantities are scaled by the largest of them, a process which does not affect the final transformation.

6.4.3.2. The QR step is performed as described in section 4.

6.4.3.3. After each QR step the iteration count is increased by one.

6.4.4. If KASE = 4 , S(M) is a converged singular value. If it is negative, it is made positive. It is then positioned among the singular values that have been computed so that they are in descending order of magnitude. M is decreased by one and ITER is set to zero for the next iteration.

6. Performance

Operation counts. The bulk of the work done by SSVDC is concentrated in three steps: the reduction to bidiagonal form, the initialization of U and V , and the iterative reduction to diagonal form. The first step is fixed overhead for all uses of the subroutine. The work involved in the second and third steps depends on the singular vector calculation requested via the parameter JOB . In particular, if no vectors are calculated (JOB = 00), steps two and three represent an insignificant part of the work. The operation counts that follow are asymptotically valid as n and p increase.

The reduction to bidiagonal form has the following floating-point multiplication count.

$$n \geq p: \quad 2\left[np^2 - \frac{p^3}{3}\right]$$

$$n \leq p: \quad 2\left[n^2p - \frac{n^3}{3}\right]$$

Approximately the same number of additions are required.

In the second step the transformations from the first step must be multiplied out to initialize U and V. Thus the amount of work involved will depend on whether V is calculated (JOB = 01), U is calculated (JOB = 10), or, in the case $n \geq p$, the first p columns of U are calculated (JOB = 20). The floating point multiplication count is summarized below.

	JOB = 01	JOB = 10	JOB = 20
$n \geq p$	$\frac{2}{3}p^3$	$\frac{2}{3}n^3-(n-p)^3$	$np^2 - \frac{p^3}{3}$
$n \leq p$	$\frac{2}{3}p^3-(p-n)^3$	$\frac{2}{3}n^3$	--

Approximately the same number of additions is required.

In the third step the rotations that are used to reduce the bidiagonal matrix to diagonal form must be multiplied into the arrays of singular vectors. Thus the amount of work depends on the total number of rotations needed to accomplish this reduction. If this number is designated by r, then we have the following multiplication counts.

JOB = 01 : 4pr

JOB = 10,20: 4nr

The number r is difficult to estimate. An iterative step to reduce the k-th superdiagonal element requires no more than k rotations. There are approximately $m = \min\{n,p\}$ superdiagonal elements that must be reduced to the point where they are considered zero by the convergence criterion (4.8). Thus if s is the maximum number of iterations required to reduce a superdiagonal element,

(6.1) $$r \leq \frac{sm^2}{2} .$$

However, if the matrix is large, it will begin to break apart, thus reducing the number of rotations required for an iteration. Moreover, the later superdiagonal elements will tend to converge faster than the earlier ones. Hence, the bound (6.1) must be regarded as a gross overestimate.

<u>Timings</u>. Extensive timing runs have been made on SSVDC . The execution times vary widely from machine to machine and from compiler to compiler on a given machine. In order to simplify this mass of raw data, we present not the times, but their ratios to the time required by a simple process of comparable magnitude (e.g. a matrix multiplication of appropriate order). This process dramatically reduces the variation across machines and systems.* The price to be paid is that the user cannot obtain actual execution times from these data, only an idea of how much more it will cost him to do the computation in question than another, conceptually simpler computation. However, we feel that the user who needs actual execution times should measure them himself, since minor changes in a computer system can have a great effect on the times.

The process that we have chosen to compare SSVDC with is the calculation of the upper triangle of X^TX , where X is n by p if $n \geq p$ and p by n otherwise. This process has an operation count comparable with the reduction to bidiagonal form, which is the minimum amount of calculation the user can request of SSVDC . The elements of X^TX were computed by a call to a BLAS dot product routine. The results for JOB = 00 are presented in Table 1, whose entries have the form

	r_m	
r_e		r_u
	s_r	

where

r_m is the average of the ratios,

r_e is the smallest ratio,

r_u is the largest ratio,

s_r is the standard deviation of the ratios.

If these ratios are compared with the ratios for SQRDC in Chapter 9, it is seen that the singular value decomposition is relatively expensive to compute and should not be asked for lightly. The results also suggest that if n is much greater than p , it will be to

---

*Machines designed to perform vector operations with high efficiency are exceptional in that they tend to give higher ratios than their more pedestrian counterparts. For this reason, we have excluded them from the summary below. For a fuller discussion of this phenomenon, see Chapter 1.

the users advantage to calculate the QR decomposition of X and then get the singular values from R (cf. Example 3 in Section 3). In many applications, such as rank estimation, a QR decomposition with column pivoting may be an adequate substitute for a singular value decomposition.

Various overheads, such as calls to the BLAS, tend to become insignificant as n increases, and this is reflected in decreasing ratios for fixed p . For fixed n , the ratios remain relatively constant. This is due to the column-oriented form of the algorithm which forces the overhead to increase with p . A strictly row-oriented algorithm would exhibit the opposite behavior as regards p and n .

In Table 2 we present times for JOB = 01, 10, and 20 -- this time normalized by the times in Table 1. The entries thus represent the factors by which the computation of singular vectors increases the amount of work. For $n \geq p$, requesting V never increases the amount of work by more than a factor of three; nor does the computation of the first p columns of U . However, some care must be taken in interpreting these ratios. For example, although the computation of V for a 5 by 100 matrix has a factor of 5.1 and the computation of U for a 100 by 5 matrix has a factor of 15.3 , reference to Table 1 shows that the actual work in the first case is 5.1x19.0 = 96.9 and in the second case 15.3x5.8 = 88.74 , which are quite comparable.

Effects of rounding error. The algorithm is quite stable. Let Σ , U , and V denote the quantities computed by SSVDC . Then if $n \geq p$

$$U^T(X+E)V = \begin{bmatrix} \Sigma \\ 0 \end{bmatrix}$$

for some matrix E satisfying

$$\frac{\|E\|_2}{\|X\|_2} \leq \phi(n,p)\varepsilon_M \quad ,$$

where $\phi(n,p)$ is a slowly growing function of n and p . A similar result holds for $n \leq p$.

It follows from this that the computed singular values differ from the true values by no more than $\phi(n,p)\|X\|_2\varepsilon_M$. Since $\|X\|_2 = \sigma_1$, the large singular values will be computed to high relative accuracy. Smaller singular values will be computed with decreasing accuracy, until they approach $\sigma_1\varepsilon_M$, at which point they need have no accuracy at all.

The statements in the last paragraph do not necessarily apply to small singular values that result from exotic scalings of X . For example if X is graded as illustrated

Table 1

$(SVD00)/(X^TX)$

n \ p	5	10	25	50	75	100
5	14.7 9.6 24.2 3.5	16.8 12.2 21.9 2.5	19.2 11.6 35.3 5.4	15.9 6.2 37.0 6.7	20.0 9.3 55.0 11.4	19.0 11.5 33.0 6.1
10	12.9 9.4 18.6 2.5	12.3 8.9 17.7 2.4	14.3 8.7 20.8 3.1	13.6 8.1 22.0 3.5	13.6 8.0 26.0 4.7	14.1 8.3 24.0 4.3
25	9.3 7.1 12.9 1.6	9.5 6.6 13.9 1.4	8.1 5.7 10.9 1.3	9.0 6.4 12.5 1.6	8.8 5.8 12.4 1.8	8.8 6.6 13.5 1.9
50	7.3 5.6 9.9 1.2	7.6 5.4 11.3 1.4	7.1 5.2 8.8 .98	6.2 4.8 8.2 .88	6.6 5.2 8.2 .86	6.8 5.3 8.4 1.1
75	6.3 4.7 9.5 1.2	6.5 5.4 8.2 .90	6.7 5.5 8.0 .85	6.0 4.9 7.3 .76	5.2 4.1 6.3 .65	5.6 4.6 6.8 .73
100	5.8 4.6 7.4 .90	5.8 4.3 7.4 .89	6.2 5.0 7.5 .80	5.7 4.7 6.7 .68	5.2 4.3 6.5 .73	4.8 3.8 5.7 .66

Table 2

(SVDAB)/(SVD00)

01 10 20
JOB = AB

n \ p	5	10	25	50	75	100
5	1.3 1.3 --	1.6 1.3 --	2.2 1.1 --	3.4 1.1 --	4.5 1.1 --	5.1 1.0 --
10	1.3 1.8 1.5	1.5 1.5 --	1.9 1.3 --	2.8 1.3 --	3.6 1.2 --	4.2 1.1 --
25	1.2 3.4 1.9	1.5 2.5 1.8	1.9 1.9 --	2.4 1.6 --	3.0 1.4 --	3.3 1.3 --
50	1.3 7.0 8.2	1.3 4.3 2.3	1.7 2.9 2.5	2.4 2.4 --	2.6 2.0 --	2.9 1.7 --
75	1.2 10.9 2.4	1.2 6.6 2.5	1.5 3.6 2.4	2.1 2.8 2.6	2.7 2.7 --	2.8 2.3 --
100	1.2 15.3 2.5	1.2 8.8 2.7	1.5 4.6 2.8	2.0 3.6 2.9	2.4 3.0 2.8	2.7 2.7 --

below

$$\begin{matrix} 1 & 10^{-1} & 10^{-2} & 10^{-3} \\ 10^{-1} & 10^{-2} & 10^{-3} & 10^{-4} \\ 10^{-2} & 10^{-3} & 10^{-4} & 10^{-5} \\ 10^{-3} & 10^{-4} & 10^{-5} & 10^{-6} \end{matrix} ,$$

the small singular values will usually be computed accurately, although counterexamples can be found.

7. Notes and References

The singular value decomposition has a venerable history, dating back at least to Sylvester (1899). The right singular vectors arise in statistical applications under the name principal components, where they are usually defined as the eigenvectors of X^TX after the columns of X have been suitably adjusted and scaled.

Golub and Kahan (1965) first pointed out the numerical problems with computing the singular values directly from X^TX. The algorithm of this chapter is a variant of the one published by Golub and Reinsch (1970). It is based on the symmetric tridiagonal QR algorithm, which has been treated in detail by Wilkinson (1965,1968).

We were faced with a difficult choice in deciding how to judge if an element is negligible. For nicely balanced matrices, it is sufficient to call an element negligible if it is less than ϵ_M times some norm of X. However, this would cause the small singular values of graded matrices to be computed with unnecessary inaccuracy. Although our more conservative criterion circumvents this difficulty, it will in some cases cause the program to perform extra iterations in order to wring accuracy out of small singular values that simply isn't there. However, because the QR algorithm converges cubically, the extra work should not be inordinately great.

The rearrangement of the singular values into descending order is accomplished by a bubble sort, which is potentially expensive -- the more so as every interchange of singular values can generate interchanges in the U and V arrays. However, since the QR algorithm tends to produce the singular values in descending order anyway, we judged that a more elaborate sorting algorithm would be unlikely to save any work and might well generate more.

No formal rounding-error analysis has been published for the algorithm of this chapter. However, the straightforward application of orthogonal transformations that it entails falls under the general analyses of Wilkinson (1965).

The bound (1.6) is derived from results given by Stewart (1977a).

Much of the current interest in the singular value decomposition has to do with its use in detecting rank degeneracies and circumventing the difficulties they cause. While we do not wish to deny its utility in many applications, it has several limitations which have not been stressed sufficiently in the literature. In the first place, it is quite expensive to compute in comparison, say, with a QR decomposition. Secondly, something it shares with all the decompositions is that what it says about rank depends on how the original matrix has been scaled; just grinding a matrix through SSVDC and looking for small singular values can give misleading results. Third, in most applications a QR decomposition with column pivoting will serve equally well to determine rank and, as we have observed, at less cost. In fact even a Cholesky decomposition of X^TX may be preferable in some cases. Finally, suppression of singular values below the error level will stabilize least squares solutions only if the significant singular values are well above the error level [cf. (1.6)]. What to do with small but significant singular values is a difficult and unsolved problem.

References

AASEN, J. O. (1971). "On the reduction of a symmetric matrix to tridiagonal form," *BIT (Nord. Tisdkr. Informations-Behandl.) 11*, 233-242.

BARTELS, R. H. (1971). "A stabilization of the simplex method," *Numer. Math 16*, 414-434.

BARWELL, V. and A. GEORGE (1976). "A comparison of algorithms for solving symmetric indefinite systems of linear equations," *ACM Trans. Math. Software 2*, 242-251.

BJÖRCK, A. (1967a). "Solving linear least squares problems by Gram-Schmidt orthonormalization," *BIT (Nord. Tidskr. Informations-Behandl.) 7*, 1-21.

BJÖRCK, A. (1967b). "Iterative refinement of linear least square solutions I," *BIT (Nord. Tidskr. Informations-Behandl.) 7*, 257-278.

BJÖRCK, A. (1968). "Iterative refinement of linear least squares solutions II," *BIT (Nord. Tidskr. Informations-Behandl.) 8*, 8-30.

BJÖRCK, A. and G. H. GOLUB (1967). "Iterative refinement of linear least square solutions by Householder transformation," *BIT (Nord. Tidskr. Informations-Behandl) 7*, 322-337.

BOYLE, J. and K. DRITZ (1974). "An automated programming system to aid the development of quality mathematical software," *IFIP Proceedings*, North Holland, 542-546.

BOYLE, J. and M. MATZ (1976). "Automating multiple program realizations," *Proceedings of the XXVI-MRI Symposium, Computer Software Engineering*, Polytechnic Press.

BUNCH, J. R. (1971). "Analysis of the diagonal pivoting method," *SIAM Numerical Analysis 8*, 656-680.

BUNCH, J. R. and L. KAUFMAN (1977). "Some stable methods for calculating inertia and solving symmetric linear systems," *Math. Comp. 31*, 163-179.

BUNCH, J. R., L. KAUFMAN and B. N. PARLETT (1976). "Decomposition of a symmetric matrix," *Numerische Mathematik 27*, 95-109.

BUNCH, J. R. and B. N. PARLETT (1971). "Direct methods for solving symmetric indefinite systems of linear equations," *SIAM Numerical Analysis 8*, 639-655.

BUSINGER, P. and G. H. GOLUB (1965). "Linear least squares solutions by Householder transformations," *Numerische Mathematik 7*, 269-276.

CLINE, A. K., C. B. MOLER, G. W. STEWART and J. H. WILKINSON (1979). "An estimate for the condition number of a matrix," *SIAM Numerical Analysis 16*, 368-375.

DANIEL, J., W. B. GRAGG, L. KAUFMAN, and G. W. STEWART (1976). "Reorthogonalization and stable algorithms for updating the Gram-Schmidt QR factorization," *Math. Comp. 30*, 772-795.

DANTZIG, G. S. (1963). *Linear Programming and Extensions*, Princeton University Press, Princeton, N.J.

DONGARRA, J. J. and A. R. HINDS (197). "Unrolling loops in Fortran," *Software-Practice and Experience 9*, 219-229.

DWYER, P. S. (1945). "The square root method and its use in correlation and regression," *J. Amer. Stat. Assoc. 40*, 493-503.

FORSYTHE, G. E., M. A. MALCOLM and C. B. MOLER (1977). *Computer Methods for Mathematical Computations*, Prentice-Hall, Englewood Cliffs, N.J.

FORSYTHE, G. E. and C. B. MOLER (1967). *Computer Solution of Linear Algebraic Systems*, Prentice-Hall, Englewood Cliffs, N.J.

GILL, P. E., G. H. GOLUB, W. MURRAY, and M. A. SAUNDERS (1974). "Methods for modifying matrix factorizations," *Math. Comp. 28*, 505-535.

GILL, P. E., W. MURRAY, and M. A. SAUNDERS (1975). "Methods for computing and modifying the LDV factors of a matrix," *Math. Comp. 29*, 1051-1077.

GOLUB, G. H. (1965). "Numerical methods for solving linear least squares problems," *Numer. Math. 7*, 206-216.

GOLUB, G. H. and W. KAHAN (1965). "Calculating the singular values and pseudo-inverse of a matrix," *SIAM Numerical Analysis 2*, 202-224.

GOLUB, G. H. and C. REINSCH (1970). "Singular value decomposition and least squares solutions," *Numer. Math. 14*, 403-420.

GOLUB, G. H. and G. P. STYAN (1973). "Numerical computations for univariate linear models," *J. Stat. Comput. Simul. 2*, 253-274.

GOLUB, G. H. and J. H. WILKINSON (1966). "Note on iterative refinement of least squares solutions," *Numer. Math. 9*, 139-148.

GOODMAN, J. T. and C. B. MOLER (1977). "Three numerical experiments with Gaussian elimination," LINPACK Working Note #8, Argonne National Laboratory, AMD Technical Memorandum No. 311.

HOUSEHOLDER, A. S. (1958). "Unitary triangularization of a non-symetric matrix," *J. Assoc. Comput. Math. 5*, 339-342.

HOUSEHOLDER, A. S. (1964). *The Theory of Matrices in Numerical Analysis*, Blaisdell, N.Y.

LAWSON, C. L. and R. J. HANSON (1974). *Solving Least Squares Problems*, Prentice-Hall, Englewood Cliffs, N.J.

LAWSON, C., R. HANSON, D. KINCAID and F. KROGH (1979). "Basic linear algebra subprograms for Fortran usage," *ACM Trans. Math. Software,* Vol. 5, No. 3, 308-371.

MIRSKY, L. (2955). *An Introduction to Linear Algebra,* Clarendon Press, Oxford.

MOLER, C. B. (1972). "Matrix computations with Fortran and paging," *Comm. A.C.M. 15,* 268-270.

MOLER, C. B. and G. W. Stewart (1978). "On the Householder-Fox algorithm for decomposing a projection," *J. Comput. Phys. 28,* 82-91.

RYDER, B. G. (2974). "The Pfort verifier," *Software Practice and Experience 4,* 359-377.

SAUNDERS, M. A. (1972). "Large scale linear programming using the Cholesky factorization," Stanford University Report STAN-CS-72-252.

SEBER, G. A. F. (1977). *Linear Regression Analysis,* John Wiley, N.Y.

STEWART, G. W. (1974). *Introduction to Matrix Computations,* Academic Press, N.Y.

STEWART, G. W. (1977). "On the perturbation of pseudo-inverses, projections, and linear least squares problems, *SIAM Rev. 4,* 634-662.

STEWART, G. W. (1977). "The effects of rounding error on an algorithm for downdating a Cholesky factorization," University of Maryland, Computer Science TR-582.

SYLVESTER, J. J.(1899). *Messenger of Math 19,* 42.

WILKINSON, J. H. (1963). *Rounding Errors in Algebraic Processes,* Prentice-Hall, Englewood Cliffs, N.J.

WILKINSON, J. H. (1965a). *The Algebraic Eigenvalue Problem,* Oxford University Press, London.

WILKINSON, J. H. (1965b). "Error analysis of transformations based on the use of matrices of the form I-2ww," in *Error in Digital Computation* (L. B. Rall, ed.), Vol. 2, pp. 77-101, John Wiley & Sons, N.Y.

WILKINSON, J. H. (1968). "Global convergence of tridiagonal QR algorithm with origin shift," *Alg. and Appl. 1,* 409-420.

WILKINSON, J. H. and C. REINSCH (1971). *Handbook for Automatic Computation, Volume II, Linear Algebra,* Springer-Verlag, Heidelberg.

Appendix A: Basic Linear Algebra Subprograms

The LINPACK routines use a collection of low-level subprograms called the Basic Linear Algebra Subprograms (BLAS) for performing basic vector operations. The operations the BLAS perform include index of the largest component, vector norms, vector copy and swap, dot product, scalar times vector plus vector, and Givens transformations. The BLAS were developed by Lawson, Hanson, Kincaid, and Krogh (1979) and this appendix is an abbreviated version of their paper. Some of the BLAS, including those that involve mixed precision arithmetic, are not used by LINPACK and so are not described here. Additional BLAS have been added, namely CSROT and all those with a "Z" in their names.

The parameters INCX and INCY allow the BLAS to operate on vectors whose elements are not contiguous in memory. However, all calls to the BLAS in LINPACK have INCX = INCY = 1 .

Type declarations for function names are as follows:

```
INTEGER ISAMAX, IDAMAX, ICAMAX, IZAMAX
REAL SDOT, SNRM2, SCNRM2, SASUM, SCASUM
DOUBLE PRECISION DDOT, DNRM2, DASUM, DZNRM2, DZASUM
COMPLEX CDOTC, CDOTU
COMPLEX*16 ZDOTC, ZDOTU
```

Type and dimension declarations for variables occurring in the subprogram specifications are as follows:

```
INTEGER N, INCX, INCY, IMAX
REAL SX(1), SY(1), SA, SC, SS, SW
DOUBLE PRECISION DX(1), DY(1), DA, DC, DS, DW
COMPLEX CX(1), CY(1), CA, CW
COMPLEX*16 ZX(1), ZY(1), ZA, ZW
```

All the BLAS supplied with LINPACK are written in ANS Fortran with the exception of routines that use COMPLEX*16 variables. The routines are portable and are coded in a way to make them efficient on most computer systems.

TABLE 1

Summary of Functions and Names
of the Basic Linear Algebra Subprograms
used in LINPACK

Function	Prefix and Suffix of Name						Root of Name
Dot Product	S-	D-	C-U	C-C	Z-U	Z-C	-DOT-
Constant Times a Vector Plus a Vector	S-	D-		C-		Z-	-AXPY
Setup Givens Rotation	S-	D-					-ROTG
Apply Rotation	S-	D-		CS-		ZD-	-ROT
Copy x into y	S-	D-		C-		Z-	-COPY
Swap x and y	S-	D-		C-		Z-	-SWAP
2-Norm (Euclidean Length)	S-	D-		SC-		DZ-	-NRM2
Sum of Absolute Values*	S-	D-		SC-		DZ-	-ASUM
Constant Times a Vector	S-	D-	CS-	C-	ZD-	Z-	-SCAL
Index of Element Having Max Absolute Value*	IS-	ID-		IC-		IZ-	-AMAX

*For complex components $z_j = x_j + iy_j$ these subprograms compute $|x_j| + |y_j|$ instead of $(x_j^2 + y_j^2)^{\frac{1}{2}}$.

Dot Product Subprograms

SW = SDOT(N,SX,INCX,SY,INCY) $\qquad w := \sum_{i=1}^{N} x_i y_i$

DW = DDOT(N,DX,INCX,DY,INCY) $\qquad w := \sum_{i=1}^{N} x_i y_i$

CW = CDOTC(N,CX,INCX,CY,INCY) $\qquad w := \sum_{i=1}^{N} \overline{x}_i y_i$

The suffix C on CDOTC indicates that the complex conjugates of the components x_i are used.

CW = CDOTU(N,CX,INCX,CY,INCY) $\qquad w := \sum_{i=1}^{N} x_i y_i$

The suffix U on CDOTU indicates that the vector components x_i are used unconjugated.

ZW = ZDOTC(N,ZX,INCX,ZY,INCY) $\qquad w := \sum_{i=1}^{N} \bar{x}_i y_i$

The suffix C on ZDOTC indicates that the complex conjugates of the components x_i are used.

ZW = ZDOTU(N,ZX,INCX,ZY,INCY) $\qquad w := \sum_{i=1}^{N} x_i y_i$

The suffix U on ZDOTU indicates that the vector components x_i are used unconjugated.

In the preceding six subprograms, the value of $\sum_{i=1}^{N}$ will be set to zero if $N \leq 0$.

Elementary Vector Operation $\quad y := ax + y$

```
CALL SAXPY(N,SA,SX,INCX,SY,INCY)
CALL DAXPY(N,DA,DX,INCX,DY,INCY)
CALL CAXPY(N,CA,CX,INCX,CY,INCY)
CALL ZAXPY(N,ZA,ZX,INCX,ZY,INCY)
```

If $a = 0$ or if $N \leq 0$ these subroutines return immediately.

Construct Givens Plane Rotation

```
CALL SROTG(SA,SB,SC,SS)
CALL DROTG(DA,DB,DC,DS)
```

Given a and b each of these subroutines computes

$$\sigma = \begin{cases} \mathrm{sgn}(a) & \text{if } |a| > |b| \\ \mathrm{sgn}(b) & \text{if } |b| \geq |a| \end{cases}$$

$$r = \sigma(a^2+b^2)^{\frac{1}{2}}$$

$$c = \begin{cases} a/r & \text{if } r \neq 0 \\ 1 & \text{if } r = 0 \end{cases}$$

$$s = \begin{cases} b/r & \text{if } r \neq 0 \\ 0 & \text{if } r = 0 \end{cases}$$

The numbers c , s , and r then satisfy the matrix equation

$$\begin{bmatrix} c & s \\ -s & c \end{bmatrix} \begin{bmatrix} a \\ b \end{bmatrix} = \begin{bmatrix} r \\ 0 \end{bmatrix} .$$

The introduction of σ is not essential to the computation of a Givens rotation matrix but its use permits later stable reconstruction of c and s from just one number.

For this purpose the subroutine also computes

$$z = \begin{cases} s & \text{if } |a| > |b| \\ 1/c & \text{if } |b| \geq |a| \text{ and } c \neq 0 \\ 1 & \text{if } c = 0 \end{cases}$$

The subroutine returns r overwriting a , and z overwriting b , as well as returning c and s .

If the user later wishes to reconstruct c and s from z it can be done as follows:

If $z = 1$ set $c = 0$ and $s = 1$

If $|z| < 1$ set $c = (1-z^2)^{\frac{1}{2}}$ and $s = z$

If $|z| > 1$ set $c = 1/z$ and $s = (1-c^2)^{\frac{1}{2}}$

<u>Apply a Plane Rotation</u>

```
CALL SROT(N,SX,INCX,SY,INCY,SC,SS)
CALL DROT(N,DX,INCX,DY,INCY,DC,DS)
CALL CSROT(N,CX,INCX,CY,INCY,SC,SS)
CALL ZDROT(N,ZX,INCX,ZY,INCY,DC,DS)
```

These subroutines compute

$$\begin{bmatrix} x_i \\ y_i \end{bmatrix} := \begin{bmatrix} c & s \\ -s & c \end{bmatrix} \cdot \begin{bmatrix} x_i \\ y_i \end{bmatrix} \quad \text{for } i = 1,\ldots,N.$$

If $N \leq 0$ or if $c = 1$ and $s = 0$ the subroutine returns immediately.

<u>Copy a Vector x to y</u> y := x

```
CALL SCOPY(N,SX,INCX,SY,INCY)
CALL DCOPY(N,DX,INCY,DY,INCY)
CALL CCOPY(N,CX,INCX,CY,INCY)
CALL ZCOPY(N,ZX,INCX,ZY,INCY)
```

Returns immediately if $N \leq 0$.

<u>Interchange Vectors x and y</u> x :=: y

```
CALL SSWAP(N,SX,INCX,SY,INCY)
CALL DSWAP(N,DX,INCY,DY,INCY)
CALL CSWAP(N,CX,INCX,CY,INCY)
CALL ZSWAP(N,ZX,INCX,ZY,INCY)
```

Returns immediately if $N \leq 0$.

Euclidean Length or ℓ_2 Norm of a Vector $\qquad w := \left[\sum_{i=1}^{N} |x_i|^2\right]^{1/2}$

```
SW = SNRM2(N,SX,INCX)
DW = DNRM2(N,DX,INCX)
SW = SCNRM2(N,CX,INCX)
DW = DZNRM2(N,ZX,INCX)
```

If $N \le 0$ the result is set to zero.

Sum of Magnitudes of Vector Components

```
SW = SASUM(N,SX,INCX)
DW = DASUM(N,DX,INCX)
SW = SCASUM(N,CX,INCX)
DW = DZASUM(N,ZX,INCX)
```

The functions SASUM and DASUM compute $w := \sum_{i=1}^{N} |x_i|$. The functions SCASUM and DZASUM compute

$$w := \sum_{i=1}^{N} \left\{ |\mathrm{Real}(x_i)| + |\mathrm{Imag}(x_i)| \right\}$$

These functions return immediately with the result set to zero if $N \le 0$.

Vector Scaling $\qquad x := ax$

```
CALL SSCAL(N,SA,SX,INCX)
CALL DSCAL(N,DA,DX,INCX)
CALL CSCAL(N,CA,CX,INCX)
CALL CSSCAL(N,SA,CX,INCX)
CALL ZSCAL(N,ZA,ZX,INCX)
CALL ZDSCAL(N,DA,ZX,INCX)
```

If $N \le 0$ the subroutines return immediately.

Find Largest Component of a Vector

```
IMAX = ISAMAX(N,SX,INCX)
IMAX = IDAMAX(N,DX,INCX)
IMAX = ICAMAX(N,CX,INCX)
IMAX = IZAMAX(N,ZX,INCX)
```

The functions ISAMAX and IDAMAX determine the smallest index i such that $|x_i| = \max\left\{ |x_j| : j = 1,\ldots,N \right\}$.

The function ICAMAX and IZAMAX determine the smallest index i such that $|x_i| = \max\left\{ |\mathrm{Real}(x_j)| + |\mathrm{Imag}(x_j)| : j = 1,\ldots,N \right\}$.

These functions set the result to zero and return immediately if $N \le 0$.

Appendix B: Timing Data

This appendix summarizes some timing data for the subroutines in chapter 1 obtained from the test sites.

The first table attempts to compare the execution times of various computer-compiler combinations. This comparison is based on essentially only one item of data from each site, namely the time required to solve a single 100 by 100 system of linear equations. The column labeled TIME gives the execution time in seconds reported by each site for one call to SGEFA, or DGEFA for 32-bit machines, plus one call to SGESL or DGESL with N = 100. (In three cases the time was obtained by extrapolation from N = 75.) The column labeled UNIT is the resulting estimate of the time 'mu' (in microseconds) required for one execution of a statement of the form

```
Y(I) = Y(I) + T*X(I)
```

This involves one floating point multiplication, one floating point addition and a few one-dimensional indexing operations and storage references. The actual statement occurs in SAXPY, which is called roughly N**2 times by S- or DGEFA and N times by S- or DGESL to operate on vectors of varying lengths. The statement is executed approximately 1/3 N**3 + N**2 times, so

```
UNIT = 10**6 TIME/( 1/3 100**3 + 100**2 )
```

Facility	TIME N=100 secs.	UNIT micro-secs.	Computer	Type	Compiler
NCAR	.049	0.14	CRAY-1	S	CFT, Assembly BLAS
LASL	.148	0.43	CDC 7600	S	FTN, Assembly BLAS
NCAR	.192	0.56	CRAY-1	S	CFT
LASL	.210	0.61	CDC 7600	S	FTN
Argonne	.297	0.86	IBM 370/195	D	H
NCAR	.359	1.05	CDC 7600	S	Local
Argonne	.388	1.33	IBM 3033	D	H
NASA Langley	.489	1.42	CDC Cyber 175	S	FTN
U. Ill. Urbana	.506	1.47	CDC Cyber 175	S	Ext. 4.6
LLL	.554	1.61	CDC 7600	S	CHAT, No optimize
SLAC	.579	1.69	IBM 370/168	D	H Ext., Fast mult.
Michigan	.631	1.84	Amdahl 470/V6	D	H
Toronto	.890	2.59	IBM 370/165	D	H Ext., Fast mult.
Northwestern	1.44	4.20	CDC 6600	S	FTN
Texas	1.93*	5.63	CDC 6600	S	RUN
China Lake	1.95*	5.69	Univac 1110	S	V
Yale	2.59	7.53	DEC KL-20	S	F20
Bell Labs	3.46	10.1	Honeywell 6080	S	Y
Wisconsin	3.49	10.1	Univac 1110	S	V
Iowa State	3.54	10.2	Itel AS/5 mod3	D	H
U. Ill. Chicago	4.10	11.9	IBM 370/158	D	G1
Purdue	5.69	16.6	CDC 6500	S	FUN
U. C. San Diego	13.1	38.2	Burroughs 6700	S	H
Yale	17.1*	49.9	DEC KA-10	S	F40

* TIME(100) = (100/75)**3 SGEFA(75) + (100/75)**2 SGESL(75)

The preceding table should not be taken too seriously. In multiprogramming environments it is often difficult to reliably measure the execution time of a single program. We trust that anyone actually evaluating machines and operating systems will gather more reliable and more representative data.

The remaining tables summarize additional details of the data from various test sites. The execution times for up to six subroutines and up to six matrix orders are given. The times are normalized by the UNIT for the particular facility and by the operation counts for the particular subroutine, that is

$$\text{table entry} = \frac{\text{actual time}}{\text{UNIT . ops}}$$

where

```
ops  = 1/3 N**3 for FA
     = N**2     for SL
```

The choice of UNIT thus leads to an entry near 1.00 in the last row of each table. The tables allow comparison of double precision and complex arithmetic execution times with single precision times, as well as measures of overhead for small matrices. The regularity of the tables also provides some indication of the internal consistency of the data.

Stanford University (SLAC), IBM 370/168, Fast multiply, H extended

N	SGEFA	SGESL	DGEFA	DGESL	CGEFA	CGESL
5	7.21	6.76	7.55	7.14	14.79	14.46
10	3.64	3.91	3.75	4.30	10.56	10.97
25	1.80	2.82	1.80	1.88	8.56	8.45
50	1.21	1.41	1.27	1.64	8.13	8.45
75	1.03	1.25	1.08	1.25	7.97	8.14
100	0.96	1.12	0.99	1.23	7.84	8.04

Lawrence Livermore Lab., CDC 7600, CHAT, No optimization

N	SGEFA	SGESL	DGEFA	DGESL	CGEFA	CGESL
5	4.86	3.97	6.72	5.55	6.07	4.91
10	2.74	2.54	4.20	3.94	4.02	3.66
25	1.54	1.49	2.87	2.75	2.79	2.72
50	1.18	1.17	2.46	2.42	2.45	2.43
75	1.05	1.06	2.32	2.31	2.33	2.30
100	1.00	1.00	2.24	2.22	2.28	2.26

Argonne National Lab., IBM 370/195, Fortran H, OPT=2

N	SGEFA	SGESL	DGEFA	DGESL	CGEFA	CGESL
5	11.77	10.09	11.56	10.09	20.66	17.82
10	6.00	6.02	6.11	5.39	13.27	12.37
25	2.91	2.50	2.82	2.89	10.69	9.82
50	1.39	1.49	1.50	1.88	8.96	8.86
75	1.06	1.22	1.12	1.35	8.56	8.67
100	0.96	1.06	0.99	1.23	8.62	8.70

Univ. Illinois at Urbana, CDC Cyber 175, Ext. Ver. 4.6, OPT=1

N	SGEFA	SGESL	DGEFA	DGESL	CGEFA	CGESL
5	11.33	10.64	12.12	11.94	10.94	10.86
10	5.56	5.43	7.06	7.26	6.11	6.79
25	2.34	2.17	4.04	4.34	3.39	4.34
50	1.47	1.63	3.22	3.26	2.54	2.71
75	1.14	1.21	2.98	3.02	2.31	2.41
100	1.00	1.15	2.75	2.85	2.22	2.24

Univ. Illinois at Chicago Circle, IBM 370/158, Fortran G1

N	SGEFA	SGESL	DGEFA	DGESL	CGEFA	CGESL
5	5.52	4.18	6.70	4.82	9.27	8.20
10	2.94	2.57	3.11	2.86	5.87	6.68
25	1.62	1.55	1.65	1.65	4.93	4.90
50	1.11	1.04	1.20	1.23	4.18	3.81
75	1.01	1.01	1.08	1.08	4.18	3.79
100	0.87	0.86	1.00	0.96	3.94	4.27

Bell Telephone Labs., Honeywell 6080, Fortran Y Optimizing

N	SGEFA	SGESL	DGEFA	DGESL	CGEFA	CGESL
5	4.91	4.37	5.46	4.85	9.82	9.62
10	2.82	2.78	3.10	3.11	7.12	7.35
25	1.51	1.43	1.79	1.91	6.12	6.36
50	1.17	1.31	1.48	1.59	5.72	5.80
75	1.06	1.13	1.37	1.43	5.85	5.85
100	1.00	1.05	1.32	1.38	5.69	5.58

Purdue University, CDC 6500, FUN

N	SGEFA	SGESL	DGEFA	DGESL	CGEFA	CGESL
5	4.94	3.96	8.73	7.44	7.78	5.87
10	2.84	2.66	6.29	5.96	4.71	4.47
25	1.62	1.45	4.60	4.64	3.28	3.19
50	1.20	1.16	4.28	4.35	2.81	2.70
75	1.07	1.06	4.12	4.16	2.64	2.58
100	1.00	0.99	4.08	4.12	2.57	2.56

University of Michigan, Amdahl 470/V6, Fortran H, OPT=2

N	SGEFA	SGESL	DGEFA	DGESL	CGEFA	CGESL
5	4.41	3.70	5.11	4.50	6.99	6.11
10	2.21	2.19	2.69	2.74	4.62	4.58
25	1.06	1.28	1.49	1.69	3.46	3.68
50	0.76	0.85	1.17	1.30	3.26	3.34
75	0.66	0.73	1.06	1.17	3.16	3.19
100	0.61	0.67	1.00	1.11	3.10	3.15

University of Toronto, IBM 370/165, Fast multiply, H extended

N	SGEFA	SGESL	DGEFA	DGESL	CGEFA	CGESL
5	6.43	4.94	6.17	5.77	12.59	11.51
10	2.84	3.42	2.82	3.44	9.26	9.45
25	1.73	2.10	1.47	2.04	7.40	8.27
50	1.18	0.52	1.20	1.54	7.22	7.72
75	1.16	0.91	1.12	1.37	7.10	7.06
100	1.08	1.03	1.00	1.16	7.05	7.06

Yale University, DEC KL-20, F20 OPT

N	SGEFA	SGESL	DGEFA	DGESL	CGEFA	CGESL
5	3.47	2.97	4.46	3.78	11.02	9.19
10	1.99	2.03	2.79	2.75	8.44	8.06
25	0.99	1.27	1.96	2.12	7.44	7.43
50	1.08	1.06	1.83	1.75	7.17	7.01
75	1.03	0.99	1.77	1.68	7.07	6.99
100	1.00	1.01	1.72	1.65	7.05	6.94

Yale University, DEC KA-10, F40

N	SGEFA	SGESL			CGEFA	CGESL
5	5.01	3.36			13.25	8.99
10	2.70	2.43			8.91	7.37
25	1.49	1.12			6.59	5.94
50	1.11	0.99			5.97	5.81
75	1.00	0.93			5.74	5.67

NASA Langley Research Center, CDC Cyber 175, FTN OPT=2

N	SGEFA	SGESL	DGEFA	DGESL	CGEFA	CGESL
5	11.86	11.46	14.15	13.26	12.67	11.68
10	6.32	6.55	8.00	7.51	6.47	6.55
25	2.43	3.37	4.58	4.49	3.64	4.49
50	1.55	1.69	3.32	3.37	2.66	2.81
75	1.14	1.37	3.01	3.12	2.45	2.62
100	1.00	1.12	2.84	2.88	2.30	2.32

Northwestern University, CDC 6600, FTN 4.6 OPT=2

N	SGEFA	SGESL	DGEFA	DGESL	CGEFA	CGESL
5	9.89	10.10	11.71	12.00	9.49	10.67
10	4.71	5.40	6.86	6.83	5.57	6.19
25	1.87	3.05	3.89	3.43	3.20	4.19
50	1.27	1.33	3.20	3.71	2.43	2.48
75	1.07	1.27	2.91	2.96	2.25	2.16
100	1.00	1.00	2.75	3.05	2.15	2.31

University of Wisconsin at Madison, Univac 1110, Fortran V

N	SGEFA	SGESL	DGEFA	DGESL	CGEFA	CGESL
5	7.73	6.81	8.48	7.44	9.64	9.02
10	4.08	4.14	4.64	4.60	5.46	5.78
25	1.97	2.21	2.40	2.36	3.48	3.78
50	1.32	1.38	1.69	1.77	2.93	3.07
75	1.11	1.17	1.46	1.52	2.75	2.87
100	1.00	1.05	1.35	1.41	2.66	2.77

Naval Weapons Center at China Lake, Univac 1110, Fortran V

N	SGEFA	SGESL	DGEFA	DGESL	CGEFA	CGESL
5	6.97	6.26	7.69	6.98	8.61	8.26
10	3.66	3.76	4.18	4.29	4.92	5.31
25	1.77	1.91	2.15	2.36	3.21	3.49
50	1.18	1.31	1.54	1.65	2.73	2.93
75	1.00	1.08	1.33	1.42	2.58	2.71

Univ. Texas at Austin, CDC 6600/6400, RUN

N	SGEFA	SGESL	DGEFA	DGESL	CGEFA	CGESL
5	7.25	6.71	9.55	9.60	9.47	7.00
10	3.69	1.66	6.13	5.33	4.97	3.43
25	2.05	0.0	3.75	4.27	2.93	0.57
50	1.21	1.00	2.78	3.34	2.43	2.13
75	1.00	1.14	2.57	2.91	2.20	1.96

Iowa State University, Itel AS/5 mod 3, Fortran H, OPT=2

N	SGEFA	SGESL	DGEFA	DGESL	CGEFA	CGESL
5	4.31	4.06	4.31	4.06	7.87	7.80
10	2.54	2.60	2.34	3.25	5.65	5.20
25	1.12	1.56	1.31	3.12	4.49	4.68
50	1.03	1.17	1.12	1.17	4.19	4.29
75	0.84	0.87	1.07	0.87	4.15	4.34
100	0.81	0.78	1.00	1.07	4.18	4.19

Univ. Calif. San Diego, Burroughs 6700, Fortran H

N	SGEFA	SGESL	DGEFA	DGESL	CGEFA	CGESL
5	3.54	2.50	3.23	2.45	6.78	5.44
10	2.01	1.50	2.06	1.61	5.30	4.95
25	1.32	1.03	1.35	1.18	4.32	4.06
50	0.99	0.85	1.28	1.25	3.86	3.86
75	0.98	0.83	1.30	1.16	4.06	3.82
100	1.00	0.83	1.22	1.17	4.11	4.24

Nat'l Center Atmospheric Research, CDC 7600, Local compiler

N	SGEFA	SGESL	CGEFA	CGESL
5	12.49	11.32	13.04	11.02
10	6.11	6.38	5.94	7.01
25	2.39	3.06	2.94	3.06
50	1.49	1.53	2.09	2.30
75	1.14	1.36	1.78	2.04
100	1.00	1.15	1.64	1.72

Nat'l Center Atmospheric Research, Cray-1, CRI, Fortran BLAS

N	SGEFA	SGESL
5	6.96	5.40
10	3.88	3.44
25	1.91	1.88
50	1.30	1.31
75	1.10	1.11
100	1.00	1.01

Nat'l Center Atmospheric Research, Cray-1, CRI, CAL BLAS

N	SGEFA	SGESL
5	18.70	15.39
10	8.55	8.00
25	3.26	3.36
50	1.70	1.82
75	1.23	1.31
100	1.00	1.06

Appendix C: Program Listings

SGECO

```
      SUBROUTINE SGECO(A,LDA,N,IPVT,RCOND,Z)
      INTEGER LDA,N,IPVT(1)
      REAL A(LDA,1),Z(1)
      REAL RCOND
C
C     SGECO FACTORS A REAL MATRIX BY GAUSSIAN ELIMINATION
C     AND ESTIMATES THE CONDITION OF THE MATRIX.
C
C     IF  RCOND  IS NOT NEEDED, SGEFA IS SLIGHTLY FASTER.
C     TO SOLVE  A*X = B , FOLLOW SGECO BY SGESL.
C     TO COMPUTE  INVERSE(A)*C , FOLLOW SGECO BY SGESL.
C     TO COMPUTE  DETERMINANT(A) , FOLLOW SGECO BY SGEDI.
C     TO COMPUTE  INVERSE(A) , FOLLOW SGECO BY SGEDI.
C
C     ON ENTRY
C
C        A       REAL(LDA, N)
C                THE MATRIX TO BE FACTORED.
C
C        LDA     INTEGER
C                THE LEADING DIMENSION OF THE ARRAY  A .
C
C        N       INTEGER
C                THE ORDER OF THE MATRIX  A .
C
C     ON RETURN
C
C        A       AN UPPER TRIANGULAR MATRIX AND THE MULTIPLIERS
C                WHICH WERE USED TO OBTAIN IT.
C                THE FACTORIZATION CAN BE WRITTEN  A = L*U  WHERE
C                L  IS A PRODUCT OF PERMUTATION AND UNIT LOWER
C                TRIANGULAR MATRICES AND  U  IS UPPER TRIANGULAR.
C
C        IPVT    INTEGER(N)
C                AN INTEGER VECTOR OF PIVOT INDICES.
C
C        RCOND   REAL
C                AN ESTIMATE OF THE RECIPROCAL CONDITION OF  A .
C                FOR THE SYSTEM  A*X = B , RELATIVE PERTURBATIONS
C                IN  A  AND  B  OF SIZE  EPSILON  MAY CAUSE
C                RELATIVE PERTURBATIONS IN  X  OF SIZE  EPSILON/RCOND .
C                IF  RCOND  IS SO SMALL THAT THE LOGICAL EXPRESSION
C                           1.0 + RCOND .EQ. 1.0
C                IS TRUE, THEN  A  MAY BE SINGULAR TO WORKING
C                PRECISION.  IN PARTICULAR,  RCOND  IS ZERO  IF
C                EXACT SINGULARITY IS DETECTED OR THE ESTIMATE
C                UNDERFLOWS.
C
C        Z       REAL(N)
C                A WORK VECTOR WHOSE CONTENTS ARE USUALLY UNIMPORTANT.
C                IF  A  IS CLOSE TO A SINGULAR MATRIX, THEN  Z  IS
C                AN APPROXIMATE NULL VECTOR IN THE SENSE THAT
C                NORM(A*Z) = RCOND*NORM(A)*NORM(Z) .
C
C     LINPACK. THIS VERSION DATED 08/14/78 .
C     CLEVE MOLER, UNIVERSITY OF NEW MEXICO, ARGONNE NATIONAL LAB.
C
C     SUBROUTINES AND FUNCTIONS
C
C     LINPACK SGEFA
C     BLAS SAXPY,SDOT,SSCAL,SASUM
```

```
C     FORTRAN ABS,AMAX1,SIGN
C
C     INTERNAL VARIABLES
C
      REAL SDOT,EK,T,WK,WKM
      REAL ANORM,S,SASUM,SM,YNORM
      INTEGER INFO,J,K,KB,KP1,L
C
C
C     COMPUTE 1-NORM OF A
C
      ANORM = 0.0E0
      DO 10 J = 1, N
         ANORM = AMAX1(ANORM,SASUM(N,A(1,J),1))
   10 CONTINUE
C
C     FACTOR
C
      CALL SGEFA(A,LDA,N,IPVT,INFO)
C
C     RCOND = 1/(NORM(A)*(ESTIMATE OF NORM(INVERSE(A)))) .
C     ESTIMATE = NORM(Z)/NORM(Y) WHERE  A*Z = Y  AND  TRANS(A)*Y = E .
C     TRANS(A)  IS THE TRANSPOSE OF A .  THE COMPONENTS OF  E  ARE
C     CHOSEN TO CAUSE MAXIMUM LOCAL GROWTH IN THE ELEMENTS OF W  WHERE
C     TRANS(U)*W = E .  THE VECTORS ARE FREQUENTLY RESCALED TO AVOID
C     OVERFLOW.
C
C     SOLVE TRANS(U)*W = E
C
      EK = 1.0E0
      DO 20 J = 1, N
         Z(J) = 0.0E0
   20 CONTINUE
      DO 100 K = 1, N
         IF (Z(K) .NE. 0.0E0) EK = SIGN(EK,-Z(K))
         IF (ABS(EK-Z(K)) .LE. ABS(A(K,K))) GO TO 30
            S = ABS(A(K,K))/ABS(EK-Z(K))
            CALL SSCAL(N,S,Z,1)
            EK = S*EK
   30    CONTINUE
         WK = EK - Z(K)
         WKM = -EK - Z(K)
         S = ABS(WK)
         SM = ABS(WKM)
         IF (A(K,K) .EQ. 0.0E0) GO TO 40
            WK = WK/A(K,K)
            WKM = WKM/A(K,K)
         GO TO 50
   40    CONTINUE
            WK = 1.0E0
            WKM = 1.0E0
   50    CONTINUE
         KP1 = K + 1
         IF (KP1 .GT. N) GO TO 90
            DO 60 J = KP1, N
               SM = SM + ABS(Z(J)+WKM*A(K,J))
               Z(J) = Z(J) + WK*A(K,J)
               S = S + ABS(Z(J))
   60       CONTINUE
            IF (S .GE. SM) GO TO 80
               T = WKM - WK
               WK = WKM
               DO 70 J = KP1, N
                  Z(J) = Z(J) + T*A(K,J)
   70          CONTINUE
```

```
   80       CONTINUE
   90    CONTINUE
         Z(K) = WK
  100 CONTINUE
      S = 1.0E0/SASUM(N,Z,1)
      CALL SSCAL(N,S,Z,1)
C
C     SOLVE TRANS(L)*Y = W
C
      DO 120 KB = 1, N
         K = N + 1 - KB
         IF (K .LT. N) Z(K) = Z(K) + SDOT(N-K,A(K+1,K),1,Z(K+1),1)
         IF (ABS(Z(K)) .LE. 1.0E0) GO TO 110
            S = 1.0E0/ABS(Z(K))
            CALL SSCAL(N,S,Z,1)
  110    CONTINUE
         L = IPVT(K)
         T = Z(L)
         Z(L) = Z(K)
         Z(K) = T
  120 CONTINUE
      S = 1.0E0/SASUM(N,Z,1)
      CALL SSCAL(N,S,Z,1)
C
      YNORM = 1.0E0
C
C     SOLVE L*V = Y
C
      DO 140 K = 1, N
         L = IPVT(K)
         T = Z(L)
         Z(L) = Z(K)
         Z(K) = T
         IF (K .LT. N) CALL SAXPY(N-K,T,A(K+1,K),1,Z(K+1),1)
         IF (ABS(Z(K)) .LE. 1.0E0) GO TO 130
            S = 1.0E0/ABS(Z(K))
            CALL SSCAL(N,S,Z,1)
            YNORM = S*YNORM
  130    CONTINUE
  140 CONTINUE
      S = 1.0E0/SASUM(N,Z,1)
      CALL SSCAL(N,S,Z,1)
      YNORM = S*YNORM
C
C     SOLVE  U*Z = V
C
      DO 160 KB = 1, N
         K = N + 1 - KB
         IF (ABS(Z(K)) .LE. ABS(A(K,K))) GO TO 150
            S = ABS(A(K,K))/ABS(Z(K))
            CALL SSCAL(N,S,Z,1)
            YNORM = S*YNORM
  150    CONTINUE
         IF (A(K,K) .NE. 0.0E0) Z(K) = Z(K)/A(K,K)
         IF (A(K,K) .EQ. 0.0E0) Z(K) = 1.0E0
         T = -Z(K)
         CALL SAXPY(K-1,T,A(1,K),1,Z(1),1)
  160 CONTINUE
C     MAKE ZNORM = 1.0
      S = 1.0E0/SASUM(N,Z,1)
      CALL SSCAL(N,S,Z,1)
      YNORM = S*YNORM
C
```

```
      IF (ANORM .NE. 0.0E0) RCOND = YNORM/ANORM
      IF (ANORM .EQ. 0.0E0) RCOND = 0.0E0
      RETURN
      END
```

```
      SUBROUTINE SGEFA(A,LDA,N,IPVT,INFO)
      INTEGER LDA,N,IPVT(1),INFO
      REAL A(LDA,1)
C
C     SGEFA FACTORS A REAL MATRIX BY GAUSSIAN ELIMINATION.
C
C     SGEFA IS USUALLY CALLED BY SGECO, BUT IT CAN BE CALLED
C     DIRECTLY WITH A SAVING IN TIME IF  RCOND  IS NOT NEEDED.
C     (TIME FOR SGECO) = (1 + 9/N)*(TIME FOR SGEFA) .
C
C     ON ENTRY
C
C        A       REAL(LDA, N)
C                THE MATRIX TO BE FACTORED.
C
C        LDA     INTEGER
C                THE LEADING DIMENSION OF THE ARRAY  A .
C
C        N       INTEGER
C                THE ORDER OF THE MATRIX  A .
C
C     ON RETURN
C
C        A       AN UPPER TRIANGULAR MATRIX AND THE MULTIPLIERS
C                WHICH WERE USED TO OBTAIN IT.
C                THE FACTORIZATION CAN BE WRITTEN  A = L*U  WHERE
C                L  IS A PRODUCT OF PERMUTATION AND UNIT LOWER
C                TRIANGULAR MATRICES AND  U  IS UPPER TRIANGULAR.
C
C        IPVT    INTEGER(N)
C                AN INTEGER VECTOR OF PIVOT INDICES.
C
C        INFO    INTEGER
C                = 0  NORMAL VALUE.
C                = K  IF  U(K,K) .EQ. 0.0 .  THIS IS NOT AN ERROR
C                     CONDITION FOR THIS SUBROUTINE, BUT IT DOES
C                     INDICATE THAT SGESL OR SGEDI WILL DIVIDE BY ZERO
C                     IF CALLED.  USE  RCOND  IN SGECO FOR A RELIABLE
C                     INDICATION OF SINGULARITY.
C
C     LINPACK. THIS VERSION DATED 08/14/78 .
C     CLEVE MOLER, UNIVERSITY OF NEW MEXICO, ARGONNE NATIONAL LAB.
C
C     SUBROUTINES AND FUNCTIONS
C
C     BLAS SAXPY,SSCAL,ISAMAX
C
C     INTERNAL VARIABLES
C
      REAL T
      INTEGER ISAMAX,J,K,KP1,L,NM1
C
C
C     GAUSSIAN ELIMINATION WITH PARTIAL PIVOTING
C
      INFO = 0
      NM1 = N - 1
      IF (NM1 .LT. 1) GO TO 70
      DO 60 K = 1, NM1
         KP1 = K + 1
C
C        FIND L = PIVOT INDEX
C
```

```
         L = ISAMAX(N-K+1,A(K,K),1) + K - 1
         IPVT(K) = L
C
C        ZERO PIVOT IMPLIES THIS COLUMN ALREADY TRIANGULARIZED
C
         IF (A(L,K) .EQ. 0.0E0) GO TO 40
C
C           INTERCHANGE IF NECESSARY
C
            IF (L .EQ. K) GO TO 10
               T = A(L,K)
               A(L,K) = A(K,K)
               A(K,K) = T
   10       CONTINUE
C
C           COMPUTE MULTIPLIERS
C
            T = -1.0E0/A(K,K)
            CALL SSCAL(N-K,T,A(K+1,K),1)
C
C           ROW ELIMINATION WITH COLUMN INDEXING
C
            DO 30 J = KP1, N
               T = A(L,J)
               IF (L .EQ. K) GO TO 20
                  A(L,J) = A(K,J)
                  A(K,J) = T
   20          CONTINUE
               CALL SAXPY(N-K,T,A(K+1,K),1,A(K+1,J),1)
   30       CONTINUE
         GO TO 50
   40    CONTINUE
            INFO = K
   50    CONTINUE
   60 CONTINUE
   70 CONTINUE
      IPVT(N) = N
      IF (A(N,N) .EQ. 0.0E0) INFO = N
      RETURN
      END
```

```
      SUBROUTINE SGESL(A,LDA,N,IPVT,B,JOB)
      INTEGER LDA,N,IPVT(1),JOB
      REAL A(LDA,1),B(1)
C
C     SGESL SOLVES THE REAL SYSTEM
C     A * X = B  OR  TRANS(A) * X = B
C     USING THE FACTORS COMPUTED BY SGECO OR SGEFA.
C
C     ON ENTRY
C
C        A       REAL(LDA, N)
C                THE OUTPUT FROM SGECO OR SGEFA.
C
C        LDA     INTEGER
C                THE LEADING DIMENSION OF THE ARRAY  A .
C
C        N       INTEGER
C                THE ORDER OF THE MATRIX  A .
C
C        IPVT    INTEGER(N)
C                THE PIVOT VECTOR FROM SGECO OR SGEFA.
C
C        B       REAL(N)
C                THE RIGHT HAND SIDE VECTOR.
C
C        JOB     INTEGER
C                = 0         TO SOLVE  A*X = B ,
C                = NONZERO   TO SOLVE  TRANS(A)*X = B  WHERE
C                            TRANS(A)  IS THE TRANSPOSE.
C
C     ON RETURN
C
C        B       THE SOLUTION VECTOR  X .
C
C     ERROR CONDITION
C
C        A DIVISION BY ZERO WILL OCCUR IF THE INPUT FACTOR CONTAINS A
C        ZERO ON THE DIAGONAL.  TECHNICALLY THIS INDICATES SINGULARITY
C        BUT IT IS OFTEN CAUSED BY IMPROPER ARGUMENTS OR IMPROPER
C        SETTING OF LDA .  IT WILL NOT OCCUR IF THE SUBROUTINES ARE
C        CALLED CORRECTLY AND IF SGECO HAS SET RCOND .GT. 0.0
C        OR SGEFA HAS SET INFO .EQ. 0 .
C
C     TO COMPUTE  INVERSE(A) * C  WHERE  C  IS A MATRIX
C     WITH  P  COLUMNS
C           CALL SGECO(A,LDA,N,IPVT,RCOND,Z)
C           IF (RCOND IS TOO SMALL) GO TO ...
C           DO 10 J = 1, P
C              CALL SGESL(A,LDA,N,IPVT,C(1,J),0)
C        10 CONTINUE
C
C     LINPACK. THIS VERSION DATED 08/14/78 .
C     CLEVE MOLER, UNIVERSITY OF NEW MEXICO, ARGONNE NATIONAL LAB.
C
C     SUBROUTINES AND FUNCTIONS
C
C     BLAS SAXPY,SDOT
C
C     INTERNAL VARIABLES
C
      REAL SDOT,T
      INTEGER K,KB,L,NM1
C
```

```
      NM1 = N - 1
      IF (JOB .NE. 0) GO TO 50
C
C        JOB = 0 , SOLVE  A * X = B
C        FIRST SOLVE  L*Y = B
C
         IF (NM1 .LT. 1) GO TO 30
         DO 20 K = 1, NM1
            L = IPVT(K)
            T = B(L)
            IF (L .EQ. K) GO TO 10
               B(L) = B(K)
               B(K) = T
   10       CONTINUE
            CALL SAXPY(N-K,T,A(K+1,K),1,B(K+1),1)
   20    CONTINUE
   30    CONTINUE
C
C        NOW SOLVE  U*X = Y
C
         DO 40 KB = 1, N
            K = N + 1 - KB
            B(K) = B(K)/A(K,K)
            T = -B(K)
            CALL SAXPY(K-1,T,A(1,K),1,B(1),1)
   40    CONTINUE
      GO TO 100
   50 CONTINUE
C
C        JOB = NONZERO, SOLVE  TRANS(A) * X = B
C        FIRST SOLVE  TRANS(U)*Y = B
C
         DO 60 K = 1, N
            T = SDOT(K-1,A(1,K),1,B(1),1)
            B(K) = (B(K) - T)/A(K,K)
   60    CONTINUE
C
C        NOW SOLVE TRANS(L)*X = Y
C
         IF (NM1 .LT. 1) GO TO 90
         DO 80 KB = 1, NM1
            K = N - KB
            B(K) = B(K) + SDOT(N-K,A(K+1,K),1,B(K+1),1)
            L = IPVT(K)
            IF (L .EQ. K) GO TO 70
               T = B(L)
               B(L) = B(K)
               B(K) = T
   70       CONTINUE
   80    CONTINUE
   90    CONTINUE
  100 CONTINUE
      RETURN
      END
```

```
      SUBROUTINE SGEDI(A,LDA,N,IPVT,DET,WORK,JOB)
      INTEGER LDA,N,IPVT(1),JOB
      REAL A(LDA,1),DET(2),WORK(1)
C
C     SGEDI COMPUTES THE DETERMINANT AND INVERSE OF A MATRIX
C     USING THE FACTORS COMPUTED BY SGECO OR SGEFA.
C
C     ON ENTRY
C
C        A       REAL(LDA, N)
C                THE OUTPUT FROM SGECO OR SGEFA.
C
C        LDA     INTEGER
C                THE LEADING DIMENSION OF THE ARRAY  A .
C
C        N       INTEGER
C                THE ORDER OF THE MATRIX  A .
C
C        IPVT    INTEGER(N)
C                THE PIVOT VECTOR FROM SGECO OR SGEFA.
C
C        WORK    REAL(N)
C                WORK VECTOR.  CONTENTS DESTROYED.
C
C        JOB     INTEGER
C                = 11   BOTH DETERMINANT AND INVERSE.
C                = 01   INVERSE ONLY.
C                = 10   DETERMINANT ONLY.
C
C     ON RETURN
C
C        A       INVERSE OF ORIGINAL MATRIX IF REQUESTED.
C                OTHERWISE UNCHANGED.
C
C        DET     REAL(2)
C                DETERMINANT OF ORIGINAL MATRIX IF REQUESTED.
C                OTHERWISE NOT REFERENCED.
C                DETERMINANT = DET(1) * 10.0**DET(2)
C                WITH  1.0 .LE. ABS(DET(1)) .LT. 10.0
C                OR  DET(1) .EQ. 0.0 .
C
C     ERROR CONDITION
C
C        A DIVISION BY ZERO WILL OCCUR IF THE INPUT FACTOR CONTAINS
C        A ZERO ON THE DIAGONAL AND THE INVERSE IS REQUESTED.
C        IT WILL NOT OCCUR IF THE SUBROUTINES ARE CALLED CORRECTLY
C        AND IF SGECO HAS SET RCOND .GT. 0.0 OR SGEFA HAS SET
C        INFO .EQ. 0 .
C
C     LINPACK. THIS VERSION DATED 08/14/78 .
C     CLEVE MOLER, UNIVERSITY OF NEW MEXICO, ARGONNE NATIONAL LAB.
C
C     SUBROUTINES AND FUNCTIONS
C
C     BLAS SAXPY,SSCAL,SSWAP
C     FORTRAN ABS,MOD
C
C     INTERNAL VARIABLES
C
      REAL T
      REAL TEN
      INTEGER I,J,K,KB,KP1,L,NM1
C
```

```
C
C     COMPUTE DETERMINANT
C
      IF (JOB/10 .EQ. 0) GO TO 70
         DET(1) = 1.0E0
         DET(2) = 0.0E0
         TEN = 10.0E0
         DO 50 I = 1, N
            IF (IPVT(I) .NE. I) DET(1) = -DET(1)
            DET(1) = A(I,I)*DET(1)
C        ...EXIT
            IF (DET(1) .EQ. 0.0E0) GO TO 60
   10       IF (ABS(DET(1)) .GE. 1.0E0) GO TO 20
               DET(1) = TEN*DET(1)
               DET(2) = DET(2) - 1.0E0
            GO TO 10
   20       CONTINUE
   30       IF (ABS(DET(1)) .LT. TEN) GO TO 40
               DET(1) = DET(1)/TEN
               DET(2) = DET(2) + 1.0E0
            GO TO 30
   40       CONTINUE
   50    CONTINUE
   60    CONTINUE
   70 CONTINUE
C
C     COMPUTE INVERSE(U)
C
      IF (MOD(JOB,10) .EQ. 0) GO TO 150
         DO 100 K = 1, N
            A(K,K) = 1.0E0/A(K,K)
            T = -A(K,K)
            CALL SSCAL(K-1,T,A(1,K),1)
            KP1 = K + 1
            IF (N .LT. KP1) GO TO 90
            DO 80 J = KP1, N
               T = A(K,J)
               A(K,J) = 0.0E0
               CALL SAXPY(K,T,A(1,K),1,A(1,J),1)
   80       CONTINUE
   90       CONTINUE
  100    CONTINUE
C
C        FORM INVERSE(U)*INVERSE(L)
C
         NM1 = N - 1
         IF (NM1 .LT. 1) GO TO 140
         DO 130 KB = 1, NM1
            K = N - KB
            KP1 = K + 1
            DO 110 I = KP1, N
               WORK(I) = A(I,K)
               A(I,K) = 0.0E0
  110       CONTINUE
            DO 120 J = KP1, N
               T = WORK(J)
               CALL SAXPY(N,T,A(1,J),1,A(1,K),1)
  120       CONTINUE
            L = IPVT(K)
            IF (L .NE. K) CALL SSWAP(N,A(1,K),1,A(1,L),1)
  130    CONTINUE
  140    CONTINUE
  150 CONTINUE
      RETURN
      END
```

```
      SUBROUTINE SGBCO(ABD,LDA,N,ML,MU,IPVT,RCOND,Z)
      INTEGER LDA,N,ML,MU,IPVT(1)
      REAL ABD(LDA,1),Z(1)
      REAL RCOND
C
C     SGBCO FACTORS A REAL BAND MATRIX BY GAUSSIAN
C     ELIMINATION AND ESTIMATES THE CONDITION OF THE MATRIX.
C
C     IF  RCOND  IS NOT NEEDED, SGBFA IS SLIGHTLY FASTER.
C     TO SOLVE  A*X = B , FOLLOW SGBCO BY SGBSL.
C     TO COMPUTE  INVERSE(A)*C , FOLLOW SGBCO BY SGBSL.
C     TO COMPUTE  DETERMINANT(A) , FOLLOW SGBCO BY SGBDI.
C
C     ON ENTRY
C
C        ABD     REAL(LDA, N)
C                CONTAINS THE MATRIX IN BAND STORAGE.  THE COLUMNS
C                OF THE MATRIX ARE STORED IN THE COLUMNS OF  ABD  AND
C                THE DIAGONALS OF THE MATRIX ARE STORED IN ROWS
C                ML+1 THROUGH 2*ML+MU+1 OF  ABD .
C                SEE THE COMMENTS BELOW FOR DETAILS.
C
C        LDA     INTEGER
C                THE LEADING DIMENSION OF THE ARRAY  ABD .
C                LDA MUST BE .GE. 2*ML + MU + 1 .
C
C        N       INTEGER
C                THE ORDER OF THE ORIGINAL MATRIX.
C
C        ML      INTEGER
C                NUMBER OF DIAGONALS BELOW THE MAIN DIAGONAL.
C                0 .LE. ML .LT. N .
C
C        MU      INTEGER
C                NUMBER OF DIAGONALS ABOVE THE MAIN DIAGONAL.
C                0 .LE. MU .LT. N .
C                MORE EFFICIENT IF  ML .LE. MU .
C
C     ON RETURN
C
C        ABD     AN UPPER TRIANGULAR MATRIX IN BAND STORAGE AND
C                THE MULTIPLIERS WHICH WERE USED TO OBTAIN IT.
C                THE FACTORIZATION CAN BE WRITTEN  A = L*U  WHERE
C                L  IS A PRODUCT OF PERMUTATION AND UNIT LOWER
C                TRIANGULAR MATRICES AND  U  IS UPPER TRIANGULAR.
C
C        IPVT    INTEGER(N)
C                AN INTEGER VECTOR OF PIVOT INDICES.
C
C        RCOND   REAL
C                AN ESTIMATE OF THE RECIPROCAL CONDITION OF  A .
C                FOR THE SYSTEM  A*X = B , RELATIVE PERTURBATIONS
C                IN  A  AND  B  OF SIZE  EPSILON  MAY CAUSE
C                RELATIVE PERTURBATIONS IN  X  OF SIZE  EPSILON/RCOND .
C                IF  RCOND  IS SO SMALL THAT THE LOGICAL EXPRESSION
C                           1.0 + RCOND .EQ. 1.0
C                IS TRUE, THEN  A  MAY BE SINGULAR TO WORKING
C                PRECISION.  IN PARTICULAR,  RCOND  IS ZERO  IF
C                EXACT SINGULARITY IS DETECTED OR THE ESTIMATE
C                UNDERFLOWS.
C
C        Z       REAL(N)
C                A WORK VECTOR WHOSE CONTENTS ARE USUALLY UNIMPORTANT.
```

```
C              IF  A  IS CLOSE TO A SINGULAR MATRIX, THEN  Z  IS
C              AN APPROXIMATE NULL VECTOR IN THE SENSE THAT
C              NORM(A*Z) = RCOND*NORM(A)*NORM(Z) .
C
C     BAND STORAGE
C
C           IF  A  IS A BAND MATRIX, THE FOLLOWING PROGRAM SEGMENT
C           WILL SET UP THE INPUT.
C
C                   ML = (BAND WIDTH BELOW THE DIAGONAL)
C                   MU = (BAND WIDTH ABOVE THE DIAGONAL)
C                   M = ML + MU + 1
C                   DO 20 J = 1, N
C                      I1 = MAX0(1, J-MU)
C                      I2 = MIN0(N, J+ML)
C                      DO 10 I = I1, I2
C                         K = I - J + M
C                         ABD(K,J) = A(I,J)
C                10    CONTINUE
C                20 CONTINUE
C
C           THIS USES ROWS  ML+1  THROUGH  2*ML+MU+1  OF  ABD .
C           IN ADDITION, THE FIRST  ML  ROWS IN  ABD  ARE USED FOR
C           ELEMENTS GENERATED DURING THE TRIANGULARIZATION.
C           THE TOTAL NUMBER OF ROWS NEEDED IN  ABD  IS  2*ML+MU+1 .
C           THE  ML+MU BY ML+MU  UPPER LEFT TRIANGLE AND THE
C           ML BY ML  LOWER RIGHT TRIANGLE ARE NOT REFERENCED.
C
C     EXAMPLE..  IF THE ORIGINAL MATRIX IS
C
C           11 12 13  0  0  0
C           21 22 23 24  0  0
C            0 32 33 34 35  0
C            0  0 43 44 45 46
C            0  0  0 54 55 56
C            0  0  0  0 65 66
C
C      THEN  N = 6, ML = 1, MU = 2, LDA .GE. 5  AND ABD SHOULD CONTAIN
C
C            *  *  *  +  +  +  , * = NOT USED
C            *  * 13 24 35 46  , + = USED FOR PIVOTING
C            * 12 23 34 45 56
C           11 22 33 44 55 66
C           21 32 43 54 65  *
C
C     LINPACK. THIS VERSION DATED 08/14/78 .
C     CLEVE MOLER, UNIVERSITY OF NEW MEXICO, ARGONNE NATIONAL LAB.
C
C     SUBROUTINES AND FUNCTIONS
C
C     LINPACK SGBFA
C     BLAS SAXPY,SDOT,SSCAL,SASUM
C     FORTRAN ABS,AMAX1,MAX0,MIN0,SIGN
C
C     INTERNAL VARIABLES
C
      REAL SDOT,EK,T,WK,WKM
      REAL ANORM,S,SASUM,SM,YNORM
      INTEGER IS,INFO,J,JU,K,KB,KP1,L,LA,LM,LZ,M,MM
C
C
C     COMPUTE 1-NORM OF A
C
```

```
      ANORM = 0.0E0
      L = ML + 1
      IS = L + MU
      DO 10 J = 1, N
         ANORM = AMAX1(ANORM,SASUM(L,ABD(IS,J),1))
         IF (IS .GT. ML + 1) IS = IS - 1
         IF (J .LE. MU) L = L + 1
         IF (J .GE. N - ML) L = L - 1
   10 CONTINUE
C
C     FACTOR
C
      CALL SGBFA(ABD,LDA,N,ML,MU,IPVT,INFO)
C
C     RCOND = 1/(NORM(A)*(ESTIMATE OF NORM(INVERSE(A)))) .
C     ESTIMATE = NORM(Z)/NORM(Y) WHERE  A*Z = Y  AND  TRANS(A)*Y = E .
C     TRANS(A)  IS THE TRANSPOSE OF A .  THE COMPONENTS OF  E  ARE
C     CHOSEN TO CAUSE MAXIMUM LOCAL GROWTH IN THE ELEMENTS OF W  WHERE
C     TRANS(U)*W = E .  THE VECTORS ARE FREQUENTLY RESCALED TO AVOID
C     OVERFLOW.
C
C     SOLVE TRANS(U)*W = E
C
      EK = 1.0E0
      DO 20 J = 1, N
         Z(J) = 0.0E0
   20 CONTINUE
      M = ML + MU + 1
      JU = 0
      DO 100 K = 1, N
         IF (Z(K) .NE. 0.0E0) EK = SIGN(EK,-Z(K))
         IF (ABS(EK-Z(K)) .LE. ABS(ABD(M,K))) GO TO 30
            S = ABS(ABD(M,K))/ABS(EK-Z(K))
            CALL SSCAL(N,S,Z,1)
            EK = S*EK
   30    CONTINUE
         WK = EK - Z(K)
         WKM = -EK - Z(K)
         S = ABS(WK)
         SM = ABS(WKM)
         IF (ABD(M,K) .EQ. 0.0E0) GO TO 40
            WK = WK/ABD(M,K)
            WKM = WKM/ABD(M,K)
         GO TO 50
   40    CONTINUE
            WK = 1.0E0
            WKM = 1.0E0
   50    CONTINUE
         KP1 = K + 1
         JU = MIN0(MAX0(JU,MU+IPVT(K)),N)
         MM = M
         IF (KP1 .GT. JU) GO TO 90
            DO 60 J = KP1, JU
               MM = MM - 1
               SM = SM + ABS(Z(J)+WKM*ABD(MM,J))
               Z(J) = Z(J) + WK*ABD(MM,J)
               S = S + ABS(Z(J))
   60       CONTINUE
            IF (S .GE. SM) GO TO 80
               T = WKM - WK
               WK = WKM
               MM = M
               DO 70 J = KP1, JU
```

```
                MM = MM - 1
                Z(J) = Z(J) + T*ABD(MM,J)
   70         CONTINUE
   80      CONTINUE
   90   CONTINUE
        Z(K) = WK
  100 CONTINUE
      S = 1.0E0/SASUM(N,Z,1)
      CALL SSCAL(N,S,Z,1)
C
C     SOLVE TRANS(L)*Y = W
C
      DO 120 KB = 1, N
         K = N + 1 - KB
         LM = MIN0(ML,N-K)
         IF (K .LT. N) Z(K) = Z(K) + SDOT(LM,ABD(M+1,K),1,Z(K+1),1)
         IF (ABS(Z(K)) .LE. 1.0E0) GO TO 110
            S = 1.0E0/ABS(Z(K))
            CALL SSCAL(N,S,Z,1)
  110    CONTINUE
         L = IPVT(K)
         T = Z(L)
         Z(L) = Z(K)
         Z(K) = T
  120 CONTINUE
      S = 1.0E0/SASUM(N,Z,1)
      CALL SSCAL(N,S,Z,1)
C
      YNORM = 1.0E0
C
C     SOLVE L*V = Y
C
      DO 140 K = 1, N
         L = IPVT(K)
         T = Z(L)
         Z(L) = Z(K)
         Z(K) = T
         LM = MIN0(ML,N-K)
         IF (K .LT. N) CALL SAXPY(LM,T,ABD(M+1,K),1,Z(K+1),1)
         IF (ABS(Z(K)) .LE. 1.0E0) GO TO 130
            S = 1.0E0/ABS(Z(K))
            CALL SSCAL(N,S,Z,1)
            YNORM = S*YNORM
  130    CONTINUE
  140 CONTINUE
      S = 1.0E0/SASUM(N,Z,1)
      CALL SSCAL(N,S,Z,1)
      YNORM = S*YNORM
C
C     SOLVE  U*Z = V
C
      DO 160 KB = 1, N
         K = N + 1 - KB
         IF (ABS(Z(K)) .LE. ABS(ABD(M,K))) GO TO 150
            S = ABS(ABD(M,K))/ABS(Z(K))
            CALL SSCAL(N,S,Z,1)
            YNORM = S*YNORM
  150    CONTINUE
         IF (ABD(M,K) .NE. 0.0E0) Z(K) = Z(K)/ABD(M,K)
         IF (ABD(M,K) .EQ. 0.0E0) Z(K) = 1.0E0
         LM = MIN0(K,M) - 1
         LA = M - LM
         LZ = K - LM
```

```
            T = -Z(K)
            CALL SAXPY(LM,T,ABD(LA,K),1,Z(LZ),1)
  160 CONTINUE
C     MAKE ZNORM = 1.0
      S = 1.0E0/SASUM(N,Z,1)
      CALL SSCAL(N,S,Z,1)
      YNORM = S*YNORM
C
      IF (ANORM .NE. 0.0E0) RCOND = YNORM/ANORM
      IF (ANORM .EQ. 0.0E0) RCOND = 0.0E0
      RETURN
      END
```

```
      SUBROUTINE SGBFA(ABD,LDA,N,ML,MU,IPVT.INFO)
      INTEGER LDA,N,ML,MU,IPVT(1),INFO
      REAL ABD(LDA,1)
C
C     SGBFA FACTORS A REAL BAND MATRIX BY GAUSSIAN ELIMINATION.
C
C     SGBFA IS USUALLY CALLED BY SGBCO, BUT IT CAN BE CALLED
C     DIRECTLY WITH A SAVING IN TIME IF  RCOND  IS NOT NEEDED.
C
C     ON ENTRY
C
C        ABD     REAL(LDA, N)
C                CONTAINS THE MATRIX IN BAND STORAGE.  THE COLUMNS
C                OF THE MATRIX ARE STORED IN THE COLUMNS OF  ABD  AND
C                THE DIAGONALS OF THE MATRIX ARE STORED IN ROWS
C                ML+1 THROUGH 2*ML+MU+1 OF  ABD .
C                SEE THE COMMENTS BELOW FOR DETAILS.
C
C        LDA     INTEGER
C                THE LEADING DIMENSION OF THE ARRAY  ABD .
C                LDA MUST BE .GE. 2*ML + MU + 1 .
C
C        N       INTEGER
C                THE ORDER OF THE ORIGINAL MATRIX.
C
C        ML      INTEGER
C                NUMBER OF DIAGONALS BELOW THE MAIN DIAGONAL.
C                0 .LE. ML .LT. N .
C
C        MU      INTEGER
C                NUMBER OF DIAGONALS ABOVE THE MAIN DIAGONAL.
C                0 .LE. MU .LT. N .
C                MORE EFFICIENT IF  ML .LE. MU .
C     ON RETURN
C
C        ABD     AN UPPER TRIANGULAR MATRIX IN BAND STORAGE AND
C                THE MULTIPLIERS WHICH WERE USED TO OBTAIN IT.
C                THE FACTORIZATION CAN BE WRITTEN  A = L*U  WHERE
C                L  IS A PRODUCT OF PERMUTATION AND UNIT LOWER
C                TRIANGULAR MATRICES AND  U  IS UPPER TRIANGULAR.
C
C        IPVT    INTEGER(N)
C                AN INTEGER VECTOR OF PIVOT INDICES.
C
C        INFO    INTEGER
C                = 0  NORMAL VALUE.
C                = K  IF  U(K,K) .EQ. 0.0 .  THIS IS NOT AN ERROR
C                     CONDITION FOR THIS SUBROUTINE, BUT IT DOES
C                     INDICATE THAT SGBSL WILL DIVIDE BY ZERO IF
C                     CALLED.  USE  RCOND  IN SGBCO FOR A RELIABLE
C                     INDICATION OF SINGULARITY.
C
C     BAND STORAGE
C
C           IF  A  IS A BAND MATRIX, THE FOLLOWING PROGRAM SEGMENT
C           WILL SET UP THE INPUT.
C
C                   ML = (BAND WIDTH BELOW THE DIAGONAL)
C                   MU = (BAND WIDTH ABOVE THE DIAGONAL)
C                   M = ML + MU + 1
C                   DO 20 J = 1, N
C                      I1 = MAX0(1, J-MU)
C                      I2 = MIN0(N, J+ML)
```

```
C                    DO 10 I = I1, I2
C                       K = I - J + M
C                       ABD(K,J) = A(I,J)
C              10    CONTINUE
C              20 CONTINUE
C
C          THIS USES ROWS  ML+1  THROUGH  2*ML+MU+1  OF  ABD .
C          IN ADDITION, THE FIRST  ML  ROWS IN  ABD  ARE USED FOR
C          ELEMENTS GENERATED DURING THE TRIANGULARIZATION.
C          THE TOTAL NUMBER OF ROWS NEEDED IN  ABD  IS  2*ML+MU+1 .
C          THE  ML+MU BY ML+MU  UPPER LEFT TRIANGLE AND THE
C          ML BY ML  LOWER RIGHT TRIANGLE ARE NOT REFERENCED.
C
C     LINPACK. THIS VERSION DATED 08/14/78 .
C     CLEVE MOLER, UNIVERSITY OF NEW MEXICO, ARGONNE NATIONAL LAB.
C
C     SUBROUTINES AND FUNCTIONS
C
C     BLAS SAXPY,SSCAL,ISAMAX
C     FORTRAN MAX0,MIN0
C
C     INTERNAL VARIABLES
C
      REAL T
      INTEGER I,ISAMAX,I0,J,JU,JZ,J0,J1,K,KP1,L,LM,M,MM,NM1
C
C
      M = ML + MU + 1
      INFO = 0
C
C     ZERO INITIAL FILL-IN COLUMNS
C
      J0 = MU + 2
      J1 = MIN0(N,M) - 1
      IF (J1 .LT. J0) GO TO 30
      DO 20 JZ = J0, J1
         I0 = M + 1 - JZ
         DO 10 I = I0, ML
            ABD(I,JZ) = 0.0E0
   10    CONTINUE
   20 CONTINUE
   30 CONTINUE
      JZ = J1
      JU = 0
C
C     GAUSSIAN ELIMINATION WITH PARTIAL PIVOTING
C
      NM1 = N - 1
      IF (NM1 .LT. 1) GO TO 130
      DO 120 K = 1, NM1
         KP1 = K + 1
C
C        ZERO NEXT FILL-IN COLUMN
C
         JZ = JZ + 1
         IF (JZ .GT. N) GO TO 50
         IF (ML .LT. 1) GO TO 50
            DO 40 I = 1, ML
               ABD(I,JZ) = 0.0E0
   40       CONTINUE
   50    CONTINUE
C
C        FIND L = PIVOT INDEX
```

```
C
         LM = MIN0(ML,N-K)
         L = ISAMAX(LM+1,ABD(M,K),1) + M - 1
         IPVT(K) = L + K - M
C
C        ZERO PIVOT IMPLIES THIS COLUMN ALREADY TRIANGULARIZED
C
         IF (ABD(L,K) .EQ. 0.0E0) GO TO 100
C
C           INTERCHANGE IF NECESSARY
C
            IF (L .EQ. M) GO TO 60
               T = ABD(L,K)
               ABD(L,K) = ABD(M,K)
               ABD(M,K) = T
   60       CONTINUE
C
C           COMPUTE MULTIPLIERS
C
            T = -1.0E0/ABD(M,K)
            CALL SSCAL(LM,T,ABD(M+1,K),1)
C
C           ROW ELIMINATION WITH COLUMN INDEXING
C
            JU = MIN0(MAX0(JU,MU+IPVT(K)),N)
            MM = M
            IF (JU .LT. KP1) GO TO 90
            DO 80 J = KP1, JU
               L = L - 1
               MM = MM - 1
               T = ABD(L,J)
               IF (L .EQ. MM) GO TO 70
                  ABD(L,J) = ABD(MM,J)
                  ABD(MM,J) = T
   70          CONTINUE
               CALL SAXPY(LM,T,ABD(M+1,K),1,ABD(MM+1,J),1)
   80       CONTINUE
   90       CONTINUE
         GO TO 110
  100    CONTINUE
            INFO = K
  110    CONTINUE
  120 CONTINUE
  130 CONTINUE
      IPVT(N) = N
      IF (ABD(M,N) .EQ. 0.0E0) INFO = N
      RETURN
      END
```

```
      SUBROUTINE SGBSL(ABD,LDA,N,ML,MU,IPVT,B,JOB)
      INTEGER LDA,N,ML,MU,IPVT(1),JOB
      REAL ABD(LDA,1),B(1)
C
C     SGBSL SOLVES THE REAL BAND SYSTEM
C     A * X = B  OR  TRANS(A) * X = B
C     USING THE FACTORS COMPUTED BY SGBCO OR SGBFA.
C
C     ON ENTRY
C
C        ABD     REAL(LDA, N)
C                THE OUTPUT FROM SGBCO OR SGBFA.
C
C        LDA     INTEGER
C                THE LEADING DIMENSION OF THE ARRAY  ABD .
C
C        N       INTEGER
C                THE ORDER OF THE ORIGINAL MATRIX.
C
C        ML      INTEGER
C                NUMBER OF DIAGONALS BELOW THE MAIN DIAGONAL.
C
C        MU      INTEGER
C                NUMBER OF DIAGONALS ABOVE THE MAIN DIAGONAL.
C
C        IPVT    INTEGER(N)
C                THE PIVOT VECTOR FROM SGBCO OR SGBFA.
C
C        B       REAL(N)
C                THE RIGHT HAND SIDE VECTOR.
C
C        JOB     INTEGER
C                = 0         TO SOLVE  A*X = B ,
C                = NONZERO   TO SOLVE  TRANS(A)*X = B , WHERE
C                            TRANS(A)  IS THE TRANSPOSE.
C
C     ON RETURN
C
C        B       THE SOLUTION VECTOR  X .
C
C     ERROR CONDITION
C
C        A DIVISION BY ZERO WILL OCCUR IF THE INPUT FACTOR CONTAINS A
C        ZERO ON THE DIAGONAL.  TECHNICALLY THIS INDICATES SINGULARITY
C        BUT IT IS OFTEN CAUSED BY IMPROPER ARGUMENTS OR IMPROPER
C        SETTING OF LDA .  IT WILL NOT OCCUR IF THE SUBROUTINES ARE
C        CALLED CORRECTLY AND IF SGBCO HAS SET RCOND .GT. 0.0
C        OR SGBFA HAS SET INFO .EQ. 0 .
C
C     TO COMPUTE  INVERSE(A) * C  WHERE  C  IS A MATRIX
C     WITH  P  COLUMNS
C           CALL SGBCO(ABD,LDA,N,ML,MU,IPVT,RCOND,Z)
C           IF (RCOND IS TOO SMALL) GO TO ...
C           DO 10 J = 1, P
C              CALL SGBSL(ABD,LDA,N,ML,MU,IPVT,C(1,J),0)
C        10 CONTINUE
C
C     LINPACK. THIS VERSION DATED 08/14/78 .
C     CLEVE MOLER, UNIVERSITY OF NEW MEXICO, ARGONNE NATIONAL LAB.
C
C     SUBROUTINES AND FUNCTIONS
C
C     BLAS SAXPY,SDOT
```

```
C     FORTRAN MINO
C
C     INTERNAL VARIABLES
C
      REAL SDOT,T
      INTEGER K,KB,L,LA,LB,LM,M,NM1
C
      M = MU + ML + 1
      NM1 = N - 1
      IF (JOB .NE. 0) GO TO 50
C
C        JOB = 0 , SOLVE  A * X = B
C        FIRST SOLVE L*Y = B
C
         IF (ML .EQ. 0) GO TO 30
         IF (NM1 .LT. 1) GO TO 30
            DO 20 K = 1, NM1
               LM = MIN0(ML,N-K)
               L = IPVT(K)
               T = B(L)
               IF (L .EQ. K) GO TO 10
                  B(L) = B(K)
                  B(K) = T
   10          CONTINUE
               CALL SAXPY(LM,T,ABD(M+1,K),1,B(K+1),1)
   20       CONTINUE
   30    CONTINUE
C
C        NOW SOLVE  U*X = Y
C
         DO 40 KB = 1, N
            K = N + 1 - KB
            B(K) = B(K)/ABD(M,K)
            LM = MIN0(K,M) - 1
            LA = M - LM
            LB = K - LM
            T = -B(K)
            CALL SAXPY(LM,T,ABD(LA,K),1,B(LB),1)
   40    CONTINUE
      GO TO 100
   50 CONTINUE
C
C        JOB = NONZERO, SOLVE  TRANS(A) * X = B
C        FIRST SOLVE  TRANS(U)*Y = B
C
         DO 60 K = 1, N
            LM = MIN0(K,M) - 1
            LA = M - LM
            LB = K - LM
            T = SDOT(LM,ABD(LA,K),1,B(LB),1)
            B(K) = (B(K) - T)/ABD(M,K)
   60    CONTINUE
C
C        NOW SOLVE TRANS(L)*X = Y
C
         IF (ML .EQ. 0) GO TO 90
         IF (NM1 .LT. 1) GO TO 90
            DO 80 KB = 1, NM1
               K = N - KB
               LM = MIN0(ML,N-K)
               B(K) = B(K) + SDOT(LM,ABD(M+1,K),1,B(K+1),1)
               L = IPVT(K)
               IF (L .EQ. K) GO TO 70
```

```
                  T = B(L)
                  B(L) = B(K)
                  B(K) = T
   70          CONTINUE
   80       CONTINUE
   90    CONTINUE
  100 CONTINUE
      RETURN
      END
```

```
      SUBROUTINE SGBDI(ABD,LDA,N,ML,MU,IPVT,DET)
      INTEGER LDA,N,ML,MU,IPVT(1)
      REAL ABD(LDA,1),DET(2)
C
C     SGBDI COMPUTES THE DETERMINANT OF A BAND MATRIX
C     USING THE FACTORS COMPUTED BY SGBCO OR SGBFA.
C     IF THE INVERSE IS NEEDED, USE SGBSL  N  TIMES.
C
C     ON ENTRY
C
C        ABD     REAL(LDA, N)
C                THE OUTPUT FROM SGBCO OR SGBFA.
C
C        LDA     INTEGER
C                THE LEADING DIMENSION OF THE ARRAY  ABD .
C
C        N       INTEGER
C                THE ORDER OF THE ORIGINAL MATRIX.
C
C        ML      INTEGER
C                NUMBER OF DIAGONALS BELOW THE MAIN DIAGONAL.
C
C        MU      INTEGER
C                NUMBER OF DIAGONALS ABOVE THE MAIN DIAGONAL.
C
C        IPVT    INTEGER(N)
C                THE PIVOT VECTOR FROM SGBCO OR SGBFA.
C
C     ON RETURN
C
C        DET     REAL(2)
C                DETERMINANT OF ORIGINAL MATRIX.
C                DETERMINANT = DET(1) * 10.0**DET(2)
C                WITH  1.0 .LE. ABS(DET(1)) .LT. 10.0
C                OR  DET(1) = 0.0 .
C
C     LINPACK. THIS VERSION DATED 08/14/78 .
C     CLEVE MOLER, UNIVERSITY OF NEW MEXICO, ARGONNE NATIONAL LAB.
C
C     SUBROUTINES AND FUNCTIONS
C
C     FORTRAN ABS
C
C     INTERNAL VARIABLES
C
      REAL TEN
      INTEGER I,M
C
C
      M = ML + MU + 1
      DET(1) = 1.0E0
      DET(2) = 0.0E0
      TEN = 10.0E0
      DO 50 I = 1, N
         IF (IPVT(I) .NE. I) DET(1) = -DET(1)
         DET(1) = ABD(M,I)*DET(1)
C     ...EXIT
         IF (DET(1) .EQ. 0.0E0) GO TO 60
   10    IF (ABS(DET(1)) .GE. 1.0E0) GO TO 20
            DET(1) = TEN*DET(1)
            DET(2) = DET(2) - 1.0E0
         GO TO 10
   20    CONTINUE
```

```
30    IF (ABS(DET(1)) .LT. TEN) GO TO 40
         DET(1) = DET(1)/TEN
         DET(2) = DET(2) + 1.0E0
      GO TO 30
40    CONTINUE
50 CONTINUE
60 CONTINUE
   RETURN
   END
```

SPOCO

```
      SUBROUTINE SPOCO(A,LDA,N,RCOND,Z,INFO)
      INTEGER LDA,N,INFO
      REAL A(LDA,1),Z(1)
      REAL RCOND
C
C     SPOCO FACTORS A REAL SYMMETRIC POSITIVE DEFINITE MATRIX
C     AND ESTIMATES THE CONDITION OF THE MATRIX.
C
C     IF  RCOND  IS NOT NEEDED, SPOFA IS SLIGHTLY FASTER.
C     TO SOLVE  A*X = B , FOLLOW SPOCO BY SPOSL.
C     TO COMPUTE  INVERSE(A)*C , FOLLOW SPOCO BY SPOSL.
C     TO COMPUTE  DETERMINANT(A) , FOLLOW SPOCO BY SPODI.
C     TO COMPUTE  INVERSE(A) , FOLLOW SPOCO BY SPODI.
C
C     ON ENTRY
C
C        A       REAL(LDA, N)
C                THE SYMMETRIC MATRIX TO BE FACTORED.  ONLY THE
C                DIAGONAL AND UPPER TRIANGLE ARE USED.
C
C        LDA     INTEGER
C                THE LEADING DIMENSION OF THE ARRAY  A .
C
C        N       INTEGER
C                THE ORDER OF THE MATRIX  A .
C
C     ON RETURN
C
C        A       AN UPPER TRIANGULAR MATRIX  R  SO THAT  A = TRANS(R)*R
C                WHERE  TRANS(R)  IS THE TRANSPOSE.
C                THE STRICT LOWER TRIANGLE IS UNALTERED.
C                IF  INFO .NE. 0 , THE FACTORIZATION IS NOT COMPLETE.
C
C        RCOND   REAL
C                AN ESTIMATE OF THE RECIPROCAL CONDITION OF  A .
C                FOR THE SYSTEM  A*X = B , RELATIVE PERTURBATIONS
C                IN  A  AND  B  OF SIZE  EPSILON  MAY CAUSE
C                RELATIVE PERTURBATIONS IN  X  OF SIZE  EPSILON/RCOND .
C                IF  RCOND  IS SO SMALL THAT THE LOGICAL EXPRESSION
C                           1.0 + RCOND .EQ. 1.0
C                IS TRUE, THEN  A  MAY BE SINGULAR TO WORKING
C                PRECISION.  IN PARTICULAR,  RCOND  IS ZERO  IF
C                EXACT SINGULARITY IS DETECTED OR THE ESTIMATE
C                UNDERFLOWS.  IF INFO .NE. 0 , RCOND IS UNCHANGED.
C
C        Z       REAL(N)
C                A WORK VECTOR WHOSE CONTENTS ARE USUALLY UNIMPORTANT.
C                IF  A  IS CLOSE TO A SINGULAR MATRIX, THEN  Z  IS
C                AN APPROXIMATE NULL VECTOR IN THE SENSE THAT
C                NORM(A*Z) = RCOND*NORM(A)*NORM(Z) .
C                IF  INFO .NE. 0 , Z  IS UNCHANGED.
C
C        INFO    INTEGER
C                = 0  FOR NORMAL RETURN.
C                = K  SIGNALS AN ERROR CONDITION.  THE LEADING MINOR
C                     OF ORDER  K  IS NOT POSITIVE DEFINITE.
C
C     LINPACK.  THIS VERSION DATED 08/14/78 .
C     CLEVE MOLER, UNIVERSITY OF NEW MEXICO, ARGONNE NATIONAL LAB.
C
C     SUBROUTINES AND FUNCTIONS
C
C     LINPACK SPOFA
```

```
C     BLAS SAXPY,SDOT,SSCAL,SASUM
C     FORTRAN ABS,AMAX1,SIGN
C
C     INTERNAL VARIABLES
C
      REAL SDOT,EK,T,WK,WKM
      REAL ANORM,S,SASUM,SM,YNORM
      INTEGER I,J,JM1,K,KB,KP1
C
C
C     FIND NORM OF A USING ONLY UPPER HALF
C
      DO 30 J = 1, N
         Z(J) = SASUM(J,A(1,J),1)
         JM1 = J - 1
         IF (JM1 .LT. 1) GO TO 20
         DO 10 I = 1, JM1
            Z(I) = Z(I) + ABS(A(I,J))
   10    CONTINUE
   20    CONTINUE
   30 CONTINUE
      ANORM = 0.0E0
      DO 40 J = 1, N
         ANORM = AMAX1(ANORM,Z(J))
   40 CONTINUE
C
C     FACTOR
C
      CALL SPOFA(A,LDA,N,INFO)
      IF (INFO .NE. 0) GO TO 180
C
C        RCOND = 1/(NORM(A)*(ESTIMATE OF NORM(INVERSE(A)))) .
C        ESTIMATE = NORM(Z)/NORM(Y) WHERE  A*Z = Y  AND  A*Y = E .
C        THE COMPONENTS OF  E  ARE CHOSEN TO CAUSE MAXIMUM LOCAL
C        GROWTH IN THE ELEMENTS OF W  WHERE  TRANS(R)*W = E .
C        THE VECTORS ARE FREQUENTLY RESCALED TO AVOID OVERFLOW.
C
C        SOLVE TRANS(R)*W = E
C
         EK = 1.0E0
         DO 50 J = 1, N
            Z(J) = 0.0E0
   50    CONTINUE
         DO 110 K = 1, N
            IF (Z(K) .NE. 0.0E0) EK = SIGN(EK,-Z(K))
            IF (ABS(EK-Z(K)) .LE. A(K,K)) GO TO 60
               S = A(K,K)/ABS(EK-Z(K))
               CALL SSCAL(N,S,Z,1)
               EK = S*EK
   60       CONTINUE
            WK = EK - Z(K)
            WKM = -EK - Z(K)
            S = ABS(WK)
            SM = ABS(WKM)
            WK = WK/A(K,K)
            WKM = WKM/A(K,K)
            KP1 = K + 1
            IF (KP1 .GT. N) GO TO 100
               DO 70 J = KP1, N
                  SM = SM + ABS(Z(J)+WKM*A(K,J))
                  Z(J) = Z(J) + WK*A(K,J)
                  S = S + ABS(Z(J))
   70          CONTINUE
```

```
               IF (S .GE. SM) GO TO 90
                  T = WKM - WK
                  WK = WKM
                  DO 80 J = KP1, N
                     Z(J) = Z(J) + T*A(K,J)
   80             CONTINUE
   90          CONTINUE
  100       CONTINUE
            Z(K) = WK
  110    CONTINUE
         S = 1.0E0/SASUM(N,Z,1)
         CALL SSCAL(N,S,Z,1)
C
C        SOLVE R*Y = W
C
         DO 130 KB = 1, N
            K = N + 1 - KB
            IF (ABS(Z(K)) .LE. A(K,K)) GO TO 120
               S = A(K,K)/ABS(Z(K))
               CALL SSCAL(N,S,Z,1)
  120       CONTINUE
            Z(K) = Z(K)/A(K,K)
            T = -Z(K)
            CALL SAXPY(K-1,T,A(1,K),1,Z(1),1)
  130    CONTINUE
         S = 1.0E0/SASUM(N,Z,1)
         CALL SSCAL(N,S,Z,1)
C
         YNORM = 1.0E0
C
C        SOLVE TRANS(R)*V = Y
C
         DO 150 K = 1, N
            Z(K) = Z(K) - SDOT(K-1,A(1,K),1,Z(1),1)
            IF (ABS(Z(K)) .LE. A(K,K)) GO TO 140
               S = A(K,K)/ABS(Z(K))
               CALL SSCAL(N,S,Z,1)
               YNORM = S*YNORM
  140       CONTINUE
            Z(K) = Z(K)/A(K,K)
  150    CONTINUE
         S = 1.0E0/SASUM(N,Z,1)
         CALL SSCAL(N,S,Z,1)
         YNORM = S*YNORM
C
C        SOLVE R*Z = V
C
         DO 170 KB = 1, N
            K = N + 1 - KB
            IF (ABS(Z(K)) .LE. A(K,K)) GO TO 160
               S = A(K,K)/ABS(Z(K))
               CALL SSCAL(N,S,Z,1)
               YNORM = S*YNORM
  160       CONTINUE
            Z(K) = Z(K)/A(K,K)
            T = -Z(K)
            CALL SAXPY(K-1,T,A(1,K),1,Z(1),1)
  170    CONTINUE
C        MAKE ZNORM = 1.0
         S = 1.0E0/SASUM(N,Z,1)
         CALL SSCAL(N,S,Z,1)
         YNORM = S*YNORM
C
```

```
      IF (ANORM .NE. 0.0E0) RCOND = YNORM/ANORM
      IF (ANORM .EQ. 0.0E0) RCOND = 0.0E0
180 CONTINUE
    RETURN
    END
```

SPOFA

```
      SUBROUTINE SPOFA(A,LDA,N,INFO)
      INTEGER LDA,N,INFO
      REAL A(LDA,1)
C
C     SPOFA FACTORS A REAL SYMMETRIC POSITIVE DEFINITE MATRIX.
C
C     SPOFA IS USUALLY CALLED BY SPOCO, BUT IT CAN BE CALLED
C     DIRECTLY WITH A SAVING IN TIME IF  RCOND  IS NOT NEEDED.
C     (TIME FOR SPOCO) = (1 + 18/N)*(TIME FOR SPOFA) .
C
C     ON ENTRY
C
C        A       REAL(LDA, N)
C                THE SYMMETRIC MATRIX TO BE FACTORED.  ONLY THE
C                DIAGONAL AND UPPER TRIANGLE ARE USED.
C
C        LDA     INTEGER
C                THE LEADING DIMENSION OF THE ARRAY  A .
C
C        N       INTEGER
C                THE ORDER OF THE MATRIX  A .
C
C     ON RETURN
C
C        A       AN UPPER TRIANGULAR MATRIX  R  SO THAT  A = TRANS(R)*R
C                WHERE  TRANS(R)  IS THE TRANSPOSE.
C                THE STRICT LOWER TRIANGLE IS UNALTERED.
C                IF  INFO .NE. 0 , THE FACTORIZATION IS NOT COMPLETE.
C
C        INFO    INTEGER
C                = 0  FOR NORMAL RETURN.
C                = K  SIGNALS AN ERROR CONDITION.  THE LEADING MINOR
C                     OF ORDER  K  IS NOT POSITIVE DEFINITE.
C
C     LINPACK.  THIS VERSION DATED 08/14/78 .
C     CLEVE MOLER, UNIVERSITY OF NEW MEXICO, ARGONNE NATIONAL LAB.
C
C     SUBROUTINES AND FUNCTIONS
C
C     BLAS SDOT
C     FORTRAN SQRT
C
C     INTERNAL VARIABLES
C
      REAL SDOT,T
      REAL S
      INTEGER J,JM1,K
C     BEGIN BLOCK WITH ...EXITS TO 40
C
C
         DO 30 J = 1, N
            INFO = J
            S = 0.0E0
            JM1 = J - 1
            IF (JM1 .LT. 1) GO TO 20
            DO 10 K = 1, JM1
               T = A(K,J) - SDOT(K-1,A(1,K),1,A(1,J),1)
               T = T/A(K,K)
               A(K,J) = T
               S = S + T*T
   10       CONTINUE
   20       CONTINUE
            S = A(J,J) - S
```

```
C       ......EXIT
              IF (S .LE. 0.0E0) GO TO 40
              A(J,J) = SQRT(S)
   30      CONTINUE
           INFO = 0
   40 CONTINUE
      RETURN
      END
```

SPOSL

```
      SUBROUTINE SPOSL(A,LDA,N,B)
      INTEGER LDA,N
      REAL A(LDA,1),B(1)
C
C     SPOSL SOLVES THE REAL SYMMETRIC POSITIVE DEFINITE SYSTEM
C     A * X = B
C     USING THE FACTORS COMPUTED BY SPOCO OR SPOFA.
C
C     ON ENTRY
C
C        A       REAL(LDA, N)
C                THE OUTPUT FROM SPOCO OR SPOFA.
C
C        LDA     INTEGER
C                THE LEADING DIMENSION OF THE ARRAY  A .
C
C        N       INTEGER
C                THE ORDER OF THE MATRIX  A .
C
C        B       REAL(N)
C                THE RIGHT HAND SIDE VECTOR.
C
C     ON RETURN
C
C        B       THE SOLUTION VECTOR  X .
C
C     ERROR CONDITION
C
C        A DIVISION BY ZERO WILL OCCUR IF THE INPUT FACTOR CONTAINS
C        A ZERO ON THE DIAGONAL.  TECHNICALLY THIS INDICATES
C        SINGULARITY BUT IT IS USUALLY CAUSED BY IMPROPER SUBROUTINE
C        ARGUMENTS.  IT WILL NOT OCCUR IF THE SUBROUTINES ARE CALLED
C        CORRECTLY AND  INFO .EQ. 0 .
C
C     TO COMPUTE  INVERSE(A) * C  WHERE  C  IS A MATRIX
C     WITH  P  COLUMNS
C           CALL SPOCO(A,LDA,N,RCOND,Z,INFO)
C           IF (RCOND IS TOO SMALL .OR. INFO .NE. 0) GO TO ...
C           DO 10 J = 1, P
C              CALL SPOSL(A,LDA,N,C(1,J))
C        10 CONTINUE
C
C     LINPACK.  THIS VERSION DATED 08/14/78 .
C     CLEVE MOLER, UNIVERSITY OF NEW MEXICO, ARGONNE NATIONAL LAB.
C
C     SUBROUTINES AND FUNCTIONS
C
C     BLAS SAXPY,SDOT
C
C     INTERNAL VARIABLES
C
      REAL SDOT,T
      INTEGER K,KB
C
C     SOLVE TRANS(R)*Y = B
C
      DO 10 K = 1, N
         T = SDOT(K-1,A(1,K),1,B(1),1)
         B(K) = (B(K) - T)/A(K,K)
   10 CONTINUE
C
C     SOLVE R*X = Y
C
```

```
      DO 20 KB = 1, N
         K = N + 1 - KB
         B(K) = B(K)/A(K,K)
         T = -B(K)
         CALL SAXPY(K-1,T,A(1,K),1,B(1),1)
   20 CONTINUE
      RETURN
      END
```

```
      SUBROUTINE SPODI(A,LDA,N,DET,JOB)
      INTEGER LDA,N,JOB
      REAL A(LDA,1)
      REAL DET(2)
C
C     SPODI COMPUTES THE DETERMINANT AND INVERSE OF A CERTAIN
C     REAL SYMMETRIC POSITIVE DEFINITE MATRIX (SEE BELOW)
C     USING THE FACTORS COMPUTED BY SPOCO, SPOFA OR SQRDC.
C
C     ON ENTRY
C
C        A       REAL(LDA, N)
C                THE OUTPUT  A  FROM SPOCO OR SPOFA
C                OR THE OUTPUT  X  FROM SQRDC.
C
C        LDA     INTEGER
C                THE LEADING DIMENSION OF THE ARRAY  A .
C
C        N       INTEGER
C                THE ORDER OF THE MATRIX  A .
C
C        JOB     INTEGER
C                = 11   BOTH DETERMINANT AND INVERSE.
C                = 01   INVERSE ONLY.
C                = 10   DETERMINANT ONLY.
C
C     ON RETURN
C
C        A       IF SPOCO OR SPOFA WAS USED TO FACTOR  A  THEN
C                SPODI PRODUCES THE UPPER HALF OF INVERSE(A) .
C                IF SQRDC WAS USED TO DECOMPOSE  X  THEN
C                SPODI PRODUCES THE UPPER HALF OF INVERSE(TRANS(X)*X)
C                WHERE TRANS(X) IS THE TRANSPOSE.
C                ELEMENTS OF  A  BELOW THE DIAGONAL ARE UNCHANGED.
C                IF THE UNITS DIGIT OF JOB IS ZERO,  A  IS UNCHANGED.
C
C        DET     REAL(2)
C                DETERMINANT OF  A  OR OF  TRANS(X)*X  IF REQUESTED.
C                OTHERWISE NOT REFERENCED.
C                DETERMINANT = DET(1) * 10.0**DET(2)
C                WITH  1.0 .LE. DET(1) .LT. 10.0
C                OR  DET(1) .EQ. 0.0 .
C
C     ERROR CONDITION
C
C        A DIVISION BY ZERO WILL OCCUR IF THE INPUT FACTOR CONTAINS
C        A ZERO ON THE DIAGONAL AND THE INVERSE IS REQUESTED.
C        IT WILL NOT OCCUR IF THE SUBROUTINES ARE CALLED CORRECTLY
C        AND IF SPOCO OR SPOFA HAS SET INFO .EQ. 0 .
C
C     LINPACK.  THIS VERSION DATED 08/14/78 .
C     CLEVE MOLER, UNIVERSITY OF NEW MEXICO, ARGONNE NATIONAL LAB.
C
C     SUBROUTINES AND FUNCTIONS
C
C     BLAS SAXPY,SSCAL
C     FORTRAN MOD
C
C     INTERNAL VARIABLES
C
      REAL T
      REAL S
      INTEGER I,J,JM1,K,KP1
```

```
C
C     COMPUTE DETERMINANT
C
      IF (JOB/10 .EQ. 0) GO TO 70
         DET(1) = 1.0E0
         DET(2) = 0.0E0
         S = 10.0E0
         DO 50 I = 1, N
            DET(1) = A(I,I)**2*DET(1)
C        ...EXIT
            IF (DET(1) .EQ. 0.0E0) GO TO 60
   10       IF (DET(1) .GE. 1.0E0) GO TO 20
               DET(1) = S*DET(1)
               DET(2) = DET(2) - 1.0E0
            GO TO 10
   20       CONTINUE
   30       IF (DET(1) .LT. S) GO TO 40
               DET(1) = DET(1)/S
               DET(2) = DET(2) + 1.0E0
            GO TO 30
   40       CONTINUE
   50    CONTINUE
   60    CONTINUE
   70 CONTINUE
C
C     COMPUTE INVERSE(R)
C
      IF (MOD(JOB,10) .EQ. 0) GO TO 140
         DO 100 K = 1, N
            A(K,K) = 1.0E0/A(K,K)
            T = -A(K,K)
            CALL SSCAL(K-1,T,A(1,K),1)
            KP1 = K + 1
            IF (N .LT. KP1) GO TO 90
            DO 80 J = KP1, N
               T = A(K,J)
               A(K,J) = 0.0E0
               CALL SAXPY(K,T,A(1,K),1,A(1,J),1)
   80       CONTINUE
   90       CONTINUE
  100    CONTINUE
C
C        FORM  INVERSE(R) * TRANS(INVERSE(R))
C
         DO 130 J = 1, N
            JM1 = J - 1
            IF (JM1 .LT. 1) GO TO 120
            DO 110 K = 1, JM1
               T = A(K,J)
               CALL SAXPY(K,T,A(1,J),1,A(1,K),1)
  110       CONTINUE
  120       CONTINUE
            T = A(J,J)
            CALL SSCAL(J,T,A(1,J),1)
  130    CONTINUE
  140 CONTINUE
      RETURN
      END
```

```
      SUBROUTINE SPPCO(AP,N,RCOND,Z,INFO)
      INTEGER N,INFO
      REAL AP(1),Z(1)
      REAL RCOND
C
C     SPPCO FACTORS A REAL SYMMETRIC POSITIVE DEFINITE MATRIX
C     STORED IN PACKED FORM
C     AND ESTIMATES THE CONDITION OF THE MATRIX.
C
C     IF  RCOND  IS NOT NEEDED, SPPFA IS SLIGHTLY FASTER.
C     TO SOLVE  A*X = B , FOLLOW SPPCO BY SPPSL.
C     TO COMPUTE  INVERSE(A)*C , FOLLOW SPPCO BY SPPSL.
C     TO COMPUTE  DETERMINANT(A) , FOLLOW SPPCO BY SPPDI.
C     TO COMPUTE  INVERSE(A) , FOLLOW SPPCO BY SPPDI.
C
C     ON ENTRY
C
C        AP      REAL (N*(N+1)/2)
C                THE PACKED FORM OF A SYMMETRIC MATRIX  A .  THE
C                COLUMNS OF THE UPPER TRIANGLE ARE STORED SEQUENTIALLY
C                IN A ONE-DIMENSIONAL ARRAY OF LENGTH  N*(N+1)/2 .
C                SEE COMMENTS BELOW FOR DETAILS.
C
C        N       INTEGER
C                THE ORDER OF THE MATRIX  A .
C
C     ON RETURN
C
C        AP      AN UPPER TRIANGULAR MATRIX  R , STORED IN PACKED
C                FORM, SO THAT  A = TRANS(R)*R WHERE TRANS(R) IS THE
                 TRANSPOSE.
C                IF  INFO .NE. 0 , THE FACTORIZATION IS NOT COMPLETE.
C
C        RCOND   REAL
C                AN ESTIMATE OF THE RECIPROCAL CONDITION OF  A .
C                FOR THE SYSTEM  A*X = B , RELATIVE PERTURBATIONS
C                IN  A  AND  B  OF SIZE  EPSILON  MAY CAUSE
C                RELATIVE PERTURBATIONS IN  X  OF SIZE  EPSILON/RCOND .
C                IF  RCOND  IS SO SMALL THAT THE LOGICAL EXPRESSION
C                           1.0 + RCOND .EQ. 1.0
C                IS TRUE, THEN  A  MAY BE SINGULAR TO WORKING
C                PRECISION.  IN PARTICULAR,  RCOND  IS ZERO  IF
C                EXACT SINGULARITY IS DETECTED OR THE ESTIMATE
C                UNDERFLOWS.  IF INFO .NE. 0 , RCOND IS UNCHANGED.
C
C        Z       REAL(N)
C                A WORK VECTOR WHOSE CONTENTS ARE USUALLY UNIMPORTANT.
C                IF  A  IS CLOSE TO A SINGULAR MATRIX  THEN  Z  IS
C                AN APPROXIMATE NULL VECTOR IN THE SENSE THAT
C                NORM(A*Z) = RCOND*NORM(A)*NORM(Z) .
C                IF  INFO .NE. 0 , Z  IS UNCHANGED.
C
C        INFO    INTEGER
C                = 0  FOR NORMAL RETURN.
C                = K  SIGNALS AN ERROR CONDITION.  THE LEADING MINOR
C                     OF ORDER  K  IS NOT POSITIVE DEFINITE.
C
C     PACKED STORAGE
C
C          THE FOLLOWING PROGRAM SEGMENT WILL PACK THE UPPER
C          TRIANGLE OF A SYMMETRIC MATRIX.
C
C                K = 0
C                DO 20 J = 1, N
```

```
C                   DO 10 I = 1, J
C                      K = K + 1
C                      AP(K) = A(I,J)
C             10    CONTINUE
C             20 CONTINUE
C
C     LINPACK.  THIS VERSION DATED 08/14/78 .
C     CLEVE MOLER, UNIVERSITY OF NEW MEXICO, ARGONNE NATIONAL LAB.
C
C     SUBROUTINES AND FUNCTIONS
C
C     LINPACK SPPFA
C     BLAS SAXPY,SDOT,SSCAL,SASUM
C     FORTRAN ABS,AMAX1,SIGN
C
C     INTERNAL VARIABLES
C
      REAL SDOT,EK,T,WK,WKM
      REAL ANORM,S,SASUM,SM,YNORM
      INTEGER I,IJ,J,JM1,J1,K,KB,KJ,KK,KP1
C
C
C     FIND NORM OF A
C
      J1 = 1
      DO 30 J = 1, N
         Z(J) = SASUM(J,AP(J1),1)
         IJ = J1
         J1 = J1 + J
         JM1 = J - 1
         IF (JM1 .LT. 1) GO TO 20
         DO 10 I = 1, JM1
            Z(I) = Z(I) + ABS(AP(IJ))
            IJ = IJ + 1
   10    CONTINUE
   20    CONTINUE
   30 CONTINUE
      ANORM = 0.0E0
      DO 40 J = 1, N
         ANORM = AMAX1(ANORM,Z(J))
   40 CONTINUE
C
C     FACTOR
C
      CALL SPPFA(AP,N,INFO)
      IF (INFO .NE. 0) GO TO 180
C
C        RCOND = 1/(NORM(A)*(ESTIMATE OF NORM(INVERSE(A)))) .
C        ESTIMATE = NORM(Z)/NORM(Y) WHERE  A*Z = Y  AND  A*Y = E .
C        THE COMPONENTS OF  E  ARE CHOSEN TO CAUSE MAXIMUM LOCAL
C        GROWTH IN THE ELEMENTS OF W  WHERE  TRANS(R)*W = E .
C        THE VECTORS ARE FREQUENTLY RESCALED TO AVOID OVERFLOW.
C
C        SOLVE TRANS(R)*W = E
C
         EK = 1.0E0
         DO 50 J = 1, N
            Z(J) = 0.0E0
   50    CONTINUE
         KK = 0
         DO 110 K = 1, N
            KK = KK + K
            IF (Z(K) .NE. 0.0E0) EK = SIGN(EK,-Z(K))
```

```
            IF (ABS(EK-Z(K)) .LE. AP(KK)) GO TO 60
               S = AP(KK)/ABS(EK-Z(K))
               CALL SSCAL(N,S,Z,1)
               EK = S*EK
   60       CONTINUE
            WK = EK - Z(K)
            WKM = -EK - Z(K)
            S = ABS(WK)
            SM = ABS(WKM)
            WK = WK/AP(KK)
            WKM = WKM/AP(KK)
            KP1 = K + 1
            KJ = KK + K
            IF (KP1 .GT. N) GO TO 100
               DO 70 J = KP1, N
                  SM = SM + ABS(Z(J)+WKM*AP(KJ))
                  Z(J) = Z(J) + WK*AP(KJ)
                  S = S + ABS(Z(J))
                  KJ = KJ + J
   70          CONTINUE
               IF (S .GE. SM) GO TO 90
                  T = WKM - WK
                  WK = WKM
                  KJ = KK + K
                  DO 80 J = KP1, N
                     Z(J) = Z(J) + T*AP(KJ)
                     KJ = KJ + J
   80             CONTINUE
   90          CONTINUE
  100       CONTINUE
            Z(K) = WK
  110    CONTINUE
         S = 1.0E0/SASUM(N,Z,1)
         CALL SSCAL(N,S,Z,1)
C
C        SOLVE R*Y = W
C
         DO 130 KB = 1, N
            K = N + 1 - KB
            IF (ABS(Z(K)) .LE. AP(KK)) GO TO 120
               S = AP(KK)/ABS(Z(K))
               CALL SSCAL(N,S,Z,1)
  120       CONTINUE
            Z(K) = Z(K)/AP(KK)
            KK = KK - K
            T = -Z(K)
            CALL SAXPY(K-1,T,AP(KK+1),1,Z(1),1)
  130    CONTINUE
         S = 1.0E0/SASUM(N,Z,1)
         CALL SSCAL(N,S,Z,1)
C
         YNORM = 1.0E0
C
C        SOLVE TRANS(R)*V = Y
C
         DO 150 K = 1, N
            Z(K) = Z(K) - SDOT(K-1,AP(KK+1),1,Z(1),1)
            KK = KK + K
            IF (ABS(Z(K)) .LE. AP(KK)) GO TO 140
               S = AP(KK)/ABS(Z(K))
               CALL SSCAL(N,S,Z,1)
               YNORM = S*YNORM
  140       CONTINUE
```

```
            Z(K) = Z(K)/AP(KK)
  150    CONTINUE
         S = 1.0E0/SASUM(N,Z,1)
         CALL SSCAL(N,S,Z,1)
         YNORM = S*YNORM
C
C        SOLVE R*Z = V
C
         DO 170 KB = 1, N
            K = N + 1 - KB
            IF (ABS(Z(K)) .LE. AP(KK)) GO TO 160
               S = AP(KK)/ABS(Z(K))
               CALL SSCAL(N,S,Z,1)
               YNORM = S*YNORM
  160       CONTINUE
            Z(K) = Z(K)/AP(KK)
            KK = KK - K
            T = -Z(K)
            CALL SAXPY(K-1,T,AP(KK+1),1,Z(1),1)
  170    CONTINUE
C        MAKE ZNORM = 1.0
         S = 1.0E0/SASUM(N,Z,1)
         CALL SSCAL(N,S,Z,1)
         YNORM = S*YNORM
C
         IF (ANORM .NE. 0.0E0) RCOND = YNORM/ANORM
         IF (ANORM .EQ. 0.0E0) RCOND = 0.0E0
  180 CONTINUE
      RETURN
      END
```

```
      SUBROUTINE SPPFA(AP,N,INFO)
      INTEGER N,INFO
      REAL AP(1)
C
C     SPPFA FACTORS A REAL SYMMETRIC POSITIVE DEFINITE MATRIX
C     STORED IN PACKED FORM.
C
C     SPPFA IS USUALLY CALLED BY SPPCO, BUT IT CAN BE CALLED
C     DIRECTLY WITH A SAVING IN TIME IF  RCOND  IS NOT NEEDED.
C     (TIME FOR SPPCO) = (1 + 18/N)*(TIME FOR SPPFA) .
C
C     ON ENTRY
C
C        AP      REAL (N*(N+1)/2)
C                THE PACKED FORM OF A SYMMETRIC MATRIX  A .  THE
C                COLUMNS OF THE UPPER TRIANGLE ARE STORED SEQUENTIALLY
C                IN A ONE-DIMENSIONAL ARRAY OF LENGTH  N*(N+1)/2 .
C                SEE COMMENTS BELOW FOR DETAILS.
C
C        N       INTEGER
C                THE ORDER OF THE MATRIX  A .
C
C     ON RETURN
C
C        AP      AN UPPER TRIANGULAR MATRIX  R , STORED IN PACKED
C                FORM, SO THAT  A = TRANS(R)*R .
C                IF  INFO .NE. 0 , THE FACTORIZATION IS NOT COMPLETE.
C
C        INFO    INTEGER
C                = 0  FOR NORMAL RETURN.
C                = K  SIGNALS AN ERROR CONDITION.  THE LEADING MINOR OF
C                     ORDER  K  IS NOT POSITIVE DEFINITE.
C
C
C     PACKED STORAGE
C
C          THE FOLLOWING PROGRAM SEGMENT WILL PACK THE UPPER
C          TRIANGLE OF A SYMMETRIC MATRIX.
C
C                K = 0
C                DO 20 J = 1, N
C                   DO 10 I = 1, J
C                      K = K + 1
C                      AP(K) = A(I,J)
C             10    CONTINUE
C             20 CONTINUE
C
C     LINPACK.  THIS VERSION DATED 08/14/78 .
C     CLEVE MOLER, UNIVERSITY OF NEW MEXICO, ARGONNE NATIONAL LAB.
C
C     SUBROUTINES AND FUNCTIONS
C
C     BLAS SDOT
C     FORTRAN SQRT
C
C     INTERNAL VARIABLES
C
      REAL SDOT,T
      REAL S
      INTEGER J,JJ,JM1,K,KJ,KK
C     BEGIN BLOCK WITH ...EXITS TO 40
C
C
         JJ = 0
```

```
         DO 30 J = 1, N
            INFO = J
            S = 0.0E0
            JM1 = J - 1
            KJ = JJ
            KK = 0
            IF (JM1 .LT. 1) GO TO 20
            DO 10 K = 1, JM1
               KJ = KJ + 1
               T = AP(KJ) - SDOT(K-1,AP(KK+1),1,AP(JJ+1),1)
               KK = KK + K
               T = T/AP(KK)
               AP(KJ) = T
               S = S + T*T
   10       CONTINUE
   20       CONTINUE
            JJ = JJ + J
            S = AP(JJ) - S
C     ......EXIT
            IF (S .LE. 0.0E0) GO TO 40
            AP(JJ) = SQRT(S)
   30    CONTINUE
         INFO = 0
   40 CONTINUE
      RETURN
      END
```

```
      SUBROUTINE SPPSL(AP,N,B)
      INTEGER N
      REAL AP(1),B(1)
C
C     SPPSL SOLVES THE REAL SYMMETRIC POSITIVE DEFINITE SYSTEM
C     A * X = B
C     USING THE FACTORS COMPUTED BY SPPCO OR SPPFA.
C
C     ON ENTRY
C
C        AP      REAL (N*(N+1)/2)
C                THE OUTPUT FROM SPPCO OR SPPFA.
C
C        N       INTEGER
C                THE ORDER OF THE MATRIX  A .
C
C        B       REAL(N)
C                THE RIGHT HAND SIDE VECTOR.
C
C     ON RETURN
C
C        B       THE SOLUTION VECTOR  X .
C
C     ERROR CONDITION
C
C        A DIVISION BY ZERO WILL OCCUR IF THE INPUT FACTOR CONTAINS
C        A ZERO ON THE DIAGONAL.  TECHNICALLY THIS INDICATES
C        SINGULARITY BUT IT IS USUALLY CAUSED BY IMPROPER SUBROUTINE
C        ARGUMENTS.  IT WILL NOT OCCUR IF THE SUBROUTINES ARE CALLED
C        CORRECTLY AND  INFO .EQ. 0 .
C
C     TO COMPUTE  INVERSE(A) * C  WHERE  C  IS A MATRIX
C     WITH  P  COLUMNS
C           CALL SPPCO(AP,N,RCOND,Z,INFO)
C           IF (RCOND IS TOO SMALL .OR. INFO .NE. 0) GO TO ...
C           DO 10 J = 1, P
C              CALL SPPSL(AP,N,C(1,J))
C        10 CONTINUE
C
C     LINPACK.  THIS VERSION DATED 08/14/78 .
C     CLEVE MOLER, UNIVERSITY OF NEW MEXICO, ARGONNE NATIONAL LAB.
C
C     SUBROUTINES AND FUNCTIONS
C
C     BLAS SAXPY,SDOT
C
C     INTERNAL VARIABLES
C
      REAL SDOT,T
      INTEGER K,KB,KK
C
      KK = 0
C
C     SOLVE TRANS(R)*Y = B
C
      DO 10 K = 1, N
         T = SDOT(K-1,AP(KK+1),1,B(1),1)
         KK = KK + K
         B(K) = (B(K) - T)/AP(KK)
```

```
   10 CONTINUE
C
C     SOLVE R*X = Y
C
      DO 20 KB = 1, N
         K = N + 1 - KB
         B(K) = B(K)/AP(KK)
         KK = KK - K
         T = -B(K)
         CALL SAXPY(K-1,T,AP(KK_1),1,B(1),1)
   20 CONTINUE
      RETURN
      END
```

```
      SUBROUTINE SPPDI(AP,N,DET,JOB)
      INTEGER N,JOB
      REAL AP(1)
      REAL DET(2)
C
C     SPPDI COMPUTES THE DETERMINANT AND INVERSE
C     OF A REAL SYMMETRIC POSITIVE DEFINITE MATRIX
C     USING THE FACTORS COMPUTED BY SPPCO OR SPPFA .
C
C     ON ENTRY
C
C        AP      REAL (N*(N+1)/2)
C                THE OUTPUT FROM SPPCO OR SPPFA.
C
C        N       INTEGER
C                THE ORDER OF THE MATRIX  A .
C
C        JOB     INTEGER
C                = 11   BOTH DETERMINANT AND INVERSE.
C                = 01   INVERSE ONLY.
C                = 10   DETERMINANT ONLY.
C
C     ON RETURN
C
C        AP      THE UPPER TRIANGULAR HALF OF THE INVERSE .
C                THE STRICT LOWER TRIANGLE IS UNALTERED.
C
C        DET     REAL(2)
C                DETERMINANT OF ORIGINAL MATRIX IF REQUESTED.
C                OTHERWISE NOT REFERENCED.
C                DETERMINANT = DET(1) * 10.0**DET(2)
C                WITH  1.0 .LE. DET(1) .LT. 10.0
C                OR  DET(1) .EQ. 0.0 .
C
C     ERROR CONDITION
C
C        A DIVISION BY ZERO WILL OCCUR IF THE INPUT FACTOR CONTAINS
C        A ZERO ON THE DIAGONAL AND THE INVERSE IS REQUESTED.
C        IT WILL NOT OCCUR IF THE SUBROUTINES ARE CALLED CORRECTLY
C        AND IF SPOCO OR SPOFA HAS SET INFO .EQ. 0 .
C
C     LINPACK.  THIS VERSION DATED 08/14/78 .
C     CLEVE MOLER, UNIVERSITY OF NEW MEXICO, ARGONNE NATIONAL LAB.
C
C     SUBROUTINES AND FUNCTIONS
C
C     BLAS SAXPY,SSCAL
C     FORTRAN MOD
C
C     INTERNAL VARIABLES
C
      REAL T
      REAL S
      INTEGER I,II,J,JJ,JM1,J1,K,KJ,KK,KP1,K1
C
C     COMPUTE DETERMINANT
C
      IF (JOB/10 .EQ. 0) GO TO 70
         DET(1) = 1.0E0
         DET(2) = 0.0E0
         S = 10.0E0
         II = 0
         DO 50 I = 1, N
```

```
            II = II + I
            DET(1) = AP(II)**2*DET(1)
C        ...EXIT
            IF (DET(1) .EQ. 0.0E0) GO TO 60
   10       IF (DET(1) .GE. 1.0E0) GO TO 20
               DET(1) = S*DET(1)
               DET(2) = DET(2) - 1.0E0
            GO TO 10
   20       CONTINUE
   30       IF (DET(1) .LT. S) GO TO 40
               DET(1) = DET(1)/S
               DET(2) = DET(2) + 1.0E0
            GO TO 30
   40       CONTINUE
   50    CONTINUE
   60    CONTINUE
   70 CONTINUE
C
C     COMPUTE INVERSE(R)
C
      IF (MOD(JOB,10) .EQ. 0) GO TO 140
         KK = 0
         DO 100 K = 1, N
            K1 = KK + 1
            KK = KK + K
            AP(KK) = 1.0E0/AP(KK)
            T = -AP(KK)
            CALL SSCAL(K-1,T,AP(K1),1)
            KP1 = K + 1
            J1 = KK + 1
            KJ = KK + K
            IF (N .LT. KP1) GO TO 90
            DO 80 J = KP1, N
               T = AP(KJ)
               AP(KJ) = 0.0E0
               CALL SAXPY(K,T,AP(K1),1,AP(J1),1)
               J1 = J1 + J
               KJ = KJ + J
   80       CONTINUE
   90       CONTINUE
  100    CONTINUE
C
C        FORM  INVERSE(R) * TRANS(INVERSE(R))
C
         JJ = 0
         DO 130 J = 1, N
            J1 = JJ + 1
            JJ = JJ + J
            JM1 = J - 1
            K1 = 1
            KJ = J1
            IF (JM1 .LT. 1) GO TO 120
            DO 110 K = 1, JM1
               T = AP(KJ)
               CALL SAXPY(K,T,AP(J1),1,AP(K1),1)
               K1 = K1 + K
               KJ = KJ + 1
  110       CONTINUE
  120       CONTINUE
            T = AP(JJ)
            CALL SSCAL(J,T,AP(J1),1)
  130    CONTINUE
  140 CONTINUE
      RETURN
      END
```

```
      SUBROUTINE SPBCO(ABD,LDA,N,M,RCOND,Z,INFO)
      INTEGER LDA,N,M,INFO
      REAL ABD(LDA,1),Z(1)
      REAL RCOND
C
C     SPBCO FACTORS A REAL SYMMETRIC POSITIVE DEFINITE MATRIX
C     STORED IN BAND FORM AND ESTIMATES THE CONDITION OF THE MATRIX.
C
C     IF  RCOND  IS NOT NEEDED, SPBFA IS SLIGHTLY FASTER.
C     TO SOLVE  A*X = B , FOLLOW SPBCO BY SPBSL.
C     TO COMPUTE  INVERSE(A)*C , FOLLOW SPBCO BY SPBSL.
C     TO COMPUTE  DETERMINANT(A) , FOLLOW SPBCO BY SPBDI.
C
C     ON ENTRY
C
C        ABD     REAL(LDA, N)
C                THE MATRIX TO BE FACTORED.  THE COLUMNS OF THE UPPER
C                TRIANGLE ARE STORED IN THE COLUMNS OF ABD AND THE
C                DIAGONALS OF THE UPPER TRIANGLE ARE STORED IN THE
C                ROWS OF ABD .  SEE THE COMMENTS BELOW FOR DETAILS.
C
C        LDA     INTEGER
C                THE LEADING DIMENSION OF THE ARRAY  ABD .
C                LDA MUST BE .GE. M + 1 .
C
C        N       INTEGER
C                THE ORDER OF THE MATRIX  A .
C
C        M       INTEGER
C                THE NUMBER OF DIAGONALS ABOVE THE MAIN DIAGONAL.
C                0 .LE. M .LT. N .
C
C     ON RETURN
C
C        ABD     AN UPPER TRIANGULAR MATRIX  R , STORED IN BAND
C                FORM, SO THAT  A = TRANS(R)*R .
C                IF  INFO .NE. 0 , THE FACTORIZATION IS NOT COMPLETE.
C
C        RCOND   REAL
C                AN ESTIMATE OF THE RECIPROCAL CONDITION OF  A .
C                FOR THE SYSTEM  A*X = B , RELATIVE PERTURBATIONS
C                IN  A  AND  B  OF SIZE  EPSILON  MAY CAUSE
C                RELATIVE PERTURBATIONS IN  X  OF SIZE  EPSILON/RCOND .
C                IF  RCOND  IS SO SMALL THAT THE LOGICAL EXPRESSION
C                           1.0 + RCOND .EQ. 1.0
C                IS TRUE, THEN  A  MAY BE SINGULAR TO WORKING
C                PRECISION.  IN PARTICULAR,  RCOND  IS ZERO  IF
C                EXACT SINGULARITY IS DETECTED OR THE ESTIMATE
C                UNDERFLOWS.  IF INFO .NE. 0 , RCOND IS UNCHANGED.
C
C        Z       REAL(N)
C                A WORK VECTOR WHOSE CONTENTS ARE USUALLY UNIMPORTANT.
C                IF  A  IS SINGULAR TO WORKING PRECISION, THEN  Z  IS
C                AN APPROXIMATE NULL VECTOR IN THE SENSE THAT
C                NORM(A*Z) = RCOND*NORM(A)*NORM(Z) .
C                IF  INFO .NE. 0 , Z  IS UNCHANGED.
C
C        INFO    INTEGER
C                = 0  FOR NORMAL RETURN.
C                = K  SIGNALS AN ERROR CONDITION.  THE LEADING MINOR
C                     OF ORDER  K  IS NOT POSITIVE DEFINITE.
C
C     BAND STORAGE
```

```
C
C          IF  A  IS A SYMMETRIC POSITIVE DEFINITE BAND MATRIX,
C          THE FOLLOWING PROGRAM SEGMENT WILL SET UP THE INPUT.
C
C                  M = (BAND WIDTH ABOVE DIAGONAL)
C                  DO 20 J = 1, N
C                     I1 = MAX0(1, J-M)
C                     DO 10 I = I1, J
C                        K = I-J+M+1
C                        ABD(K,J) = A(I,J)
C               10    CONTINUE
C               20 CONTINUE
C
C          THIS USES  M + 1  ROWS OF  A , EXCEPT FOR THE  M BY M
C          UPPER LEFT TRIANGLE, WHICH IS IGNORED.
C
C     EXAMPLE..  IF THE ORIGINAL MATRIX IS
C
C          11 12 13  0  0  0
C          12 22 23 24  0  0
C          13 23 33 34 35  0
C           0 24 34 44 45 46
C           0  0 35 45 55 56
C           0  0  0 46 56 66
C
C     THEN  N = 6 , M = 2  AND  ABD  SHOULD CONTAIN
C
C           *  * 13 24 35 46
C           * 12 23 34 45 56
C          11 22 33 44 55 66
C
C     LINPACK.  THIS VERSION DATED 08/14/78 .
C     CLEVE MOLER, UNIVERSITY OF NEW MEXICO, ARGONNE NATIONAL LAB.
C
C     SUBROUTINES AND FUNCTIONS
C
C     LINPACK SPBFA
C     BLAS SAXPY,SDOT,SSCAL,SASUM
C     FORTRAN ABS,AMAX1,MAX0,MIN0,SIGN
C
C     INTERNAL VARIABLES
C
      REAL SDOT,EK,T,WK,WKM
      REAL ANORM,S,SASUM,SM,YNORM
      INTEGER I,J,J2,K,KB,KP1,L,LA,LB,LM,MU
C
C
C     FIND NORM OF A
C
      DO 30 J = 1, N
         L = MIN0(J,M+1)
         MU = MAX0(M+2-J,1)
         Z(J) = SASUM(L,ABD(MU,J),1)
         K = J - L
         IF (M .LT. MU) GO TO 20
         DO 10 I = MU, M
            K = K + 1
            Z(K) = Z(K) + ABS(ABD(I,J))
   10    CONTINUE
   20    CONTINUE
   30 CONTINUE
      ANORM = 0.0E0
      DO 40 J = 1, N
```

```
            ANORM = AMAX1(ANORM,Z(J))
   40 CONTINUE
C
C     FACTOR
C
      CALL SPBFA(ABD,LDA,N,M,INFO)
      IF (INFO .NE. 0) GO TO 180
C
C        RCOND = 1/(NORM(A)*(ESTIMATE OF NORM(INVERSE(A)))) .
C        ESTIMATE = NORM(Z)/NORM(Y) WHERE  A*Z = Y  AND  A*Y = E .
C        THE COMPONENTS OF  E  ARE CHOSEN TO CAUSE MAXIMUM LOCAL
C        GROWTH IN THE ELEMENTS OF W  WHERE  TRANS(R)*W = E .
C        THE VECTORS ARE FREQUENTLY RESCALED TO AVOID OVERFLOW.
C
C        SOLVE TRANS(R)*W = E
C
         EK = 1.0E0
         DO 50 J = 1, N
            Z(J) = 0.0E0
   50    CONTINUE
         DO 110 K = 1, N
            IF (Z(K) .NE. 0.0E0) EK = SIGN(EK,-Z(K))
            IF (ABS(EK-Z(K)) .LE. ABD(M+1,K)) GO TO 60
               S = ABD(M+1,K)/ABS(EK-Z(K))
               CALL SSCAL(N,S,Z,1)
               EK = S*EK
   60       CONTINUE
            WK = EK - Z(K)
            WKM = -EK - Z(K)
            S = ABS(WK)
            SM = ABS(WKM)
            WK = WK/ABD(M+1,K)
            WKM = WKM/ABD(M+1,K)
            KP1 = K + 1
            J2 = MIN0(K+M,N)
            I = M + 1
            IF (KP1 .GT. J2) GO TO 100
               DO 70 J = KP1, J2
                  I = I - 1
                  SM = SM + ABS(Z(J)+WKM*ABD(I,J))
                  Z(J) = Z(J) + WK*ABD(I,J)
                  S = S + ABS(Z(J))
   70          CONTINUE
               IF (S .GE. SM) GO TO 90
                  T = WKM - WK
                  WK = WKM
                  I = M + 1
                  DO 80 J = KP1, J2
                     I = I - 1
                     Z(J) = Z(J) + T*ABD(I,J)
   80             CONTINUE
   90          CONTINUE
  100       CONTINUE
            Z(K) = WK
  110    CONTINUE
         S = 1.0E0/SASUM(N,Z,1)
         CALL SSCAL(N,S,Z,1)
C
C        SOLVE  R*Y = W
C
         DO 130 KB = 1, N
            K = N + 1 - KB
            IF (ABS(Z(K)) .LE. ABD(M+1,K)) GO TO 120
```

```
            S = ABD(M+1,K)/ABS(Z(K))
            CALL SSCAL(N,S,Z,1)
  120    CONTINUE
         Z(K) = Z(K)/ABD(M+1,K)
         LM = MIN0(K-1,M)
         LA = M + 1 - LM
         LB = K - LM
         T = -Z(K)
         CALL SAXPY(LM,T,ABD(LA,K),1,Z(LB),1)
  130 CONTINUE
      S = 1.0E0/SASUM(N,Z,1)
      CALL SSCAL(N,S,Z,1)
C
      YNORM = 1.0E0
C
C     SOLVE TRANS(R)*V = Y
C
      DO 150 K = 1, N
         LM = MIN0(K-1,M)
         LA = M + 1 - LM
         LB = K - LM
         Z(K) = Z(K) - SDOT(LM,ABD(LA,K),1,Z(LB),1)
         IF (ABS(Z(K)) .LE. ABD(M+1,K)) GO TO 140
            S = ABD(M+1,K)/ABS(Z(K))
            CALL SSCAL(N,S,Z,1)
            YNORM = S*YNORM
  140    CONTINUE
         Z(K) = Z(K)/ABD(M+1,K)
  150 CONTINUE
      S = 1.0E0/SASUM(N,Z,1)
      CALL SSCAL(N,S,Z,1)
      YNORM = S*YNORM
C
C     SOLVE  R*Z = V
C
      DO 170 KB = 1, N
         K = N + 1 - KB
         IF (ABS(Z(K)) .LE. ABD(M+1,K)) GO TO 160
            S = ABD(M+1,K)/ABS(Z(K))
            CALL SSCAL(N,S,Z,1)
            YNORM = S*YNORM
  160    CONTINUE
         Z(K) = Z(K)/ABD(M+1,K)
         LM = MIN0(K-1,M)
         LA = M + 1 - LM
         LB = K - LM
         T = -Z(K)
         CALL SAXPY(LM,T,ABD(LA,K),1,Z(LB),1)
  170 CONTINUE
C     MAKE ZNORM = 1.0
      S = 1.0E0/SASUM(N,Z,1)
      CALL SSCAL(N,S,Z,1)
      YNORM = S*YNORM
C
      IF (ANORM .NE. 0.0E0) RCOND = YNORM/ANORM
      IF (ANORM .EQ. 0.0E0) RCOND = 0.0E0
  180 CONTINUE
      RETURN
      END
```

```
      SUBROUTINE SPBFA(ABD,LDA,N,M,INFO)
      INTEGER LDA,N,M,INFO
      REAL ABD(LDA,1)
C
C     SPBFA FACTORS A REAL SYMMETRIC POSITIVE DEFINITE MATRIX
C     STORED IN BAND FORM.
C
C     SPBFA IS USUALLY CALLED BY SPBCO, BUT IT CAN BE CALLED
C     DIRECTLY WITH A SAVING IN TIME IF  RCOND  IS NOT NEEDED.
C
C     ON ENTRY
C
C        ABD     REAL(LDA, N)
C                THE MATRIX TO BE FACTORED.  THE COLUMNS OF THE UPPER
C                TRIANGLE ARE STORED IN THE COLUMNS OF ABD AND THE
C                DIAGONALS OF THE UPPER TRIANGLE ARE STORED IN THE
C                ROWS OF ABD .  SEE THE COMMENTS BELOW FOR DETAILS.
C
C        LDA     INTEGER
C                THE LEADING DIMENSION OF THE ARRAY  ABD .
C                LDA MUST BE .GE. M + 1 .
C
C        N       INTEGER
C                THE ORDER OF THE MATRIX  A .
C
C        M       INTEGER
C                THE NUMBER OF DIAGONALS ABOVE THE MAIN DIAGONAL.
C                0 .LE. M .LT. N .
C
C     ON RETURN
C
C        ABD     AN UPPER TRIANGULAR MATRIX  R , STORED IN BAND
C                FORM, SO THAT  A = TRANS(R)*R .
C
C        INFO    INTEGER
C                = 0  FOR NORMAL RETURN.
C                = K  IF THE LEADING MINOR OF ORDER  K  IS NOT
C                     POSITIVE DEFINITE.
C
C     BAND STORAGE
C
C           IF  A  IS A SYMMETRIC POSITIVE DEFINITE BAND MATRIX,
C           THE FOLLOWING PROGRAM SEGMENT WILL SET UP THE INPUT.
C
C                   M = (BAND WIDTH ABOVE DIAGONAL)
C                   DO 20 J = 1, N
C                      I1 = MAX0(1, J-M)
C                      DO 10 I = I1, J
C                         K = I-J+M+1
C                         ABD(K,J) = A(I,J)
C                10    CONTINUE
C                20 CONTINUE
C
C     LINPACK.  THIS VERSION DATED 08/14/78 .
C     CLEVE MOLER, UNIVERSITY OF NEW MEXICO, ARGONNE NATIONAL LAB.
C
C     SUBROUTINES AND FUNCTIONS
C
C     BLAS SDOT
C     FORTRAN MAX0,SQRT
C
C     INTERNAL VARIABLES
C
```

```
      REAL SDOT,T
      REAL S
      INTEGER IK,J,JK,K,MU
C     BEGIN BLOCK WITH ...EXITS TO 40
C
C
         DO 30 J = 1, N
            INFO = J
            S = 0.0E0
            IK = M + 1
            JK = MAX0(J-M,1)
            MU = MAX0(M+2-J,1)
            IF (M .LT. MU) GO TO 20
            DO 10 K = MU, M
               T = ABD(K,J) - SDOT(K-MU,ABD(IK,JK),1,ABD(MU,J),1)
               T = T/ABD(M+1,JK)
               ABD(K,J) = T
               S = S + T*T
               IK = IK - 1
               JK = JK + 1
   10       CONTINUE
   20       CONTINUE
            S = ABD(M+1,J) - S
C     ......EXIT
            IF (S .LE. 0.0E0) GO TO 40
            ABD(M+1,J) = SQRT(S)
   30    CONTINUE
         INFO = 0
   40 CONTINUE
      RETURN
      END
```

SPBSL

```
      SUBROUTINE SPBSL(ABD,LDA,N,M,B)
      INTEGER LDA,N,M
      REAL ABD(LDA,1),B(1)
C
C     SPBSL SOLVES THE REAL SYMMETRIC POSITIVE DEFINITE BAND
C     SYSTEM  A*X = B
C     USING THE FACTORS COMPUTED BY SPBCO OR SPBFA.
C
C     ON ENTRY
C
C        ABD     REAL(LDA, N)
C                THE OUTPUT FROM SPBCO OR SPBFA.
C
C        LDA     INTEGER
C                THE LEADING DIMENSION OF THE ARRAY  ABD .
C
C        N       INTEGER
C                THE ORDER OF THE MATRIX  A .
C
C        M       INTEGER
C                THE NUMBER OF DIAGONALS ABOVE THE MAIN DIAGONAL.
C
C        B       REAL(N)
C                THE RIGHT HAND SIDE VECTOR.
C
C     ON RETURN
C
C        B       THE SOLUTION VECTOR  X .
C
C     ERROR CONDITION
C
C        A DIVISION BY ZERO WILL OCCUR IF THE INPUT FACTOR CONTAINS
C        A ZERO ON THE DIAGONAL.  TECHNICALLY THIS INDICATES
C        SINGULARITY BUT IT IS USUALLY CAUSED BY IMPROPER SUBROUTINE
C        ARGUMENTS.  IT WILL NOT OCCUR IF THE SUBROUTINES ARE CALLED
C        CORRECTLY AND  INFO .EQ. 0 .
C
C     TO COMPUTE  INVERSE(A) * C  WHERE  C  IS A MATRIX
C     WITH  P  COLUMNS
C           CALL SPBCO(ABD,LDA,N,M,RCOND,Z,INFO)
C           IF (RCOND IS TOO SMALL .OR. INFO .NE. 0) GO TO ...
C           DO 10 J = 1, P
C              CALL SPBSL(ABD,LDA,N,M,C(1,J))
C        10 CONTINUE
C
C     LINPACK.  THIS VERSION DATED 08/14/78 .
C     CLEVE MOLER, UNIVERSITY OF NEW MEXICO, ARGONNE NATIONAL LAB.
C
C     SUBROUTINES AND FUNCTIONS
C
C     BLAS SAXPY,SDOT
C     FORTRAN MIN0
C
C     INTERNAL VARIABLES
C
      REAL SDOT,T
      INTEGER K,KB,LA,LB,LM
C
C     SOLVE TRANS(R)*Y = B
C
      DO 10 K = 1, N
         LM = MIN0(K-1,M)
         LA = M + 1 - LM
```

```
         LB = K - LM
         T = SDOT(LM,ABD(LA,K),1,B(LB),1)
         B(K) = (B(K) - T)/ABD(M+1,K)
   10 CONTINUE
C
C     SOLVE R*X = Y
C
      DO 20 KB = 1, N
         K = N + 1 - KB
         LM = MIN0(K-1,M)
         LA = M + 1 - LM
         LB = K - LM
         B(K) = B(K)/ABD(M+1,K)
         T = -3(K)
         CALL SAXPY(LM,T,ABD(LA,K),1,B(LB),1)
   20 CONTINUE
      RETURN
      END
```

```
      SUBROUTINE SPBDI(ABD,LDA,N,M,DET)
      INTEGER LDA,N,M
      REAL ABD(LDA,1)
      REAL DET(2)
C
C     SPBDI COMPUTES THE DETERMINANT
C     OF A REAL SYMMETRIC POSITIVE DEFINITE BAND MATRIX
C     USING THE FACTORS COMPUTED BY SPBCO OR SPBFA.
C     IF THE INVERSE IS NEEDED, USE SPBSL  N  TIMES.
C
C     ON ENTRY
C
C        ABD     REAL(LDA, N)
C                THE OUTPUT FROM SPBCO OR SPBFA.
C
C        LDA     INTEGER
C                THE LEADING DIMENSION OF THE ARRAY  ABD .
C
C        N       INTEGER
C                THE ORDER OF THE MATRIX  A .
C
C        M       INTEGER
C                THE NUMBER OF DIAGONALS ABOVE THE MAIN DIAGONAL.
C
C     ON RETURN
C
C        DET     REAL(2)
C                DETERMINANT OF ORIGINAL MATRIX IN THE FORM
C                DETERMINANT = DET(1) * 10.0**DET(2)
C                WITH  1.0 .LE. DET(1) .LT. 10.0
C                OR  DET(1) .EQ. 0.0 .
C
C     LINPACK.  THIS VERSION DATED 08/14/78 .
C     CLEVE MOLER, UNIVERSITY OF NEW MEXICO, ARGONNE NATIONAL LAB.
C
C     SUBROUTINES AND FUNCTIONS
C
C
C     INTERNAL VARIABLES
C
      REAL S
      INTEGER I
C
C     COMPUTE DETERMINANT
C
      DET(1) = 1.0E0
      DET(2) = 0.0E0
      S = 10.0E0
      DO 50 I = 1, N
         DET(1) = ABD(M+1,I)**2*DET(1)
C     ...EXIT
         IF (DET(1) .EQ. 0.0E0) GO TO 60
   10    IF (DET(1) .GE. 1.0E0) GO TO 20
            DET(1) = S*DET(1)
            DET(2) = DET(2) - 1.0E0
         GO TO 10
   20    CONTINUE
   30    IF (DET(1) .LT. S) GO TO 40
            DET(1) = DET(1)/S
            DET(2) = DET(2) + 1.0E0
         GO TO 30
   40    CONTINUE
   50 CONTINUE
```

```
   60 CONTINUE
      RETURN
      END
```

```
      SUBROUTINE SSICO(A,LDA,N,KPVT,RCOND,Z)
      INTEGER LDA,N,KPVT(1)
      REAL A(LDA,1),Z(1)
      REAL RCOND
C
C     SSICO FACTORS A REAL SYMMETRIC MATRIX BY ELIMINATION WITH
C     SYMMETRIC PIVOTING AND ESTIMATES THE CONDITION OF THE MATRIX.
C
C     IF  RCOND  IS NOT NEEDED, SSIFA IS SLIGHTLY FASTER.
C     TO SOLVE  A*X = B , FOLLOW SSICO BY SSISL.
C     TO COMPUTE  INVERSE(A)*C , FOLLOW SSICO BY SSISL.
C     TO COMPUTE  INVERSE(A) , FOLLOW SSICO BY SSIDI.
C     TO COMPUTE  DETERMINANT(A) , FOLLOW SSICO BY SSIDI.
C     TO COMPUTE  INERTIA(A), FOLLOW SSICO BY SSIDI.
C
C     ON ENTRY
C
C        A       REAL(LDA, N)
C                THE SYMMETRIC MATRIX TO BE FACTORED.
C                ONLY THE DIAGONAL AND UPPER TRIANGLE ARE USED.
C
C        LDA     INTEGER
C                THE LEADING DIMENSION OF THE ARRAY  A .
C
C        N       INTEGER
C                THE ORDER OF THE MATRIX  A .
C
C     OUTPUT
C
C        A       A BLOCK DIAGONAL MATRIX AND THE MULTIPLIERS WHICH
C                WERE USED TO OBTAIN IT.
C                THE FACTORIZATION CAN BE WRITTEN  A = U*D*TRANS(U)
C                WHERE  U  IS A PRODUCT OF PERMUTATION AND UNIT
C                UPPER TRIANGULAR MATRICES , TRANS(U) IS THE
C                TRANSPOSE OF  U , AND  D  IS BLOCK DIAGONAL
C                WITH 1 BY 1 AND 2 BY 2 BLOCKS.
C
C        KPVT    INTEGER(N)
C                AN INTEGER VECTOR OF PIVOT INDICES.
C
C        RCOND   REAL
C                AN ESTIMATE OF THE RECIPROCAL CONDITION OF  A .
C                FOR THE SYSTEM  A*X = B , RELATIVE PERTURBATIONS
C                IN  A  AND  B  OF SIZE  EPSILON  MAY CAUSE
C                RELATIVE PERTURBATIONS IN  X  OF SIZE  EPSILON/RCOND .
C                IF  RCOND  IS SO SMALL THAT THE LOGICAL EXPRESSION
C                           1.0 + RCOND .EQ. 1.0
C                IS TRUE, THEN  A  MAY BE SINGULAR TO WORKING
C                PRECISION.  IN PARTICULAR,  RCOND  IS ZERO  IF
C                EXACT SINGULARITY IS DETECTED OR THE ESTIMATE
C                UNDERFLOWS.
C
C        Z       REAL(N)
C                A WORK VECTOR WHOSE CONTENTS ARE USUALLY UNIMPORTANT.
C                IF  A  IS CLOSE TO A SINGULAR MATRIX, THEN  Z  IS
C                AN APPROXIMATE NULL VECTOR IN THE SENSE THAT
C                NORM(A*Z) = RCOND*NORM(A)*NORM(Z) .
C
C     LINPACK. THIS VERSION DATED 08/14/78 .
C     CLEVE MOLER, UNIVERSITY OF NEW MEXICO, ARGONNE NATIONAL LAB.
C
C     SUBROUTINES AND FUNCTIONS
C
```

```
C     LINPACK SSIFA
C     BLAS SAXPY,SDOT,SSCAL,SASUM
C     FORTRAN ABS,AMAX1,IABS,SIGN
C
C     INTERNAL VARIABLES
C
      REAL AK,AKM1,BK,BKM1,SDOT,DENOM,EK,T
      REAL ANORM,S,SASUM,YNORM
      INTEGER I,INFO,J,JM1,K,KP,KPS,KS
C
C
C     FIND NORM OF A USING ONLY UPPER HALF
C
      DO 30 J = 1, N
         Z(J) = SASUM(J,A(1,J),1)
         JM1 = J - 1
         IF (JM1 .LT. 1) GO TO 20
         DO 10 I = 1, JM1
            Z(I) = Z(I) + ABS(A(I,J))
   10    CONTINUE
   20    CONTINUE
   30 CONTINUE
      ANORM = 0.0E0
      DO 40 J = 1, N
         ANORM = AMAX1(ANORM,Z(J))
   40 CONTINUE
C
C     FACTOR
C
      CALL SSIFA(A,LDA,N,KPVT,INFO)
C
C     RCOND = 1/(NORM(A)*(ESTIMATE OF NORM(INVERSE(A)))) .
C     ESTIMATE = NORM(Z)/NORM(Y) WHERE  A*Z = Y  AND  A*Y = E .
C     THE COMPONENTS OF  E  ARE CHOSEN TO CAUSE MAXIMUM LOCAL
C     GROWTH IN THE ELEMENTS OF W  WHERE  D*W = U*E .
C     THE VECTORS ARE FREQUENTLY RESCALED TO AVOID OVERFLOW.
C
C     SOLVE U*D*W = E
C
      EK = 1.0E0
      DO 50 J = 1, N
         Z(J) = 0.0E0
   50 CONTINUE
      K = N
   60 IF (K .EQ. 0) GO TO 120
         KS = 1
         IF (KPVT(K) .LT. 0) KS = 2
         KP = IABS(KPVT(K))
         KPS = K + 1 - KS
         IF (KP .EQ. KPS) GO TO 70
            T = Z(KPS)
            Z(KPS) = Z(KP)
            Z(KP) = T
   70    CONTINUE
         IF (Z(K) .NE. 0.0E0) EK = SIGN(EK,Z(K))
         Z(K) = Z(K) + EK
         CALL SAXPY(K-KS,Z(K),A(1,K),1,Z(1),1)
         IF (KS .EQ. 1) GO TO 80
            IF (Z(K-1) .NE. 0.0E0) EK = SIGN(EK,Z(K-1))
            Z(K-1) = Z(K-1) + EK
            CALL SAXPY(K-KS,Z(K-1),A(1,K-1),1,Z(1),1)
   80    CONTINUE
         IF (KS .EQ. 2) GO TO 100
```

```
            IF (ABS(Z(K)) .LE. ABS(A(K,K))) GO TO 90
               S = ABS(A(K,K))/ABS(Z(K))
               CALL SSCAL(N,S,Z,1)
               EK = S*EK
   90       CONTINUE
            IF (A(K,K) .NE. 0.0E0) Z(K) = Z(K)/A(K,K)
            IF (A(K,K) .EQ. 0.0E0) Z(K) = 1.0E0
         GO TO 110
  100    CONTINUE
            AK = A(K,K)/A(K-1,K)
            AKM1 = A(K-1,K-1)/A(K-1,K)
            BK = Z(K)/A(K-1,K)
            BKM1 = Z(K-1)/A(K-1,K)
            DENOM = AK*AKM1 - 1.0E0
            Z(K) = (AKM1*BK - BKM1)/DENOM
            Z(K-1) = (AK*BKM1 - BK)/DENOM
  110    CONTINUE
         K = K - KS
      GO TO 60
  120 CONTINUE
      S = 1.0E0/SASUM(N,Z,1)
      CALL SSCAL(N,S,Z,1)
C
C     SOLVE TRANS(U)*Y = W
C
      K = 1
  130 IF (K .GT. N) GO TO 160
         KS = 1
         IF (KPVT(K) .LT. 0) KS = 2
         IF (K .EQ. 1) GO TO 150
            Z(K) = Z(K) + SDOT(K-1,A(1,K),1,Z(1),1)
            IF (KS .EQ. 2)
     *         Z(K+1) = Z(K+1) + SDOT(K-1,A(1,K+1),1,Z(1),1)
            KP = IABS(KPVT(K))
            IF (KP .EQ. K) GO TO 140
               T = Z(K)
               Z(K) = Z(KP)
               Z(KP) = T
  140       CONTINUE
  150    CONTINUE
         K = K + KS
      GO TO 130
  160 CONTINUE
      S = 1.0E0/SASUM(N,Z,1)
      CALL SSCAL(N,S,Z,1)
C
      YNORM = 1.0E0
C
C     SOLVE U*D*V = Y
C
      K = N
  170 IF (K .EQ. 0) GO TO 230
         KS = 1
         IF (KPVT(K) .LT. 0) KS = 2
         IF (K .EQ. KS) GO TO 190
            KP = IABS(KPVT(K))
            KPS = K + 1 - KS
            IF (KP .EQ. KPS) GO TO 180
               T = Z(KPS)
               Z(KPS) = Z(KP)
               Z(KP) = T
  180       CONTINUE
            CALL SAXPY(K-KS,Z(K),A(1,K),1,Z(1),1)
```

```
            IF (KS .EQ. 2) CALL SAXPY(K-KS,Z(K-1),A(1,K-1),1,Z(1),1)
  190    CONTINUE
         IF (KS .EQ. 2) GO TO 210
            IF (ABS(Z(K)) .LE. ABS(A(K,K))) GO TO 200
               S = ABS(A(K,K))/ABS(Z(K))
               CALL SSCAL(N,S,Z,1)
               YNORM = S*YNORM
  200       CONTINUE
            IF (A(K,K) .NE. 0.0E0) Z(K) = Z(K)/A(K,K)
            IF (A(K,K) .EQ. 0.0E0) Z(K) = 1.0E0
         GO TO 220
  210    CONTINUE
            AK = A(K,K)/A(K-1,K)
            AKM1 = A(K-1,K-1)/A(K-1,K)
            BK = Z(K)/A(K-1,K)
            BKM1 = Z(K-1)/A(K-1,K)
            DENOM = AK*AKM1 - 1.0E0
            Z(K) = (AKM1*BK - BKM1)/DENOM
            Z(K-1) = (AK*BKM1 - BK)/DENOM
  220    CONTINUE
         K = K - KS
      GO TO 170
  230 CONTINUE
      S = 1.0E0/SASUM(N,Z,1)
      CALL SSCAL(N,S,Z,1)
      YNORM = S*YNORM
C
C     SOLVE TRANS(U)*Z = V
C
      K = 1
  240 IF (K .GT. N) GO TO 270
         KS = 1
         IF (KPVT(K) .LT. 0) KS = 2
         IF (K .EQ. 1) GO TO 260
            Z(K) = Z(K) + SDOT(K-1,A(1,K),1,Z(1),1)
            IF (KS .EQ. 2)
     *         Z(K+1) = Z(K+1) + SDOT(K-1,A(1,K+1),1,Z(1),1)
            KP = IABS(KPVT(K))
            IF (KP .EQ. K) GO TO 250
               T = Z(K)
               Z(K) = Z(KP)
               Z(KP) = T
  250       CONTINUE
  260    CONTINUE
         K = K + KS
      GO TO 240
  270 CONTINUE
C     MAKE ZNORM = 1.0
      S = 1.0E0/SASUM(N,Z,1)
      CALL SSCAL(N,S,Z,1)
      YNORM = S*YNORM
C
      IF (ANORM .NE. 0.0E0) RCOND = YNORM/ANORM
      IF (ANORM .EQ. 0.0E0) RCOND = 0.0E0
      RETURN
      END
```

```
      SUBROUTINE SSIFA(A,LDA,N,KPVT,INFO)
      INTEGER LDA,N,KPVT(1),INFO
      REAL A(LDA,1)
C
C     SSIFA FACTORS A REAL SYMMETRIC MATRIX BY ELIMINATION
C     WITH SYMMETRIC PIVOTING.
C
C     TO SOLVE  A*X = B , FOLLOW SSIFA BY SSISL.
C     TO COMPUTE  INVERSE(A)*C , FOLLOW SSIFA BY SSISL.
C     TO COMPUTE  DETERMINANT(A) , FOLLOW SSIFA BY SSIDI.
C     TO COMPUTE  INERTIA(A) , FOLLOW SSIFA BY SSIDI.
C     TO COMPUTE  INVERSE(A) , FOLLOW SSIFA BY SSIDI.
C
C     ON ENTRY
C
C        A       REAL(LDA,N)
C                THE SYMMETRIC MATRIX TO BE FACTORED.
C                ONLY THE DIAGONAL AND UPPER TRIANGLE ARE USED.
C
C        LDA     INTEGER
C                THE LEADING DIMENSION OF THE ARRAY  A .
C
C        N       INTEGER
C                THE ORDER OF THE MATRIX  A .
C
C     ON RETURN
C
C        A       A BLOCK DIAGONAL MATRIX AND THE MULTIPLIERS WHICH
C                WERE USED TO OBTAIN IT.
C                THE FACTORIZATION CAN BE WRITTEN  A = U*D*TRANS(U)
C                WHERE  U  IS A PRODUCT OF PERMUTATION AND UNIT
C                UPPER TRIANGULAR MATRICES , TRANS(U) IS THE
C                TRANSPOSE OF  U , AND  D  IS BLOCK DIAGONAL
C                WITH 1 BY 1 AND 2 BY 2 BLOCKS.
C
C        KPVT    INTEGER(N)
C                AN INTEGER VECTOR OF PIVOT INDICES.
C
C        INFO    INTEGER
C                = 0  NORMAL VALUE.
C                = K  IF THE K-TH PIVOT BLOCK IS SINGULAR. THIS IS
C                     NOT AN ERROR CONDITION FOR THIS SUBROUTINE,
C                     BUT IT DOES INDICATE THAT SSISL OR SSIDI MAY
C                     DIVIDE BY ZERO IF CALLED.
C
C     LINPACK. THIS VERSION DATED 08/14/78 .
C     JAMES BUNCH, UNIV. CALIF. SAN DIEGO, ARGONNE NAT. LAB.
C
C     SUBROUTINES AND FUNCTIONS
C
C     BLAS SAXPY,SSWAP,ISAMAX
C     FORTRAN ABS,AMAX1,SQRT
C
C     INTERNAL VARIABLES
C
      REAL AK,AKM1,BK,BKM1,DENOM,MULK,MULKM1,T
      REAL ABSAKK,ALPHA,COLMAX,ROWMAX
      INTEGER IMAX,IMAXP1,J,JJ,JMAX,K,KM1,KM2,KSTEP,ISAMAX
      LOGICAL SWAP
C
C
C     INITIALIZE
C
```

```
C     ALPHA IS USED IN CHOOSING PIVOT BLOCK SIZE.
      ALPHA = (1.0E0 + SQRT(17.0E0))/8.0E0
C
      INFO = 0
C
C     MAIN LOOP ON K, WHICH GOES FROM N TO 1.
C
      K = N
   10 CONTINUE
C
C        LEAVE THE LOOP IF K=0 OR K=1.
C
C     ...EXIT
         IF (K .EQ. 0) GO TO 200
         IF (K .GT. 1) GO TO 20
            KPVT(1) = 1
            IF (A(1,1) .EQ. 0.0E0) INFO = 1
C     ......EXIT
            GO TO 200
   20    CONTINUE
C
C        THIS SECTION OF CODE DETERMINES THE KIND OF
C        ELIMINATION TO BE PERFORMED.  WHEN IT IS COMPLETED,
C        KSTEP WILL BE SET TO THE SIZE OF THE PIVOT BLOCK, AND
C        SWAP WILL BE SET TO .TRUE. IF AN INTERCHANGE IS
C        REQUIRED.
C
         KM1 = K - 1
         ABSAKK = ABS(A(K,K))
C
C        DETERMINE THE LARGEST OFF-DIAGONAL ELEMENT IN
C        COLUMN K.
C
         IMAX = ISAMAX(K-1,A(1,K),1)
         COLMAX = ABS(A(IMAX,K))
         IF (ABSAKK .LT. ALPHA*COLMAX) GO TO 30
            KSTEP = 1
            SWAP = .FALSE.
         GO TO 90
   30    CONTINUE
C
C           DETERMINE THE LARGEST OFF-DIAGONAL ELEMENT IN
C           ROW IMAX.
C
            ROWMAX = 0.0E0
            IMAXP1 = IMAX + 1
            DO 40 J = IMAXP1, K
               ROWMAX = AMAX1(ROWMAX,ABS(A(IMAX,J)))
   40       CONTINUE
            IF (IMAX .EQ. 1) GO TO 50
               JMAX = ISAMAX(IMAX-1,A(1,IMAX),1)
               ROWMAX = AMAX1(ROWMAX,ABS(A(JMAX,IMAX)))
   50       CONTINUE
            IF (ABS(A(IMAX,IMAX)) .LT. ALPHA*ROWMAX) GO TO 60
               KSTEP = 1
               SWAP = .TRUE.
            GO TO 80
   60       CONTINUE
            IF (ABSAKK .LT. ALPHA*COLMAX*(COLMAX/ROWMAX)) GO TO 70
               KSTEP = 1
               SWAP = .FALSE.
            GO TO 80
   70       CONTINUE
```

```
               KSTEP = 2
               SWAP = IMAX .NE. KM1
   80       CONTINUE
   90    CONTINUE
         IF (AMAX1(ABSAKK,COLMAX) .NE. 0.0E0) GO TO 100
C
C           COLUMN K IS ZERO.  SET INFO AND ITERATE THE LOOP.
C
            KPVT(K) = K
            INFO = K
         GO TO 190
  100    CONTINUE
         IF (KSTEP .EQ. 2) GO TO 140
C
C           1 X 1 PIVOT BLOCK.
C
            IF (.NOT.SWAP) GO TO 120
C
C              PERFORM AN INTERCHANGE.
C
               CALL SSWAP(IMAX,A(1,IMAX),1,A(1,K),1)
               DO 110 JJ = IMAX, K
                  J = K + IMAX - JJ
                  T = A(J,K)
                  A(J,K) = A(IMAX,J)
                  A(IMAX,J) = T
  110          CONTINUE
  120       CONTINUE
C
C           PERFORM THE ELIMINATION.
C
            DO 130 JJ = 1, KM1
               J = K - JJ
               MULK = -A(J,K)/A(K,K)
               T = MULK
               CALL SAXPY(J,T,A(1,K),1,A(1,J),1)
               A(J,K) = MULK
  130       CONTINUE
C
C           SET THE PIVOT ARRAY.
C
            KPVT(K) = K
            IF (SWAP) KPVT(K) = IMAX
         GO TO 190
  140    CONTINUE
C
C           2 X 2 PIVOT BLOCK.
C
            IF (.NOT.SWAP) GO TO 160
C
C              PERFORM AN INTERCHANGE.
C
               CALL SSWAP(IMAX,A(1,IMAX),1,A(1,K-1),1)
               DO 150 JJ = IMAX, KM1
                  J = KM1 + IMAX - JJ
                  T = A(J,K-1)
                  A(J,K-1) = A(IMAX,J)
                  A(IMAX,J) = T
  150          CONTINUE
               T = A(K-1,K)
               A(K-1,K) = A(IMAX,K)
               A(IMAX,K) = T
  160       CONTINUE
```

```
C
C           PERFORM THE ELIMINATION.
C
            KM2 = K - 2
            IF (KM2 .EQ. 0) GO TO 180
               AK = A(K,K)/A(K-1,K)
               AKM1 = A(K-1,K-1)/A(K-1,K)
               DENOM = 1.0E0 - AK*AKM1
               DO 170 JJ = 1, KM2
                  J = KM1 - JJ
                  BK = A(J,K)/A(K-1,K)
                  BKM1 = A(J,K-1)/A(K-1,K)
                  MULK = (AKM1*BK - BKM1)/DENOM
                  MULKM1 = (AK*BKM1 - BK)/DENOM
                  T = MULK
                  CALL SAXPY(J,T,A(1,K),1,A(1,J),1)
                  T = MULKM1
                  CALL SAXPY(J,T,A(1,K-1),1,A(1,J),1)
                  A(J,K) = MULK
                  A(J,K-1) = MULKM1
  170          CONTINUE
  180       CONTINUE
C
C           SET THE PIVOT ARRAY.
C
            KPVT(K) = 1 - K
            IF (SWAP) KPVT(K) = -IMAX
            KPVT(K-1) = KPVT(K)
  190    CONTINUE
         K = K - KSTEP
      GO TO 10
  200 CONTINUE
      RETURN
      END
```

```
      SUBROUTINE SSISL(A,LDA,N,KPVT,B)
      INTEGER LDA,N,KPVT(1)
      REAL A(LDA,1),B(1)
C
C     SSISL SOLVES THE REAL SYMMETRIC SYSTEM
C     A * X = B
C     USING THE FACTORS COMPUTED BY SSICO or SSIFA.
C
C     ON ENTRY
C
C        A       REAL(LDA,N)
C                THE OUTPUT FROM SSICO or SSIFA.
C
C        LDA     INTEGER
C                THE LEADING DIMENSION OF THE ARRAY  A .
C
C        N       INTEGER
C                THE ORDER OF THE MATRIX  A .
C
C        KPVT    INTEGER(N)
C                THE PIVOT VECTOR FROM SSICO or SSIFA.
C
C        B       REAL(N)
C                THE RIGHT HAND SIDE VECTOR.
C
C     ON RETURN
C
C        B       THE SOLUTION VECTOR  X .
C
C     ERROR CONDITION
C
C        A DIVISION BY ZERO MAY OCCUR IF  SSICO  HAS SET RCOND .EQ. 0.0
C        OR  SSIFA  HAS SET INFO .NE. 0  .
C
C     TO COMPUTE  INVERSE(A) * C  WHERE  C  IS A MATRIX
C     WITH  P  COLUMNS
C           CALL SSIFA(A,LDA,N,KPVT,INFO)
C           IF (INFO .NE. 0) GO TO ...
C           DO 10 J = 1, P
C              CALL SSISL(A,LDA,N,KPVT,C(1,J))
C        10 CONTINUE
C
C     LINPACK. THIS VERSION DATED 08/14/78 .
C     JAMES BUNCH, UNIV. CALIF. SAN DIEGO, ARGONNE NAT. LAB.
C
C     SUBROUTINES AND FUNCTIONS
C
C     BLAS SAXPY,SDOT
C     FORTRAN IABS
C
C     INTERNAL VARIABLES.
C
      REAL AK,AKM1,BK,BKM1,SDOT,DENOM,TEMP
      INTEGER K,KP
C
C     LOOP BACKWARD APPLYING THE TRANSFORMATIONS AND
C     D INVERSE TO B.
C
      K = N
   10 IF (K .EQ. 0) GO TO 80
         IF (KPVT(K) .LT. 0) GO TO 40
C
C           1 X 1 PIVOT BLOCK.
```

```
C
            IF (K .EQ. 1) GO TO 30
               KP = KPVT(K)
               IF (KP .EQ. K) GO TO 20
C
C                 INTERCHANGE.
C
                  TEMP = B(K)
                  B(K) = B(KP)
                  B(KP) = TEMP
   20          CONTINUE
C
C              APPLY THE TRANSFORMATION.
C
               CALL SAXPY(K-1,B(K),A(1,K),1,B(1),1)
   30       CONTINUE
C
C           APPLY D INVERSE.
C
            B(K) = B(K)/A(K,K)
            K = K - 1
         GO TO 70
   40    CONTINUE
C
C           2 X 2 PIVOT BLOCK.
C
            IF (K .EQ. 2) GO TO 60
               KP = IABS(KPVT(K))
               IF (KP .EQ. K - 1) GO TO 50
C
C                 INTERCHANGE.
C
                  TEMP = B(K-1)
                  B(K-1) = B(KP)
                  B(KP) = TEMP
   50          CONTINUE
C
C              APPLY THE TRANSFORMATION.
C
               CALL SAXPY(K-2,B(K),A(1,K),1,B(1),1)
               CALL SAXPY(K-2,B(K-1),A(1,K-1),1,B(1),1)
   60       CONTINUE
C
C           APPLY D INVERSE.
C
            AK = A(K,K)/A(K-1,K)
            AKM1 = A(K-1,K-1)/A(K-1,K)
            BK = B(K)/A(K-1,K)
            BKM1 = B(K-1)/A(K-1,K)
            DENOM = AK*AKM1 - 1.0E0
            B(K) = (AKM1*BK - BKM1)/DENOM
            B(K-1) = (AK*BKM1 - BK)/DENOM
            K = K - 2
   70    CONTINUE
      GO TO 10
   80 CONTINUE
C
C     LOOP FORWARD APPLYING THE TRANSFORMATIONS.
C
      K = 1
   90 IF (K .GT. N) GO TO 160
         IF (KPVT(K) .LT. 0) GO TO 120
C
```

```
C            1 X 1 PIVOT BLOCK.
C
             IF (K .EQ. 1) GO TO 110
C
C               APPLY THE TRANSFORMATION.
C
                B(K) = B(K) + SDOT(K-1,A(1,K),1,B(1),1)
                KP = KPVT(K)
                IF (KP .EQ. K) GO TO 100
C
C                  INTERCHANGE.
C
                   TEMP = B(K)
                   B(K) = B(KP)
                   B(KP) = TEMP
  100           CONTINUE
  110        CONTINUE
             K = K + 1
          GO TO 150
  120     CONTINUE
C
C            2 X 2 PIVOT BLOCK.
C
             IF (K .EQ. 1) GO TO 140
C
C               APPLY THE TRANSFORMATION.
C
                B(K) = B(K) + SDOT(K-1,A(1,K),1,B(1),1)
                B(K+1) = B(K+1) + SDOT(K-1,A(1,K+1),1,B(1),1)
                KP = IABS(KPVT(K))
                IF (KP .EQ. K) GO TO 130
C
C                  INTERCHANGE.
C
                   TEMP = B(K)
                   B(K) = B(KP)
                   B(KP) = TEMP
  130           CONTINUE
  140        CONTINUE
             K = K + 2
  150     CONTINUE
       GO TO 90
  160 CONTINUE
       RETURN
       END
```

```
      SUBROUTINE SSIDI(A,LDA,N,KPVT,DET,INERT,WORK,JOB)
      INTEGER LDA,N,JOB
      REAL A(LDA,1),WORK(1)
      REAL DET(2)
      INTEGER KPVT(1),INERT(3)
C
C     SSIDI COMPUTES THE DETERMINANT, INERTIA AND INVERSE
C     OF A REAL SYMMETRIC MATRIX USING THE FACTORS FROM SSICO or SSIFA.
C
C     ON ENTRY
C
C        A       REAL(LDA,N)
C                THE OUTPUT FROM SSICO or SSIFA.
C
C        LDA     INTEGER
C                THE LEADING DIMENSION OF THE ARRAY A.
C
C        N       INTEGER
C                THE ORDER OF THE MATRIX A.
C
C        KPVT    INTEGER(N)
C                THE PIVOT VECTOR FROM SSICO or SSIFA.
C
C        WORK    REAL(N)
C                WORK VECTOR.  CONTENTS DESTROYED.
C
C        JOB     INTEGER
C                JOB HAS THE DECIMAL EXPANSION  ABC  WHERE
C                   IF  C .NE. 0, THE INVERSE IS COMPUTED,
C                   IF  B .NE. 0, THE DETERMINANT IS COMPUTED,
C                   IF  A .NE. 0, THE INERTIA IS COMPUTED.
C
C                FOR EXAMPLE, JOB = 111  GIVES ALL THREE.
C
C     ON RETURN
C
C        VARIABLES NOT REQUESTED BY JOB ARE NOT USED.
C
C        A      CONTAINS THE UPPER TRIANGLE OF THE INVERSE OF
C               THE ORIGINAL MATRIX.  THE STRICT LOWER TRIANGLE
C               IS NEVER REFERENCED.
C
C        DET    REAL(2)
C               DETERMINANT OF ORIGINAL MATRIX.
C               DETERMINANT = DET(1) * 10.0**DET(2)
C               WITH 1.0 .LE. ABS(DET(1)) .LT. 10.0
C               OR DET(1) = 0.0.
C
C        INERT  INTEGER(3)
C               THE INERTIA OF THE ORIGINAL MATRIX.
C               INERT(1)  =  NUMBER OF POSITIVE EIGENVALUES.
C               INERT(2)  =  NUMBER OF NEGATIVE EIGENVALUES.
C               INERT(3)  =  NUMBER OF ZERO EIGENVALUES.
C
C     ERROR CONDITION
C
C        A DIVISION BY ZERO MAY OCCUR IF THE INVERSE IS REQUESTED
C        AND  SSICO  HAS SET RCOND .EQ. 0.0
C        OR  SSIFA  HAS SET  INFO .NE. 0 .
C
C     LINPACK. THIS VERSION DATED 08/14/78 .
C     JAMES BUNCH, UNIV. CALIF. SAN DIEGO, ARGONNE NAT. LAB
C
```

```
C     SUBROUTINES AND FUNCTIONS
C
C     BLAS SAXPY,SCOPY,SDOT,SSWAP
C     FORTRAN ABS,IABS,MOD
C
C     INTERNAL VARIABLES.
C
      REAL AKKP1,SDOT,TEMP
      REAL TEN,D,T,AK,AKP1
      INTEGER J,JB,K,KM1,KS,KSTEP
      LOGICAL NOINV,NODET,NOERT
C
      NOINV = MOD(JOB,10) .EQ. 0
      NODET = MOD(JOB,100)/10 .EQ. 0
      NOERT = MOD(JOB,1000)/100 .EQ. 0
C
      IF (NODET .AND. NOERT) GO TO 140
         IF (NOERT) GO TO 10
            INERT(1) = 0
            INERT(2) = 0
            INERT(3) = 0
   10    CONTINUE
         IF (NODET) GO TO 20
            DET(1) = 1.0E0
            DET(2) = 0.0E0
            TEN = 10.0E0
   20    CONTINUE
         T = 0.0E0
         DO 130 K = 1, N
            D = A(K,K)
C
C           CHECK IF 1 BY 1
C
            IF (KPVT(K) .GT. 0) GO TO 50
C
C              2 BY 2 BLOCK
C              USE DET (D  S)  =  (D/T * C - T) * T  ,  T = ABS(S)
C                      (S  C)
C              TO AVOID UNDERFLOW/OVERFLOW TROUBLES.
C              TAKE TWO PASSES THROUGH SCALING.  USE  T  FOR FLAG.
C
               IF (T .NE. 0.0E0) GO TO 30
                  T = ABS(A(K,K+1))
                  D = (D/T)*A(K+1,K+1) - T
               GO TO 40
   30          CONTINUE
                  D = T
                  T = 0.0E0
   40          CONTINUE
   50       CONTINUE
C
            IF (NOERT) GO TO 60
               IF (D .GT. 0.0E0) INERT(1) = INERT(1) + 1
               IF (D .LT. 0.0E0) INERT(2) = INERT(2) + 1
               IF (D .EQ. 0.0E0) INERT(3) = INERT(3) + 1
   60       CONTINUE
C
            IF (NODET) GO TO 120
               DET(1) = D*DET(1)
               IF (DET(1) .EQ. 0.0E0) GO TO 110
   70             IF (ABS(DET(1)) .GE. 1.0E0) GO TO 80
                     DET(1) = TEN*DET(1)
                     DET(2) = DET(2) - 1.0E0
```

```
                  GO TO 70
   80             CONTINUE
   90             IF (ABS(DET(1)) .LT. TEN) GO TO 100
                     DET(1) = DET(1)/TEN
                     DET(2) = DET(2) + 1.0E0
                  GO TO 90
  100             CONTINUE
  110          CONTINUE
  120       CONTINUE
  130    CONTINUE
  140 CONTINUE
C
C     COMPUTE INVERSE(A)
C
      IF (NOINV) GO TO 270
         K = 1
  150    IF (K .GT. N) GO TO 260
            KM1 = K - 1
            IF (KPVT(K) .LT. 0) GO TO 180
C
C              1 BY 1
C
               A(K,K) = 1.0E0/A(K,K)
               IF (KM1 .LT. 1) GO TO 170
                  CALL SCOPY(KM1,A(1,K),1,WORK,1)
                  DO 160 J = 1, KM1
                     A(J,K) = SDOT(J,A(1,J),1,WORK,1)
                     CALL SAXPY(J-1,WORK(J),A(1,J),1,A(1,K),1)
  160             CONTINUE
                  A(K,K) = A(K,K) + SDOT(KM1,WORK,1,A(1,K),1)
  170          CONTINUE
               KSTEP = 1
            GO TO 220
  180       CONTINUE
C
C              2 BY 2
C
               T = ABS(A(K,K+1))
               AK = A(K,K)/T
               AKP1 = A(K+1,K+1)/T
               AKKP1 = A(K,K+1)/T
               D = T*(AK*AKP1 - 1.0E0)
               A(K,K) = AKP1/D
               A(K+1,K+1) = AK/D
               A(K,K+1) = -AKKP1/D
               IF (KM1 .LT. 1) GO TO 210
                  CALL SCOPY(KM1,A(1,K+1),1,WORK,1)
                  DO 190 J = 1, KM1
                     A(J,K+1) = SDOT(J,A(1,J),1,WORK,1)
                     CALL SAXPY(J-1,WORK(J),A(1,J),1,A(1,K+1),1)
  190             CONTINUE
                  A(K+1,K+1) = A(K+1,K+1) + SDOT(KM1,WORK,1,A(1,K+1),1)
                  A(K,K+1) = A(K,K+1) + SDOT(KM1,A(1,K),1,A(1,K+1),1)
                  CALL SCOPY(KM1,A(1,K),1,WORK,1)
                  DO 200 J = 1, KM1
                     A(J,K) = SDOT(J,A(1,J),1,WORK,1)
                     CALL SAXPY(J-1,WORK(J),A(1,J),1,A(1,K),1)
  200             CONTINUE
                  A(K,K) = A(K,K) + SDOT(KM1,WORK,1,A(1,K),1)
  210          CONTINUE
               KSTEP = 2
  220       CONTINUE
C
```

```
C           SWAP
C
            KS = IABS(KPVT(K))
            IF (KS .EQ. K) GO TO 250
               CALL SSWAP(KS,A(1,KS),1,A(1,K),1)
               DO 230 JB = KS, K
                  J = K + KS - JB
                  TEMP = A(J,K)
                  A(J,K) = A(KS,J)
                  A(KS,J) = TEMP
  230          CONTINUE
               IF (KSTEP .EQ. 1) GO TO 240
                  TEMP = A(KS,K+1)
                  A(KS,K+1) = A(K,K+1)
                  A(K,K+1) = TEMP
  240          CONTINUE
  250       CONTINUE
            K = K + KSTEP
         GO TO 150
  260    CONTINUE
  270 CONTINUE
      RETURN
      END
```

```
      SUBROUTINE SSPCO(AP,N,KPVT,RCOND,Z)
      INTEGER N,KPVT(1)
      REAL AP(1),Z(1)
      REAL RCOND
C
C     SSPCO FACTORS A REAL SYMMETRIC MATRIX STORED IN PACKED
C     FORM BY ELIMINATION WITH SYMMETRIC PIVOTING AND ESTIMATES
C     THE CONDITION OF THE MATRIX.
C
C     IF  RCOND  IS NOT NEEDED, SSPFA IS SLIGHTLY FASTER.
C     TO SOLVE  A*X = B , FOLLOW SSPCO BY SSPSL.
C     TO COMPUTE  INVERSE(A)*C , FOLLOW SSPCO BY SSPSL.
C     TO COMPUTE  INVERSE(A) , FOLLOW SSPCO BY SSPDI.
C     TO COMPUTE  DETERMINANT(A) , FOLLOW SSPCO BY SSPDI.
C     TO COMPUTE  INERTIA(A), FOLLOW SSPCO BY SSPDI.
C
C     ON ENTRY
C
C        AP      REAL (N*(N+1)/2)
C                THE PACKED FORM OF A SYMMETRIC MATRIX  A .  THE
C                COLUMNS OF THE UPPER TRIANGLE ARE STORED SEQUENTIALLY
C                IN A ONE-DIMENSIONAL ARRAY OF LENGTH  N*(N+1)/2 .
C                SEE COMMENTS BELOW FOR DETAILS.
C
C        N       INTEGER
C                THE ORDER OF THE MATRIX  A .
C
C     OUTPUT
C
C        AP      A BLOCK DIAGONAL MATRIX AND THE MULTIPLIERS WHICH
C                WERE USED TO OBTAIN IT STORED IN PACKED FORM.
C                THE FACTORIZATION CAN BE WRITTEN  A = U*D*TRANS(U)
C                WHERE  U  IS A PRODUCT OF PERMUTATION AND UNIT
C                UPPER TRIANGULAR MATRICES , TRANS(U) IS THE
C                TRANSPOSE OF  U , AND  D  IS BLOCK DIAGONAL
C                WITH 1 BY 1 AND 2 BY 2 BLOCKS.
C
C        KPVT    INTEGER(N)
C                AN INTEGER VECTOR OF PIVOT INDICES.
C
C        RCOND   REAL
C                AN ESTIMATE OF THE RECIPROCAL CONDITION OF  A .
C                FOR THE SYSTEM  A*X = B , RELATIVE PERTURBATIONS
C                IN  A  AND  B  OF SIZE  EPSILON  MAY CAUSE
C                RELATIVE PERTURBATIONS IN  X  OF SIZE  EPSILON/RCOND .
C                IF  RCOND  IS SO SMALL THAT THE LOGICAL EXPRESSION
C                           1.0 + RCOND .EQ. 1.0
C                IS TRUE, THEN  A  MAY BE SINGULAR TO WORKING
C                PRECISION.  IN PARTICULAR,  RCOND  IS ZERO  IF
C                EXACT SINGULARITY IS DETECTED OR THE ESTIMATE
C                UNDERFLOWS.
C
C        Z       REAL(N)
C                A WORK VECTOR WHOSE CONTENTS ARE USUALLY UNIMPORTANT.
C                IF  A  IS CLOSE TO A SINGULAR MATRIX, THEN  Z  IS
C                AN APPROXIMATE NULL VECTOR IN THE SENSE THAT
C                NORM(A*Z) = RCOND*NORM(A)*NORM(Z) .
C
C     PACKED STORAGE
C
C          THE FOLLOWING PROGRAM SEGMENT WILL PACK THE UPPER
C          TRIANGLE OF A SYMMETRIC MATRIX.
C
```

```
C                 K = 0
C                 DO 20 J = 1, N
C                    DO 10 I = 1, J
C                       K = K + 1
C                       AP(K) = A(I,J)
C               10    CONTINUE
C               20 CONTINUE
C
C     LINPACK. THIS VERSION DATED 08/14/78 .
C     CLEVE MOLER, UNIVERSITY OF NEW MEXICO, ARGONNE NATIONAL LAB.
C
C     SUBROUTINES AND FUNCTIONS
C
C     LINPACK SSPFA
C     BLAS SAXPY,SDOT,SSCAL,SASUM
C     FORTRAN ABS,AMAX1,IABS,SIGN
C
C     INTERNAL VARIABLES
C
      REAL AK,AKM1,BK,BKM1,SDOT,DENOM,EK,T
      REAL ANORM,S,SASUM,YNORM
      INTEGER I,IJ,IK,IKM1,IKP1,INFO,J,JM1,J1
      INTEGER K,KK,KM1K,KM1KM1,KP,KPS,KS
C
C
C     FIND NORM OF A USING ONLY UPPER HALF
C
      J1 = 1
      DO 30 J = 1, N
         Z(J) = SASUM(J,AP(J1),1)
         IJ = J1
         J1 = J1 + J
         JM1 = J - 1
         IF (JM1 .LT. 1) GO TO 20
         DO 10 I = 1, JM1
            Z(I) = Z(I) + ABS(AP(IJ))
            IJ = IJ + 1
   10    CONTINUE
   20    CONTINUE
   30 CONTINUE
      ANORM = 0.0E0
      DO 40 J = 1, N
         ANORM = AMAX1(ANORM,Z(J))
   40 CONTINUE
C
C     FACTOR
C
      CALL SSPFA(AP,N,KPVT,INFO)
C
C     RCOND = 1/(NORM(A)*(ESTIMATE OF NORM(INVERSE(A)))) .
C     ESTIMATE = NORM(Z)/NORM(Y) WHERE  A*Z = Y  AND  A*Y = E .
C     THE COMPONENTS OF  E  ARE CHOSEN TO CAUSE MAXIMUM LOCAL
C     GROWTH IN THE ELEMENTS OF W  WHERE  U*D*W = E .
C     THE VECTORS ARE FREQUENTLY RESCALED TO AVOID OVERFLOW.
C
C     SOLVE U*D*W = E
C
      EK = 1.0E0
      DO 50 J = 1, N
         Z(J) = 0.0E0
   50 CONTINUE
      K = N
      IK = (N*(N - 1))/2
```

```
   60 IF (K .EQ. 0) GO TO 120
         KK = IK + K
         IKM1 = IK - (K - 1)
         KS = 1
         IF (KPVT(K) .LT. 0) KS = 2
         KP = IABS(KPVT(K))
         KPS = K + 1 - KS
         IF (KP .EQ. KPS) GO TO 70
            T = Z(KPS)
            Z(KPS) = Z(KP)
            Z(KP) = T
   70    CONTINUE
         IF (Z(K) .NE. 0.0E0) EK = SIGN(EK,Z(K))
         Z(K) = Z(K) + EK
         CALL SAXPY(K-KS,Z(K),AP(IK+1),1,Z(1),1)
         IF (KS .EQ. 1) GO TO 80
            IF (Z(K-1) .NE. 0.0E0) EK = SIGN(EK,Z(K-1))
            Z(K-1) = Z(K-1) + EK
            CALL SAXPY(K-KS,Z(K-1),AP(IKM1+1),1,Z(1),1)
   80    CONTINUE
         IF (KS .EQ. 2) GO TO 100
            IF (ABS(Z(K)) .LE. ABS(AP(KK))) GO TO 90
               S = ABS(AP(KK))/ABS(Z(K))
               CALL SSCAL(N,S,Z,1)
               EK = S*EK
   90       CONTINUE
            IF (AP(KK) .NE. 0.0E0) Z(K) = Z(K)/AP(KK)
            IF (AP(KK) .EQ. 0.0E0) Z(K) = 1.0E0
         GO TO 110
  100    CONTINUE
            KM1K = IK + K - 1
            KM1KM1 = IKM1 + K - 1
            AK = AP(KK)/AP(KM1K)
            AKM1 = AP(KM1KM1)/AP(KM1K)
            BK = Z(K)/AP(KM1K)
            BKM1 = Z(K-1)/AP(KM1K)
            DENOM = AK*AKM1 - 1.0E0
            Z(K) = (AKM1*BK - BKM1)/DENOM
            Z(K-1) = (AK*BKM1 - BK)/DENOM
  110    CONTINUE
         K = K - KS
         IK = IK - K
         IF (KS .EQ. 2) IK = IK - (K + 1)
      GO TO 60
  120 CONTINUE
      S = 1.0E0/SASUM(N,Z,1)
      CALL SSCAL(N,S,Z,1)
C
C     SOLVE TRANS(U)*Y = W
C
      K = 1
      IK = 0
  130 IF (K .GT. N) GO TO 160
         KS = 1
         IF (KPVT(K) .LT. 0) KS = 2
         IF (K .EQ. 1) GO TO 150
            Z(K) = Z(K) + SDOT(K-1,AP(IK+1),1,Z(1),1)
            IKP1 = IK + K
            IF (KS .EQ. 2)
     *         Z(K+1) = Z(K+1) + SDOT(K-1,AP(IKP1+1),1,Z(1),1)
            KP = IABS(KPVT(K))
            IF (KP .EQ. K) GO TO 140
               T = Z(K)
```

```
            Z(K) = Z(KP)
            Z(KP) = T
  140     CONTINUE
  150   CONTINUE
        IK = IK + K
        IF (KS .EQ. 2) IK = IK + (K + 1)
        K = K + KS
      GO TO 130
  160 CONTINUE
      S = 1.0E0/SASUM(N,Z,1)
      CALL SSCAL(N,S,Z,1)
C
      YNORM = 1.0E0
C
C     SOLVE U*D*V = Y
C
      K = N
      IK = N*(N - 1)/2
  170 IF (K .EQ. 0) GO TO 230
        KK = IK + K
        IKM1 = IK - (K - 1)
        KS = 1
        IF (KPVT(K) .LT. 0) KS = 2
        IF (K .EQ. KS) GO TO 190
          KP = IABS(KPVT(K))
          KPS = K + 1 - KS
          IF (KP .EQ. KPS) GO TO 180
            T = Z(KPS)
            Z(KPS) = Z(KP)
            Z(KP) = T
  180     CONTINUE
          CALL SAXPY(K-KS,Z(K),AP(IK+1),1,Z(1),1)
          IF (KS .EQ. 2) CALL SAXPY(K-KS,Z(K-1),AP(IKM1+1),1,Z(1),1)
  190   CONTINUE
        IF (KS .EQ. 2) GO TO 210
          IF (ABS(Z(K)) .LE. ABS(AP(KK))) GO TO 200
            S = ABS(AP(KK))/ABS(Z(K))
            CALL SSCAL(N,S,Z,1)
            YNORM = S*YNORM
  200     CONTINUE
          IF (AP(KK) .NE. 0.0E0) Z(K) = Z(K)/AP(KK)
          IF (AP(KK) .EQ. 0.0E0) Z(K) = 1.0E0
        GO TO 220
  210   CONTINUE
          KM1K = IK + K - 1
          KM1KM1 = IKM1 + K - 1
          AK = AP(KK)/AP(KM1K)
          AKM1 = AP(KM1KM1)/AP(KM1K)
          BK = Z(K)/AP(KM1K)
          BKM1 = Z(K-1)/AP(KM1K)
          DENOM = AK*AKM1 - 1.0E0
          Z(K) = (AKM1*BK - BKM1)/DENOM
          Z(K-1) = (AK*BKM1 - BK)/DENOM
  220   CONTINUE
        K = K - KS
        IK = IK - K
        IF (KS .EQ. 2) IK = IK - (K + 1)
      GO TO 170
  230 CONTINUE
      S = 1.0E0/SASUM(N,Z,1)
      CALL SSCAL(N,S,Z,1)
      YNORM = S*YNORM
C
```

```
C     SOLVE TRANS(U)*Z = V
C
      K = 1
      IK = 0
  240 IF (K .GT. N) GO TO 270
         KS = 1
         IF (KPVT(K) .LT. 0) KS = 2
         IF (K .EQ. 1) GO TO 260
            Z(K) = Z(K) + SDOT(K-1,AP(IK+1),1,Z(1),1)
            IKP1 = IK + K
            IF (KS .EQ. 2)
     *         Z(K+1) = Z(K+1) + SDOT(K-1,AP(IKP1+1),1,Z(1),1)
            KP = IABS(KPVT(K))
            IF (KP .EQ. K) GO TO 250
               T = Z(K)
               Z(K) = Z(KP)
               Z(KP) = T
  250       CONTINUE
  260    CONTINUE
         IK = IK + K
         IF (KS .EQ. 2) IK = IK + (K + 1)
         K = K + KS
      GO TO 240
  270 CONTINUE
C     MAKE ZNORM = 1.0
      S = 1.0E0/SASUM(N,Z,1)
      CALL SSCAL(N,S,Z,1)
      YNORM = S*YNORM
C
      IF (ANORM .NE. 0.0E0) RCOND = YNORM/ANORM
      IF (ANORM .EQ. 0.0E0) RCOND = 0.0E0
      RETURN
      END
```

```
      SUBROUTINE SSPFA(AP,N,KPVT,INFO)
      INTEGER N,KPVT(1),INFO
      REAL AP(1)
C
C     SSPFA FACTORS A REAL SYMMETRIC MATRIX STORED IN
C     PACKED FORM BY ELIMINATION WITH SYMMETRIC PIVOTING.
C
C     TO SOLVE  A*X = B , FOLLOW SSPFA BY SSPSL.
C     TO COMPUTE  INVERSE(A)*C , FOLLOW SSPFA BY SSPSL.
C     TO COMPUTE  DETERMINANT(A) , FOLLOW SSPFA BY SSPDI.
C     TO COMPUTE  INERTIA(A) , FOLLOW SSPFA BY SSPDI.
C     TO COMPUTE  INVERSE(A) , FOLLOW SSPFA BY SSPDI.
C
C     ON ENTRY
C
C        AP      REAL (N*(N+1)/2)
C                THE PACKED FORM OF A SYMMETRIC MATRIX  A .  THE
C                COLUMNS OF THE UPPER TRIANGLE ARE STORED SEQUENTIALLY
C                IN A ONE-DIMENSIONAL ARRAY OF LENGTH  N*(N+1)/2 .
C                SEE COMMENTS BELOW FOR DETAILS.
C
C        N       INTEGER
C                THE ORDER OF THE MATRIX  A .
C
C     OUTPUT
C
C        AP      A BLOCK DIAGONAL MATRIX AND THE MULTIPLIERS WHICH
C                WERE USED TO OBTAIN IT STORED IN PACKED FORM.
C                THE FACTORIZATION CAN BE WRITTEN  A = U*D*TRANS(U)
C                WHERE  U  IS A PRODUCT OF PERMUTATION AND UNIT
C                UPPER TRIANGULAR MATRICES , TRANS(U) IS THE
C                TRANSPOSE OF  U , AND  D  IS BLOCK DIAGONAL
C                WITH 1 BY 1 AND 2 BY 2 BLOCKS.
C
C        KPVT    INTEGER(N)
C                AN INTEGER VECTOR OF PIVOT INDICES.
C
C        INFO    INTEGER
C                = 0  NORMAL VALUE.
C                = K  IF THE K-TH PIVOT BLOCK IS SINGULAR. THIS IS
C                     NOT AN ERROR CONDITION FOR THIS SUBROUTINE,
C                     BUT IT DOES INDICATE THAT SSPSL OR SSPDI MAY
C                     DIVIDE BY ZERO IF CALLED.
C
C     PACKED STORAGE
C
C          THE FOLLOWING PROGRAM SEGMENT WILL PACK THE UPPER
C          TRIANGLE OF A SYMMETRIC MATRIX.
C
C                K = 0
C                DO 20 J = 1, N
C                   DO 10 I = 1, J
C                      K = K + 1
C                      AP(K)  = A(I,J)
C            10    CONTINUE
C            20 CONTINUE
C
C     LINPACK. THIS VERSION DATED 08/14/78 .
C     JAMES BUNCH, UNIV. CALIF. SAN DIEGO, ARGONNE NAT. LAB.
C
C     SUBROUTINES AND FUNCTIONS
C
C     BLAS SAXPY,SSWAP,ISAMAX
```

```
C     FORTRAN ABS,AMAX1,SQRT
C
C     INTERNAL VARIABLES
C
      REAL AK,AKM1,BK,BKM1,DENOM,MULK,MULKM1,T
      REAL ABSAKK,ALPHA,COLMAX,ROWMAX
      INTEGER ISAMAX,IJ,IJJ,IK,IKM1,IM,IMAX,IMAXP1,IMIM,IMJ,IMK
      INTEGER J,JJ,JK,JKM1,JMAX,JMIM,K,KK,KM1,KM1K,KM1KM1,KM2,KSTEP
      LOGICAL SWAP
C
C
C     INITIALIZE
C
C     ALPHA IS USED IN CHOOSING PIVOT BLOCK SIZE.
      ALPHA = (1.0E0 + SQRT(17.0E0))/8.0E0
C
      INFO = 0
C
C     MAIN LOOP ON K, WHICH GOES FROM N TO 1.
C
      K = N
      IK = (N*(N - 1))/2
   10 CONTINUE
C
C        LEAVE THE LOOP IF K=0 OR K=1.
C
C     ...EXIT
         IF (K .EQ. 0) GO TO 200
         IF (K .GT. 1) GO TO 20
            KPVT(1) = 1
            IF (AP(1) .EQ. 0.0E0) INFO = 1
C     ......EXIT
            GO TO 200
   20    CONTINUE
C
C        THIS SECTION OF CODE DETERMINES THE KIND OF
C        ELIMINATION TO BE PERFORMED.  WHEN IT IS COMPLETED,
C        KSTEP WILL BE SET TO THE SIZE OF THE PIVOT BLOCK, AND
C        SWAP WILL BE SET TO .TRUE. IF AN INTERCHANGE IS
C        REQUIRED.
C
         KM1 = K - 1
         KK = IK + K
         ABSAKK = ABS(AP(KK))
C
C        DETERMINE THE LARGEST OFF-DIAGONAL ELEMENT IN
C        COLUMN K.
C
         IMAX = ISAMAX(K-1,AP(IK+1),1)
         IMK = IK + IMAX
         COLMAX = ABS(AP(IMK))
         IF (ABSAKK .LT. ALPHA*COLMAX) GO TO 30
            KSTEP = 1
            SWAP = .FALSE.
         GO TO 90
   30    CONTINUE
C
C           DETERMINE THE LARGEST OFF-DIAGONAL ELEMENT IN
C           ROW IMAX.
C
            ROWMAX = 0.0E0
            IMAXP1 = IMAX + 1
            IM = IMAX*(IMAX - 1)/2
```

```
            IMJ = IM + 2*IMAX
            DO 40 J = IMAXP1, K
               ROWMAX = AMAX1(ROWMAX,ABS(AP(IMJ)))
               IMJ = IMJ + J
   40       CONTINUE
            IF (IMAX .EQ. 1) GO TO 50
               JMAX = ISAMAX(IMAX-1,AP(IM+1),1)
               JMIM = JMAX + IM
               ROWMAX = AMAX1(ROWMAX,ABS(AP(JMIM)))
   50       CONTINUE
            IMIM = IMAX + IM
            IF (ABS(AP(IMIM)) .LT. ALPHA*ROWMAX) GO TO 60
               KSTEP = 1
               SWAP = .TRUE.
            GO TO 80
   60       CONTINUE
            IF (ABSAKK .LT. ALPHA*COLMAX*(COLMAX/ROWMAX)) GO TO 70
               KSTEP = 1
               SWAP = .FALSE.
            GO TO 80
   70       CONTINUE
               KSTEP = 2
               SWAP = IMAX .NE. KM1
   80       CONTINUE
   90    CONTINUE
         IF (AMAX1(ABSAKK,COLMAX) .NE. 0.0E0) GO TO 100
C
C           COLUMN K IS ZERO.  SET INFO AND ITERATE THE LOOP.
C
            KPVT(K) = K
            INFO = K
         GO TO 190
  100    CONTINUE
         IF (KSTEP .EQ. 2) GO TO 140
C
C           1 X 1 PIVOT BLOCK.
C
            IF (.NOT.SWAP) GO TO 120
C
C              PERFORM AN INTERCHANGE.
C
               CALL SSWAP(IMAX,AP(IM+1),1,AP(IK+1),1)
               IMJ = IK + IMAX
               DO 110 JJ = IMAX, K
                  J = K + IMAX - JJ
                  JK = IK + J
                  T = AP(JK)
                  AP(JK) = AP(IMJ)
                  AP(IMJ) = T
                  IMJ = IMJ - (J - 1)
  110          CONTINUE
  120       CONTINUE
C
C           PERFORM THE ELIMINATION.
C
            IJ = IK - (K - 1)
            DO 130 JJ = 1, KM1
               J = K - JJ
               JK = IK + J
               MULK = -AP(JK)/AP(KK)
               T = MULK
               CALL SAXPY(J,T,AP(IK+1),1,AP(IJ+1),1)
               IJJ = IJ + J
```

```
               AP(JK) = MULK
               IJ = IJ - (J - 1)
  130       CONTINUE
C
C           SET THE PIVOT ARRAY.
C
            KPVT(K) = K
            IF (SWAP) KPVT(K) = IMAX
         GO TO 190
  140    CONTINUE
C
C           2 X 2 PIVOT BLOCK.
C
            KM1K = IK + K - 1
            IKM1 = IK - (K - 1)
            IF (.NOT.SWAP) GO TO 160
C
C              PERFORM AN INTERCHANGE.
C
               CALL SSWAP(IMAX,AP(IM+1),1,AP(IKM1+1),1)
               IMJ = IKM1 + IMAX
               DO 150 JJ = IMAX, KM1
                  J = KM1 + IMAX - JJ
                  JKM1 = IKM1 + J
                  T = AP(JKM1)
                  AP(JKM1) = AP(IMJ)
                  AP(IMJ) = T
                  IMJ = IMJ - (J - 1)
  150          CONTINUE
               T = AP(KM1K)
               AP(KM1K) = AP(IMK)
               AP(IMK) = T
  160       CONTINUE
C
C           PERFORM THE ELIMINATION.
C
            KM2 = K - 2
            IF (KM2 .EQ. 0) GO TO 180
               AK = AP(KK)/AP(KM1K)
               KM1KM1 = IKM1 + K - 1
               AKM1 = AP(KM1KM1)/AP(KM1K)
               DENOM = 1.0E0 - AK*AKM1
               IJ = IK - (K - 1) - (K - 2)
               DO 170 JJ = 1, KM2
                  J = KM1 - JJ
                  JK = IK + J
                  BK = AP(JK)/AP(KM1K)
                  JKM1 = IKM1 + J
                  BKM1 = AP(JKM1)/AP(KM1K)
                  MULK = (AKM1*BK - BKM1)/DENOM
                  MULKM1 = (AK*BKM1 - BK)/DENOM
                  T = MULK
                  CALL SAXPY(J,T,AP(IK+1),1,AP(IJ+1),1)
                  T = MULKM1
                  CALL SAXPY(J,T,AP(IKM1+1),1,AP(IJ+1),1)
                  AP(JK) = MULK
                  AP(JKM1) = MULKM1
                  IJJ = IJ + J
                  IJ = IJ - (J - 1)
  170          CONTINUE
  180       CONTINUE
C
C           SET THE PIVOT ARRAY.
```

```
C
            KPVT(K) = 1 - K
            IF (SWAP) KPVT(K) = -IMAX
            KPVT(K-1) = KPVT(K)
  190    CONTINUE
         IK = IK - (K - 1)
         IF (KSTEP .EQ. 2) IK = IK - (K - 2)
         K = K - KSTEP
      GO TO 10
  200 CONTINUE
      RETURN
      END
```

```
      SUBROUTINE SSPSL(AP,N,KPVT,B)
      INTEGER N,KPVT(1)
      REAL AP(1),B(1)
C
C     SSISL SOLVES THE REAL SYMMETRIC SYSTEM
C     A * X = B
C     USING THE FACTORS COMPUTED BY SSPCO or SSPFA.
C
C     ON ENTRY
C
C        AP      REAL(N*(N+1)/2)
C                THE OUTPUT FROM SSPCO or SSPFA.
C
C        N       INTEGER
C                THE ORDER OF THE MATRIX  A .
C
C        KPVT    INTEGER(N)
C                THE PIVOT VECTOR FROM SSPCO or SSPFA.
C
C        B       REAL(N)
C                THE RIGHT HAND SIDE VECTOR.
C
C     ON RETURN
C
C        B       THE SOLUTION VECTOR  X .
C
C     ERROR CONDITION
C
C        A DIVISION BY ZERO MAY OCCUR IF  SSPCO  HAS SET RCOND .EQ. 0.0
C        OR  SSPFA  HAS SET INFO .NE. 0   .
C
C     TO COMPUTE  INVERSE(A) * C  WHERE  C  IS A MATRIX
C     WITH  P  COLUMNS
C           CALL SSPFA(AP,N,KPVT,INFO)
C           IF (INFO .NE. 0) GO TO ...
C           DO 10 J = 1, P
C              CALL SSPSL(AP,N,KPVT,C(1,J))
C        10 CONTINUE
C
C     LINPACK. THIS VERSION DATED 08/14/78 .
C     JAMES BUNCH, UNIV. CALIF. SAN DIEGO, ARGONNE NAT. LAB.
C
C     SUBROUTINES AND FUNCTIONS
C
C     BLAS SAXPY,SDOT
C     FORTRAN IABS
C
C     INTERNAL VARIABLES.
C
      REAL AK,AKM1,BK,BKM1,SDOT,DENOM,TEMP
      INTEGER IK,IKM1,IKP1,K,KK,KM1K,KM1KM1,KP
C
C     LOOP BACKWARD APPLYING THE TRANSFORMATIONS AND
C     D INVERSE TO B.
C
      K = N
      IK = (N*(N - 1))/2
   10 IF (K .EQ. 0) GO TO 80
         KK = IK + K
         IF (KPVT(K) .LT. 0) GO TO 40
C
C           1 X 1 PIVOT BLOCK.
C
```

```
            IF (K .EQ. 1) GO TO 30
               KP = KPVT(K)
               IF (KP .EQ. K) GO TO 20
C
C                 INTERCHANGE.
C
                  TEMP = B(K)
                  B(K) = B(KP)
                  B(KP) = TEMP
   20          CONTINUE
C
C              APPLY THE TRANSFORMATION.
C
               CALL SAXPY(K-1,B(K),AP(IK+1),1,B(1),1)
   30       CONTINUE
C
C           APPLY D INVERSE.
C
            B(K) = B(K)/AP(KK)
            K = K - 1
            IK = IK - K
         GO TO 70
   40    CONTINUE
C
C           2 X 2 PIVOT BLOCK.
C
            IKM1 = IK - (K - 1)
            IF (K .EQ. 2) GO TO 60
               KP = IABS(KPVT(K))
               IF (KP .EQ. K - 1) GO TO 50
C
C                 INTERCHANGE.
C
                  TEMP = B(K-1)
                  B(K-1) = B(KP)
                  B(KP) = TEMP
   50          CONTINUE
C
C              APPLY THE TRANSFORMATION.
C
               CALL SAXPY(K-2,B(K),AP(IK+1),1,B(1),1)
               CALL SAXPY(K-2,B(K-1),AP(IKM1+1),1,B(1),1)
   60       CONTINUE
C
C           APPLY D INVERSE.
C
            KM1K = IK + K - 1
            KK = IK + K
            AK = AP(KK)/AP(KM1K)
            KM1KM1 = IKM1 + K - 1
            AKM1 = AP(KM1KM1)/AP(KM1K)
            BK = B(K)/AP(KM1K)
            BKM1 = B(K-1)/AP(KM1K)
            DENOM = AK*AKM1 - 1.0E0
            B(K) = (AKM1*BK - BKM1)/DENOM
            B(K-1) = (AK*BKM1 - BK)/DENOM
            K = K - 2
            IK = IK - (K + 1) - K
   70    CONTINUE
      GO TO 10
   80 CONTINUE
C
C     LOOP FORWARD APPLYING THE TRANSFORMATIONS.
```

```
C
      K = 1
      IK = 0
   90 IF (K .GT. N) GO TO 160
         IF (KPVT(K) .LT. 0) GO TO 120
C
C           1 X 1 PIVOT BLOCK.
C
            IF (K .EQ. 1) GO TO 110
C
C              APPLY THE TRANSFORMATION.
C
               B(K) = B(K) + SDOT(K-1,AP(IK+1),1,B(1),1)
               KP = KPVT(K)
               IF (KP .EQ. K) GO TO 100
C
C                 INTERCHANGE.
C
                  TEMP = B(K)
                  B(K) = B(KP)
                  B(KP) = TEMP
  100          CONTINUE
  110       CONTINUE
            IK = IK + K
            K = K + 1
         GO TO 150
  120    CONTINUE
C
C           2 X 2 PIVOT BLOCK.
C
            IF (K .EQ. 1) GO TO 140
C
C              APPLY THE TRANSFORMATION.
C
               B(K) = B(K) + SDOT(K-1,AP(IK+1),1,B(1),1)
               IKP1 = IK + K
               B(K+1) = B(K+1) + SDOT(K-1,AP(IKP1+1),1,B(1),1)
               KP = IABS(KPVT(K))
               IF (KP .EQ. K) GO TO 130
C
C                 INTERCHANGE.
C
                  TEMP = B(K)
                  B(K) = B(KP)
                  B(KP) = TEMP
  130          CONTINUE
  140       CONTINUE
            IK = IK + K + K + 1
            K = K + 2
  150    CONTINUE
      GO TO 90
  160 CONTINUE
      RETURN
      END
```

SSPDI

```
      SUBROUTINE SSPDI(AP,N,KPVT,DET,INERT,WORK,JOB)
      INTEGER N,JOB
      REAL AP(1),WORK(1)
      REAL DET(2)
      INTEGER KPVT(1),INERT(3)
C
C     SSPDI COMPUTES THE DETERMINANT, INERTIA AND INVERSE
C     OF A REAL SYMMETRIC MATRIX USING THE FACTORS FROM SSPCO or SSPFA,
C     WHERE THE MATRIX IS STORED IN PACKED FORM.
C
C     ON ENTRY
C
C        AP      REAL (N*(N+1)/2)
C                THE OUTPUT FROM SSPCO or SSPFA.
C
C        N       INTEGER
C                THE ORDER OF THE MATRIX A.
C
C        KPVT    INTEGER(N)
C                THE PIVOT VECTOR FROM SSPCO or SSPFA.
C
C        WORK    REAL(N)
C                WORK VECTOR.  CONTENTS IGNORED.
C
C        JOB     INTEGER
C                JOB HAS THE DECIMAL EXPANSION  ABC  WHERE
C                   IF  C .NE. 0, THE INVERSE IS COMPUTED,
C                   IF  B .NE. 0, THE DETERMINANT IS COMPUTED,
C                   IF  A .NE. 0, THE INERTIA IS COMPUTED.
C
C                FOR EXAMPLE, JOB = 111  GIVES ALL THREE.
C
C     ON RETURN
C
C        VARIABLES NOT REQUESTED BY JOB ARE NOT USED.
C
C        AP     CONTAINS THE UPPER TRIANGLE OF THE INVERSE OF
C               THE ORIGINAL MATRIX, STORED IN PACKED FORM.
C               THE COLUMNS OF THE UPPER TRIANGLE ARE STORED
C               SEQUENTIALLY IN A ONE-DIMENSIONAL ARRAY.
C
C        DET    REAL(2)
C               DETERMINANT OF ORIGINAL MATRIX.
C               DETERMINANT = DET(1) * 10.0**DET(2)
C               WITH 1.0 .LE. ABS(DET(1)) .LT. 10.0
C               OR DET(1) = 0.0.
C
C        INERT  INTEGER(3)
C               THE INERTIA OF THE ORIGINAL MATRIX.
C               INERT(1)  =  NUMBER OF POSITIVE EIGENVALUES.
C               INERT(2)  =  NUMBER OF NEGATIVE EIGENVALUES.
C               INERT(3)  =  NUMBER OF ZERO EIGENVALUES.
C
C     ERROR CONDITION
C
C        A DIVISION BY ZERO WILL OCCUR IF THE INVERSE IS REQUESTED
C        AND  SSPCO  HAS SET RCOND .EQ. 0.0
C        OR  SSPFA  HAS SET  INFO .NE. 0 .
C
C     LINPACK. THIS VERSION DATED 08/14/78 .
C     JAMES BUNCH, UNIV. CALIF. SAN DIEGO, ARGONNE NAT. LAB.
C
C     SUBROUTINES AND FUNCTIONS
```

```
C
C     BLAS SAXPY,SCOPY,SDOT,SSWAP
C     FORTRAN ABS,IABS,MOD
C
C     INTERNAL VARIABLES.
C
      REAL AKKP1,SDOT,TEMP
      REAL TEN,D,T,AK,AKP1
      INTEGER IJ,IK,IKP1,IKS,J,JB,JK,JKP1
      INTEGER K,KK,KKP1,KM1,KS,KSJ,KSKP1,KSTEP
      LOGICAL NOINV,NODET,NOERT
C
      NOINV = MOD(JOB,10) .EQ. 0
      NODET = MOD(JOB,100)/10 .EQ. 0
      NOERT = MOD(JOB,1000)/100 .EQ. 0
C
      IF (NODET .AND. NOERT) GO TO 140
         IF (NOERT) GO TO 10
            INERT(1) = 0
            INERT(2) = 0
            INERT(3) = 0
   10    CONTINUE
         IF (NODET) GO TO 20
            DET(1) = 1.0E0
            DET(2) = 0.0E0
            TEN = 10.0E0
   20    CONTINUE
         T = 0.0E0
         IK = 0
         DO 130 K = 1, N
            KK = IK + K
            D = AP(KK)
C
C           CHECK IF 1 BY 1
C
            IF (KPVT(K) .GT. 0) GO TO 50
C
C              2 BY 2 BLOCK
C              USE DET (D  S)  =  (D/T * C - T) * T  ,  T = ABS(S)
C                      (S  C)
C              TO AVOID UNDERFLOW/OVERFLOW TROUBLES.
C              TAKE TWO PASSES THROUGH SCALING.  USE  T  FOR FLAG.
C
               IF (T .NE. 0.0E0) GO TO 30
                  IKP1 = IK + K
                  KKP1 = IKP1 + K
                  T = ABS(AP(KKP1))
                  D = (D/T)*AP(KKP1+1) - T
               GO TO 40
   30          CONTINUE
                  D = T
                  T = 0.0E0
   40          CONTINUE
   50       CONTINUE
C
            IF (NOERT) GO TO 60
               IF (D .GT. 0.0E0) INERT(1) = INERT(1) + 1
               IF (D .LT. 0.0E0) INERT(2) = INERT(2) + 1
               IF (D .EQ. 0.0E0) INERT(3) = INERT(3) + 1
   60       CONTINUE
C
            IF (NODET) GO TO 120
               DET(1) = D*DET(1)
```

```
               IF (DET(1) .EQ. 0.0E0) GO TO 110
   70             IF (ABS(DET(1)) .GE. 1.0E0) GO TO 80
                     DET(1) = TEN*DET(1)
                     DET(2) = DET(2) - 1.0E0
                  GO TO 70
   80             CONTINUE
   90             IF (ABS(DET(1)) .LT. TEN) GO TO 100
                     DET(1) = DET(1)/TEN
                     DET(2) = DET(2) + 1.0E0
                  GO TO 90
  100             CONTINUE
  110          CONTINUE
  120       CONTINUE
            IK = IK + K
  130    CONTINUE
  140 CONTINUE
C
C     COMPUTE INVERSE(A)
C
      IF (NOINV) GO TO 270
         K = 1
         IK = 0
  150    IF (K .GT. N) GO TO 260
            KM1 = K - 1
            KK = IK + K
            IKP1 = IK + K
            KKP1 = IKP1 + K
            IF (KPVT(K) .LT. 0) GO TO 180
C
C              1 BY 1
C
               AP(KK) = 1.0E0/AP(KK)
               IF (KM1 .LT. 1) GO TO 170
                  CALL SCOPY(KM1,AP(IK+1),1,WORK,1)
                  IJ = 0
                  DO 160 J = 1, KM1
                     JK = IK + J
                     AP(JK) = SDOT(J,AP(IJ+1),1,WORK,1)
                     CALL SAXPY(J-1,WORK(J),AP(IJ+1),1,AP(IK+1),1)
                     IJ = IJ + J
  160             CONTINUE
                  AP(KK) = AP(KK) + SDOT(KM1,WORK,1,AP(IK+1),1)
  170          CONTINUE
               KSTEP = 1
            GO TO 220
  180       CONTINUE
C
C              2 BY 2
C
               T = ABS(AP(KKP1))
               AK = AP(KK)/T
               AKP1 = AP(KKP1+1)/T
               AKKP1 = AP(KKP1)/T
               D = T*(AK*AKP1 - 1.0E0)
               AP(KK) = AKP1/D
               AP(KKP1+1) = AK/D
               AP(KKP1) = -AKKP1/D
               IF (KM1 .LT. 1) GO TO 210
                  CALL SCOPY(KM1,AP(IKP1+1),1,WORK,1)
                  IJ = 0
                  DO 190 J = 1, KM1
                     JKP1 = IKP1 + J
                     AP(JKP1) = SDOT(J,AP(IJ+1),1,WORK,1)
```

```
                  CALL SAXPY(J-1,WORK(J),AP(IJ+1),1,AP(IKP1+1),1)
                  IJ = IJ + J
  190          CONTINUE
               AP(KKP1+1) = AP(KKP1+1)
     *                      + SDOT(KM1,WORK,1,AP(IKP1+1),1)
               AP(KKP1) = AP(KKP1)
     *                    + SDOT(KM1,AP(IK+1),1,AP(IKP1+1),1)
               CALL SCOPY(KM1,AP(IK+1),1,WORK,1)
               IJ = 0
               DO 200 J = 1, KM1
                  JK = IK + J
                  AP(JK) = SDOT(J,AP(IJ+1),1,WORK,1)
                  CALL SAXPY(J-1,WORK(J),AP(IJ+1),1,AP(IK+1),1)
                  IJ = IJ + J
  200          CONTINUE
               AP(KK) = AP(KK) + SDOT(KM1,WORK,1,AP(IK+1),1)
  210       CONTINUE
            KSTEP = 2
  220    CONTINUE
C
C        SWAP
C
         KS = IABS(KPVT(K))
         IF (KS .EQ. K) GO TO 250
            IKS = (KS*(KS - 1))/2
            CALL SSWAP(KS,AP(IKS+1),1,AP(IK+1),1)
            KSJ = IK + KS
            DO 230 JB = KS, K
               J = K + KS - JB
               JK = IK + J
               TEMP = AP(JK)
               AP(JK) = AP(KSJ)
               AP(KSJ) = TEMP
               KSJ = KSJ - (J - 1)
  230       CONTINUE
            IF (KSTEP .EQ. 1) GO TO 240
               KSKP1 = IKP1 + KS
               TEMP = AP(KSKP1)
               AP(KSKP1) = AP(KKP1)
               AP(KKP1) = TEMP
  240       CONTINUE
  250    CONTINUE
         IK = IK + K
         IF (KSTEP .EQ. 2) IK = IK + K + 1
         K = K + KSTEP
      GO TO 150
  260 CONTINUE
  270 CONTINUE
      RETURN
      END
```

```
      SUBROUTINE STRCO(T,LDT,N,RCOND,Z,JOB)
      INTEGER LDT,N,JOB
      REAL T(LDT,1),Z(1)
      REAL RCOND
C
C     STRCO ESTIMATES THE CONDITION OF A REAL TRIANGULAR MATRIX.
C
C     ON ENTRY
C
C        T       REAL(LDT,N)
C                T CONTAINS THE TRIANGULAR MATRIX. THE ZERO
C                ELEMENTS OF THE MATRIX ARE NOT REFERENCED, AND
C                THE CORRESPONDING ELEMENTS OF THE ARRAY CAN BE
C                USED TO STORE OTHER INFORMATION.
C
C        LDT     INTEGER
C                LDT IS THE LEADING DIMENSION OF THE ARRAY T.
C
C        N       INTEGER
C                N IS THE ORDER OF THE MATRIX.
C
C        JOB     INTEGER
C                = 0         T  IS LOWER TRIANGULAR.
C                = NONZERO   T  IS UPPER TRIANGULAR.
C
C     ON RETURN
C
C        RCOND   REAL
C                AN ESTIMATE OF THE RECIPROCAL CONDITION OF  T .
C                FOR THE SYSTEM  T*X = B , RELATIVE PERTURBATIONS
C                IN  T  AND  B  OF SIZE  EPSILON  MAY CAUSE
C                RELATIVE PERTURBATIONS IN  X  OF SIZE  EPSILON/RCOND
C                IF  RCOND  IS SO SMALL THAT THE LOGICAL EXPRESSION
C                           1.0 + RCOND .EQ. 1.0
C                IS TRUE, THEN  T  MAY BE SINGULAR TO WORKING
C                PRECISION.  IN PARTICULAR,  RCOND  IS ZERO  IF
C                EXACT SINGULARITY IS DETECTED OR THE ESTIMATE
C                UNDERFLOWS.
C
C        Z       REAL(N)
C                A WORK VECTOR WHOSE CONTENTS ARE USUALLY UNIMPORTANT.
C                IF  T  IS CLOSE TO A SINGULAR MATRIX, THEN  Z  IS
C                AN APPROXIMATE NULL VECTOR IN THE SENSE THAT
C                NORM(A*Z) = RCOND*NORM(A)*NORM(Z) .
C
C     LINPACK. THIS VERSION DATED 08/14/78 .
C     CLEVE MOLER, UNIVERSITY OF NEW MEXICO, ARGONNE NATIONAL LAB.
C
C     SUBROUTINES AND FUNCTIONS
C
C     BLAS SAXPY,SSCAL,SASUM
C     FORTRAN ABS,AMAX1,SIGN
C
C     INTERNAL VARIABLES
C
      REAL W,WK,WKM,EK
      REAL TNORM,YNORM,S,SM,SASUM
      INTEGER I1,J,J1,J2,K,KK,L
      LOGICAL LOWER
C
      LOWER = JOB .EQ. 0
C
C     COMPUTE 1-NORM OF T
```

```
C
      TNORM = 0.0E0
      DO 10 J = 1, N
         L = J
         IF (LOWER) L = N + 1 - J
         I1 = 1
         IF (LOWER) I1 = J
         TNORM = AMAX1(TNORM,SASUM(L,T(I1,J),1))
   10 CONTINUE
C
C     RCOND = 1/(NORM(T)*(ESTIMATE OF NORM(INVERSE(T)))) .
C     ESTIMATE = NORM(Z)/NORM(Y) WHERE  T*Z = Y  AND  TRANS(T)*Y = E .
C     TRANS(T)  IS THE TRANSPOSE OF T .
C     THE COMPONENTS OF  E  ARE CHOSEN TO CAUSE MAXIMUM LOCAL
C     GROWTH IN THE ELEMENTS OF Y
C     THE VECTORS ARE FREQUENTLY RESCALED TO AVOID OVERFLOW.
C
C     SOLVE TRANS(T)*Y = E
C
      EK = 1.0E0
      DO 20 J = 1, N
         Z(J) = 0.0E0
   20 CONTINUE
      DO 100 KK = 1, N
         K = KK
         IF (LOWER) K = N + 1 - KK
         IF (Z(K) .NE. 0.0E0) EK = SIGN(EK,-Z(K))
         IF (ABS(EK-Z(K)) .LE. ABS(T(K,K))) GO TO 30
            S = ABS(T(K,K))/ABS(EK-Z(K))
            CALL SSCAL(N,S,Z,1)
            EK = S*EK
   30    CONTINUE
         WK = EK - Z(K)
         WKM = -EK - Z(K)
         S = ABS(WK)
         SM = ABS(WKM)
         IF (T(K,K) .EQ. 0.0E0) GO TO 40
            WK = WK/T(K,K)
            WKM = WKM/T(K,K)
         GO TO 50
   40    CONTINUE
            WK = 1.0E0
            WKM = 1.0E0
   50    CONTINUE
         IF (KK .EQ. N) GO TO 90
            J1 = K + 1
            IF (LOWER) J1 = 1
            J2 = N
            IF (LOWER) J2 = K - 1
            DO 60 J = J1, J2
               SM = SM + ABS(Z(J)+WKM*T(K,J))
               Z(J) = Z(J) + WK*T(K,J)
               S = S + ABS(Z(J))
   60       CONTINUE
            IF (S .GE. SM) GO TO 80
               W = WKM - WK
               WK = WKM
               DO 70 J = J1, J2
                  Z(J) = Z(J) + W*T(K,J)
   70          CONTINUE
   80       CONTINUE
   90    CONTINUE
         Z(K) = WK
```

```
  100 CONTINUE
      S = 1.0E0/SASUM(N,Z,1)
      CALL SSCAL(N,S,Z,1)
C
      YNORM = 1.0E0
C
C     SOLVE T*Z = Y
C
      DO 130 KK = 1, N
         K = N + 1 - KK
         IF (LOWER) K = KK
         IF (ABS(Z(K)) .LE. ABS(T(K,K))) GO TO 110
            S = ABS(T(K,K))/ABS(Z(K))
            CALL SSCAL(N,S,Z,1)
            YNORM = S*YNORM
  110    CONTINUE
         IF (T(K,K) .NE. 0.0E0) Z(K) = Z(K)/T(K,K)
         IF (T(K,K) .EQ. 0.0E0) Z(K) = 1.0E0
         I1 = 1
         IF (LOWER) I1 = K + 1
         IF (KK .GE. N) GO TO 120
            W = -Z(K)
            CALL SAXPY(N-KK,W,T(I1,K),1,Z(I1),1)
  120    CONTINUE
  130 CONTINUE
C     MAKE ZNORM = 1.0
      S = 1.0E0/SASUM(N,Z,1)
      CALL SSCAL(N,S,Z,1)
      YNORM = S*YNORM
C
      IF (TNORM .NE. 0.0E0) RCOND = YNORM/TNORM
      IF (TNORM .EQ. 0.0E0) RCOND = 0.0E0
      RETURN
      END
```

```
      SUBROUTINE STRSL(T,LDT,N,B,JOB,INFO)
      INTEGER LDT,N,JOB,INFO
      REAL T(LDT,1),B(1)
C
C
C     STRSL SOLVES SYSTEMS OF THE FORM
C
C                   T * X = B
C     OR
C                   TRANS(T) * X = B
C
C     WHERE T IS A TRIANGULAR MATRIX OF ORDER N. HERE TRANS(T)
C     DENOTES THE TRANSPOSE OF THE MATRIX T.
C
C     ON ENTRY
C
C         T         REAL(LDT,N)
C                   T CONTAINS THE MATRIX OF THE SYSTEM. THE ZERO
C                   ELEMENTS OF THE MATRIX ARE NOT REFERENCED, AND
C                   THE CORRESPONDING ELEMENTS OF THE ARRAY CAN BE
C                   USED TO STORE OTHER INFORMATION.
C
C         LDT       INTEGER
C                   LDT IS THE LEADING DIMENSION OF THE ARRAY T.
C
C         N         INTEGER
C                   N IS THE ORDER OF THE SYSTEM.
C
C         B         REAL(N)
C                   B CONTAINS THE RIGHT HAND SIDE OF THE SYSTEM.
C
C         JOB       INTEGER
C                   JOB SPECIFIES WHAT KIND OF SYSTEM IS TO BE SOLVED.
C                   IF JOB IS
C
C                        00   SOLVE T*X=B, T LOWER TRIANGULAR,
C                        01   SOLVE T*X=B, T UPPER TRIANGULAR,
C                        10   SOLVE TRANS(T)*X=B, T LOWER TRIANGULAR,
C                        11   SOLVE TRANS(T)*X=B, T UPPER TRIANGULAR.
C
C     ON RETURN
C
C         B         B CONTAINS THE SOLUTION, IF INFO .EQ. 0.
C                   OTHERWISE B IS UNALTERED.
C
C         INFO      INTEGER
C                   INFO CONTAINS ZERO IF THE SYSTEM IS NONSINGULAR.
C                   OTHERWISE INFO CONTAINS THE INDEX OF
C                   THE FIRST ZERO DIAGONAL ELEMENT OF T.
C
C     LINPACK. THIS VERSION DATED 08/14/78 .
C     G. W. STEWART, UNIVERSITY OF MARYLAND, ARGONNE NATIONAL LAB.
C
C     SUBROUTINES AND FUNCTIONS
C
C     BLAS SAXPY,SDOT
C     FORTRAN MOD
C
C     INTERNAL VARIABLES
C
      REAL SDOT,TEMP
      INTEGER CASE,J,JJ
C
```

```
C        BEGIN BLOCK PERMITTING ...EXITS TO 150
C
C           CHECK FOR ZERO DIAGONAL ELEMENTS.
C
            DO 10 INFO = 1, N
C        ......EXIT
               IF (T(INFO,INFO) .EQ. 0.0E0) GO TO 150
   10       CONTINUE
            INFO = 0
C
C           DETERMINE THE TASK AND GO TO IT.
C
            CASE = 1
            IF (MOD(JOB,10) .NE. 0) CASE = 2
            IF (MOD(JOB,100)/10 .NE. 0) CASE = CASE + 2
            GO TO (20,50,80,110), CASE
C
C           SOLVE T*X=B FOR T LOWER TRIANGULAR.
C
   20       CONTINUE
               B(1) = B(1)/T(1,1)
               IF (N .LT. 2) GO TO 40
               DO 30 J = 2, N
                  TEMP = -B(J-1)
                  CALL SAXPY(N-J+1,TEMP,T(J,J-1),1,B(J),1)
                  B(J) = B(J)/T(J,J)
   30          CONTINUE
   40          CONTINUE
            GO TO 140
C
C           SOLVE T*X=B FOR T UPPER TRIANGULAR.
C
   50       CONTINUE
               B(N) = B(N)/T(N,N)
               IF (N .LT. 2) GO TO 70
               DO 60 JJ = 2, N
                  J = N - JJ + 1
                  TEMP = -B(J+1)
                  CALL SAXPY(J,TEMP,T(1,J+1),1,B(1),1)
                  B(J) = B(J)/T(J,J)
   60          CONTINUE
   70          CONTINUE
            GO TO 140
C
C           SOLVE TRANS(T)*X=B FOR T LOWER TRIANGULAR.
C
   80       CONTINUE
               B(N) = B(N)/T(N,N)
               IF (N .LT. 2) GO TO 100
               DO 90 JJ = 2, N
                  J = N - JJ + 1
                  B(J) = B(J) - SDOT(JJ-1,T(J+1,J),1,B(J+1),1)
                  B(J) = B(J)/T(J,J)
   90          CONTINUE
  100          CONTINUE
            GO TO 140
C
C           SOLVE TRANS(T)*X=B FOR T UPPER TRIANGULAR.
C
  110       CONTINUE
               B(1) = B(1)/T(1,1)
               IF (N .LT. 2) GO TO 130
               DO 120 J = 2, N
```

```
            B(J) = B(J) - SDOT(J-1,T(1,J),1,B(1),1)
            B(J) = B(J)/T(J,J)
120       CONTINUE
130       CONTINUE
140    CONTINUE
150 CONTINUE
    RETURN
    END
```

STRDI

```
      SUBROUTINE STRDI(T,LDT,N,DET,JOB,INFO)
      INTEGER LDT,N,JOB,INFO
      REAL T(LDT,1),DET(2)
C
C     STRDI COMPUTES THE DETERMINANT AND INVERSE OF A REAL
C     TRIANGULAR MATRIX.
C
C     ON ENTRY
C
C        T       REAL(LDT,N)
C                T CONTAINS THE TRIANGULAR MATRIX. THE ZERO
C                ELEMENTS OF THE MATRIX ARE NOT REFERENCED, AND
C                THE CORRESPONDING ELEMENTS OF THE ARRAY CAN BE
C                USED TO STORE OTHER INFORMATION.
C
C        LDT     INTEGER
C                LDT IS THE LEADING DIMENSION OF THE ARRAY T.
C
C        N       INTEGER
C                N IS THE ORDER OF THE MATRIX.
C
C        JOB     INTEGER
C                = 010       NO DET, INVERSE OF LOWER TRIANGULAR.
C                = 011       NO DET, INVERSE OF UPPER TRIANGULAR.
C                = 100       DET, NO INVERSE.
C                = 110       DET, INVERSE OF LOWER TRIANGULAR.
C                = 111       DET, INVERSE OF UPPER TRIANGULAR.
C
C     ON RETURN
C
C        T       INVERSE OF ORIGINAL MATRIX IF REQUESTED.
C                OTHERWISE UNCHANGED.
C
C        DET     REAL(2)
C                DETERMINANT OF ORIGINAL MATRIX IF REQUESTED.
C                OTHERWISE NOT REFERENCED.
C                DETERMINANT = DET(1) * 10.0**DET(2)
C                WITH  1.0 .LE. ABS(DET(1)) .LT. 10.0
C                OR  DET(1) .EQ. 0.0 .
C
C        INFO    INTEGER
C                INFO CONTAINS ZERO IF THE SYSTEM IS NONSINGULAR
C                AND THE INVERSE IS REQUESTED.
C                OTHERWISE INFO CONTAINS THE INDEX OF
C                A ZERO DIAGONAL ELEMENT OF T.
C
C
C     LINPACK. THIS VERSION DATED 08/14/78 .
C     CLEVE MOLER, UNIVERSITY OF NEW MEXICO, ARGONNE NATIONAL LAB.
C
C     SUBROUTINES AND FUNCTIONS
C
C     BLAS SAXPY,SSCAL
C     FORTRAN ABS,MOD
C
C     INTERNAL VARIABLES
C
      REAL TEMP
      REAL TEN
      INTEGER I,J,K,KB,KM1,KP1
C
C     BEGIN BLOCK PERMITTING ...EXITS TO 180
C
```

```
C        COMPUTE DETERMINANT
C
         IF (JOB/100 .EQ. 0) GO TO 70
            DET(1) = 1.0E0
            DET(2) = 0.0E0
            TEN = 10.0E0
            DO 50 I = 1, N
               DET(1) = T(I,I)*DET(1)
C           ...EXIT
               IF (DET(1) .EQ. 0.0E0) GO TO 60
   10          IF (ABS(DET(1)) .GE. 1.0E0) GO TO 20
                  DET(1) = TEN*DET(1)
                  DET(2) = DET(2) - 1.0E0
               GO TO 10
   20          CONTINUE
   30          IF (ABS(DET(1)) .LT. TEN) GO TO 40
                  DET(1) = DET(1)/TEN
                  DET(2) = DET(2) + 1.0E0
               GO TO 30
   40          CONTINUE
   50       CONTINUE
   60       CONTINUE
   70    CONTINUE
C
C        COMPUTE INVERSE OF UPPER TRIANGULAR
C
         IF (MOD(JOB/10,10) .EQ. 0) GO TO 170
            IF (MOD(JOB,10) .EQ. 0) GO TO 120
C              BEGIN BLOCK PERMITTING ...EXITS TO 110
                  DO 100 K = 1, N
                     INFO = K
C              ......EXIT
                     IF (T(K,K) .EQ. 0.0E0) GO TO 110
                     T(K,K) = 1.0E0/T(K,K)
                     TEMP = -T(K,K)
                     CALL SSCAL(K-1,TEMP,T(1,K),1)
                     KP1 = K + 1
                     IF (N .LT. KP1) GO TO 90
                     DO 80 J = KP1, N
                        TEMP = T(K,J)
                        T(K,J) = 0.0E0
                        CALL SAXPY(K,TEMP,T(1,K),1,T(1,J),1)
   80                CONTINUE
   90                CONTINUE
  100             CONTINUE
                  INFO = 0
  110          CONTINUE
            GO TO 160
  120       CONTINUE
C
C              COMPUTE INVERSE OF LOWER TRIANGULAR
C
               DO 150 KB = 1, N
                  K = N + 1 - KB
                  INFO = K
C     ............EXIT
                  IF (T(K,K) .EQ. 0.0E0) GO TO 180
                  T(K,K) = 1.0E0/T(K,K)
                  TEMP = -T(K,K)
                  IF (K .NE. N) CALL SSCAL(N-K,TEMP,T(K+1,K),1)
                  KM1 = K - 1
                  IF (KM1 .LT. 1) GO TO 140
                  DO 130 J = 1, KM1
```

```
                  TEMP = T(K,J)
                  T(K,J) = 0.0E0
                  CALL SAXPY(N-K+1,TEMP,T(K,K),1,T(K,J),1)
  130          CONTINUE
  140          CONTINUE
  150       CONTINUE
            INFO = 0
  160    CONTINUE
  170 CONTINUE
  180 CONTINUE
      RETURN
      END
```

```
      SUBROUTINE SGTSL(N,C,D,E,B,INFO)
      INTEGER N, INFO
      REAL C(1),D(1),E(1),B(1)
C
C     SGTSL GIVEN A GENERAL TRIDIAGONAL MATRIX AND A RIGHT HAND SIDE WILL
C     FIND THE SOLUTION OF THE ASSOCIATED SYSTEM OF LINEAR EQUATIONS.
C
C     ON ENTRY
C
C        N       INTEGER
C                IS THE ORDER OF THE TRIDIAGONAL MATRIX.
C
C        C       REAL(N)
C                IS THE SUBDIAGONAL OF THE TRIDIAGONAL MATRIX.
C                C(2) THROUGH C(N) SHOULD CONTAIN THE SUBDIAGONAL.
C                ON OUTPUT C IS DESTROYED.
C
C        D       REAL(N)
C                IS THE DIAGONAL OF THE TRIDIAGONAL MATRIX.
C                ON OUTPUT D IS DESTROYED.
C
C        E       REAL(N)
C                IS THE SUPERDIAGONAL OF THE TRIDIAGONAL MATRIX.
C                E(1) THROUGH E(N-1) SHOULD CONTAIN THE SUPERDIAGONAL.
C                ON OUTPUT E IS DESTROYED.
C
C        B       REAL(N)
C                IS THE RIGHT HAND SIDE VECTOR.
C
C     ON RETURN
C
C        B       IS THE SOLUTION VECTOR.
C
C        INFOR   INTEGER
C                = 0 NORMAL VALUE.
C                = K IF THE K-TH PIVOT ELEMENT BECOMES EXACTLY
C                    ZERO.  THE SUBROUTINE RETURNS WHEN THIS IS
C                    DETECTED.
C
C     LINPACK.  THIS VERSION DATED 08/14/78 .
C     JACK DONGARRA, ARGONNE NATIONAL LABORATORY.
C
C     NO EXTERNALS
C     FORTRAN ABS
C
C     INTERNAL VARIABLES
C
      INTEGER K,KB,KP1,NM1,NM2
      REAL T
C     BEGIN BLOCK PERMITTING ...EXITS TO 100
C
         INFO = 0
         C(1) = D(1)
         NM1 = N - 1
         IF (NM1 .LT. 1) GO TO 40
            D(1) = E(1)
            E(1) = 0.0E0
            E(N) = 0.0E0
C
            DO 30 K= 1, NM1
               KP1 = K + 1
C
C              FIND THE LARGEST OF THE TWO ROWS
```

```
C
               IF (ABS(C(KP1)) .LT. ABS(C(K))) GO TO 10
C
C                 INTERCHANGE ROW
C
                  T = C(KP1)
                  C(KP1) = C(K)
                  C(K) = T
                  T = D(KP1)
                  D(KP1) = D(K)
                  D(K) = T
                  T = E(KP1)
                  E(KP1) = E(K)
                  E(K) = T
                  T = B(KP1)
                  B(KP1) = B(K)
                  B(K) = T
   10          CONTINUE
C
C              ZERO ELEMENTS
C
               IF (C(K) .NE. 0.0E0) GO TO 20
                  INFO = K
C     ............EXIT
                  GO TO 100
   20          CONTINUE
               T = -C(KP1 )/C(K)
               C(KP1) = D(KP1) + T*D(K)
               D(KP1) = E(KP1) + T*E(K)
               E(KP1) = 0.0E0
               B(KP1) = B(KP1) + T*B(K)
   30       CONTINUE
   40    CONTINUE
         IF (C(N) .NE. 0.0E0) GO TO 50
            INFO = N
         GO TO 90
   50    CONTINUE
C
C           BACK SOLVE
C
            NM2 = N - 2
            B(N) = B(N)/C(N)
            IF (N .EQ. 1) GO TO 80
               B(NM1) = (B(NM1) - D(NM1)*B(N))/C(NM1)
               IF (NM2 .LT. 1) GO TO 70
               DO 60 KB = 1, NM2
                  K = NM2 - KB + 1
                  B(K) = (B(K) - D(K)*B(K+1) - E(K)*B(K+2))/C(K)
   60          CONTINUE
   70          CONTINUE
   80       CONTINUE
   90    CONTINUE
  100 CONTINUE
C
      RETURN
      END
```

```
      SUBROUTINE SPTSL(N,D,E,B)
      INTEGER N
      REAL D(1),E(1),B(1)
C
C     SPTSL GIVEN A POSITIVE DEFINITE TRIDIAGONAL MATRIX AND A RIGHT HAND
C     SIDE WILL FIND THE SOLUTION OF THE ASSOCIATED SET OF LINEAR EQUATIONS.
C
C     ON ENTRY
C
C        N         INTEGER
C                  IS THE ORDER OF THE TRIDIAGONAL MATRIX.
C
C        D         REAL(N)
C                  IS THE DIAGONAL OF THE TRIDIAGONAL MATRIX.
C                  ON OUTPUT D IS DESTROYED.
C
C        E         REAL(N)
C                  IS THE OFFDIAGONAL OF THE TRIDIAGONAL MATRIX.
C                  E(1) THROUGH E(N-1) SHOULD CONTAIN THE
C                  OFFDIAGONAL.
C
C        B         REAL(N)
C                  IS THE RIGHT HAND SIDE VECTOR.
C
C     ON RETURN
C
C        B         CONTAINS THE SOLUTION.
C
C     LINPACK. THIS VERSION DATED 08/14/78 .
C     JACK DONGARRA, ARGONNE NATIONAL LABORATORY.
C
C     NO EXTERNALS
C     FORTRAN MOD
C
C     INTERNAL VARIABLES
C
      INTEGER K,KBM1,KE,KF,KP1,NM1,NM1D2
      REAL T1,T2
C
C     CHECK FOR 1 X 1 CASE
C
      IF (N .NE. 1) GO TO 10
         B(1) = B(1)/D(1)
      GO TO 70
   10 CONTINUE
         NM1 = N - 1
         NM1D2 = NM1/2
         IF (N .EQ. 2) GO TO 30
            KBM1 = N - 1
C
C           ZERO TOP HALF OF SUBDIAGONAL AND BOTTOM HALF OF
C           SUPERDIAGONAL
C
            DO 20 K = 1, NM1D2
               T1 = E(K)/D(K)
               D(K+1) = D(K+1) - T1*E(K)
               B(K+1) = B(K+1) - T1*B(K)
               T2 = E(KBM1)/D(KBM1+1)
               D(KBM1) = D(KBM1) - T2*E(KBM1)
               B(KBM1) = B(KBM1) - T2*B(KBM1+1)
               KBM1 = KBM1 - 1
   20       CONTINUE
   30    CONTINUE
```

```
      KP1 = NM1D2 + 1
C
C     CLEAN UP FOR POSSIBLE 2 X 2 BLOCK AT CENTER
C
      IF (MOD(N,2) .NE. 0) GO TO 40
         T1 = E(KP1)/D(KP1)
         D(KP1+1) = D(KP1+1) - T1*E(KP1)
         B(KP1+1) = B(KP1+1) - T1*B(KP1)
         KP1 = KP1 + 1
   40 CONTINUE
C
C     BACK SOLVE STARTING AT THE CENTER, GOING TOWARDS THE TOP
C     AND BOTTOM
C
      B(KP1) = B(KP1)/D(KP1)
      IF (N .EQ. 2) GO TO 60
         K = KP1 - 1
         KE = KP1 + NM1D2 - 1
         DO 50 KF = KP1, KE
            B(K) = (B(K) - E(K)*B(K+1))/D(K)
            B(KF+1) = (B(KF+1) - E(KF)*B(KF))/D(KF+1)
            K = K - 1
   50    CONTINUE
   60 CONTINUE
      IF (MOD(N,2) .EQ. 0) B(1) = (B(1) - E(1)*B(2))/D(1)
   70 CONTINUE
      RETURN
      END
```

```
      SUBROUTINE SCHDC(A,LDA,P,WORK,JPVT,JOB,INFO)
      INTEGER LDA,P,JPVT(1),JOB,INFO
      REAL A(LDA,1),WORK(1)
C
C     SCHDC COMPUTES THE CHOLESKY DECOMPOSITION OF A POSITIVE DEFINITE
C     MATRIX.  A PIVOTING OPTION ALLOWS THE USER TO ESTIMATE THE
C     CONDITION OF A POSITIVE DEFINITE MATRIX OR DETERMINE THE RANK
C     OF A POSITIVE SEMIDEFINITE MATRIX.
C
C     ON ENTRY
C
C         A      REAL(LDA,P).
C                A CONTAINS THE MATRIX WHOSE DECOMPOSITION IS TO
C                BE COMPUTED.  ONLY THE UPPER HALF OF A NEED BE STORED.
C                THE LOWER PART OF THE ARRAY A IS NOT REFERENCED.
C
C         LDA    INTEGER.
C                LDA IS THE LEADING DIMENSION OF THE ARRAY A.
C
C         P      INTEGER.
C                P IS THE ORDER OF THE MATRIX.
C
C         WORK   REAL.
C                WORK IS A WORK ARRAY.
C
C         JPVT   INTEGER(P).
C                JPVT CONTAINS INTEGERS THAT CONTROL THE SELECTION
C                OF THE PIVOT ELEMENTS, IF PIVOTING HAS BEEN REQUESTED.
C                EACH DIAGONAL ELEMENT A(K,K)
C                IS PLACED IN ONE OF THREE CLASSES ACCORDING TO THE
C                VALUE OF JPVT(K).
C
C                   IF JPVT(K) .GT. 0, THEN A(K,K) IS AN INITIAL
C                                      ELEMENT.
C
C                   IF JPVT(K) .EQ. 0, THEN A(K,K) IS A FREE ELEMENT.
C
C                   IF JPVT(K) .LT. 0, THEN A(K,K) IS A FINAL ELEMENT.
C
C                BEFORE THE DECOMPOSITION IS COMPUTED, INITIAL ELEMENTS
C                ARE MOVED BY SYMMETRIC ROW AND COLUMN INTERCHANGES TO
C                THE BEGINNING OF THE ARRAY A AND FINAL
C                ELEMENTS TO THE END.  BOTH INITIAL AND FINAL ELEMENTS
C                ARE FROZEN IN PLACE DURING THE COMPUTATION AND ONLY
C                FREE ELEMENTS ARE MOVED.  AT THE K-TH STAGE OF THE
C                REDUCTION, IF A(K,K) IS OCCUPIED BY A FREE ELEMENT
C                IT IS INTERCHANGED WITH THE LARGEST FREE ELEMENT
C                A(L,L) WITH L .GE. K.  JPVT IS NOT REFERENCED IF
C                JOB .EQ. 0.
C
C        JOB     INTEGER.
C                JOB IS AN INTEGER THAT INITIATES PIVOTING.
C                IF JOB .EQ. 0, NO PIVOTING IS DONE.
C                IF JOB .NE. 0, PIVOTING IS DONE.
C
C     ON RETURN
C
C         A      A CONTAINS IN ITS UPPER HALF THE CHOLESKY FACTOR
C                OF THE MATRIX A AS IT HAS BEEN PERMUTED BY PIVOTING.
C
C         JPVT   JPVT(J) CONTAINS THE INDEX OF THE DIAGONAL ELEMENT
C                OF A THAT WAS MOVED INTO THE J-TH POSITION,
C                PROVIDED PIVOTING WAS REQUESTED.
```

```
C
C         INFO    CONTAINS THE INDEX OF THE LAST POSITIVE DIAGONAL
C                 ELEMENT OF THE CHOLESKY FACTOR.
C
C     FOR POSITIVE DEFINITE MATRICES INFO = P IS THE NORMAL RETURN.
C     FOR PIVOTING WITH POSITIVE SEMIDEFINITE MATRICES INFO WILL
C     IN GENERAL BE LESS THAN P.  HOWEVER, INFO MAY BE GREATER THAN
C     THE RANK OF A, SINCE ROUNDING ERROR CAN CAUSE AN OTHERWISE ZERO
C     ELEMENT TO BE POSITIVE. INDEFINITE SYSTEMS WILL ALWAYS CAUSE
C     INFO TO BE LESS THAN P.
C
C     LINPACK. THIS VERSION DATED 08/14/78 .
C     J.J. DONGARRA AND G.W. STEWART, ARGONNE NATIONAL LABORATORY AND
C     UNIVERSITY OF MARYLAND.
C
C
C     BLAS SAXPY,SSWAP
C     FORTRAN SQRT
C
C     INTERNAL VARIABLES
C
      INTEGER PU,PL,PLP1,J,JP,JT,K,KB,KM1,KP1,L,MAXL
      REAL TEMP
      REAL MAXDIA
      LOGICAL SWAPK,NEGK
C
      PL = 1
      PU = 0
      INFO = P
      IF (JOB .EQ. 0) GO TO 160
C
C        PIVOTING HAS BEEN REQUESTED. REARRANGE
C        THE ELEMENTS ACCORDING TO JPVT.
C
         DO 70 K = 1, P
            SWAPK = JPVT(K) .GT. 0
            NEGK = JPVT(K) .LT. 0
            JPVT(K) = K
            IF (NEGK) JPVT(K) = -JPVT(K)
            IF (.NOT.SWAPK) GO TO 60
               IF (K .EQ. PL) GO TO 50
                  CALL SSWAP(PL-1,A(1,K),1,A(1,PL),1)
                  TEMP = A(K,K)
                  A(K,K) = A(PL,PL)
                  A(PL,PL) = TEMP
                  PLP1 = PL + 1
                  IF (P .LT. PLP1) GO TO 40
                  DO 30 J = PLP1, P
                     IF (J .GE. K) GO TO 10
                        TEMP = A(PL,J)
                        A(PL,J) = A(J,K)
                        A(J,K) = TEMP
                     GO TO 20
   10                CONTINUE
                     IF (J .EQ. K) GO TO 20
                        TEMP = A(K,J)
                        A(K,J) = A(PL,J)
                        A(PL,J) = TEMP
   20                CONTINUE
   30             CONTINUE
   40             CONTINUE
                  JPVT(K) = JPVT(PL)
                  JPVT(PL) = K
```

```
   50          CONTINUE
               PL = PL + 1
   60       CONTINUE
   70    CONTINUE
         PU = P
         IF (P .LT. PL) GO TO 150
         DO 140 KB = PL, P
            K = P - KB + PL
            IF (JPVT(K) .GE. 0) GO TO 130
               JPVT(K) = -JPVT(K)
               IF (PU .EQ. K) GO TO 120
                  CALL SSWAP(K-1,A(1,K),1,A(1,PU),1)
                  TEMP = A(K,K)
                  A(K,K) = A(PU,PU)
                  A(PU,PU) = TEMP
                  KP1 = K + 1
                  IF (P .LT. KP1) GO TO 110
                  DO 100 J = KP1, P
                     IF (J .GE. PU) GO TO 80
                        TEMP = A(K,J)
                        A(K,J) = A(J,PU)
                        A(J,PU) = TEMP
                     GO TO 90
   80                CONTINUE
                     IF (J .EQ. PU) GO TO 90
                        TEMP = A(K,J)
                        A(K,J) = A(PU,J)
                        A(PU,J) = TEMP
   90                CONTINUE
  100             CONTINUE
  110             CONTINUE
                  JT = JPVT(K)
                  JPVT(K) = JPVT(PU)
                  JPVT(PU) = JT
  120          CONTINUE
               PU = PU - 1
  130       CONTINUE
  140    CONTINUE
  150    CONTINUE
  160 CONTINUE
      DO 270 K = 1, P
C
C        REDUCTION LOOP.
C
         MAXDIA = A(K,K)
         KP1 = K + 1
         MAXL = K
C
C        DETERMINE THE PIVOT ELEMENT.
C
         IF (K .LT. PL .OR. K .GE. PU) GO TO 190
            DO 180 L = KP1, PU
               IF (A(L,L) .LE. MAXDIA) GO TO 170
                  MAXDIA = A(L,L)
                  MAXL = L
  170          CONTINUE
  180       CONTINUE
  190    CONTINUE
C
C        QUIT IF THE PIVOT ELEMENT IS NOT POSITIVE.
C
         IF (MAXDIA .GT. 0.0E0) GO TO 200
            INFO = K - 1
```

```
C     ......EXIT
            GO TO 280
  200    CONTINUE
         IF (K .EQ. MAXL) GO TO 210
C
C           START THE PIVOTING AND UPDATE JPVT.
C
            KM1 = K - 1
            CALL SSWAP(KM1,A(1,K),1,A(1,MAXL),1)
            A(MAXL,MAXL) = A(K,K)
            A(K,K) = MAXDIA
            JP = JPVT(MAXL)
            JPVT(MAXL) = JPVT(K)
            JPVT(K) = JP
  210    CONTINUE
C
C        REDUCTION STEP. PIVOTING IS CONTINUED ACROSS THE ROWS.
C
         WORK(K) = SQRT(A(K,K))
         A(K,K) = WORK(K)
         IF (P .LT. KP1) GO TO 260
         DO 250 J = KP1, P
            IF (K .EQ. MAXL) GO TO 240
               IF (J .GE. MAXL) GO TO 220
                  TEMP = A(K,J)
                  A(K,J) = A(J,MAXL)
                  A(J,MAXL) = TEMP
               GO TO 230
  220          CONTINUE
               IF (J .EQ. MAXL) GO TO 230
                  TEMP = A(K,J)
                  A(K,J) = A(MAXL,J)
                  A(MAXL,J) = TEMP
  230          CONTINUE
  240       CONTINUE
            A(K,J) = A(K,J)/WORK(K)
            WORK(J) = A(K,J)
            TEMP = -A(K,J)
            CALL SAXPY(J-K,TEMP,WORK(KP1),1,A(KP1,J),1)
  250    CONTINUE
  260    CONTINUE
  270 CONTINUE
  280 CONTINUE
      RETURN
      END
```

```
      SUBROUTINE SQRDC(X,LDX,N,P,QRAUX,JPVT,WORK,JOB)
      INTEGER LDX,N,P,JOB
      INTEGER JPVT(1)
      REAL X(LDX,1),QRAUX(1),WORK(1)
C
C     SQRDC USES HOUSEHOLDER TRANSFORMATIONS TO COMPUTE THE QR
C     DECOMPOSITION OF AN N BY P MATRIX X.  COLUMN PIVOTING
C     BASED ON THE 2-NORMS OF THE REDUCED COLUMNS MAY BE
C     PERFORMED AT THE USERS OPTION.
C
C     ON ENTRY
C
C        X       REAL(LDX,P), WHERE LDX .GE. N.
C                X CONTAINS THE MATRIX WHOSE DECOMPOSITION IS TO BE
C                COMPUTED.
C
C        LDX     INTEGER.
C                LDX IS THE LEADING DIMENSION OF THE ARRAY X.
C
C        N       INTEGER.
C                N IS THE NUMBER OF ROWS OF THE MATRIX X.
C
C        P       INTEGER.
C                P IS THE NUMBER OF COLUMNS OF THE MATRIX X.
C
C        JPVT    INTEGER(P).
C                JPVT CONTAINS INTEGERS THAT CONTROL THE SELECTION
C                OF THE PIVOT COLUMNS.  THE K-TH COLUMN X(K) OF X
C                IS PLACED IN ONE OF THREE CLASSES ACCORDING TO THE
C                VALUE OF JPVT(K).
C
C                   IF JPVT(K) .GT. 0, THEN X(K) IS AN INITIAL
C                                      COLUMN.
C
C                   IF JPVT(K) .EQ. 0, THEN X(K) IS A FREE COLUMN.
C
C                   IF JPVT(K) .LT. 0, THEN X(K) IS A FINAL COLUMN.
C
C                BEFORE THE DECOMPOSITION IS COMPUTED, INITIAL COLUMNS
C                ARE MOVED TO THE BEGINNING OF THE ARRAY X AND FINAL
C                COLUMNS TO THE END.  BOTH INITIAL AND FINAL COLUMNS
C                ARE FROZEN IN PLACE DURING THE COMPUTATION AND ONLY
C                FREE COLUMNS ARE MOVED.  AT THE K-TH STAGE OF THE
C                REDUCTION, IF X(K) IS OCCUPIED BY A FREE COLUMN
C                IT IS INTERCHANGED WITH THE FREE COLUMN OF LARGEST
C                REDUCED NORM.  JPVT IS NOT REFERENCED IF
C                JOB .EQ. 0.
C
C        WORK    REAL(P).
C                WORK IS A WORK ARRAY.  WORK IS NOT REFERENCED IF
C                JOB .EQ. 0.
C
C        JOB     INTEGER.
C                JOB IS AN INTEGER THAT INITIATES COLUMN PIVOTING.
C                IF JOB .EQ. 0, NO PIVOTING IS DONE.
C                IF JOB .NE. 0, PIVOTING IS DONE.
C
C     ON RETURN
C
C        X       X CONTAINS IN ITS UPPER TRIANGLE THE UPPER
C                TRIANGULAR MATRIX R OF THE QR DECOMPOSITION
C                BELOW ITS DIAGONAL X CONTAINS INFORMATION FROM
C                WHICH THE ORTHOGONAL PART OF THE DECOMPOSITION
```

```
C                 CAN BE RECOVERED.  NOTE THAT IF PIVOTING HAS
C                 BEEN REQUESTED, THE DECOMPOSITION IS NOT THAT
C                 OF THE ORIGINAL MATRIX X BUT THAT OF X
C                 WITH ITS COLUMNS PERMUTED AS DESCRIBED BY JPVT.
C
C        QRAUX    REAL(P).
C                 QRAUX CONTAINS FURTHER INFORMATION REQUIRED TO RECOVER
C                 THE ORTHOGONAL PART OF THE DECOMPOSITION.
C
C        JPVT     JPVT(K) CONTAINS THE INDEX OF THE COLUMN OF THE
C                 ORIGINAL MATRIX THAT HAS BEEN INTERCHANGED INTO
C                 THE K-TH COLUMN, IF PIVOTING WAS REQUESTED.
C
C     LINPACK. THIS VERSION DATED 08/14/78 .
C     G.W. STEWART, UNIVERSITY OF MARYLAND, ARGONNE NATIONAL LAB.
C
C     SQRDC USES THE FOLLOWING FUNCTIONS AND SUBROUTINES.
C
C     BLAS SAXPY,SDOT,SSCAL,SSWAP,SNRM2
C     FORTRAN ABS,AMAX1,MIN0,SQRT,SIGN
C
C     INTERNAL VARIABLES
C
      INTEGER J,JP,L,LP1,LUP,MAXJ,PL,PU
      REAL MAXNRM,SNRM2,TT
      REAL SDOT,NRMXL,T
      LOGICAL NEGJ,SWAPJ
C
C
      PL = 1
      PU = 0
      IF (JOB .EQ. 0) GO TO 60
C
C        PIVOTING HAS BEEN REQUESTED.  REARRANGE THE COLUMNS
C        ACCORDING TO JPVT.
C
         DO 20 J = 1, P
            SWAPJ = JPVT(J) .GT. 0
            NEGJ = JPVT(J) .LT. 0
            JPVT(J) = J
            IF (NEGJ) JPVT(J) = -J
            IF (.NOT.SWAPJ) GO TO 10
               IF (J .NE. PL) CALL SSWAP(N,X(1,PL),1,X(1,J),1)
               JPVT(J) = JPVT(PL)
               JPVT(PL) = J
               PL = PL + 1
   10       CONTINUE
   20    CONTINUE
         PU = P
         DO 50 JJ = 1, P
            J = P - JJ + 1
            IF (JPVT(J) .GE. 0) GO TO 40
               JPVT(J) = -JPVT(J)
               IF (J .EQ. PU) GO TO 30
                  CALL SSWAP(N,X(1,PU),1,X(1,J),1)
                  JP = JPVT(PU)
                  JPVT(PU) = JPVT(J)
                  JPVT(J) = JP
   30          CONTINUE
               PU = PU - 1
   40       CONTINUE
   50    CONTINUE
   60 CONTINUE
```

```
C
C     COMPUTE THE NORMS OF THE FREE COLUMNS.
C
      IF (PU .LT. PL) GO TO 80
      DO 70 J = PL, PU
         QRAUX(J) = SNRM2(N,X(1,J),1)
         WORK(J) = QRAUX(J)
   70 CONTINUE
   80 CONTINUE
C
C     PERFORM THE HOUSEHOLDER REDUCTION OF X.
C
      LUP = MIN0(N,P)
      DO 200 L = 1, LUP
         IF (L .LT. PL .OR. L .GE. PU) GO TO 120
C
C           LOCATE THE COLUMN OF LARGEST NORM AND BRING IT
C           INTO THE PIVOT POSITION.
C
            MAXNRM = 0.0E0
            MAXJ = L
            DO 100 J = L, PU
               IF (QRAUX(J) .LE. MAXNRM) GO TO 90
                  MAXNRM = QRAUX(J)
                  MAXJ = J
   90          CONTINUE
  100       CONTINUE
            IF (MAXJ .EQ. L) GO TO 110
               CALL SSWAP(N,X(1,L),1,X(1,MAXJ),1)
               QRAUX(MAXJ) = QRAUX(L)
               WORK(MAXJ) = WORK(L)
               JP = JPVT(MAXJ)
               JPVT(MAXJ) = JPVT(L)
               JPVT(L) = JP
  110       CONTINUE
  120    CONTINUE
         QRAUX(L) = 0.0E0
         IF (L .EQ. N) GO TO 190
C
C           COMPUTE THE HOUSEHOLDER TRANSFORMATION FOR COLUMN L.
C
            NRMXL = SNRM2(N-L+1,X(L,L),1)
            IF (NRMXL .EQ. 0.0E0) GO TO 180
               IF (X(L,L) .NE. 0.0E0) NRMXL = SIGN(NRMXL,X(L,L))
               CALL SSCAL(N-L+1,1.0E0/NRMXL,X(L,L),1)
               X(L,L) = 1.0E0 + X(L,L)
C
C              APPLY THE TRANSFORMATION TO THE REMAINING COLUMNS,
C              UPDATING THE NORMS.
C
               LP1 = L + 1
               IF (P .LT. LP1) GO TO 170
               DO 160 J = LP1, P
                  T = -SDOT(N-L+1,X(L,L),1,X(L,J),1)/X(L,L)
                  CALL SAXPY(N-L+1,T,X(L,L),1,X(L,J),1)
                  IF (J .LT. PL .OR. J .GT. PU) GO TO 150
                  IF (QRAUX(J) .EQ. 0.0E0) GO TO 150
                     TT = 1.0E0 - (ABS(X(L,J))/QRAUX(J))**2
                     TT = AMAX1(TT,0.0E0)
                     T = TT
                     TT = 1.0E0 + 0.05E0*TT*(QRAUX(J)/WORK(J))**2
                     IF (TT .EQ. 1.0E0) GO TO 130
                        QRAUX(J) = QRAUX(J)*SQRT(T)
```

```
                  GO TO 140
  130             CONTINUE
                     QRAUX(J) = SNRM2(N-L,X(L+1,J),1)
                     WORK(J) = QRAUX(J)
  140             CONTINUE
  150          CONTINUE
  160       CONTINUE
  170       CONTINUE
C
C           SAVE THE TRANSFORMATION.
C
            QRAUX(L) = X(L,L)
            X(L,L) = -NRMXL
  180    CONTINUE
  190 CONTINUE
  200 CONTINUE
      RETURN
      END
```

```
      SUBROUTINE SQRSL(X,LDX,N,K,QRAUX,Y,QY,QTY,B,RSD,XB,JOB,INFO)
      INTEGER LDX,N,K,JOB,INFO
      REAL X(LDX,1),QRAUX(1),Y(1),QY(1),QTY(1),B(1),RSD(1),XB(1)
C
C     SQRSL APPLIES THE OUTPUT OF SQRDC TO COMPUTE COORDINATE
C     TRANSFORMATIONS, PROJECTIONS, AND LEAST SQUARES SOLUTIONS.
C     FOR K .LE. MIN(N,P), LET XK BE THE MATRIX
C
C            XK = (X(JPVT(1)),X(JPVT(2)), ... ,X(JPVT(K)))
C
C     FORMED FROM COLUMNS  JPVT(1), ... ,JPVT(K) OF THE ORIGINAL
C     N X P MATRIX X THAT WAS INPUT TO SQRDC (IF NO PIVOTING WAS
C     DONE, XK CONSISTS OF THE FIRST K COLUMNS OF X IN THEIR
C     ORIGINAL ORDER).  SQRDC PRODUCES A FACTORED ORTHOGONAL MATRIX Q
C     AND AN UPPER TRIANGULAR MATRIX R SUCH THAT
C
C              XK = Q * (R)
C                       (0)
C
C     THIS INFORMATION IS CONTAINED IN CODED FORM IN THE ARRAYS
C     X AND QRAUX.
C
C     ON ENTRY
C
C        X      REAL(LDX,P).
C               X CONTAINS THE OUTPUT OF SQRDC.
C
C        LDX    INTEGER.
C               LDX IS THE LEADING DIMENSION OF THE ARRAY X.
C
C        N      INTEGER.
C               N IS THE NUMBER OF ROWS OF THE MATRIX XK.  IT MUST
C               HAVE THE SAME VALUE AS N IN SQRDC.
C
C        K      INTEGER.
C               K IS THE NUMBER OF COLUMNS OF THE MATRIX XK.  K
C               MUST  NOT BE GREATER THAN MIN(N,P), WHERE P IS THE
C               SAME AS IN THE CALLING SEQUENCE TO SQRDC.
C
C        QRAUX  REAL(P).
C               QRAUX CONTAINS THE AUXILIARY OUTPUT FROM SQRDC.
C
C        Y      REAL(N)
C               Y CONTAINS AN N-VECTOR THAT IS TO BE MANIPULATED
C               BY SQRSL.
C
C        JOB    INTEGER.
C               JOB SPECIFIES WHAT IS TO BE COMPUTED.  JOB HAS
C               THE DECIMAL EXPANSION ABCDE, WITH THE FOLLOWING
C               MEANING.
C
C                    IF A.NE.0, COMPUTE QY.
C                    IF B,C,D, OR E .NE. 0, COMPUTE QTY.
C                    IF C.NE.0, COMPUTE B.
C                    IF D.NE.0, COMPUTE RSD.
C                    IF E.NE.0, COMPUTE XB.
C
C               NOTE THAT A REQUEST TO COMPUTE B, RSD, OR XB
C               AUTOMATICALLY TRIGGERS THE COMPUTATION OF QTY, FOR
C               WHICH AN ARRAY MUST BE PROVIDED IN THE CALLING
C               SEQUENCE.
C
C     ON RETURN
```

```
C
C        QY      REAL(N).
C                QY  CONTAINS  Q*Y, IF ITS COMPUTATION HAS BEEN
C                REQUESTED.
C
C        QTY     REAL(N).
C                QTY CONTAINS TRANS(Q)*Y, IF ITS COMPUTATION HAS
C                BEEN REQUESTED.  HERE TRANS(Q) IS THE
C                TRANSPOSE OF THE MATRIX Q.
C
C        B       REAL(K)
C                B CONTAINS THE SOLUTION OF THE LEAST SQUARES PROBLEM
C
C                     MINIMIZE NORM2(Y - XK*B),
C
C                IF ITS COMPUTATION HAS BEEN REQUESTED.  (NOTE THAT
C                IF PIVOTING WAS REQUESTED IN SQRDC, THE J-TH
C                COMPONENT OF B WILL BE ASSOCIATED WITH COLUMN JPVT(J)
C                OF THE ORIGINAL MATRIX X THAT WAS INPUT INTO SQRDC.)
C
C        RSD     REAL(N).
C                RSD CONTAINS THE LEAST SQUARES RESIDUAL Y - XK*B,
C                IF ITS COMPUTATION HAS BEEN REQUESTED.  RSD IS
C                ALSO THE ORTHOGONAL PROJECTION OF Y ONTO THE
C                ORTHOGONAL COMPLEMENT OF THE COLUMN SPACE OF XK.
C
C        XB      REAL(N).
C                XB CONTAINS THE LEAST SQUARES APPROXIMATION XK*B,
C                IF ITS COMPUTATION HAS BEEN REQUESTED.  XB IS ALSO
C                THE ORTHOGONAL PROJECTION OF Y ONTO THE COLUMN SPACE
C                OF X.
C
C        INFO    INTEGER.
C                INFO IS ZERO UNLESS THE COMPUTATION OF B HAS
C                BEEN REQUESTED AND R IS EXACTLY SINGULAR.  IN
C                THIS CASE, INFO IS THE INDEX OF THE FIRST ZERO
C                DIAGONAL ELEMENT OF R AND B IS LEFT UNALTERED.
C
C     THE PARAMETERS QY, QTY, B, RSD, AND XB ARE NOT REFERENCED
C     IF THEIR COMPUTATION IS NOT REQUESTED AND IN THIS CASE
C     CAN BE REPLACED BY DUMMY VARIABLES IN THE CALLING PROGRAM.
C     TO SAVE STORAGE, THE USER MAY IN SOME CASES USE THE SAME
C     ARRAY FOR DIFFERENT PARAMETERS IN THE CALLING SEQUENCE.  A
C     FREQUENTLY OCCURRING EXAMPLE IS WHEN ONE WISHES TO COMPUTE
C     ANY OF B, RSD, OR XB AND DOES NOT NEED Y OR QTY.  IN THIS
C     CASE ONE MAY IDENTIFY Y, QTY, AND ONE OF B, RSD, OR XB, WHILE
C     PROVIDING SEPARATE ARRAYS FOR ANYTHING ELSE THAT IS TO BE
C     COMPUTED.  THUS THE CALLING SEQUENCE
C
C          CALL SQRSL(X,LDX,N,K,QRAUX,Y,DUM,Y,B,Y,DUM,110,INFO)
C
C     WILL RESULT IN THE COMPUTATION OF B AND RSD, WITH RSD
C     OVERWRITING Y.  MORE GENERALLY, EACH ITEM IN THE FOLLOWING
C     LIST CONTAINS GROUPS OF PERMISSIBLE IDENTIFICATIONS FOR
C     A SINGLE CALLING  SEQUENCE.
C
C          1. (Y,QTY,B) (RSD) (XB) (QY)
C
C          2. (Y,QTY,RSD) (B) (XB) (QY)
C
C          3. (Y,QTY,XB) (B) (RSD) (QY)
C
C          4. (Y,QY) (QTY,B) (RSD) (XB)
```

```
C
C         5. (Y,QY) (QTY,RSD) (B) (XB)
C
C         6. (Y,QY) (QTY,XB) (B) (RSD)
C
C     IN ANY GROUP THE VALUE RETURNED IN THE ARRAY ALLOCATED TO
C     THE GROUP CORRESPONDS TO THE LAST MEMBER OF THE GROUP.
C
C     LINPACK. THIS VERSION DATED 08/14/78 .
C     G.W. STEWART, UNIVERSITY OF MARYLAND, ARGONNE NATIONAL LAB.
C
C     SQRSL USES THE FOLLOWING FUNCTIONS AND SUBROUTINES.
C
C     BLAS SAXPY,SCOPY,SDOT
C     FORTRAN MIN0,MOD
C
C     INTERNAL VARIABLES
C
      INTEGER I,J,JJ,JU,KP1
      REAL SDOT,T,TEMP
      LOGICAL CB,CQY,CQTY,CR,CXB
C
C
C     SET INFO FLAG.
C
      INFO = 0
C
C     DETERMINE WHAT IS TO BE COMPUTED.
C
      CQY = JOB/10000 .NE. 0
      CQTY = MOD(JOB,10000) .NE. 0
      CB = MOD(JOB,1000)/100 .NE. 0
      CR = MOD(JOB,100)/10 .NE. 0
      CXB = MOD(JOB,10) .NE. 0
      JU = MIN0(K,N-1)
C
C     SPECIAL ACTION WHEN N=1.
C
      IF (JU .NE. 0) GO TO 40
         IF (CQY) QY(1) = Y(1)
         IF (CQTY) QTY(1) = Y(1)
         IF (CXB) XB(1) = Y(1)
         IF (.NOT.CB) GO TO 30
            IF (X(1,1) .NE. 0.0E0) GO TO 10
               INFO = 1
            GO TO 20
   10       CONTINUE
               B(1) = Y(1)/X(1,1)
   20       CONTINUE
   30    CONTINUE
         IF (CR) RSD(1) = 0.0E0
      GO TO 250
   40 CONTINUE
C
C        SET UP TO COMPUTE QY OR TRANS (Q)*Y.
C
         IF (CQY) CALL SCOPY(N,Y,1,QY,1)
         IF (CQTY) CALL SCOPY(N,Y,1,QTY,1)
         IF (.NOT.CQY) GO TO 70
C
C           COMPUTE QY.
C
            DO 60 JJ = 1, JU
```

```
                  J = JU - JJ + 1
                  IF (QRAUX(J) .EQ. 0,0E0) GO TO 50
                     TEMP = X(J,J)
                     X(J,J) = QRAUX(J)
                     T = -SDOT(N-J+1,X(J,J),1,QY(J),1)/X(J,J)
                     CALL SAXPY(N-J+1,T,X(J,J),1,QY(J),1)
                     X(J,J) = TEMP
   50             CONTINUE
   60          CONTINUE
   70       CONTINUE
            IF (.NOT.CQTY) GO TO 100
C
C              COMPUTE TRANS(Q)*Y.
C
               DO 90 J = 1, JU
                  IF (QRAUX(J) .EQ. 0.0E0) GO TO 80
                     TEMP = X(J,J)
                     X(J,J) = QRAUX(J)
                     T = -SDOT(N-J+1,X(J,J),1,QTY(J),1)/X(J,J)
                     CALL SAXPY(N-J+1,T,X(J,J),1,QTY(J),1)
                     X(J,J) = TEMP
   80             CONTINUE
   90          CONTINUE
  100       CONTINUE
C
C           SET UP TO COMPUTE B, RSD, OR XB.
C
            IF (CB) CALL SCOPY(K,QTY,1,B,1)
            KP1 = K + 1
            IF (CXB) CALL SCOPY(K,QTY,1,XB,1)
            IF (CR .AND. K .LT. N) CALL SCOPY(N-K,QTY(KP1),1,RSD(KP1),1)
            IF (.NOT.CXB .OR. KP1 .GT. N) GO TO 120
               DO 110 I = KP1, N
                  XB(I) = 0.0E0
  110          CONTINUE
  120       CONTINUE
            IF (.NOT.CR) GO TO 140
               DO 130 I = 1, K
                  RSD(I) = 0.0E0
  130          CONTINUE
  140       CONTINUE
            IF (.NOT.CB) GO TO 190
C
C              COMPUTE B.
C
               DO 170 JJ = 1, K
                  J = K - JJ + 1
                  IF (X(J,J) .NE. 0.0E0) GO TO 150
                     INFO = J
C              ......EXIT
                     GO TO 180
  150             CONTINUE
                  B(J) = B(J)/X(J,J)
                  IF (J .EQ. 1) GO TO 160
                     T = -B(J)
                     CALL SAXPY(J-1,T,X(1,J),1,B,1)
  160             CONTINUE
  170          CONTINUE
  180          CONTINUE
  190       CONTINUE
            IF (.NOT.CR .AND. .NOT.CXB) GO TO 240
C
C              COMPUTE RSD OR XB AS REQUIRED.
```

```
C
            DO 230 JJ = 1, JU
               J = JU - JJ + 1
               IF (QRAUX(J) .EQ. 0.0E0) GO TO 220
                  TEMP = X(J,J)
                  X(J,J) = QRAUX(J)
                  IF (.NOT.CR) GO TO 200
                     T = -SDOT(N-J+1,X(J,J),1,RSD(J),1)/X(J,J)
                     CALL SAXPY(N-J+1,T,X(J,J),1,RSD(J),1)
  200             CONTINUE
                  IF (.NOT.CXB) GO TO 210
                     T = -SDOT(N-J+1,X(J,J),1,XB(J),1)/X(J,J)
                     CALL SAXPY(N-J+1,T,X(J,J),1,XB(J),1)
  210             CONTINUE
                  X(J,J) = TEMP
  220          CONTINUE
  230       CONTINUE
  240    CONTINUE
  250 CONTINUE
      RETURN
      END
```

```
      SUBROUTINE SCHUD(R,LDR,P,X,Z,LDZ,NZ,Y,RHO,C,S)
      INTEGER LDR,P,LDZ,NZ
      REAL RHO(1),C(1)
      REAL R(LDR,1),X(1),Z(LDZ,1),Y(1),S(1)
C
C     SCHUD UPDATES AN AUGMENTED CHOLESKY DECOMPOSITION OR THE
C     TRIANGULAR PART OF AN AUGMENTED QR DECOMPOSITION.  SPECIFICALLY,
C     GIVEN AN UPPER TRIANGULAR MATRIX R OF ORDER P, A ROW VECTOR
C     X, A COLUMN VECTOR Z, AND A SCALAR Y, SCHUD DETERMINES A
C     UNITARY MATRIX U AND A SCALAR ZETA SUCH THAT
C
C
C                              (R  Z)     (RR   ZZ )
C                        U  * (     )  = (          ) ,
C                              (X  Y)     ( 0  ZETA)
C
C     WHERE RR IS UPPER TRIANGULAR.  IF R AND Z HAVE BEEN
C     OBTAINED FROM THE FACTORIZATION OF A LEAST SQUARES
C     PROBLEM, THEN RR AND ZZ ARE THE FACTORS CORRESPONDING TO
C     THE PROBLEM WITH THE OBSERVATION (X,Y) APPENDED.  IN THIS
C     CASE, IF RHO IS THE NORM OF THE RESIDUAL VECTOR, THEN THE
C     NORM OF THE RESIDUAL VECTOR OF THE UPDATED PROBLEM IS
C     SQRT(RHO**2 + ZETA**2).  SCHUD WILL SIMULTANEOUSLY UPDATE
C     SEVERAL TRIPLETS (Z,Y,RHO).
C     FOR A LESS TERSE DESCRIPTION OF WHAT SCHUD DOES AND HOW IT
C     MAY BE APPLIED, SEE THE LINPACK GUIDE.
C
C     THE MATRIX U IS DETERMINED AS THE PRODUCT U(P)*...*U(1),
C     WHERE U(I) IS A ROTATION IN THE (I,P+1) PLANE OF THE
C     FORM
C
C                       (     C(I)      S(I) )
C                       (                    ) .
C                       (    -S(I)      C(I) )
C
C     THE ROTATIONS ARE CHOSEN SO THAT C(I) IS REAL.
C
C     ON ENTRY
C
C         R      REAL(LDR,P), WHERE LDR .GE. P.
C                R CONTAINS THE UPPER TRIANGULAR MATRIX
C                THAT IS TO BE UPDATED.  THE PART OF R
C                BELOW THE DIAGONAL IS NOT REFERENCED.
C
C         LDR    INTEGER.
C                LDR IS THE LEADING DIMENSION OF THE ARRAY R.
C
C         P      INTEGER.
C                P IS THE ORDER OF THE MATRIX R.
C
C         X      REAL(P).
C                X CONTAINS THE ROW TO BE ADDED TO R.  X IS
C                NOT ALTERED BY SCHUD.
C
C         Z      REAL(LDZ,NZ), WHERE LDZ .GE. P.
C                Z IS AN ARRAY CONTAINING NZ P-VECTORS TO
C                BE UPDATED WITH R.
C
C         LDZ    INTEGER.
C                LDZ IS THE LEADING DIMENSION OF THE ARRAY Z.
C
C         NZ     INTEGER.
C                NZ IS THE NUMBER OF VECTORS TO BE UPDATED.
```

```
C                NZ MAY BE ZERO, IN WHICH CASE Z, Y, AND RHO
C                ARE NOT REFERENCED.
C
C        Y       REAL(NZ).
C                Y CONTAINS THE SCALARS FOR UPDATING THE VECTORS
C                Z.  Y IS NOT ALTERED BY SCHUD.
C
C        RHO     REAL(NZ).
C                RHO CONTAINS THE NORMS OF THE RESIDUAL
C                VECTORS THAT ARE TO BE UPDATED.  IF RHO(J)
C                IS NEGATIVE, IT IS LEFT UNALTERED.
C
C     ON RETURN
C
C        R
C        RHO     CONTAIN THE UPDATED QUANTITIES.
C        Z
C
C        C       REAL(P).
C                C CONTAINS THE COSINES OF THE TRANSFORMING
C                ROTATIONS.
C
C        S       REAL(P).
C                S CONTAINS THE SINES OF THE TRANSFORMING
C                ROTATIONS.
C
C     LINPACK. THIS VERSION DATED 08/14/78.
C     G.W. STEWART, UNIVERSITY OF MARYLAND, ARGONNE NATIONAL LAB.
C
C     SCHUD USES THE FOLLOWING FUNCTIONS AND SUBROUTINES.
C
C     EXTENDED BLAS SROTG
C     FORTRAN SQRT
C
      INTEGER I,J,JM1
      REAL AZETA,SCALE
      REAL T,XJ,ZETA
C
C     UPDATE R.
C
      DO 30 J = 1, P
         XJ = X(J)
C
C        APPLY THE PREVIOUS ROTATIONS.
C
         JM1 = J - 1
         IF (JM1 .LT. 1) GO TO 20
         DO 10 I = 1, JM1
            T = C(I)*R(I,J) + S(I)*XJ
            XJ = C(I)*XJ - S(I)*R(I,J)
            R(I,J) = T
   10    CONTINUE
   20    CONTINUE
C
C        COMPUTE THE NEXT ROTATION.
C
         CALL SROTG(R(J,J),XJ,C(J),S(J))
   30 CONTINUE
C
C     IF REQUIRED, UPDATE Z AND RHO.
C
      IF (NZ .LT. 1) GO TO 70
      DO 60 J = 1, NZ
```

```
      ZETA = Y(J)
      DO 40 I = 1, P
         T = C(I)*Z(I,J) + S(I)*ZETA
         ZETA = C(I)*ZETA - S(I)*Z(I,J)
         Z(I,J) = T
40    CONTINUE
      AZETA = ABS(ZETA)
      IF (AZETA .EQ. 0.0E0 .OR. RHO(J) .LT. 0.0E0) GO TO 50
         SCALE = AZETA + RHO(J)
         RHO(J) = SCALE*SQRT((AZETA/SCALE)**2+(RHO(J)/SCALE)**2)
50    CONTINUE
60 CONTINUE
70 CONTINUE
   RETURN
   END
```

```
      SUBROUTINE SCHDD(R,LDR,P,X,Z,LDZ,NZ,Y,RHO,C,S,INFO)
      INTEGER LDR,P,LDZ,NZ,INFO
      REAL R(LDR,1),X(1),Z(LDZ,1),Y(1),S(1)
      REAL RHO(1),C(1)
C
C     SCHDD DOWNDATES AN AUGMENTED CHOLESKY DECOMPOSITION OR THE
C     TRIANGULAR FACTOR OF AN AUGMENTED QR DECOMPOSITION.
C     SPECIFICALLY, GIVEN AN UPPER TRIANGULAR MATRIX R OF ORDER P, A
C     ROW VECTOR X, A COLUMN VECTOR Z, AND A SCALAR Y, SCHDD
C     DETERMINES  A ORTHOGONAL MATRIX U AND A SCALAR ZETA SUCH THAT
C
C                        (R   Z )     (RR  ZZ)
C                    U * (       )  = (       ) ,
C                        (0 ZETA)     ( X   Y)
C
C     WHERE RR IS UPPER TRIANGULAR.  IF R AND Z HAVE BEEN OBTAINED
C     FROM THE FACTORIZATION OF A LEAST SQUARES PROBLEM, THEN
C     RR AND ZZ ARE THE FACTORS CORRESPONDING TO THE PROBLEM
C     WITH THE OBSERVATION (X,Y) REMOVED.  IN THIS CASE, IF RHO
C     IS THE NORM OF THE RESIDUAL VECTOR, THEN THE NORM OF
C     THE RESIDUAL VECTOR OF THE DOWNDATED PROBLEM IS
C     SQRT(RHO**2 - ZETA**2). SCHDD WILL SIMULTANEOUSLY DOWNDATE
C     SEVERAL TRIPLETS (Z,Y,RHO) ALONG WITH R.
C     FOR A LESS TERSE DESCRIPTION OF WHAT SCHDD DOES AND HOW IT
C     MAY BE APPLIED, SEE THE LINPACK GUIDE.
C
C     THE MATRIX U IS DETERMINED AS THE PRODUCT U(1)*...*U(P)
C     WHERE U(I) IS A ROTATION IN THE (P+1,I)-PLANE OF THE
C     FORM
C
C                       ( C(I)     -S(I)     )
C                       (                    ) .
C                       ( S(I)       C(I)    )
C
C     THE ROTATIONS ARE CHOSEN SO THAT C(I) IS REAL.
C
C     THE USER IS WARNED THAT A GIVEN DOWNDATING PROBLEM MAY
C     BE IMPOSSIBLE TO ACCOMPLISH OR MAY PRODUCE
C     INACCURATE RESULTS.  FOR EXAMPLE, THIS CAN HAPPEN
C     IF X IS NEAR A VECTOR WHOSE REMOVAL WILL REDUCE THE
C     RANK OF R.  BEWARE.
C
C     ON ENTRY
C
C        R      REAL(LDR,P), WHERE LDR .GE. P.
C               R CONTAINS THE UPPER TRIANGULAR MATRIX
C               THAT IS TO BE DOWNDATED.  THE PART OF  R
C               BELOW THE DIAGONAL IS NOT REFERENCED.
C
C        LDR    INTEGER.
C               LDR IS THE LEADING DIMENSION OF THE ARRAY R.
C
C        P      INTEGER.
C               P IS THE ORDER OF THE MATRIX R.
C
C        X      REAL(P).
C               X CONTAINS THE ROW VECTOR THAT IS TO
C               BE REMOVED FROM R.  X IS NOT ALTERED BY SCHDD.
C
C        Z      REAL(LDZ,NZ), WHERE LDZ .GE. P.
C               Z IS AN ARRAY OF NZ P-VECTORS WHICH
C               ARE TO BE DOWNDATED ALONG WITH R.
C
```

```
C         LDZ     INTEGER.
C                 LDZ IS THE LEADING DIMENSION OF THE ARRAY Z.
C
C         NZ      INTEGER.
C                 NZ IS THE NUMBER OF VECTORS TO BE DOWNDATED.
C                 NZ MAY BE ZERO, IN WHICH CASE Z, Y, AND RHO
C                 ARE NOT REFERENCED.
C
C         Y       REAL(NZ).
C                 Y CONTAINS THE SCALARS FOR THE DOWNDATING
C                 OF THE VECTORS Z.  Y IS NOT ALTERED BY SCHDD.
C
C         RHO     REAL(NZ).
C                 RHO CONTAINS THE NORMS OF THE RESIDUAL
C                 VECTORS THAT ARE TO BE DOWNDATED.
C
C     ON RETURN
C
C         R
C         Z       CONTAIN THE DOWNDATED QUANTITIES.
C         RHO
C
C         C       REAL(P).
C                 C CONTAINS THE COSINES OF THE TRANSFORMING
C                 ROTATIONS.
C
C         S       REAL(P).
C                 S CONTAINS THE SINES OF THE TRANSFORMING
C                 ROTATIONS.
C
C         INFO    INTEGER.
C                 INFO IS SET AS FOLLOWS.
C
C                    INFO = 0  IF THE ENTIRE DOWNDATING
C                              WAS SUCCESSFUL.
C
C                    INFO =-1  IF R COULD NOT BE DOWNDATED.
C                              IN THIS CASE, ALL QUANTITIES
C                              ARE LEFT UNALTERED.
C
C                    INFO = 1  IF SOME RHO COULD NOT BE
C                              DOWNDATED.  THE OFFENDING RHOS ARE
C                              SET TO -1.
C
C     LINPACK. THIS VERSION DATED 08/14/78.
C     G.W. STEWART, UNIVERSITY OF MARYLAND, ARGONNE NATIONAL LAB.
C
C     SCHDD USES THE FOLLOWING FUNCTIONS AND SUBPROGRAMS.
C
C     FORTRAN ABS,SQRT
C     BLAS SDOT, SNRM2
C
      INTEGER I,II,J
      REAL A,ALPHA,AZETA,NORM,SNRM2
      REAL SDOT,T,ZETA,B,XX
C
C     SOLVE THE SYSTEM TRANS(R)*A = X, PLACING THE RESULT
C     IN THE ARRAY S.
C
      INFO = 0
      S(1) = X(1)/R(1,1)
      IF (P .LT. 2) GO TO 20
      DO 10 J = 2, P
```

```
            S(J) = X(J) - SDOT(J-1,R(1,J),1,S,1)
            S(J) = S(J)/R(J,J)
   10    CONTINUE
   20    CONTINUE
         NORM = SNRM2(P,S,1)
         IF (NORM .LT. 1.0E0) GO TO 30
            INFO = -1
         GO TO 120
   30    CONTINUE
            ALPHA = SQRT(1.0E0-NORM**2)
C
C           DETERMINE THE TRANSFORMATIONS.
C
            DO 40 II = 1, P
               I = P - II + 1
               SCALE = ALPHA + ABS(S(I))
               A = ALPHA/SCALE
               B = S(I)/SCALE
               NORM = SQRT(A**2+B**2)
               C(I) = A/NORM
               S(I) = B/NORM
               ALPHA = SCALE*NORM
   40       CONTINUE
C
C           APPLY THE TRANSFORMATIONS TO R.
C
            DO 60 J = 1, P
               XX = 0.0E0
               DO 50 II = 1, J
                  I = J - II + 1
                  T = C(I)*XX + S(I)*R(I,J)
                  R(I,J) = C(I)*R(I,J) - S(I)*XX
                  XX = T
   50          CONTINUE
   60       CONTINUE
C
C           IF REQUIRED, DOWNDATE Z AND RHO.
C
            IF (NZ .LT. 1) GO TO 110
            DO 100 J = 1, NZ
               ZETA = Y(J)
               DO 70 I = 1, P
                  Z(I,J) = (Z(I,J) - S(I)*ZETA)/C(I)
                  ZETA = C(I)*ZETA - S(I)*Z(I,J)
   70          CONTINUE
               AZETA = ABS(ZETA)
               IF (AZETA .LE. RHO(J)) GO TO 80
                  INFO = 1
                  RHO(J) = -1.0E0
               GO TO 90
   80          CONTINUE
                  RHO(J) = RHO(J)*SQRT(1.0E0-(AZETA/RHO(J))**2)
   90          CONTINUE
  100       CONTINUE
  110       CONTINUE
  120    CONTINUE
         RETURN
         END
```

```
      SUBROUTINE SCHEX(R,LDR,P,K,L,Z,LDZ,NZ,C,S,JOB)
      INTEGER LDR,P,K,L,LDZ,NZ,JOB
      REAL R(LDR,1),Z(LDZ,1),S(1)
      REAL C(1)
C
C     SCHEX UPDATES THE CHOLESKY FACTORIZATION
C
C                   A = TRANS(R)*R
C
C     OF A POSITIVE DEFINITE MATRIX A OF ORDER P UNDER DIAGONAL
C     PERMUTATIONS OF THE FORM
C
C                   TRANS(E)*A*E
C
C     WHERE E IS A PERMUTATION MATRIX.  SPECIFICALLY, GIVEN
C     AN UPPER TRIANGULAR MATRIX R AND A PERMUTATION MATRIX
C     E (WHICH IS SPECIFIED BY K, L, AND JOB), SCHEX DETERMINES
C     AN ORTHOGONAL MATRIX U SUCH THAT
C
C                           U*R*E = RR,
C
C     WHERE RR IS UPPER TRIANGULAR.  AT THE USERS OPTION, THE
C     TRANSFORMATION U WILL BE MULTIPLIED INTO THE ARRAY Z.
C     IF A = TRANS(X)*X, SO THAT R IS THE TRIANGULAR PART OF THE
C     QR FACTORIZATION OF X, THEN RR IS THE TRIANGULAR PART OF THE
C     QR FACTORIZATION OF X*E, I.E. X WITH ITS COLUMNS PERMUTED.
C     FOR A LESS TERSE DESCRIPTION OF WHAT SCHEX DOES AND HOW IT MAY
C     BE APPLIED, SEE THE LINPACK GUIDE.
C
C     THE MATRIX Q IS DETERMINED AS THE PRODUCT U(L-K)*...*U(1)
C     OF PLANE ROTATIONS OF THE FORM
C
C                           (    C(I)       S(I) )
C                           (                    ) ,
C                           (    -S(I)      C(I) )
C
C     WHERE C(I) IS REAL. THE ROWS THESE ROTATIONS OPERATE ON
C     ARE DESCRIBED BELOW.
C
C     THERE ARE TWO TYPES OF PERMUTATIONS, WHICH ARE DETERMINED
C     BY THE VALUE OF JOB.
C
C     1. RIGHT CIRCULAR SHIFT (JOB = 1).
C
C         THE COLUMNS ARE REARRANGED IN THE FOLLOWING ORDER.
C
C                1,...,K-1,L,K,K+1,...,L-1,L+1,...,P.
C
C
C         U IS THE PRODUCT OF L-K ROTATIONS U(I), WHERE U(I)
C         ACTS IN THE (L-I,L-I+1)-PLANE.
C
C     2. LEFT CIRCULAR SHIFT (JOB = 2).
C
C         THE COLUMNS ARE REARRANGED IN THE FOLLOWING ORDER
C
C                1,...,K-1,K+1,K+2,...,L,K,L+1,...,P.
C
C         U IS THE PRODUCT OF L-K ROTATIONS U(I), WHERE U(I)
C         ACTS IN THE (K+I-1,K+I)-PLANE.
C
C     ON ENTRY
C
C         R      REAL(LDR,P), WHERE LDR.GE.P.
C                R CONTAINS THE UPPER TRIANGULAR FACTOR
```

```
C               THAT IS TO BE UPDATED.  ELEMENTS OF R
C               BELOW THE DIAGONAL ARE NOT REFERENCED.
C
C        LDR    INTEGER.
C               LDR IS THE LEADING DIMENSION OF THE ARRAY R.
C
C        P      INTEGER.
C               P IS THE ORDER OF THE MATRIX R.
C
C        K      INTEGER.
C               K IS THE FIRST COLUMN TO BE PERMUTED.
C
C        L      INTEGER.
C               L IS THE LAST COLUMN TO BE PERMUTED.
C               L MUST BE STRICTLY GREATER THAN K.
C
C        Z      REAL(LDZ,NZ), WHERE LDZ.GE.P.
C               Z IS AN ARRAY OF NZ P-VECTORS INTO WHICH THE
C               TRANSFORMATION U IS MULTIPLIED.  Z IS
C               NOT REFERENCED IF NZ = 0.
C
C        LDZ    INTEGER.
C               LDZ IS THE LEADING DIMENSION OF THE ARRAY Z.
C
C        NZ     INTEGER.
C               NZ IS THE NUMBER OF COLUMNS OF THE MATRIX Z.
C
C        JOB    INTEGER.
C               JOB DETERMINES THE TYPE OF PERMUTATION.
C                      JOB = 1  RIGHT CIRCULAR SHIFT.
C                      JOB = 2  LEFT CIRCULAR SHIFT.
C
C     ON RETURN
C
C        R      CONTAINS THE UPDATED FACTOR.
C
C        Z      CONTAINS THE UPDATED MATRIX Z.
C
C        C      REAL(P).
C               C CONTAINS THE COSINES OF THE TRANSFORMING ROTATIONS.
C
C        S      REAL(P).
C               S CONTAINS THE SINES OF THE TRANSFORMING ROTATIONS.
C
C      LINPACK. THIS VERSION DATED 08/14/78.
C      G.W. STEWART, UNIVERSITY OF MARYLAND, ARGONNE NATIONAL LAB.
C
C     SCHEX USES THE FOLLOWING FUNCTIONS AND SUBROUTINES.
C
C     BLAS SROTG
C     FORTRAN MIN0,MAX0
C
      INTEGER I,II,IL,IU,J,JJ,KM1,KP1,LMK,LM1
      REAL T
C
C     INITIALIZE
C
      KM1 = K - 1
      KP1 = K + 1
      LMK = L - K
      LM1 = L - 1
C
C     PERFORM THE APPROPRIATE TASK.
```

```
C
      GO TO (10,130), JOB
C
C     RIGHT CIRCULAR SHIFT.
C
   10 CONTINUE
C
C        REORDER THE COLUMNS.
C
         DO 20 I = 1, L
            II = L - I + 1
            S(I) = R(II,L)
   20    CONTINUE
         DO 40 JJ = K, LM1
            J = LM1 - JJ + K
            DO 30 I = 1, J
               R(I,J+1) = R(I,J)
   30       CONTINUE
            R(J+1,J+1) = 0.0E0
   40    CONTINUE
         IF (K .EQ. 1) GO TO 60
            DO 50 I = 1, KM1
               II = L - I + 1
               R(I,K) = S(II)
   50       CONTINUE
   60    CONTINUE
C
C        CALCULATE THE ROTATIONS.
C
         T = S(1)
         DO 70 I = 1, LMK
            CALL SROTG(S(I+1),T,C(I),S(I))
            T = S(I+1)
   70    CONTINUE
         R(K,K) = T
         DO 90 J = KP1, P
            IL = MAX0(1,L-J+1)
            DO 80 II = IL, LMK
               I = L - II
               T = C(II)*R(I,J) + S(II)*R(I+1,J)
               R(I+1,J) = C(II)*R(I+1,J) - S(II)*R(I,J)
               R(I,J) = T
   80       CONTINUE
   90    CONTINUE
C
C        IF REQUIRED, APPLY THE TRANSFORMATIONS TO Z.
C
         IF (NZ .LT. 1) GO TO 120
         DO 110 J = 1, NZ
            DO 100 II = 1, LMK
               I = L - II
               T = C(II)*Z(I,J) + S(II)*Z(I+1,J)
               Z(I+1,J) = C(II)*Z(I+1,J) - S(II)*Z(I,J)
               Z(I,J) = T
  100       CONTINUE
  110    CONTINUE
  120    CONTINUE
      GO TO 260
C
C     LEFT CIRCULAR SHIFT.
C
  130 CONTINUE
C
```

```
C        REORDER THE COLUMNS.
C
         DO 140 I = 1, K
            II = LMK + I
            S(II) = R(I,K)
  140    CONTINUE
         DO 160 J = K, LM1
            DO 150 I = 1, J
               R(I,J) = R(I,J+1)
  150       CONTINUE
            JJ = J - KM1
            S(JJ) = R(J+1,J+1)
  160    CONTINUE
         DO 170 I = 1, K
            II = LMK + I
            R(I,L) = S(II)
  170    CONTINUE
         DO 180 I = KP1, L
            R(I,L) = 0.0E0
  180    CONTINUE
C
C        REDUCTION LOOP.
C
         DO 220 J = K, P
            IF (J .EQ. K) GO TO 200
C
C              APPLY THE ROTATIONS.
C
               IU = MIN0(J-1,L-1)
               DO 190 I = K, IU
                  II = I - K + 1
                  T = C(II)*R(I,J) + S(II)*R(I+1,J)
                  R(I+1,J) = C(II)*R(I+1,J) - S(II)*R(I,J)
                  R(I,J) = T
  190          CONTINUE
  200       CONTINUE
            IF (J .GE. L) GO TO 210
               JJ = J - K + 1
               T = S(JJ)
               CALL SROTG(R(J,J),T,C(JJ),S(JJ))
  210       CONTINUE
  220    CONTINUE
C
C        APPLY THE ROTATIONS TO Z.
C
         IF (NZ .LT. 1) GO TO 250
         DO 240 J = 1, NZ
            DO 230 I = K, LM1
               II = I - KM1
               T = C(II)*Z(I,J) + S(II)*Z(I+1,J)
               Z(I+1,J) = C(II)*Z(I+1,J) - S(II)*Z(I,J)
               Z(I,J) = T
  230       CONTINUE
  240    CONTINUE
  250    CONTINUE
  260 CONTINUE
      RETURN
      END
```

```
      SUBROUTINE SSVDC(X,LDX,N,P,S,E,U,LDU,V,LDV,WORK,JOB,INFO)
      INTEGER LDX,N,P,LDU,LDV,JOB,INFO
      REAL X(LDX,1),S(1),E(1),U(LDU,1),V(LDV,1),WORK(1)
C
C
C     SSVDC IS A SUBROUTINE TO REDUCE A REAL NXP MATRIX X BY
C     ORTHOGONAL TRANSFORMATIONS U AND V TO DIAGONAL FORM.  THE
C     DIAGONAL ELEMENTS S(I) ARE THE SINGULAR VALUES OF X.  THE
C     COLUMNS OF U ARE THE CORRESPONDING LEFT SINGULAR VECTORS,
C     AND THE COLUMNS OF V THE RIGHT SINGULAR VECTORS.
C
C     ON ENTRY
C
C         X         REAL(LDX,P), WHERE LDX.GE.N.
C                   X CONTAINS THE MATRIX WHOSE SINGULAR VALUE
C                   DECOMPOSITION IS TO BE COMPUTED.  X IS
C                   DESTROYED BY SSVDC.
C
C         LDX       INTEGER.
C                   LDX IS THE LEADING DIMENSION OF THE ARRAY X.
C
C         N         INTEGER.
C                   N IS THE NUMBER OF ROWS OF THE MATRIX X.
C
C         P         INTEGER.
C                   P IS THE NUMBER OF COLUMNS OF THE MATRIX X.
C
C         LDU       INTEGER.
C                   LDU IS THE LEADING DIMENSION OF THE ARRAY U.
C                   (SEE BELOW).
C
C         LDV       INTEGER.
C                   LDV IS THE LEADING DIMENSION OF THE ARRAY V.
C                   (SEE BELOW).
C
C         WORK      REAL(N).
C                   WORK IS A SCRATCH ARRAY.
C
C         JOB       INTEGER.
C                   JOB CONTROLS THE COMPUTATION OF THE SINGULAR
C                   VECTORS.  IT HAS THE DECIMAL EXPANSION AB
C                   WITH THE FOLLOWING MEANING
C
C                        A.EQ.0    DO NOT COMPUTE THE LEFT SINGULAR
C                                  VECTORS.
C                        A.EQ.1    RETURN THE N LEFT SINGULAR VECTORS
C                                  IN U.
C                        A.GE.2    RETURN THE FIRST MIN(N,P) LEFT
C                                  SINGULAR VECTORS IN U.
C                        B.EQ.0    DO NOT COMPUTE THE RIGHT SINGULAR
C                                  VECTORS.
C                        B.EQ.1    RETURN THE RIGHT SINGULAR VECTORS
C                                  IN V.
C
C     ON RETURN
C
C         S         REAL(MM), WHERE MM=MIN(N+1,P).
C                   THE FIRST MIN(N,P) ENTRIES OF S CONTAIN THE
C                   SINGULAR VALUES OF X ARRANGED IN DESCENDING
C                   ORDER.
C
C         E         REAL(P)
C                   E ORDINARILY CONTAINS ZEROS.  HOWEVER SEE THE
```

```
C                 DISCUSSION OF INFO FOR EXCEPTIONS.
C
C        U        REAL(LDU,K), WHERE LDU.GE.N.  IF JOBA.EQ.1 THEN
C                 K.EQ.N, IF JOBA.GE.2 THEN K.EQ.MIN(N,P).
C                 U CONTAINS THE MATRIX OF  LEFT SINGULAR VECTORS.
C                 U IS NOT REFERENCED IF JOBA.EQ.0.  IF N.LE.P
C                 OR IF JOBA.EQ.2, THEN U MAY BE IDENTIFIED WITH X
C                 IN THE SUBROUTINE CALL.
C
C        V        REAL(LDV,P), WHERE LDV.GE.P.
C                 V CONTAINS THE MATRIX OF RIGHT SINGULAR VECTORS.
C                 V IS NOT REFERENCED IF JOBB.EQ.0.  IF P.LE.N,
C                 THEN V MAY BE IDENTIFIED WITH X IN THE
C                 SUBROUTINE CALL.
C
C        INFO     INTEGER.
C                 THE SINGULAR VALUES (AND THEIR CORRESPONDING
C                 SINGULAR VECTORS) S(INFO+1),S(INFO+2),...,S(M)
C                 ARE CORRECT (HERE M=MIN(N,P)).  THUS IF
C                 INFO.EQ.0, ALL THE SINGULAR VALUES AND THEIR
C                 VECTORS ARE CORRECT.  IN ANY EVENT, THE MATRIX
C                 B = TRANS(U)*X*V IS THE BIDIAGONAL MATRIX
C                 WITH THE ELEMENTS OF S ON ITS DIAGONAL AND THE
C                 ELEMENTS OF E ON ITS SUPER-DIAGONAL (TRANS(U)
C                 IS THE TRANSPOSE OF U).  THUS THE SINGULAR
C                 VALUES OF X AND B ARE THE SAME.
C
C     LINPACK. THIS VERSION DATED 08/14/78 .
C     G.W. STEWART, UNIVERSITY OF MARYLAND, ARGONNE NATIONAL LAB.
C
C     SSVDC USES THE FOLLOWING FUNCTIONS AND SUBROUTINES.
C
C     EXTERNAL SROT
C     BLAS SAXPY,SDOT,SSCAL,SSWAP,SNRM2,SROTG
C     FORTRAN ABS,AMAX1,MAX0,MIN0,MOD,SQRT
C
C     INTERNAL VARIABLES
C
      INTEGER I,ITER,J,JOBU,K,KASE,KK,L,LL,LLS,LM1,LP1,LS,LU,M,MAXIT,
     *        MM,MM1,MP1,NCT,NCTP1,NCU,NRT,NRTP1
      REAL SDOT,T
      REAL B,C,CS,EL,EMM1,F,G,SNRM2,SCALE,SHIFT,SL,SM,SN,SMM1,T1,TEST,
     *     ZTEST
      LOGICAL WANTU,WANTV
C
C
C     SET THE MAXIMUM NUMBER OF ITERATIONS.
C
      MAXIT = 30
C
C     DETERMINE WHAT IS TO BE COMPUTED.
C
      WANTU = .FALSE.
      WANTV = .FALSE.
      JOBU = MOD(JOB,100)/10
      NCU = N
      IF (JOBU .GT. 1) NCU = MIN0(N,P)
      IF (JOBU .NE. 0) WANTU = .TRUE.
      IF (MOD(JOB,10) .NE. 0) WANTV = .TRUE.
C
C     REDUCE X TO BIDIAGONAL FORM, STORING THE DIAGONAL ELEMENTS
C     IN S AND THE SUPER-DIAGONAL ELEMENTS IN E.
C
```

```
      INFO = 0
      NCT = MIN0(N-1,P)
      NRT = MAX0(0,MIN0(P-2,N))
      LU = MAX0(NCT,NRT)
      IF (LU .LT. 1) GO TO 170
      DO 160 L = 1, LU
         LP1 = L + 1
         IF (L .GT. NCT) GO TO 20
C
C           COMPUTE THE TRANSFORMATION FOR THE L-TH COLUMN AND
C           PLACE THE L-TH DIAGONAL IN S(L).
C
            S(L) = SNRM2(N-L+1,X(L,L),1)
            IF (S(L) .EQ. 0.0E0) GO TO 10
               IF (X(L,L) .NE. 0.0E0) S(L) = SIGN(S(L),X(L,L))
               CALL SSCAL(N-L+1,1.0E0/S(L),X(L,L),1)
               X(L,L) = 1.0E0 + X(L,L)
   10       CONTINUE
            S(L) = -S(L)
   20    CONTINUE
         IF (P .LT. LP1) GO TO 50
         DO 40 J = LP1, P
            IF (L .GT. NCT) GO TO 30
            IF (S(L) .EQ. 0.0E0) GO TO 30
C
C              APPLY THE TRANSFORMATION.
C
               T = -SDOT(N-L+1,X(L,L),1,X(L,J),1)/X(L,L)
               CALL SAXPY(N-L+1,T,X(L,L),1,X(L,J),1)
   30       CONTINUE
C
C           PLACE THE L-TH ROW OF X INTO  E FOR THE
C           SUBSEQUENT CALCULATION OF THE ROW TRANSFORMATION.
C
            E(J) = X(L,J)
   40    CONTINUE
   50    CONTINUE
         IF (.NOT.WANTU .OR. L .GT. NCT) GO TO 70
C
C           PLACE THE TRANSFORMATION IN U FOR SUBSEQUENT BACK
C           MULTIPLICATION.
C
            DO 60 I = L, N
               U(I,L) = X(I,L)
   60       CONTINUE
   70    CONTINUE
         IF (L .GT. NRT) GO TO 150
C
C           COMPUTE THE L-TH ROW TRANSFORMATION AND PLACE THE
C           L-TH SUPER-DIAGONAL IN E(L).
C
            E(L) = SNRM2(P-L,E(LP1),1)
            IF (E(L) .EQ. 0.0E0) GO TO 80
               IF (E(LP1) .NE. 0.0E0) E(L) = SIGN(E(L),E(LP1))
               CALL SSCAL(P-L,1.0E0/E(L),E(LP1),1)
               E(LP1) = 1.0E0 + E(LP1)
   80       CONTINUE
            E(L) = -E(L)
            IF (LP1 .GT. N .OR. E(L) .EQ. 0.0E0) GO TO 120
C
C              APPLY THE TRANSFORMATION.
C
               DO 90 I = LP1, N
```

```
                  WORK(I) = 0.0E0
   90          CONTINUE
               DO 100 J = LP1, P
                  CALL SAXPY(N-L,E(J),X(LP1,J),1,WORK(LP1),1)
  100          CONTINUE
               DO 110 J = LP1, P
                  CALL SAXPY(N-L,-E(J)/E(LP1),WORK(LP1),1,X(LP1,J),1)
  110          CONTINUE
  120       CONTINUE
            IF (.NOT.WANTV) GO TO 140
C
C              PLACE THE TRANSFORMATION IN V FOR SUBSEQUENT
C              BACK MULTIPLICATION.
C
               DO 130 I = LP1, P
                  V(I,L) = E(I)
  130          CONTINUE
  140       CONTINUE
  150    CONTINUE
  160 CONTINUE
  170 CONTINUE
C
C     SET UP THE FINAL BIDIAGONAL MATRIX OF ORDER M.
C
      M = MIN0(P,N+1)
      NCTP1 = NCT + 1
      NRTP1 = NRT + 1
      IF (NCT .LT. P) S(NCTP1) = X(NCTP1,NCTP1)
      IF (N .LT. M) S(M) = 0.0E0
      IF (NRTP1 .LT. M) E(NRTP1) = X(NRTP1,M)
      E(M) = 0.0E0
C
C     IF REQUIRED, GENERATE U.
C
      IF (.NOT.WANTU) GO TO 300
         IF (NCU .LT. NCTP1) GO TO 200
         DO 190 J = NCTP1, NCU
            DO 180 I = 1, N
               U(I,J) = 0.0E0
  180       CONTINUE
            U(J,J) = 1.0E0
  190    CONTINUE
  200    CONTINUE
         IF (NCT .LT. 1) GO TO 290
         DO 280 LL = 1, NCT
            L = NCT - LL + 1
            IF (S(L) .EQ. 0.0E0) GO TO 250
               LP1 = L + 1
               IF (NCU .LT. LP1) GO TO 220
               DO 210 J = LP1, NCU
                  T = -SDOT(N-L+1,U(L,L),1,U(L,J),1)/U(L,L)
                  CALL SAXPY(N-L+1,T,U(L,L),1,U(L,J),1)
  210          CONTINUE
  220          CONTINUE
               CALL SSCAL(N-L+1,-1.0E0,U(L,L),1)
               U(L,L) = 1.0E0 + U(L,L)
               LM1 = L - 1
               IF (LM1 .LT. 1) GO TO 240
               DO 230 I = 1, LM1
                  U(I,L) = 0.0E0
  230          CONTINUE
  240          CONTINUE
            GO TO 270
```

```
  250          CONTINUE
                  DO 260 I = 1, N
                     U(I,L) = 0.0E0
  260             CONTINUE
                  U(L,L) = 1.0E0
  270          CONTINUE
  280       CONTINUE
  290    CONTINUE
  300 CONTINUE
C
C     IF IT IS REQUIRED, GENERATE V.
C
      IF (.NOT.WANTV) GO TO 350
         DO 340 LL = 1, P
            L = P - LL + 1
            LP1 = L + 1
            IF (L .GT. NRT) GO TO 320
            IF (E(L) .EQ. 0.0E0) GO TO 320
               DO 310 J = LP1, P
                  T = -SDOT(P-L,V(LP1,L),1,V(LP1,J),1)/V(LP1,L)
                  CALL SAXPY(P-L,T,V(LP1,L),1,V(LP1,J),1)
  310          CONTINUE
  320       CONTINUE
            DO 330 I = 1, P
               V(I,L) = 0.0E0
  330       CONTINUE
            V(L,L) = 1.0E0
  340    CONTINUE
  350 CONTINUE
C
C     MAIN ITERATION LOOP FOR THE SINGULAR VALUES.
C
      MM = M
      ITER = 0
  360 CONTINUE
C
C        QUIT IF ALL THE SINGULAR VALUES HAVE BEEN FOUND.
C
C     ...EXIT
         IF (M .EQ. 0) GO TO 620
C
C        IF TOO MANY ITERATIONS HAVE BEEN PERFORMED, SET
C        FLAG AND RETURN.
C
         IF (ITER .LT. MAXIT) GO TO 370
            INFO = M
C     ......EXIT
            GO TO 620
  370    CONTINUE
C
C        THIS SECTION OF THE PROGRAM INSPECTS FOR
C        NEGLIGIBLE ELEMENTS IN THE S AND E ARRAYS.  ON
C        COMPLETION THE VARIABLES KASE AND L ARE SET AS FOLLOWS.
C
C           KASE = 1     IF S(M) AND E(L-1) ARE NEGLIGIBLE AND L.LT.M
C           KASE = 2     IF S(L) IS NEGLIGIBLE AND L.LT.M
C           KASE = 3     IF E(L-1) IS NEGLIGIBLE, L.LT.M, AND
C                        S(L), ..., S(M) ARE NOT NEGLIGIBLE (QR STEP).
C           KASE = 4     IF E(M-1) IS NEGLIGIBLE (CONVERGENCE).
C
         DO 390 LL = 1, M
            L = M - LL
C        ...EXIT
```

```
            IF (L .EQ. 0) GO TO 400
            TEST = ABS(S(L)) + ABS(S(L+1))
            ZTEST = TEST + ABS(E(L))
            IF (ZTEST .NE. TEST) GO TO 380
               E(L) = 0.0E0
C        ......EXIT
               GO TO 400
  380       CONTINUE
  390    CONTINUE
  400    CONTINUE
         IF (L .NE. M - 1) GO TO 410
            KASE = 4
         GO TO 480
  410    CONTINUE
            LP1 = L + 1
            MP1 = M + 1
            DO 430 LLS = LP1, MP1
               LS = M - LLS + LP1
C           ...EXIT
               IF (LS .EQ. L) GO TO 440
               TEST = 0.0E0
               IF (LS .NE. M) TEST = TEST + ABS(E(LS))
               IF (LS .NE. L + 1) TEST = TEST + ABS(E(LS-1))
               ZTEST = TEST + ABS(S(LS))
               IF (ZTEST .NE. TEST) GO TO 420
                  S(LS) = 0.0E0
C           ......EXIT
                  GO TO 440
  420          CONTINUE
  430       CONTINUE
  440       CONTINUE
            IF (LS .NE. L) GO TO 450
               KASE = 3
            GO TO 470
  450       CONTINUE
            IF (LS .NE. M) GO TO 460
               KASE = 1
            GO TO 470
  460       CONTINUE
               KASE = 2
               L = LS
  470       CONTINUE
  480    CONTINUE
         L = L + 1
C
C        PERFORM THE TASK INDICATED BY KASE.
C
         GO TO (490,520,540,570), KASE
C
C        DEFLATE NEGLIGIBLE S(M).
C
  490    CONTINUE
            MM1 = M - 1
            F = E(M-1)
            E(M-1) = 0.0E0
            DO 510 KK = L, MM1
               K = MM1 - KK + L
               T1 = S(K)
               CALL SROTG(T1,F,CS,SN)
               S(K) = T1
               IF (K .EQ. L) GO TO 500
                  F = -SN*E(K-1)
                  E(K-1) = CS*E(K-1)
```

```
  500          CONTINUE
               IF (WANTV) CALL SROT(P,V(1,K),1,V(1,M),1,CS,SN)
  510       CONTINUE
         GO TO 610
C
C        SPLIT AT NEGLIGIBLE S(L).
C
  520    CONTINUE
            F = E(L-1)
            E(L-1) = 0.0E0
            DO 530 K = L, M
               T1 = S(K)
               CALL SROTG(T1,F,CS,SN)
               S(K) = T1
               F = -SN*E(K)
               E(K) = CS*E(K)
               IF (WANTU) CALL SROT(N,U(1,K),1,U(1,L-1),1,CS,SN)
  530       CONTINUE
         GO TO 610
C
C        PERFORM ONE QR STEP.
C
  540    CONTINUE
C
C           CALCULATE THE SHIFT.
C
            SCALE = AMAX1(ABS(S(M)),ABS(S(M-1)),ABS(E(M-1)),ABS(S(L)),
     *                    ABS(E(L)))
            SM = S(M)/SCALE
            SMM1 = S(M-1)/SCALE
            EMM1 = E(M-1)/SCALE
            SL = S(L)/SCALE
            EL = E(L)/SCALE
            B = ((SMM1 + SM)*(SMM1 - SM) + EMM1**2)/2.0E0
            C = (SM*EMM1)**2
            SHIFT = 0.0E0
            IF (B .EQ. 0.0E0 .AND. C .EQ. 0.0E0) GO TO 550
               SHIFT = SQRT(B**2+C)
               IF (B .LT. 0.0E0) SHIFT = -SHIFT
               SHIFT = C/(B + SHIFT)
  550       CONTINUE
            F = (SL + SM)*(SL - SM) - SHIFT
            G = SL*EL
C
C           CHASE ZEROS.
C
            MM1 = M - 1
            DO 560 K = L, MM1
               CALL SROTG(F,G,CS,SN)
               IF (K .NE. L) E(K-1) = F
               F = CS*S(K) + SN*E(K)
               E(K) = CS*E(K) - SN*S(K)
               G = SN*S(K+1)
               S(K+1) = CS*S(K+1)
               IF (WANTV) CALL SROT(P,V(1,K),1,V(1,K+1),1,CS,SN)
               CALL SROTG(F,G,CS,SN)
               S(K) = F
               F = CS*E(K) + SN*S(K+1)
               S(K+1) = -SN*E(K) + CS*S(K+1)
               G = SN*E(K+1)
               E(K+1) = CS*E(K+1)
               IF (WANTU .AND. K .LT. N)
     *            CALL SROT(N,U(1,K),1,U(1,K+1),1,CS,SN)
```

```
  560         CONTINUE
              E(M-1) = F
              ITER = ITER + 1
           GO TO 610
C
C          CONVERGENCE.
C
  570      CONTINUE
C
C             MAKE THE SINGULAR VALUE  POSITIVE.
C
              IF (S(L) .GE. 0.0E0) GO TO 580
                 S(L) = -S(L)
                 IF (WANTV) CALL SSCAL(P,-1.0E0,V(1,L),1)
  580         CONTINUE
C
C             ORDER THE SINGULAR VALUE.
C
  590         IF (L .EQ. MM) GO TO 600
C             ...EXIT
                 IF (S(L) .GE. S(L+1)) GO TO 600
                 T = S(L)
                 S(L) = S(L+1)
                 S(L+1) = T
                 IF (WANTV .AND. L .LT. P)
     *              CALL SSWAP(P,V(1,L),1,V(1,L+1),1)
                 IF (WANTU .AND. L .LT. N)
     *              CALL SSWAP(N,U(1,L),1,U(1,L+1),1)
                 L = L + 1
              GO TO 590
  600         CONTINUE
              ITER = 0
              M = M - 1
  610      CONTINUE
        GO TO 360
  620 CONTINUE
      RETURN
      END
```

Appendix D: BLA Listings

ISAMAX

```
      INTEGER FUNCTION ISAMAX(N,SX,INCX)
C
C     FINDS THE INDEX OF ELEMENT HAVING MAX. ABSOLUTE VALUE.
C     JACK DONGARRA, LINPACK, 3/11/78.
C
      REAL SX(1),SMAX
      INTEGER I,INCX,IX,N
C
      ISAMAX = 0
      IF( N .LT. 1 ) RETURN
      ISAMAX = 1
      IF(N.EQ.1)RETURN
      IF(INCX.EQ.1)GO TO 20
C
C        CODE FOR INCREMENT NOT EQUAL TO 1
C
      IX = 1
      SMAX = ABS(SX(1))
      IX = IX + INCX
      DO 10 I = 2,N
         IF(ABS(SX(IX)).LE.SMAX) GO TO 5
         ISAMAX = I
         SMAX = ABS(SX(IX))
    5    IX = IX + INCX
   10 CONTINUE
      RETURN
C
C        CODE FOR INCREMENT EQUAL TO 1
C
   20 SMAX = ABS(SX(1))
      DO 30 I = 2,N
         IF(ABS(SX(I)).LE.SMAX) GO TO 30
         ISAMAX = I
         SMAX = ABS(SX(I))
   30 CONTINUE
      RETURN
      END
```

SASUM

```
      REAL FUNCTION SASUM(N,SX,INCX)
C
C     TAKES THE SUM OF THE ABSOLUTE VALUES.
C     USES UNROLLED LOOPS FOR INCREMENT EQUAL TO ONE.
C     JACK DONGARRA, LINPACK, 3/11/78.
C
      REAL SX(1),STEMP
      INTEGER I,INCX,M,MP1,N,NINCX
C
      SASUM = 0.0E0
      STEMP = 0.0E0
      IF(N.LE.0)RETURN
      IF(INCX.EQ.1)GO TO 20
C
C        CODE FOR INCREMENT NOT EQUAL TO 1
C
      NINCX = N*INCX
      DO 10 I = 1,NINCX,INCX
        STEMP = STEMP + ABS(SX(I))
   10 CONTINUE
      SASUM = STEMP
      RETURN
C
C        CODE FOR INCREMENT EQUAL TO 1
C
C
C        CLEAN-UP LOOP
C
   20 M = MOD(N,6)
      IF( M .EQ. 0 ) GO TO 40
      DO 30 I = 1,M
        STEMP = STEMP + ABS(SX(I))
   30 CONTINUE
      IF( N .LT. 6 ) GO TO 60
   40 MP1 = M + 1
      DO 50 I = MP1,N,6
        STEMP = STEMP + ABS(SX(I)) + ABS(SX(I + 1)) + ABS(SX(I + 2))
     *  + ABS(SX(I + 3)) + ABS(SX(I + 4)) + ABS(SX(I + 5))
   50 CONTINUE
   60 SASUM = STEMP
      RETURN
      END
```

SAXPY

```
      SUBROUTINE SAXPY(N,SA,SX,INCX,SY,INCY)
C
C     CONSTANT TIMES A VECTOR PLUS A VECTOR.
C     USES UNROLLED LOOPSFOR INCREMENTS EQUAL TO ONE.
C     JACK DONGARRA, LINPACK, 3/11/78.
C
      REAL SX(1),SY(1),SA
      INTEGER I,INCX,INCY,IX,IY,M,MP1,N
C
      IF(N.LE.0)RETURN
      IF (SA .EQ. 0.0) RETURN
      IF(INCX.EQ.1.AND.INCY.EQ.1)GO TO 20
C
C        CODE FOR UNEQUAL INCREMENTS OR EQUAL INCREMENTS
C          NOT EQUAL TO 1
C
      IX = 1
      IY = 1
      IF(INCX.LT.0)IX = (-N+1)*INCX + 1
      IF(INCY.LT.0)IY = (-N+1)*INCY + 1
      DO 10 I = 1,N
        SY(IY) = SY(IY) + SA*SX(IX)
        IX = IX + INCX
        IY = IY + INCY
   10 CONTINUE
      RETURN
C
C        CODE FOR BOTH INCREMENTS EQUAL TO 1
C
C
C        CLEAN-UP LOOP
C
   20 M = MOD(N,4)
      IF( M .EQ. 0 ) GO TO 40
      DO 30 I = 1,M
        SY(I) = SY(I) + SA*SX(I)
   30 CONTINUE
      IF( N .LT. 4 ) RETURN
   40 MP1 = M + 1
      DO 50 I = MP1,N,4
        SY(I) = SY(I) + SA*SX(I)
        SY(I + 1) = SY(I + 1) + SA*SX(I + 1)
        SY(I + 2) = SY(I + 2) + SA*SX(I + 2)
        SY(I + 3) = SY(I + 3) + SA*SX(I + 3)
   50 CONTINUE
      RETURN
      END
```

```
      SUBROUTINE  SCOPY(N,SX,INCX,SY,INCY)
C
C     COPIES A VECTOR, X, TO A VECTOR, Y.
C     USES UNROLLED LOOPS FOR INCREMENTS EQUAL TO 1.
C     JACK DONGARRA, LINPACK, 3/11/78.
C
      REAL SX(1),SY(1)
      INTEGER I,INCX,INCY,IX,IY,M,MP1,N
C
      IF(N.LE.0)RETURN
      IF(INCX.EQ.1.AND.INCY.EQ.1)GO TO 20
C
C        CODE FOR UNEQUAL INCREMENTS OR EQUAL INCREMENTS
C          NOT EQUAL TO 1
C
      IX = 1
      IY = 1
      IF(INCX.LT.0)IX = (-N+1)*INCX + 1
      IF(INCY.LT.0)IY = (-N+1)*INCY + 1
      DO 10 I = 1,N
        SY(IY) = SX(IX)
        IX = IX + INCX
        IY = IY + INCY
   10 CONTINUE
      RETURN
C
C        CODE FOR BOTH INCREMENTS EQUAL TO 1
C
C
C        CLEAN-UP LOOP
C
   20 M = MOD(N,7)
      IF( M .EQ. 0 ) GO TO 40
      DO 30 I = 1,M
        SY(I) = SX(I)
   30 CONTINUE
      IF( N .LT. 7 ) RETURN
   40 MP1 = M + 1
      DO 50 I = MP1,N,7
        SY(I) = SX(I)
        SY(I + 1) = SX(I + 1)
        SY(I + 2) = SX(I + 2)
        SY(I + 3) = SX(I + 3)
        SY(I + 4) = SX(I + 4)
        SY(I + 5) = SX(I + 5)
        SY(I + 6) = SX(I + 6)
   50 CONTINUE
      RETURN
      END
```

SDOT

```
      REAL FUNCTION SDOT(N,SX,INCX,SY,INCY)
C
C     FORMS THE DOT PRODUCT OF TWO VECTORS.
C     USES UNROLLED LOOPS FOR INCREMENTS EQUAL TO ONE.
C     JACK DONGARRA, LINPACK, 3/11/78.
C
      REAL SX(1),SY(1),STEMP
      INTEGER I,INCX,INCY,IX,IY,M,MP1,N
C
      STEMP = 0.0E0
      SDOT = 0.0E0
      IF(N.LE.0)RETURN
      IF(INCX.EQ.1.AND.INCY.EQ.1)GO TO 20
C
C        CODE FOR UNEQUAL INCREMENTS OR EQUAL INCREMENTS
C          NOT EQUAL TO 1
C
      IX = 1
      IY = 1
      IF(INCX.LT.0)IX = (-N+1)*INCX + 1
      IF(INCY.LT.0)IY = (-N+1)*INCY + 1
      DO 10 I = 1,N
        STEMP = STEMP + SX(IX)*SY(IY)
        IX = IX + INCX
        IY = IY + INCY
   10 CONTINUE
      SDOT = STEMP
      RETURN
C
C        CODE FOR BOTH INCREMENTS EQUAL TO 1
C
C
C        CLEAN-UP LOOP
C
   20 M = MOD(N,5)
      IF( M .EQ. 0 ) GO TO 40
      DO 30 I = 1,M
        STEMP = STEMP + SX(I)*SY(I)
   30 CONTINUE
      IF( N .LT. 5 ) GO TO 60
   40 MP1 = M + 1
      DO 50 I = MP1,N,5
        STEMP = STEMP + SX(I)*SY(I) + SX(I + 1)*SY(I + 1) +
     *   SX(I + 2)*SY(I + 2) + SX(I + 3)*SY(I + 3) + SX(I + 4)*SY(I + 4)
   50 CONTINUE
   60 SDOT = STEMP
      RETURN
      END
```

```
      REAL FUNCTION SNRM2 ( N, SX, INCX)
      INTEGER          NEXT
      REAL   SX(1),  CUTLO, CUTHI, HITEST, SUM, XMAX, ZERO, ONE
      DATA   ZERO, ONE /0.0E0, 1.0E0/
C
C     EUCLIDEAN NORM OF THE N-VECTOR STORED IN SX() WITH STORAGE
C     INCREMENT INCX .
C     IF    N .LE. 0 RETURN WITH RESULT = 0.
C     IF N .GE. 1 THEN INCX MUST BE .GE. 1
C
C           C.L.LAWSON, 1978 JAN 08
C
C     FOUR PHASE METHOD     USING TWO BUILT-IN CONSTANTS THAT ARE
C     HOPEFULLY APPLICABLE TO ALL MACHINES.
C         CUTLO = MAXIMUM OF  SQRT(U/EPS)  OVER ALL KNOWN MACHINES.
C         CUTHI = MINIMUM OF  SQRT(V)      OVER ALL KNOWN MACHINES.
C     WHERE
C         EPS = SMALLEST NO. SUCH THAT EPS + 1. .GT. 1.
C         U   = SMALLEST POSITIVE NO.   (UNDERFLOW LIMIT)
C         V   = LARGEST  NO.            (OVERFLOW  LIMIT)
C
C     BRIEF OUTLINE OF ALGORITHM..
C
C     PHASE 1    SCANS ZERO COMPONENTS.
C     MOVE TO PHASE 2 WHEN A COMPONENT IS NONZERO AND .LE. CUTLO
C     MOVE TO PHASE 3 WHEN A COMPONENT IS .GT. CUTLO
C     MOVE TO PHASE 4 WHEN A COMPONENT IS .GE. CUTHI/M
C     WHERE M = N FOR X() REAL AND M = 2*N FOR COMPLEX.
C
C     VALUES FOR CUTLO AND CUTHI..
C     FROM THE ENVIRONMENTAL PARAMETERS LISTED IN THE IMSL CONVERTER
C     DOCUMENT THE LIMITING VALUES ARE AS FOLLOWS..
C     CUTLO, S.P.   U/EPS = 2**(-102) FOR  HONEYWELL.  CLOSE SECONDS ARE
C                   UNIVAC AND DEC AT 2**(-103)
C                   THUS CUTLO = 2**(-51) = 4.44089E-16
C     CUTHI, S.P.   V = 2**127 FOR UNIVAC, HONEYWELL, AND DEC.
C                   THUS CUTHI = 2**(63.5) = 1.30438E19
C     CUTLO, D.P.   U/EPS = 2**(-67) FOR HONEYWELL AND DEC.
C                   THUS CUTLO = 2**(-33.5) = 8.23181D-11
C     CUTHI, D.P.   SAME AS S.P.  CUTHI = 1.30438D19
C     DATA CUTLO, CUTHI / 8.232D-11,  1.304D19 /
C     DATA CUTLO, CUTHI / 4.441E-16,  1.304E19 /
      DATA CUTLO, CUTHI / 4.441E-16,  1.304E19 /
C
      IF(N .GT. 0) GO TO 10
         SNRM2  = ZERO
         GO TO 300
C
   10 ASSIGN 30 TO NEXT
      SUM = ZERO
      NN = N * INCX
C                                                 BEGIN MAIN LOOP
      I = 1
   20    GO TO NEXT,(30, 50, 70, 110)
   30 IF( ABS(SX(I)) .GT. CUTLO) GO TO 85
      ASSIGN 50 TO NEXT
      XMAX = ZERO
C
C                        PHASE 1.  SUM IS ZERO
C
   50 IF( SX(I) .EQ. ZERO) GO TO 200
      IF( ABS(SX(I)) .GT. CUTLO) GO TO 85
C
```

```
C                                     PREPARE FOR PHASE 2.
      ASSIGN 70 TO NEXT
      GO TO 105
C
C                                     PREPARE FOR PHASE 4.
C
  100 I = J
      ASSIGN 110 TO NEXT
      SUM = (SUM / SX(I)) / SX(I)
  105 XMAX = ABS(SX(I))
      GO TO 115
C
C                   PHASE 2.  SUM IS SMALL.
C                             SCALE TO AVOID DESTRUCTIVE UNDERFLOW.
C
   70 IF( ABS(SX(I)) .GT. CUTLO ) GO TO 75
C
C                     COMMON CODE FOR PHASES 2 AND 4.
C                     IN PHASE 4 SUM IS LARGE.  SCALE TO AVOID OVERFLOW.
C
  110 IF( ABS(SX(I)) .LE. XMAX ) GO TO 115
         SUM = ONE + SUM * (XMAX / SX(I))**2
         XMAX = ABS(SX(I))
         GO TO 200
C
  115 SUM = SUM + (SX(I)/XMAX)**2
      GO TO 200
C
C
C                  PREPARE FOR PHASE 3.
C
   75 SUM = (SUM * XMAX) * XMAX
C
C
C     FOR REAL OR D.P. SET HITEST = CUTHI/N
C     FOR COMPLEX      SET HITEST = CUTHI/(2*N)
C
   85 HITEST = CUTHI/FLOAT( N )
C
C                   PHASE 3.  SUM IS MID-RANGE.  NO SCALING.
C
      DO 95 J =I,NN,INCX
      IF(ABS(SX(J)) .GE. HITEST) GO TO 100
   95    SUM = SUM + SX(J)**2
      SNRM2 = SQRT( SUM )
      GO TO 300
C
  200 CONTINUE
      I = I + INCX
      IF ( I .LE. NN ) GO TO 20
C
C              END OF MAIN LOOP.
C
C              COMPUTE SQUARE ROOT AND ADJUST FOR SCALING.
C
      SNRM2 = XMAX * SQRT(SUM)
  300 CONTINUE
      RETURN
      END
```

```
      SUBROUTINE  SROT (N,SX,INCX,SY,INCY,C,S)
C
C     APPLIES A PLANE ROTATION.
C     JACK DONGARRA, LINPACK, 3/11/78.
C
      REAL SX(1),SY(1),STEMP,C,S
      INTEGER I,INCX,INCY,IX,IY,N
C
      IF(N.LE.0)RETURN
      IF(INCX.EQ.1.AND.INCY.EQ.1)GO TO 20
C
C       CODE FOR UNEQUAL INCREMENTS OR EQUAL INCREMENTS NOT EQUAL
C         TO 1
C
      IX = 1
      IY = 1
      IF(INCX.LT.0)IX = (-N+1)*INCX + 1
      IF(INCY.LT.0)IY = (-N+1)*INCY + 1
      DO 10 I = 1,N
        STEMP = C*SX(IX) + S*SY(IY)
        SY(IY) = C*SY(IY) - S*SX(IX)
        SX(IX) = STEMP
        IX = IX + INCX
        IY = IY + INCY
   10 CONTINUE
      RETURN
C
C       CODE FOR BOTH INCREMENTS EQUAL TO 1
C
   20 DO 30 I = 1,N
        STEMP = C*SX(I) + S*SY(I)
        SY(I) = C*SY(I) - S*SX(I)
        SX(I) = STEMP
   30 CONTINUE
      RETURN
      END
```

SROTG

```
      SUBROUTINE SROTG(SA,SB,C,S)
C
C     CONSTRUCT GIVENS PLANE ROTATION.
C     JACK DONGARRA, LINPACK, 3/11/78.
C
      REAL SA,SB,C,S,ROE,SCALE,R,Z
C
      ROE = SB
      IF( ABS(SA) .GT. ABS(SB) ) ROE = SA
      SCALE = ABS(SA) + ABS(SB)
      IF( SCALE .NE. 0.0 ) GO TO 10
         C = 1.0
         S = 0.0
         R = 0.0
         GO TO 20
   10 R = SCALE*SQRT((SA/SCALE)**2 + (SB/SCALE)**2)
      R = SIGN(1.0,ROE)*R
      C = SA/R
      S = SB/R
   20 Z = 1.0
      IF( ABS(SA) .GT. ABS(SB) ) Z = S
      IF( ABS(SB) .GE. ABS(SA) .AND. C .NE. 0.0 ) Z = 1.0/C
      SA = R
      SB = Z
      RETURN
      END
```

```
      SUBROUTINE  SSCAL(N,SA,SX,INCX)
C
C     SCALES A VECTOR BY A CONSTANT.
C     USES UNROLLED LOOPS FOR INCREMENT EQUAL TO 1.
C     JACK DONGARRA, LINPACK, 3/11/78.
C
      REAL SA,SX(1)
      INTEGER I,INCX,M,MP1,N,NINCX
C
      IF(N.LE.0)RETURN
      IF(INCX.EQ.1)GO TO 20
C
C        CODE FOR INCREMENT NOT EQUAL TO 1
C
      NINCX = N*INCX
      DO 10 I = 1,NINCX,INCX
        SX(I) = SA*SX(I)
   10 CONTINUE
      RETURN
C
C        CODE FOR INCREMENT EQUAL TO 1
C
C
C        CLEAN-UP LOOP
C
   20 M = MOD(N,5)
      IF( M .EQ. 0 ) GO TO 40
      DO 30 I = 1,M
        SX(I) = SA*SX(I)
   30 CONTINUE
      IF( N .LT. 5 ) RETURN
   40 MP1 = M + 1
      DO 50 I = MP1,N,5
        SX(I) = SA*SX(I)
        SX(I + 1) = SA*SX(I + 1)
        SX(I + 2) = SA*SX(I + 2)
        SX(I + 3) = SA*SX(I + 3)
        SX(I + 4) = SA*SX(I + 4)
   50 CONTINUE
      RETURN
      END
```

SSWAP

```
      SUBROUTINE  SSWAP (N,SX,INCX,SY,INCY)
C
C     INTERCHANGES TWO VECTORS.
C     USES UNROLLED LOOPS FOR INCREMENTS EQUAL TO 1.
C     JACK DONGARRA, LINPACK, 3/11/78.
C
      REAL SX(1),SY(1),STEMP
      INTEGER I,INCX,INCY,IX,IY,M,MP1,N
C
      IF(N.LE.0)RETURN
      IF(INCX.EQ.1.AND.INCY.EQ.1)GO TO 20
C
C       CODE FOR UNEQUAL INCREMENTS OR EQUAL INCREMENTS NOT EQUAL
C         TO 1
C
      IX = 1
      IY = 1
      IF(INCX.LT.0)IX = (-N+1)*INCX + 1
      IF(INCY.LT.0)IY = (-N+1)*INCY + 1
      DO 10 I = 1,N
        STEMP = SX(IX)
        SX(IX) = SY(IY)
        SY(IY) = STEMP
        IX = IX + INCX
        IY = IY + INCY
   10 CONTINUE
      RETURN
C
C       CODE FOR BOTH INCREMENTS EQUAL TO 1
C
C
C       CLEAN-UP LOOP
C
   20 M = MOD(N,3)
      IF( M .EQ. 0 ) GO TO 40
      DO 30 I = 1,M
        STEMP = SX(I)
        SX(I) = SY(I)
        SY(I) = STEMP
   30 CONTINUE
      IF( N .LT. 3 ) RETURN
   40 MP1 = M + 1
      DO 50 I = MP1,N,3
        STEMP = SX(I)
        SX(I) = SY(I)
        SY(I) = STEMP
        STEMP = SX(I + 1)
        SX(I + 1) = SY(I + 1)
        SY(I + 1) = STEMP
        STEMP = SX(I + 2)
        SX(I + 2) = SY(I + 2)
        SY(I + 2) = STEMP
   50 CONTINUE
      RETURN
      END
```

Chapter	Page	Name	Parameters
1	2	SGECO	(A,LDA,N,IPVT,RCOND,Z)
1	3	SGEFA	(A,LDA,N,IPVT,INFO)
1	4	SGESL	(A,LDA,N,IPVT,B,JOB)
1	4	SGEDI	(A,LDA,N,IPVT,DET,WORK,JOB)
2	3	SGBCO	(ABD,LDA,N,ML,MU,IPVT,RCOND,Z)
2	4	SGBFA	(ABD,LDA,N,ML,MU,IPVT,INFO)
2	5	SGBSL	(ABD,LDA,N,ML,MU,IPVT,B,JOB)
2	6	SGBDI	(ABD,LDA,N,ML,MU,IPVT,DET)
3	2	SPOCO	(A,LDA,N,RCOND,Z,INFO)
3	3	SPOFA	(A,LDA,N,INFO)
3	4	SPOSL	(A,LDA,N,B)
3	4	SPODI	(A,LDA,N,DET,JOB)
3	6	SPPCO	(AP,N,RCOND,Z,INFO)
3	6	SPPFA	(AP,N,INFO)
3	6	SPPSL	(AP,N,B)
3	6	SPPDI	(AP,N,DET,JOB)
4	3	SPBCO	(ABD,LDA,N,M,RCOND,Z,INFO)
4	4	SPBFA	(ABD,LDA,N,M,INFO)
4	4	SPBSL	(ABD,LDA,N,M,B)
4	5	SPBDI	(ABD,LDA,N,M,DET)
5	3	SSICO	(A,LDA,N,KPVT,RCOND,Z)
5	4	SSIFA	(A,LDA,N,KPVT,INFO)
5	5	SSISL	(A,LDA,N,KPVT,B)
5	6	SSIDI	(A,LDA,N,KPVT,DET,INERT,WORK,JOB)
5	7	SSPCO	(AP,N,KPVT,RCOND,Z)
5	7	SSPFA	(AP,N,KPVT,INFO)
5	7	SSPSL	(AP,N,KPVT,B)
5	7	SSPDI	(AP,N,KPVT,DET,INERT,WORK,JOB)
5	8	CHICO	(A,LDA,N,KPVT,RCOND,Z)
5	8	CHIFA	(A,LDA,N,KPVT,INFO)
5	8	CHISL	(A,LDA,N,KPVT,B)
5	8	CHIDI	(A,LDA,N,KPVT,DET,INERT,WORK,JOB)
5	8	CHPCO	(AP,N,KPVT,RCOND,Z)
5	8	CHPFA	(AP,N,KPVT,INFO)
5	8	CHPSL	(AP,N,KPVT,B)
5	8	CHPDI	(AP,N,KPVT,DET,INERT,WORK,JOB)
6	1	STRCO	(T,LDT,N,RCOND,Z,JOB)
6	2	STRSL	(T,LDT,N,B,JOB,INFO)
6	3	STRDI	(T,LDT,N,DET,JOB,INFO)
7	1	SGTSL	(N,C,D,E,B,INFO)
7	2	SPTSL	(N,D,E,B)
8	5	SCHDC	(A,LDA,P,WORK,JPVT,JOB,INFO)
9	6	SQRDC	(X,LDX,N,P,QRAUX,JPVT,WORK,JOB)
9	7	SQRSL	(X,LDX,N,K,QRAUX,Y,QY,QTY,B,RSD,XB,JOB,INFO)
10	4	SCHUD	(R,LDR,P,X,Z,LDZ,NZ,Y,RHO,C,S)
10	5	SCHDD	(R,LDR,P,X,Z,LDZ,NZ,Y,RHO,C,S,INFO)
10	6	SCHEX	(R,LDR,P,K,L,Z,LDZ,NZ,C,S,JOB)
11	4	SSVDC	(X,LDX,N,P,S,E,U,LDU,V,LDV,WORK,JOB,INFO)

The leading S in the subroutine name may be changed to D or C . On some computers, the leading S or C may be changed to Z .

LINPACK
Users' Guide

J.J. Dongarra
J.R. Bunch
C.B. Moler
G.W. Stewart

1/L -1/L

1/I -1/I

1/N -1/N

1/P -1/P

1/A -1/A

1/C -1/C

1/K

Here is a guide to LINPACK—a unique collection of Fortran subroutines for analyzing and solving systems of linear algebraic equations and linear least squares problems. LINPACK is designed to be machine-independent, portable, and to operate at optimum efficiency in most cases. The package is intended for both the casual user who simply requires a library subroutine and the specialist who wishes to modify or extend the code to handle special problems. The guide supports these two groups by providing introductory sections with calling sequences and examples followed by more advanced sections spelling out the technical details. The guide should also be useful in the classroom.